BREVARD CHILDS BIBLICAL THEOLOGIAN

For the Church's One Bible

Daniel R. Driver

Baker Academic
a division of Baker Publishing Group
Grand Rapids, Michigan

Published by Baker Academic
a division of Baker Publishing Group
P.O. Box 6287, Grand Rapids, MI 49516-6287
www.bakeracademic.com

Baker Academic edition published with revisions and new appendix in 2012. Originally published as *Brevard Childs, Biblical Theologian: For the Church's One Bible,* Forschungen zum Alten Testament, 2. Reihe, 2010 by Mohr Siebeck, Tübingen, Germany.

Printed in the United States of America

Library of Congress Cataloging-in-Publication Data

Driver, Daniel R., 1979–
Brevard Childs, biblical theologian : for the church's one Bible / Daniel R. Driver.
p. cm.
Originally published : Tübingen : Mohr Siebeck, 2010.
Revision of the author's thesis—St. Mary's College, University of St. Andrews, 2008.
Includes bibliographical references (p.) and indexes.
ISBN 978-0-8010-3975-1 (pbk.)
1. Bible—Criticism, interpretation, etc. 2. Childs, Brevard S. I. Title.
BS511.3.D75 2012
220.6092—dc23 2011050904

To Adriel
who has been my help
much as God is hers

Contents

Preface to the North American Edition

Last winter I read a reputable study that is just about as old as I am, authored by a careful biblical scholar and published by a sterling press. I was amused and relieved to spot a number of errors in the text. In a day when the authors of limited-run monographs are asked to perform their own typesetting and copy editing, it is easy to imagine that they inflict a new order of scribal griefs upon their readers. Perhaps they do nothing new. Or perhaps the real grief has merely transferred from the authors, who once had someone convenient to blame for the indifference their manuscripts seemed to suffer, to the publishers, who now know they could produce better books in less time.

In the case of the present edition, I know only that the circle of those who have tended to the work has grown. First, half a dozen people responded to my request to be notified of *errata*. Special mention must be made of Richard Briggs, who produced the longest list, and who was one of the few to notice that footnote numbers restart at random points in the first edition. I have corrected as many errors as I know about, including a great many references to footnotes in the indexes. Second, I am grateful to Baker Academic Press, and especially to James Ernest and Christina Jasko, for the willingness, encouragement and work to bring out an edition more accessible to a North American audience. Most important in this regard is an appendix of English translations of the untranslated German that appears throughout the study. This addition has not been worked into the body for two reasons: to keep pagination aligned with the first edition, and to reinforce the point about how deeply European scholarship informed Childs' own. Credit for the translation in Appendix 2 belongs to M. Eugene Boring, who I am also very glad to thank.

April 2012 (Eastertide) *Daniel R. Driver*

Preface to the First Edition

This book represents a thorough revision and updating of a PhD thesis written at St Mary's College, University of St Andrews, between 2005 and 2008. It was defended in October 2008 under the title "Brevard Childs: The Logic of Scripture's Textual Authority in the Mystery of Christ" and resubmitted with only typographical changes. However, in part because in the present edition not a single chapter has been left as it was, and new material amounting to more than one long chapter has been added, I have given the study a new title.

Many factors spurred my revisions. First, my examination committee made sharp observations and challenges. Prof Walter Moberly, the external, pushed to keep the quality and charitableness of engagement high in all parts. And Dr Grant Macaskill, the internal, persuaded me that the order of two chapters needed to be reversed. Second, Mohr Siebeck's FAT series editors expect much, and I am grateful to Profs Bernd Janowski, Mark S. Smith and Hermann Spieckermann for accepting this work for publication. Prof Smith in particular made extensive comments that prompted me to reconsider a crucial part of the argument. I have labored to take all feedback into consideration, although naturally the judgments and faults that remain are mine. Third, a few important sources of new "data" have been examined and incorporated into the discussion. Childs' posthumously published book on the Pauline letters appeared just before my *viva voce*. Equally, I had not then read some of Childs' earliest work, including a 1952 graduate seminar paper for Walter Baumgartner that Childs lodged, along with other unique items, in an archival box at the Princeton Seminary library. Special thanks to Travis Bott for drawing my attention to this fascinating material, and to Ken Henke, reference archivist at Princeton, for providing copies. In the intervening time, too, I have been in touch with members of Childs' family, some of whom uncovered and shared a letter sent from Basel in 1953. I will long remember a warm and lucid conversation with Childs' sister, Anne Hummel, at her home in Old Saybrook.

Some of the debts that a person acquires in higher education are impossible to repay. First for me is a debt of gratitude to my primary supervisor, Dr Nathan MacDonald, who in 2004 picked up an MPhil proposal that bears no resemblance to the PhD that eventuated. He proved an excellent guide, sharpening my interests through coursework and attentive supervision. I was glad to revisit his last set of comments on the thesis while reshaping it for this book.

Dr Mark Elliott, my secondary supervisor, competently stood in the gap during a sabbatical and showed me the meaning of polymath while yet remaining a source of encouragement. Another formative part of my years in St Andrews, and one that has directly influenced this project, was the Scripture & Theology seminar founded by Prof Christopher Seitz. In it I had the opportunity to present early drafts of two chapters and to receive engaging feedback from mentors and peers. Studies in the reception of the Psalms and Habakkuk also stand out as some of the most energizing collaborations of my student career. Beyond the seminar, Prof Seitz helpfully supplied documents pertaining to Childs that could not otherwise have been obtained.

Additionally, some outside St Andrews enriched my research by helping to make it a truly international experience. Prof Brevard Childs gave an interview at his Cambridge home in the Spring of 2006. Prof Georg Steins courteously engaged a draft of my criticism of his *Habilitation* and later shared his impressions of Childs' impact on German language scholarship over coffee in Vienna. On a coastal walk in the the East Neuk of Fife, Dr Stephen Chapman recalled his experience at Yale with Childs and Frei. My wife and I are especially grateful to Fr Michael Regan of the Fondation Catholique Ecossaise for funds to improve our French at the ICP, in Paris. And where would this work be without Frau Bahr, who fifteen years ago guided my first encounters with German language and culture?

Since moving to Toronto, unanticipated but significant encouragement to finish has come from the little congregation of St Matthew's, Riverdale. I can only name Dr Ephraim Radner, who read an uncooperative section and gave good advice, and Fr Ajit John, whose ministry is grace. My Tyndale colleague Dr Benjamin Reynolds commiserated in various ways and read a draft of the new first chapter with care. Throughout all, though, my wife Adriel has been a source of refreshment and perspective, and a tolerant and loving companion. She has lived with this work for a very long time, and her support is unfailing. I dedicate it to her on the occasion of her thirtieth birthday.

Finally, in terms of this book's production, Dr Henning Ziebritzki has been a professional director. His keen-eyed assistant Ilse König has been highly accommodating. I also thank Thomas Carr, who read the proofs closely and compiled the indexes. Still, the task of preparing a photo-ready PDF is a little daunting, leaving no hands to blame for *errata* but mine. I would be grateful to you, dear reader, for directing such matters and others of more substance to my attention. A companion webpage — http://www.danieldriver.com/bsc/ — has been built with that purpose in mind. I offer in addition my personal email address: mail@danieldriver.com.

January 2010 (Epiphany) *Daniel R. Driver*

Abbreviations

Titles by Brevard S. Childs:

Myth and Reality	*Myth and Reality in the Old Testament.* Studies in Biblical Theology 27. London: SCM, 1960, ^{2}1962.
Memory and Tradition	*Memory and Tradition in Israel.* Studies in Biblical Theology 37. London: SCM, 1962.
Assyrian Crisis	*Isaiah and the Assyrian Crisis.* Studies in Biblical Theology, Second Series 3. London: SCM, 1967.
BTh in Crisis	*Biblical Theology in Crisis.* Philadelphia: Westminster, 1970.
Exodus	*The Book of Exodus: A Critical, Theological Commentary.* Louisville: Westminster, 1974.
OT Books	*Old Testament Books for Pastor and Teacher.* Philadelphia: Westminster, 1977.
Introduction to the OT	*Introduction to the Old Testament as Scripture.* Philadelphia: Fortress, 1979.
NT Introduction	*The New Testament as Canon: An Introduction.* Philadelphia: Fortress, 1984.
OT Theology	*Old Testament Theology in a Canonical Context.* Philadelphia: Fortress, 1985.
Biblical Theology	*Biblical Theology of the Old and New Testaments: Theological Reflection on the Christian Bible.* Minneapolis: Fortress, 1992.
Einen Bibel	*Die Theologie der einen Bibel. Bd. 1: Grundstrukturen; Bd. 2: Hauptthemen.* Translated by Manfred and Christiane Oeming. 2 vols. Freiburg: Herder, 1994–1996.
Isaiah	*Isaiah: A Commentary.* Louisville: Westminster John Knox, 2001.
Struggle	*The Struggle to Understand Isaiah as Christian Scripture.* Grand Rapids: Eerdmans, 2004.
Pauline Corpus	*The Church's Guide for Reading Paul: The Canonical Shaping of the Pauline Corpus.* Grand Rapids: Eerdmans, 2008.

Other abbreviations of key titles not listed in *The SBL Handbook of Style*:

Holy Scripture	Barr, James. *Holy Scripture: Canon, Authority, Criticism*. Oxford: Oxford University Press, 1983.
Concept of BTh	Barr, James. *The Concept of Biblical Theology: An Old Testament Perspective*. Minneapolis: Fortress, 1999.
CD 1/2	Barth, Karl. *Church Dogmatics, 1/2: The Doctrine of the Word of God*. Tr. by G. T. Thomson and Harold Knight. Edinburgh: T&T Clark, 1956.
Reading	Barton, John. *Reading the Old Testament: Method in Biblical Study*. London: Darton, Longman & Todd, 1984.
Crisis?	Brett, Mark G. *Biblical Criticism in Crisis? The Impact of the Canonical Approach on Old Testament Studies*. Cambridge: Cambridge University Press, 1991.
JBTh	*Jahrbuch für Biblische Theologie*
Canonical Approach	Noble, Paul R. *The Canonical Approach: A Critical Reconstruction of the Hermeneutics of Brevard S. Childs*. Biblical Interpretation Series 16. Leiden: Brill, 1995.
Canonical HB	Rendtorff, Rolf. *The Canonical Hebrew Bible: A Theology of the Old Testament*. Tr. by David E. Orton. Leiderdorp: Deo, 2005.
ügP	Rendtorff, Rolf. *Das überlieferungsgeschichtliche Problem des Pentateuch*. BZAW 147. Berlin: Walter de Gruyter, 1977.
Bindung	Steins, Georg. *Die "Bindung Isaaks" im Kanon (Gen 22): Grundlagen und Programm einer Kanonisch-Intertextuellen Lektüre*. Herders Biblische Studien 20. Freiburg: Herder, 1999.

CHAPTER 1

Introduction

In fact ... canonical criticism ... is simplistic. Basically it has only one idea: the controlling place of the canon. To others this may fall apart into several conflicting ideas, but to the canonical critic himself it is all one idea. There is of course complexity even in the canon, but all that complexity can be dealt with by the one simple idea... [T]he canonical principle leaves the believer at peace, alone with his Bible.
— James Barr

Criticism of my understanding of canon emerges as a recurrent theme in some of the responses of my colleagues. It is occasionally claimed that it is imprecise, unanalytical, and encompasses a variety of different phenomena. I feel that the complexity of the process being described within the OT has been underestimated, and that one is asking for an algebraic solution to a problem requiring calculus.
— Brevard Childs

Locating the work of Brevard Childs (1923–2007) can be difficult. A great deal has been written about what his canonical approach amounts to, not all of it sympathetic, not all of it helpful (critics can of course be either one without being the other). The fact that many of the portraits on offer do not much resemble Childs' self-presentation tends to obscure the scholar's actual voice, and it exacerbates the attempt to situate his contribution. Nowhere is this truer than in the multitudinous detractions of James Barr (1924–2006), who charges that "canonical criticism [sic] ... is simplistic," that the only thing its several features have in common is that they co-exist in the same mind.[1] For Barr the term canon stands not for a workable approach to biblical exegesis, but instead masks profound confusion. Childs, on the other hand, maintains against criticism like this that he would not offer "an algebraic solution to a problem requiring calculus."[2] Readers of Childs' work and of the controversy it has provoked thus face rather stark alternatives. Is the canonical approach a methodological train wreck, or is it a sophisticated attempt to address complicated hermeneutical problems?

In answering this question some have split the difference. Childs offers important insights, it is affirmed, and yet due to the confusion in and unwork-

[1] Barr, *Holy Scripture*, 168. Barr uses "canonical cricitism" despite Childs' protests. On its limitations as a descriptor for Childs' approach, see Sheppard, Canonical Criticism (in *ABD*).

[2] Childs, Response to Reviewers, 52.

ability of his program, his method must be thoroughly rebuilt. The canonical approach is flawed but can be salvaged.[3] Still others have welcomed Childs' proposals as highly salubrious. Christopher Seitz, for example, counts himself with those who judge Childs' Biblical Theology "as the most brilliant proposal for theological exegesis offered in recent memory" (if "one unlikely to gain the sort of foothold necessary to transform the church in its use of scripture").[4] But the relationship between student and teacher is less than straightforward in this instance, as evidenced by the way Seitz and Childs inform one another's work on Isaiah. Seitz dedicates his 1991 study *Zion's Final Destiny* to three honored teachers, one of whom is Childs, even as the book reconsiders Childs' main work on Isaiah up to that point (*Isaiah and the Assyrian Crisis*, 1967).[5] Childs in turn dedicates his 2001 Isaiah commentary to Seitz but does not hesitate there to probe and challenge the argument of *Destiny*. It hardly simplifies matters that Childs' sharpest critics and his strongest advocates share in the testing and refinement of Childs' thought over decades.

Gerald Sheppard, another of Childs' students, aptly describes part of the challenge here. "Childs has shown an ability to change his mind on issues and approaches over time. Ambiguities or lacunae at later stages in his work cannot be uncritically clarified by appeal to earlier positions. Yet what persists from his earlier work may remain presupposed by later formulations."[6] To take just one instance, the 1970s argument from "midrash" seen in the late addition of Psalm titles is essential background to the argument for "canonical shaping," a ubiquitous theme in Childs' *oeuvre*. At the same time, the term "midrash" itself is increasingly rejected. Through the 1980s Childs came to view it as a mode inappropriate for modern Christian exegetes.[7] Then again, care should be taken not to exaggerate this change dynamic. Seitz also emphasizes major strands of continuity in Childs' work over the years, and he qualifies "that already in 1970 Childs had laid out the basic defining features of the approach. These have been modified only subtly or in extending efforts…" He rightly points to no less than five instances of "durable and sustained interest" to be found starting with *Biblical Theology in Crisis*: (1) critique of historical criticism, (2) special prioritization of the final form, (3) "observations on the status of the Hebrew and Greek text-traditions," (4) critical but appreciative attention to pre-Enlightenment exegesis, and (5) "biblical theological handling of the two Testaments, in which the Old retains its voice as Christian Scripture, and Biblical Theology is more than a sensitive appreciation of how the New han-

[3] Representatives of this position will be discussed in chapter two.

[4] Seitz, Not Prophets, 109.

[5] Seitz, *Destiny*, x: "Ironically, much of Childs's own later work on canon has had a decided influence on the sorts of questions and modifications I have proposed here, vis-à-vis his original work."

[6] Sheppard, Childs, 575.

[7] See chapter six for details on this development.

the possibility that Childs' promotion of canon as a governing framework need not be seen as dogmatism, obstinacy or the mutterings of a simpleton, but can be appreciated as a knowledgeable embrace of an intricate, knotty subject. Then, in a third section, I will summarize this study's outline and prospect.

A. Childs as Biblical Theologian

Childs ventured into many cognate fields over his academic career. After completing four years of doctoral work at the University of Basel — this period included a semester at Heidelberg in 1951 as well — he began teaching Old Testament at a small Wisconsin seminary (now defunct) in 1954. Four years later, in 1958, he accepted a post at Yale University where he taught until his retirement in 1999.[14] For some years he studied Jewish midrash in earnest, first with a local rabbi and then with Judah Goldin at Yale.[15] In the meanwhile he produced a series of form critical studies in the vein of his German-speaking instructors. Later, upon writing his introduction to the OT, he devoted no less than five years to researching an introduction to the NT. The aim was to "read as widely as possible in an effort to do justice to the integrity of this discipline."[16] His next step toward biblical theology was the comparatively slim *Old Testament Theology in a Canonical Context* (1985). After finally realizing a Biblical Theology of both testaments in the same year he was made Sterling Professor of Divinity (1992), he returned to the OT proper by writing a technical commentary on Isaiah, despite a series of health issues that he feared would keep him from completing the task. Reprieves in his illness permitted him to give a focussed kind of attention to church history, moving far beyond his early work in the history of exegesis, for which the Exodus commentary (1974) is commonly remembered, with *The Struggle to Understand Isaiah as Christian Scripture* (2004). A notable theme in the latter title is the problem of allegory in Christian exposition of the OT. Finally, he once again turned his eye to the NT with the posthumously published *The Church's Guide for Reading Paul: The Canonical Shaping of the Pauline Corpus* (2008). The manuscript had been sent to the publisher just days before his death on 23 June 2007, at the age of 83.

How should one classify ranging work of this sort? Looking for precedents, something like Rudolf Smend's study of the work of W. M. L. de Wette presents a possibility. That study falls into two parts: there is de Wette the *Alttesta-*

[14] The best previous account of Childs' biography is found in Harrisville and Sundberg, *The Bible*, 309–310. Though brief, it incorporates a personal correspondence with Childs about his life. Sheppard's earlier, longer account in *Historical Handbook of Major Biblical Interpreters* is still useful but contains a few errors. See also Driver and MacDonald, s.v. "Childs, Brevard" in *The Encyclopedia of the Bible and Its Reception* (forthcoming).

[15] See the letter that begins section B of chapter six, below.

[16] *NT Introduction*, xvi.

mentler (part one), and then de Wette the *Neutestamentler* (part two).[17] The neat division does not suit Childs very well, however, and actually is not broad enough. In my judgment a more general and slightly ambiguous title is most appropriate in his case — Childs as biblical theologian.[18] Each part of this study comes under the biblical theological umbrella in some way. Because the designation is contested, though, it calls for a little explanation.

To begin with, Childs freely acknowledges that difficulties attend the genres he undertook. Note what he says about the task of writing an OT Theology, for instance. The context is a symposium on Jewish-Christian dialogue held in early January 1985, the year *OT Theology* appeared:

> Seit ihrer Entstehung war es ein Charakteristikum der Disziplin alttestamentlicher Theologie, dass sie immer mit ernsten methodologischen Unsicherheiten zu kämpfen hatte. Obschon sie oft als Krone der ganzen Disziplin bezeichnet wurde, sah es so aus, als ob ihre führenden Vertreter immer wieder einen unsicheren Blick auf andere Gebiete des Unternehmens werfen würden, voller Angst, ob nicht irgendeine neue literarische, historische oder philologische Entdeckung das Unternehmen gefährde… Nicht nur, dass die Disziplin locker definiert und in ständiger Revision war, sondern *gewisse grundlegende Spannungen* stellen nach wie vor ihre Gestalt in Frage. Ist die Disziplin alttestamentlicher Theologie nur deskriptiv oder enthält sie ebenso ein notwendiges Element konstruktiver Theologie? Was ist die Beziehung zwischen einer alttestamentlichen Theologie und einer Geschichte Israels? Sind ihrer Aufbauprinzipien historisch, systematisch oder eine eklektische Kombination beider? Und schliesslich: was ist die Beziehung zwischen jüdischen und christlichen theologischen Interpretationen der Hebräischen Schriften?[19]

These are all among the questions he takes up at various points in his work, although it is worth underscoring that his driving concern at this juncture is theology of just the first testament. He admits that it would be "supremely arrogant" to propose a quick solution to a nest of problems so complex they seem to inhere in the discipline. Nonetheless, he commends an approach to scripture marked by constitutive features of *Christian* exposition, features which to his satisfaction have not been adequately pursued in the critical or post-critical era. "Ich möchte so in einer anderen Weise einige dieser quälenden methodologischen Fragen angehen."[20] A key element of the prescription is a reminder that OT theology has almost always been — is perhaps irreducibly — a Christian preoccupation. If so, the ecumenical dilemma for OT exegetes becomes how to appropriately handle a Jewish canon already functioning as OT within the operations of church theology.

---

[17] Smend, *WML de Wettes Arbeit*.

[18] Childs refers to himself as a biblical theologian at least once (*Exodus*, 88). As for the term itself, I have attempted to follow James Barr's practice of capitalizing Biblical Theology when I mean a specific instance of the genre and not otherwise. The same distinction applies to Introductions to or Theologies of either OT or NT individually.

[19] Childs, Jüdischen Kanons, 271–272, my emphasis.

[20] Ibid., 272.

Biblical theology itself — more than just Old plus New, "as if one could spend the first semester with Eichrodt and von Rad and the second with Bultmann and Jeremias!"[21] — is for Childs fundamentally a bridge-building exercise, an arena for theological reflection on the entire Christian Bible in which biblical scholarship and dogmatic theology meet to illuminate the object they share. Its "major function … is to provide a bridge for two-way traffic between biblical exegesis and systematic theology's reflection on the subject matter."[22] Childs obviously enters this space as an OT specialist, and by his own admission he was not as successful coming up to speed in systematics as in the NT. "In spite of the challenge of trying to gain competence in both testaments, this task paled into insignificance before the difficulty of gaining entrance into the field of dogmatic/systematic theology. Anyone who has ever studied under Karl Barth is left with the lasting sense of inadequacy just from remembering the standards of thoroughness which he required of his students."[23] That is, Childs never attempted a Church Dogmatics. I doubt that his ambition ever reached that far. He made efforts at proficiency in the formal discipline of theology, although these struck him as inadequate.[24] Yet biblical theology's connecting purpose is to rejoin scripture and theology. It serves something other than dialogue for its own sake, or whatever other goals might be desirable in a strictly academic context. It arises first from a church situation, and as such it principally serves the unity of the Christian confession of one God. This ecclesial context drives Childs' concern for "the oneness of the biblical witness," or the "oneness of scripture's scope" that he insists "is not a rival to the multiple voices within the canon."[25] Exactly how to articulate scripture's unity, at both the exegetical level and the hermeneutical or theological level, admits a range of answers, but for Childs the basic confessional imperative inherent in the question is experienced and voiced at every turn.

So when Gerhard Ebeling writes of an "inner unity" to the discipline in a now classic essay on the meaning of biblical theology (1955), Childs picks up the language: "The Christian church responded to [the canonical scriptures] as the authoritative word of God, and it remains existentially committed to an inquiry into its inner unity because of its confession of the one gospel of Jesus Christ which it proclaims to the world."[26] At least three points of clarification need to be made about this claim. First, it is fair to say that the Ebeling-Childs

---

[21] *Biblical Theology*, xv.

[22] Ibid., 481, cf. 551. See also Helmer, Biblical Theology: Bridge Over Many Waters.

[23] *Biblical Theology*, xvi.

[24] "From my library shelves the great volumes of the Fathers, Schoolmen, and Reformers look down invitingly. I have also acquired over the years many of the great classics of the Reformed and Lutheran post-Reformation tradition. However, life is too short for a biblical specialist to do more than read selectively and dabble here and there" (ibid.).

[25] Ibid., 719, 725.

[26] Ibid., 8.

line, which foregrounds unity, reverses the priorities of J. P. Gabler, who for convenience's sake is often credited with calling biblical theology into existence.[27] Childs admits this by calling Ebeling's definition a redefinition, and "a return to a pre-Gabler position in so far as he once again joins the historical and theological elements."[28] Gabler had advocated a sharp distinction in his inaugural lecture at Altdorf in 1787, a distinction between religion and theology, between things of "historical origin" and "didactic origin," between "the simplicity of what they call biblical theology" and "the subtlety of dogmatic theology."[29] Procedurally this entails further distinctions, not only between OT and NT, but also Paul and the gospel writers, right down to the level of each individual author.[30] Yet Gabler does not envision the final divorce of biblical from dogmatic theology, and one can only guess how he might have addressed the evaporation of his hope to eliminate "doubtful readings" of scripture in pursuit of "the Christian religion of all times."[31] Ebeling and Childs reflect very different historical moments than Gabler. Furthermore, it would be a serious mistake to assume that Childs (the only one of the three actually to attempt a Biblical Theology) nullifies all distinctions in the name of unity. We have already seen evidence of the way he accords Jewish studies, OT and NT scholarship, and systematic theology their own integrity as disciplines. His language of "discrete witnesses" is also relevant here. Perhaps it is not too trivial a generalization to say that, in the centuries between Gabler and Childs, the burden of keeping Christian theology intact came to overwhelm the need to keep its domains apart. As Ebeling's essay concludes,

> the concept "biblical theology," the false understanding of which caused theology — contrary to the original intention — to split up into different disciplines, when rightly understood points back again to the unity of theology — not of course a unity achieved by abolishing the different disciplines, but a unity consisting in the right theological use of the different disciplines, each of which has its own peculiar task and yet each is "theology" in the sense of participating in the scientific expression of the Word of God.[32]

The task is to hear "the inner unity of the manifold testimony of the Bible," and the call is for "the intensive co-operation of Old and New Testament scholars" and indeed of all theological specialists, including dogmaticians and church historians. Should collaboration be achieved, Ebeling observes that "'biblical theology' would not then be a rival substitute for dogmatics and would hardly correspond either to the pietistic ideal of a 'simple' theology, but would be an

---

[27] As Ebeling and others have shown, the first use of the term "biblical theology" goes back somewhat further than Gabler.

[28] Ibid., 7.

[29] Gabler, J. P. Gabler and the Distinction, 137.

[30] In order to establish proper comparisons of biblical ideas to "universal notions," he prescribes first "diligently isolating the opinions of each author" (ibid., 142).

[31] Ibid., 143.

[32] Ebeling, The Meaning, 96.

uncommonly complex exercise in historical theology."[33] This ideal counters the trend toward hyper-specialization and realigns a standard view of biblical theology; simultaneously, it denies the simplicity of pure notions that Gabler desired. In each of these respects Childs stands with Ebeling.

Second, Childs is quite frank about what constitutes the "inner unity," and it is far from the old enthusiasm for universal religion: a biblical theologian has to do with "inner unity because of … the one gospel of Jesus Christ." At the center of Childs' approach, then, is a startlingly specific confession of the lordship of Jesus Christ. To be sure, he is not the first biblical theologian to make this move. In the end there is an expressly christological side to Old Testament inquiry for one of his teachers, Gerhard von Rad, however reluctantly acknowledged by von Rad himself, however often overlooked by von Rad's other students and successors. Yet for Childs the *Christuszeugnis* of scripture's witness is fully embraced by 1992 and forms the heart of his *gesamtbiblische* theology.[34] Sometimes the utter difficulty of the assertion sounds out loudest. "Allerdings bleibt schwer bestimmbar, was es bedeutet, im Alten Testament einen Hinweis auf Christus zu finden, und das Ringen mit diesem Problem führt ins Herz der Biblischen Theologie."[35] Just how should one move from the verbal or literal sense of the the OT to its true theological substance, identified by Childs as knowledge of God in the face of Christ? Most traditional Christian exegetes do so readily. Von Rad's hesitancy in the twentieth century, and Childs' in its own way, is symptomatic of a dilemma facing biblical scholars who feel compelled to take similar steps in a critical age. All the same, *Biblical Theology* undertakes the search for, and upholds the proclamation of, one thing from two testaments, namely, the gospel of Jesus Christ.

Third, specificity about Christ puts extra strain on the biblical theologian's ecumenical obligations. If OT theology was once presumed the crown of OT scholarship, this has not been the case since about the time Childs first waved the tattered banner of biblical theology, in 1970. Jon Levenson, in an essay exploring shortcomings in the OT Theologies of Eichrodt and von Rad, effectively describes the less certain climate that has gained predominance over the field of historical critical scholarship.

> In North America, the emergence of religion departments and Jewish studies programs and departments has further contributed to the dethronement of Christian theology, indeed *any* theology, as the organizing paradigm for the study of the Hebrew Bible. As a consequence, in the elite academic world, those for whom the term "Old Testament" is more than vestigial have

---

[33] Ibid. He continues, "then it would be able also for its part to assist dogmatics towards a clearer grasp of the question of what constitutes scriptural dogmatics."

[34] See below for Childs on von Rad, *gesamtbiblische* theology and the *Christuszeugnis* of the OT (especially chapters three, six and seven).

[35] Childs, Biblische Theologie, 24, and compare idem, von Rad.

been put into the unenviable position of an ex-emperor who now must learn how to be a good neighbor.[36]

Given these circumstances, one can appreciate why a theologically minded Lutheran Old Testament scholar like Fretheim judges the 1992 *Biblical Theology* as "a theological retrenchment" — a failure precisely in its ability to cope with the new climate — and "more as a somewhat belated end of an era than as … an imaginative venture that charts new directions."[37] Fretheim probably underestimates the extent to which Childs broke with those he gladly claimed as his teachers (interestingly, Levenson quotes Childs in support of his critique of von Rad). But by voicing deeper misgivings about the ability of *Biblical Theology* to address "the complex realities of the contemporary world," Fretheim makes a potentially damaging point that Childs' tendency to dismiss newer theological efforts by liberation, process, feminist or postmodern theologians leaves him out of touch.[38] The canonical approach is just too traditional to have relevance or impact. Are most historic forms of Christianity automatically out of touch, though? The attempt simply to clear and restore old paths — much older than von Rad, or even Gabler — does not exclude the possibility of dialogue with those cutting other trails. Commenting from a Jewish perspective, Levenson sees potential, if only partly actualized: "Founded upon a historical particularity — the Protestant canon — Childs's method harbors a potential for respect for other historically particular traditions."[39] This despite (or seemingly because of) the fact that a frank confessionalism comes built in, with high liability for offense. "The role of canon often calls for a parting of the ways," writes Childs near the front of his last book.[40] How much capacity does Childs' work have to advance in-house or inter-religious dialogue? Readers will be of different minds, though fairly quickly one confronts real limits on the possibility for consensus. There is still the option Levenson advances, that creedal particularity set the foundation for a more substantive exchange than Gabler could have imagined, although if so, the most productive front is likely to be the one shared by people who wish to heal the breach between scripture and tradition rather than to celebrate or even exploit it. Protestant though he be, it is hardly by accident that Childs has been relatively well received by certain Jewish and Catholic biblical specialists.[41]

The full title of this study is *Brevard Childs, Biblical Theologian: For the Church's One Bible*. The above discussion should clarify the sense of its terms,

[36] Levenson, *Hebrew Bible*, 32.

[37] Fretheim, Review of *Biblical Theology*, 324.

[38] Ibid., 326.

[39] Levenson, *Hebrew Bible*, 122.

[40] *Pauline Corpus*, 44.

[41] By no means all Catholic and Jewish biblicists, though see chapters two and six for examples of each.

from the vocational designation "biblical theologian," to the ecclesial locus of Childs' work, to the oneness of the Bible's scope as grounded in christology. Naturally, more remains to be said on each score. First, though, another thing shown by this preliminary tour bears repeating. Childs took his project very seriously, never underestimating the difficulty of mastering so many different subject areas. Though he was uncommonly studious, he owns up to limitations in the broad personal competence he sought. We have seen the acknowledgement, too, of "quälenden methodologischen Fragen" in the operations of OT theology, as well as genuine hesitation about what it means "im Alten Testament einen Hinweis auf Christus zu finden," particularly with respect to what has been called the double reception of the Hebrew Bible. If we can credit statements like these, if he truly feels the weight of "agonizing methodological questions" including those in the list cited above, and if with him we share an impression of the number and width of historical, religious and disciplinary chasms to be spanned, then there may be some sense in talking about calculus after all.

B. Canon and History

Generally speaking, generosity toward constructive theological work with canon runs against the prevailing mood. The canonical approach is a non-starter, according to a common worry, because biblical scholarship oriented by or to church teaching blocks the free investigation of historical periods and sources that is central to the biblical scholar's mandate. Robert Kraft, for example, speaks of the "tyranny of canonical assumptions." For him, and for not a few members of the Society of Biblical Literature he addresses, to speak of canon at all is to introduce a seriously distorting anachronism. "Historically responsible philological work, of course, does not pay attention to these boundaries, either as limits … or as touchstones."[42] Kraft's view is as straightforward as it is widespread: history trumps canon.

This attitude has not helped Childs' reception, reinforcing a habit of incredulity toward the logic and self-presentation of the canonical approach visible especially in the literature on Childs' so-called method. Criticism has been so severe at times that one senses why in his later work he wants to "resist the practice of some immediately to characterize [his] approach as 'canonical,' since the label has only engendered confusion."[43] Yet in the end he neither abandons the term nor amends his use of it along the lines suggested by his

[42] Kraft, Para-mania, 17–18.

[43] Childs, *Isaiah*, xii. He continues, "I hope that this commentary will be judged on its own merits apart from any prior concept of what a 'canonical' reading ought to entail." The same request could well preface all of his work now.

critics. Therefore, to clear the ground for a better hearing, it will be helpful at this early stage to outline the trajectory of his thought on the relationship of canon and history — categories that stay in tension to the very last: in that sense canon *never* trumps history for him — and then to suggest the advantage of canon as an umbrella term. In other words, my purpose in this section is to clarify Childs' thought at a crucial point where it has often been misunderstood. The hope is to forestall premature dismissal of a proposal that has proved so counter-intuitive that it is commonly rejected out of hand. Is not the recourse to canon a retreat from history into dogma (a "dogmatische Flucht aus den Schwierigkeiten des historischen Geschäfts," in the words of Manfred Oeming[44])? If not, why not? How can Childs' dogmatic (in the word's more positive sense), theological deployment of canon accommodate all that we know about the extremely complicated history of canon?

Those who instinctively associate "canonical criticism" with anti-historical dogmatism would do well to consider when and where Childs went to school. True enough, in the background was the sort of conservatism that resists the incursions of "higher" criticism. As the mature Childs puts it in a correspondence with Harrisville and Sundberg, "it took me some years to get beyond Hodge and Warfield."[45] It is hard to say exactly when he overcame the legacy of old Princeton, which he probably knew first in the Presbyterian church his family attended in Queens, New York,[46] but there is solid evidence that it happened before he had his doctorate. Like many of his peers, Childs' formal education was interrupted by World War II. Anticipating the draft, he elected to start at Queens College, near home, rather than to go away to university. He was there little more than a year. In October 1942 Childs enlisted in the US Army.[47] Barely nineteen, he prepared to sail for Europe. On his sister's account, he had by then already taken a serious interest in theology, aided by the leader of a student group at Queens who helped guide his extracurricular reading.[48] Recollecting the weekly letters she exchanged with her brother during the war, the sister tells how Childs worked to teach himself Greek while aboard the RMS Queen Mary.[49] He returned to the United States in 1945 for

---

[44] Oeming, *Gesamtbiblische*, 195–196 = ^{3}204–205, cf. 209 = ^{3}216. For a fuller discussion see the section on Oeming in chapter two.

[45] Cited in Harrisville and Sundberg, *The Bible*, 310.

[46] Childs was born in Columbia, South Carolina, on 2 September 1923 and soon baptized Episcopalian, but the family moved North because of the father's poor health.

[47] According to Army enlistment records (The National Archives, http://aad.archives.gov/, accessed 23 October 2009), Childs enlisted in New York on 17 October 1942.

[48] Did it include Hodge or Warfield?

[49] "I always have that picture, of this nineteen year old heading into war, and he was teaching himself Greek. And he said, everybody was gambling — they had crap tables going and the money was this high — and here's Bard, working away. There was something so typical about Bard's determination" (recording of a personal communication with Anne Childs Hummel, 22 November 2008). During the war, while moving from France into Germany — he

redeployment to Japan, but Truman's atom bomb kept this from happening (he was on leave, visiting his sister, when it fell). As he waited to be demobilized, Childs completed several correspondence courses through the Army Education Program, earning enough credit through the University of Michigan to graduate with an AB and an MA in 1947. From there he went to Princeton Theological Seminary (Bachelor of Divinity, 1950), and then back to Europe, to Switzerland and Germany.

Against this backdrop, it is interesting to think about what motivated Childs' selection of material when, in the summer of 1995, he submitted a small box to the Princeton Seminary archives. In addition to later papers, letters and manuscripts, there is a syllabus from an introduction to the New Testament taught by Bruce Metzger in 1948. And there are Childs' own scrupulous notes from a course on the parables of Jesus, with Otto Piper in 1949. Apart from a copy of his Basel dissertation (1955),[50] the only other testament to his student days is a paper written for Walter Baumgartner in 1952, with Baumgartner's feedback in the margins. A hardworking *source critical analysis* of Exodus 13:17–15:21 that searches out the hand of L, J, E or P verse by verse (at the end Baumgartner praised it as a "sorgfältige und wohlüberlegte Arbeit mit verständigem Urteil"), the paper indicates something important about the early direction of Childs' work in the Old Testament. If initially Childs inclined toward Greek and the New Testament, he left Princeton with something else in view. (By Harrisville and Sundberg's report, his influences at Princeton were "few" and "largely negative."[51]) The paper also shows clearly that Childs went to Basel for what it had to offer in the Old Testament, not for Karl Barth.[52] Finally, whatever parallels one might be tempted to draw between Childs' years of study on the European Continent and those of Charles Hodge a century and a quarter before, the most obvious are disanalogous. In terms of their attitude to German criticism, the outcomes for these two learned men were fundamentally different.[53] Was there symbolism for

---

was in transportation, not the infantry, though according to Hummel he advanced with the front into Germany — his sister was in school at Wellesley College. She remembers writing for advice on a required, year long course on the Bible. The course introduced her to biblical criticism, and it shook her confidence in scripture. She wrote to her older brother about the issues it raised several times, sometimes twice a week. Childs responded regularly, reassuring his sister. "It was the content of what he said, but more than that it was the assurance that this wasn't the only way to look at it, that gave me great confidence," Hummel recalls. Unfortunately, the correspondence itself has not survived.

[50] See page 40, below, for details on why this was re-written in English.

[51] Harrisville and Sundberg, *The Bible*, 310.

[52] The relationship of Childs to Barth has been widely misunderstood. As will be seen in chapter three, Childs cautiously warms to Barth only later, at Yale, although he heard Barth lecture in his student days.

[53] See the published form of a dissertation Childs directed: Taylor, *The OT in the Old Princeton School (1812–1929)*, esp. 50–55 and 74–79 on Hodge.

Childs, with respect either to the famous old Princeton school or the seminary he would have remembered, in leaving this particular paper in its archives?

I. Early and Late Attitudes to History: From 1952 to 2008

Entitled "The Deliverance of Israel at the Crossing of the Sea," the Baumgartner paper bears a curious relation to Childs' subsequent work. Let me give some indication of its flavor. The piece begins by making detailed observations about the chosen text, noting alternate readings from the old Greek, the Syriac, the Samaritan Pentateuch, and so on. Exodus 13:20, for instance, is judged to be "very corrupt." In a subsequent note on literary analysis the same verse is ascribed to P, because P has the most developed geographical tradition (he is following Baentsch, Holzinger and Noth, against Beer and Eissfeldt). Other verses are separated into two or more strands, though P is said to be hard to distinguish from E. Next, Childs reconstructs two main sources under the headings "The Account of the Yahwist" and "The Account of EP." The first lacks any account of Israelites crossing the sea. Much of the subsequent discussion concerns "geographical-historical problems," such as the meaning and location of the יַם־סוּף in different traditions. With von Rad and especially Noth, Childs decides that the "localization" of the sea is secondary, that in fact accounts of the Exodus contain two distinct localizations. All of this is standard historical critical stuff, of course, conversant with the best research of the day. Given the approach for which Childs is now known, what is most remarkable here is his rejection of ostensibly more conservative options. Noth's account of incongruous traditions is preferred to Pedersen's case that the whole of Exodus 1–14 is a historicized "passah festival." A twenty-eight year old Childs writes,

> It has been convincingly demonstrated that the slaughter of sheep, the smearing of its blood on the tent posts, and the eating of bitter herbs, belonged to the ancient nomadic sacrifice customs. However, while this connection is clear, the weak point in Pedersen's argument is the actual connection between the passah legend and the exodus tradition. To be sure, *in its present form, the passah legend is a preparation for the exodus*, and the passah festival is a "Gedächtnisfeier." *But an organic, primary connection fails between the traditions.* Noth sees this correctly, in my opinion, when he criticizes Pedersen at this point…
>
> The Passah festival was originally a sacrifice customary among the "weidewechselnde Wanderhirten" before the departure for the summer pasturage. The yearly "exodus" was historified and took on the meaning of the once-and-for-all departure out of Egypt. Once the relation was created between the festival and the exodus tradition, the historifying was carried out all along the line.[54]

Apart from seven short notes on undiscussed problems, this is where the essay ends. Remarkably, its basic analysis was rehearsed twice in Childs' later work, finally being reworked for the appropriate chapter in his Exodus commentary.

---

[54] Childs, Deliverance of Israel, 12–13, my emphasis.

Two years before that, in 1972, Childs (then aged forty-eight) also used the paper as the backbone for the fourth lecture (of five) in the James Sprunt Lectures at Union Theological Seminary in Virginia. Something had shifted, though. The title for the lecture series that year was "Canon and Criticism: The Old Testament as Scripture of the Church," and session four was called "The Crossing of the Sea in its Canonical Context."[55]

What changed? In due course I will give my account of major threads of continuity and change across Childs' work. The first of two big turns happens on the road to *BTh in Crisis* — 1970 is a convenient marker. (The other is reflected in the break between chapter six, on the "mystery of Israel," and chapter seven, on the "mystery of Christ." It happens in the early 1980s.) Initially, though, it is important to say that the change is more subtle than has often been supposed. The double reworking of the Basel paper is a case in point.

First, the 1972 Sprunt Lectures. Lecture four uses Exodus 14 to explore an instance of "one of the most difficult problems of faith and history."[56] The existence of sources is presupposed. There are "two basically complete, and yet different, accounts of the event at the sea," though Childs pleads for "more flexibility in describing them than is often allowed."[57] Then, in language straight from the old postgraduate paper, the J account is given under one heading, and the P(E) account under the next. After this, however, the analysis pushes in a new direction.

> [F]ollowing the source analysis, the historical critical interpreter usually makes some comparisons of the two accounts and tries then to draw historical and theological conclusions. In my judgment, before any such move it is basic to seek to understand the whole account in its final form. There is another witness which must be heard, namely the final redaction. How does the chapter function as a whole?[58]

This question was not asked in 1952. Quite the contrary. Now, though, he attends to "the present form of the biblical text," arguing that "the final form of the story has an integrity of its own."[59] Is the earlier account undone? Has he inadvertently joined leagues with the likes of Pedersen, or even surpassed him in the move toward harmonization?

---

[55] Copies of all but the first lecture are housed at Princeton. The first is "The Canon as a Historical and Theological Problem," and I cannot say whether its exclusion is deliberate. Papers two, three and five are, respectively, "'II Isaiah' in the Context of the Canon," "The Canonical Shape of the Psalter" and "Daniel in the Context of the Canon." Revisions of all this material made its way into subsequent publications.

[56] Sprunt Lectures, 26.

[57] Ibid., 27. "This reservation is simply to share the feeling of many Old Testament scholars that the minute divisions have often gone beyond the evidence."

[58] Ibid., 28.

[59] Ibid., 31.

Not necessarily. Importantly, Childs suggests "that there is a canonical integrity which cannot be identified with simply literary unity."[60] And in the run-up to *Exodus* is other closely related work that does not directly reprise the Basel paper. The most sophisticated is "A Traditio-historical Study of the Reed Sea Tradition" (1970), which makes some adjustments to the slightly earlier "Deuteronomic Formulae of the Exodus Traditions" (1967, in a Festschrift for Baumgartner, actually). In the later essay Childs articulates his view that the Song of the Sea in Exodus 15 is dependent on the conquest tradition: "it seems highly probable that the influence stems from the Jordan tradition which has been projected back to the earlier event rather than in the reverse direction."[61] For J, the event at the sea was part of the wilderness tradition, but through a variety of influences, including the Deuteronomic concern for centralization, it became linked (in P) to Israel's primary saving event, the Exodus, with consequences for how Passover was understood. The analysis in 1970 is more up to date. It includes Frank Cross and George Coats, for instance. Notably, though, Noth is still preferred to Pedersen. What has been introduced to the discussion for the 1972 lecture, in full awareness of complex underlying sources, is an historical and theological account of the contribution of the redactor. "The biblical writer is aware, both of the variety within the tradition, and the two levels of divine activity, which combined ordinary [J] and wonderful [P] elements." To leave the account arrayed according to "a pattern of historical development runs counter to the intention of the final narrative."[62] At one level this is simply an historical observation. At another, the text's full history stands as a warning against the hegemony of historical development as the only critical framework. "The canonical redaction operates as a critical judgment against such moves and bears witness how the various parts are to be understood."[63] At yet another (higher?) level — from a theological vantage — the "critical judgment" of the canon aligns with scripture's witness to the church, a major theme of his Sprunt Lectures.

> The work of God is not buried in past events which are dependent on the scholar's reconstruction, but testified to plainly by the law and the prophets. That which the historian characterizes as a late literary fiction, the church confesses to be the full witness of God's redemption made possible through the continued activity of the Holy Spirit within the community of faith…
>
> To the question, how then did God redeem Israel at the sea, the Christian can only reply: read the Scriptures. Here is found the beginning of the story of God's redemption which brought the Church into being and continues to provide her with life.[64]

---

[60] Ibid., 27.

[61] Reed Sea, 414, cf. 410.

[62] Sprunt Lectures, 31.

[63] Ibid., 32.

[64] Ibid.

History raises some troubling theological questions for a person of faith (what if the Exodus did not "actually" happen?), and Childs acknowledges the issue without attempting to address it. What he does instead is complexify what counts for history in the first place. After the final form, there is the long history of effects in "the community of faith" — synagogue as well as church, as he often says elsewhere, though his own native context is patent — a variegated history with its own sets of context and reality.

By 1974 all this research and reflection had been drawn into a much larger project. Chapter nine of *Exodus*, "The Deliverance at the Sea (13:17–14:31)," repeats the basic juxtaposition of contexts.[65] It introduces a third recension of the J and P(E) accounts (the only one published), and then incorporates and builds on exegetical observations from 1972. Oddly enough, we arrive at a position from which to see the development of Childs' template for *Exodus.* Chapters start with a bibliography and a translation of the text under consideration. Most then have six sections, some omitting one or more of the last three:

1. Textual and Philological Notes
2. Literary and Traditio-Historical Problems
3. Old Testament Context
4. New Testament Context
5. History of Exegesis
6. Theological Reflection[66]

A way of investigating items 1 and 2 had been established at Basel in the early 1950s. Subsequently, for reasons that will have to be explored later, an array of biblical theological preoccupations fills out the scope of investigation. To the extent that reorientation of 3 to the received text was novel, it must also be said that Childs' emphasis on "final form" surfaces with a broad complement of orienting theological concerns. This required (and suited, presumably) someone who was in certain measure an autodidact, and in the preface to *Exodus* we catch a glimpse of the route taken:

> My academic interest in the book of Exodus goes back some twenty years to an unforgettable seminar on Moses which was conducted by Professor Walter Baumgartner of Basel in the summer semester of 1952. Well-worn copies of Dillmann, Gressmann, Driver, and Noth indicate their constant use over two decades. Active work on this commentary extends over ten years. During that period I have gone through many different stages in my own thinking. Somewhere *en route* I discovered that Calvin and Drusius, Rashi and Ibn Ezra, belong among the giants. I have tried to show why these great expositors — the term 'pre-critical' is both naïve and arrogant — need to be heard in concert with Wellhausen and Gunkel.[67]

---

[65] "There is some value in rehearsing the story according to each of the two main sources. However, the case will be made in the exegesis for the integrity of the composite accounts" (*Exodus*, 220).

[66] See the rationale given in ibid., xiv–xvi.

[67] Ibid., x.

"Somewhere *en route*" is vague language — maybe deliberately so. However Childs may have discovered the importance of the tradition, the essential point is twofold: Calvin and Drusius, Rashi and Ibn Ezra quite concretely fill out language of "the community of faith"; and, again, they add further historical dimension to a text that has so very many historical dimensions.

It has been said that *Exodus* represents the source critical Childs, allegedly distinct from a New Critical or final form Childs known elsewhere.[68] Actually, after Basel the acknowledgment of reconstructed biblical history *never* goes away.[69] Some will be surprised to learn how permanently Childs commits himself to an investigation of the diachronic, even though he refuses to let it have the last word. A 2008 comment about Acts, for instance, sounds almost intensely historicist. "The canonical function of Acts in relation to the whole New Testament, but especially in relation to the Pauline corpus, can be correctly described *only* when one reconstructs the historical process leading to its canonization."[70] In fact, the statement lines up with a major purpose of his final study, which is to explore the relationship of two sometimes contradictory histories of canon. Although earlier works refer to Martin Kähler's understanding of "Geschichte" and "Historie," *Pauline Corpus* develops the relation of this pair of words to an extent that surpasses all Childs' previous discussions. The terms signal overlap and divergence "between critical, historical exegesis and confessional, canonical understanding of biblical interpretation."[71] He defines them this way: "*Geschichte* is the historical reflections on events and conditions carried on within a confessing community of faith. *Historie* is the attempt to understand events from an objective, scientific analysis, applying ordinary human experience, apart from any confessional content, as the measure of its credibility."[72] Maintaining the tension between these perspectives is essential. Those who dissolve the tension tend to give maximalist or minimalist accounts of *Historie* on the assumption that *Geschichte* stands or falls with it, evoking either way Childs' characteristic dissatisfaction with options on the "right" and "left" of the theological spectrum. Thus Kähler's terms are also linked to conservatism, which fuses *Historie* and *Geschichte*, and liberalism, which separates them permanently.[73] For Childs, in contrast to both, canon and history are neither antinomies nor twins.

---

[68] See chapters two and three, below.

[69] Reconstructed history mostly means tradition history, in Continental style, although sometimes one finds judgments about "what actually happened." On the historicity of the crossing of the sea in particular, see *Biblical Theology*, 100, cited below.

[70] *Pauline Corpus*, 223, my emphasis.

[71] Ibid., 16.

[72] Ibid., 165.

[73] It is interesting to see the reasons Childs distances himself from Scott Hafemann's maximalist account of Paul and history, for instance (ibid., 125–126). For a fuller account of Childs between "left" and "right" see Driver, Later Childs.

Put differently, tension between *Historie* and *Geschichte* parallels a tension between secular history and sacred history, mirrored in a life spent working in the modern university for the sake of the church. In a sense the theological problematic is not new, except insofar as a different and sharper dialectic emerges after the rise of critical biblical scholarship. Church fathers and reformers sometimes wondered about how to handle scripture if it came into real conflict with good science (consider Augustine's last commentary on Genesis), though none anticipate the hermeneutical reversal described in Hans Frei's *Eclipse of Biblical Narrative* (1974). And when Childs speaks of "canon" and "community of faith" in the singular, as opposed to the plurals commonly seen in literature oriented more exclusively to secular history, it is fair to spot a rough analog to Augustine's "city of God."[74] As a theological category, canon bespeaks the unity that governs Childs' description of the Bible's function as a testimony to one God in church and world. One might as well speak of "canon" and "canons" as *Geschichte* and *Historie*.

Then again, standing on the other side of a hermeneutical watershed, Childs' work is deeply marked by the gap that opens between what Frei calls the "history-likeness (literal meaning) and history (ostensive reference)" of biblical narrative.[75] Much as his thought overlaps with Frei's at this point, though, Childs prefers to speak of reading the Bible as "witness" versus as "source." The most obvious departure from categories of realistic narrative: "witness" implies a confession. As Childs explains while introducing Old Testament aspects of his *Biblical Theology*, "The contrast lies in viewing history from Israel's confessional stance, from within a community of faith, rather than from a neutral, phenomenological reconstruction. However, in spite of insisting on a basic distinction in the way of viewing history, the problem remains that a subtle relationship continues to obtain between these two perspectives." Thus another difference from Frei, as from nearly all exegetes working before the Enlightenment, is Childs' readiness to make critical judgements about the relationship of history on its canonical presentation to history as reconstructed by modern scholars. It can range from high correspondence to almost total non-correspondence.

At times Israel's confessional witness overlaps fully with a common public testimony, and a confirmation of an event such as the destruction of Jerusalem in the sixth century can be elicited even from foreign and hostile nations (Ezek. 26.15ff.; 36.16ff.). At other times there is virtually no relation between Israel's witness (e.g. the crossing of the sea, Ex. 14) and extra-biblical sources. Usually there emerges some sort of connection, even when remote or contradic-

[74] Writing of *City of God* in this connection, Childs explains: "The effect of this Augustinian typology was to develop a powerful theological thesis respecting the unity of God's purpose within history. However, history as such remained fully subordinated to theology. It is, therefore, not by chance that no serious attention to the history of Israel for its own sake emerged until the Renaissance" (*Biblical Theology*, 196).

[75] *Eclipse*, 12.

tory (cf. the manna stories of Exodus and Numbers). The theological challenge is to pursue an exegesis of these passages in such a way as to avoid the rationalistic assumption of a common reality behind all religious expression or the threat of super-naturalism which would deny in principle any relation between an outer and inner side of historical events.[76]

There are good reasons why Childs calls this a "canonical approach," though again he can sit loose to the phrase when he feels it distracts from his point. Hearing the confession (more than making one himself) is the bedrock:

The goal of a new approach is to seek to do justice to the theological integrity of Israel's witness while at the same time freely acknowledging the complexities of all human knowledge and the serious challenge of modernity to any claims of revelation. Whether one calls a new approach 'canonical,' 'kerygmatic,' or 'post-critical' is largely irrelevant. I would only reject the categories of mediating theology (*Vermittlungstheologie*) which seeks simply to fuse elements of orthodoxy and liberalism without doing justice to either. The fact that one falls back on the problematic term 'dialectic' is merely a sign that there is no comprehensive philosophical or hermeneutical system available which can adequately resolve with one proposal the whole range of problems arising from the historical critical method.[77]

The contrast, then, is not properly between liberalism and conservatism. Instead, the need is for biblical theologians "to work in a theologically responsible exegetical fashion,"[78] a duty with at least two major dimensions. On the one hand, "the biblical material" must be handled "in a way which is critically responsible."[79] This mode gives attention to the discrete witnesses of both Testaments and their constituent parts. It also resists "biblicist, external appropriation of the various parts of the Christian Bible without the required exegetical rigour of the theological discipline."[80] On the other hand, the material calls for a response. It makes a "coercion … on the reader. There is a 'reader response' required by any responsible theological reflection."[81] Christians feel this coercion differently than Jews, and those who adopt an inside perspective feel it differently than those outside. From his Christian position Childs affirms a "struggle of faith by the church and the individual Christian of today [that] continues to focus on God's promises in his word," though this too must come to expression within "disciplined theological reflection."[82]

At issue is how to let Christian discourse on the Bible be at once public and faithful. Orthodoxy can be broad, though it comes under strain once biblical history and ostensive history drift apart. It becomes an acute "struggle" when the half-measures propped up by a residual Christendom finally collapse — when emperors are deposed and face the prospect of learning to be good

[76] *Biblical Theology*, 100.
[77] Ibid., 99.
[78] Ibid.
[79] Ibid., 94.
[80] Ibid., 336.
[81] Ibid., 335. Admittedly, this is a peculiar way of using the phrase "reader response."
[82] Ibid., 336.

neighbors, as Levenson has it, or when the institutional space left for faithful pursuit of Christian theological disciplines at elite schools diminishes to such an extent that it may be wondered just how much public real estate remains. If historicists successfully overthrow the "tyranny of canonical assumptions" it might turn out that Childs will be seen as one of the last representatives of a bygone era. This remains to be seen.[83] Whatever the outcome, the fraught ground between sacred and secular is the conceptual space Childs attempts to occupy. If the ecclesial context of his work is fundamental, as I suggest, the university context is no less important. His commitment to both institutions explains why he simply must grapple with history, including history in reconstructed rather than merely final form.

II. Canons Broad and Narrow

Given what has already been said, it is appropriate to inquire after canon as an historical concept before offering an account of canon as a live dogmatic concept. What is canon from the vantage of *Historie*? Canons inhabit history, after all, if they are real. Can Childs' meta-canon cope with the many canonical facts on the ground? Scholars of biblical canon formation regularly say that there are as many canons as there are religious communities, and there is truth in this. For many it is also axiomatic that canon must be sharply distinguished from scripture, in part because most communities that cherish a canon stand at some remove from the communities that produced the scriptures in it (and frequently in other canons besides). If canon is late, relative to scripture, then there is at least a possibility that a given community's theology of its canon is arbitrary, or at least non-essential to scholars who are trying to account for the theology in or arising from the scripture preserved in canons. It seems like a classic case where free historical investigation could overturn the established orthodoxy.

There are arguments for and against the strict separation of scripture from canon. In the English-speaking world the argument for such a distinction stems from Albert Sundberg's influential *The Old Testament of the Early Church* (1964), and it has been advanced in various ways by James Sanders,

---

[83] Levenson (*Hebrew Bible*, especially 117–124) makes a fascinating comparison of Childs to the scholar who became the face of the Old Testament at Yale following Childs' retirement, John Collins. In Levenson's judgment Childs' "canonical method" is better equipped to face the challenges of religious discourse in a pluralistic setting "than Collins's revision of nineteenth-century historicism." The reason? Particular religious commitment is a better place from which to engage people of other particular commitments. "For a biblical canon is always either Jewish or Samaritan or Eastern Orthodox or Roman Catholic or Protestant — but never generic, never universal" (122, cf. 79–81). Collins' response to Levenson (*Encounters*, 3–4) is cursory. He is right that the issue concerns "the nature of the conversation in which we wish to participate" (4), but the "we" glosses over more basic questions. Who in particular does he have in mind? For whom is he speaking? The antecedent of "we" is never specified.

John Barton, Eugene Ulrich, Lee McDonald, and a host of others. Elsewhere and in an earlier day Theodor Zahn had looked for the church to have its core canon in place by the end of the first century, but Adolf von Harnack argued persuasively for a second century date. Today there is a near-consensus that the fourth century is the proper terminus. It is in line with this that McDonald and Sanders ask, introducing their hefty compendium *The Canon Debate* (2002), "With such a long delay in the church's use of the term 'canon' to describe a closed body of Christian scriptures, one may well ask why there was an emergence of 'canon consciousness' in the church of the fourth century C.E. and little evidence of it before?"[84] Examples of this position could easily be multiplied, and another will be given shortly.

But then another historical assessment sees a consciousness of canon emerging far earlier, coincident in meaningful ways with the distinct concept scripture. In 1953 Isac L. Seeligmann spoke of a *Kanonbewußtsein* within the Jewish Bible itself, tacitly expressed in what might now be called inner-biblical exegesis or proto-midrash. By 1967 Childs had noted Seeligmann's argument and soon began to adapt the notion of "canon consciousness" within scripture in his own proposals.[85] A dissenting minority has followed this alternate (and prior) usage of "canon consciousness," including some of Childs' former students.[86] One also thinks of Continental scholars such as Christoph Dohmen. Although he knows that the first clear references to the canon as a list of books do not appear until the fourth century — the Muratorian fragment aside, Athanasius lists twenty-seven canonical books of the New Testament in 367 — Dohmen defends an alternate definition of canon: "vielmehr hebt der Begriff auf die Funktion ab, Maßstab oder Norm der Bücher und Buchsammlungen zu sein, die schon vorliegen und mit wechselnden Begriffen wie *Schrift, Heilige Schriften/Bücher, Miqra, Gesetz, Tora, Propheten* bezeichnet werden."[87] By these lights "canon" emerges much earlier than the fourth century CE. It is something the early church inherits, in incipient form at least, from the pre-Christian synagogue.

How to make sense of the difference between these two trajectories, each of which seeks to account for the same body of historical evidence? Possibly the single greatest difference hinges on narrow and broad definitions of canon. An anxiety shared by many who incline toward narrower usage is that broader use

[84] *Canon Debate*, 13.

[85] See chapter six for an account of Seeligmann, Midraschexegese, and of the place of this important essay in the early development of Childs' approach.

[86] See the 2005 taxonomy of literature on canon in Childs, Reflections on an Era (discussed below, in section A of chapter two). Of special note are Chapman, *Law and Prophets*, especially 106–110, and most recently Seitz, *Goodly Fellowship*. The latter speaks of an "achievement of association" in the formation of the Book of the Twelve by which "one is made conscious of the reality of affiliation and association within a diverse witness" (53, cf. 43–45).

[87] C. Dohmen, *Die Bibel und ihre Auslegung* (3rd, rev. ed.; Munich: C. H. Beck, 2006), 20.

imports anachronistic dogma by applying the term too early.[88] In the extreme one might even say that the the ascription of canonicity always belies the historical situation. Canon is not a real concept at all but sheer ideology. And one can find representatives of this extreme view. Writing of John Van Seters' critique of the redactor, Thomas Römer asserts: "I agree with Van Seters, that one should not use the term redactor for the editors of the 'final form' of a text, *since such a final form never existed*."[89] As the remark is neither qualified nor explained, it is difficult to know what he means. Manifestly final forms do exist. For the Hebrew Bible the Leningrad Codex is an obvious and splendid example. Taking this for granted, Römer appears more to mean that "final form" is an empty concept, wholly alien to the biblical situation. Canon, then, intrudes on history; or to be precise, it intrudes on the sort of history that would see editions of Deuteronomistic History (so-called) as a more basic textual and historical reality than Former Prophets. Römer's hyperbole permits a stark division between canon and history, but this actually seems rather rare among scholars of canon formation (given his interests, one can legitimately doubt whether Römer numbers among them). Most operate with at least a tacit awareness of their stake in the appropriateness of a community's theology of its Holy Writ. If canon is rejected, in other words, it is typically because canon is a *false* dogmatic concept, not because it is not history. Canon is not replaced by history, but by the evidently more suitable category scripture. Scripture then stands in the breach, inviting a historically chastened theology of, say, the Protestant church's Bible. My point is that, rhetorical flourishes to the side, it is unusual to pit raw history against dogma in the debate about canon; more often, an irregular exercise of negative theology takes place (not canon!) by which something deemed too rigid is supplanted by something broader and more flexible. For the most part the bifurcated use of "canon consciousness" that stems either from Seeligmann or from Sundberg is not explained by the rejection of dogma, but by divergent formulations of right dogma.[90]

---

[88] As Georg Steins quite rightly insists (in Ballhorn and Steins, eds., *Bibelkanon*, 115, contra Frankemölle, *Frühjudentum*), an early application of the term canon is not automatically anachronistic, so long as the way the concept is defined fits the situation it describes.

[89] Römer, *Deuteronomistic History*, 49n10, my emphasis. Toward the end of the book is an acknowledgment that something eventually changes. There is a "transformation of the book of Deuteronomy [which] was the end of the Deuteronomistic History," and the beginning of the "Former Prophets" (182). Absent any explanation of this transformation, however, the reader is left with the impression that the change lacks deep logic and is therefore mostly arbitrary.

[90] In addition to John Webster's skill as a dogmatician, one advantage of his "frankly dogmatic" account in "The Dogmatic Location of the Canon" is precisely that it is frank. He "assumes the truth of the church's confession of the gospel, regarding that confession as a point from which we move rather than a point towards which we proceed" (11). Studies of canon formation have different goals, but relative to Webster they have a methodological weakness if an ostensibly historical category, scripture, is made a surrogate for a more obviously dogmatic category, and then becomes the unacknowledged vehicle for dogmatic judgments.

Adoption of a broad semantic range for canon has made Childs and those who follow him outliers in recent discussions. As a striking example consider the impasse that halts traffic between Childs' work on the Pauline corpus (2008) and Craig Allert's *A High View of Scripture? The Authority of the Bible and the Formation of the New Testament Canon* (2007), titles which would appear to coincide as much in theme as time. Allert, a Canadian and self-described evangelical,[91] follows his more technical first monograph with a pastorally minded book about "how an understanding of the formation of the New Testament canon may inform an evangelical doctrine of Scripture."[92] Childs, as we have seen, navigates from the historical Paul to the canonical Paul with the aim of elevating regard for theological aspects of an historically shaped corpus. Both authors define "canon" early in their books, where some pretty fundamental disagreement begins. As from 1970 and counter to a "narrow, history-of-religions definition," Childs defends "a far broader definition that does justice to the theological dimension of the term. The early Christian church was never without a canon since it assumed Israel's Scriptures as normative."[93] Allert, on the other hand, takes for granted that "canon" should be restricted to mean "a closed collection of texts to which nothing can be added and from which nothing can be taken."[94] He also states flatly at one point: "The church existed before the Bible."[95] In each case the goal is obviously sound dogma rather than no dogma. What is at stake in this in-house debate about the character of Christian scripture?[96] And from a wider perspective — with regard to those who insist on bracketing religious commitments, insofar as that is possible — what does it matter if one broadens canon or abandons it for scripture? Is history distorted in either case? A brief comparison of Childs and Allert can shed light on both questions. Childs' approach is far from the only way to handle the difficult intersection of history and theology at the point of what the church's canon is and does, but I do hope to raise the possibility that the broad use of canon which has bemused so many of Childs' readers is at once theologically advantageous and historically defensible.

Falling in line behind Sanders and McDonald, then, Allert defines "canon consciousness" as the express knowledge of a closed list of canonical scriptures and so as something that does not properly emerge in the church until the

[91] Evangelical in Allert's sense should of course be distinguished from *evangelisch* in the German sense (and as adopted by the likes of Webster).

[92] *High View?*, 173, cf. 10. His first title, which Brill carried in 2002: *Revelation, Truth, Canon, and Interpretation: Studies in Justin Martyr's Dialogue with Trypho.*

[93] *Pauline Corpus*, 4n4, cf. 253.

[94] *High View?*, 9n1, cf. 37.

[95] Ibid., 76.

[96] This formulation echoes the title of a forthcoming book by Seitz.

fourth century.[97] More uniquely, he makes additional efforts to reform a semi-popular evangelical understanding of the Bible as having quite definite boundaries: sixty six books in total, inerrant in the original autographs. Against this Allert brings evidence of how much apocryphal literature is cited by the very Fathers who set parameters on the church's New Testament, and of how broad the Fathers' sense of inspiration tends to be. North American evangelicals need a thicker ecclesiology, he insists, by which they stand to gain an appreciation of the historically porous boundaries between canonical and non-canonical scripture, and ultimately between scripture and tradition. This is the setting for a "realization that the Bible grew up in the cradle of the church," which leads to his clam that "[t]he church existed before the Bible."[98] At this point, however, he ventures into awkward historical-theological territory. If the target is just a "Bible, Holy Spirit and me" view of *sola scriptura*, then one can see his point. If, on the other hand, he is making a theological claim of the first order, then the claim is open to question. Even on strict historical grounds, what weight does one give to the fact that the early church took as its theological inheritance and point of reference the Jewish scriptures? Allert makes much of the notion that the church did not receive a canon but rather scriptures on the way to canon — does this mean the church had no Bible? Or what does 1 Corinthians 15 mean in saying that Christ died according to the scriptures? On a few occasions Allert refers to the "content of Christianity," but the crucial question goes unasked: before and as the NT came into being, how did the church apprehend this content? St Augustine can hardly settle the matter, yet it is challenging to remember that even at the brink of the fifth century he sees in the OT "such a strong prediction and pre-announcement of the New Testament that nothing is found in the teaching of the Evangelists and the apostles, however exalted and divine the precepts and promises, that is lacking in those ancient books."[99] In short, in Allert's work the role of the Old Testament in the crucial first centuries of the church's life is not adequately explained.[100]

---

[97] Ibid., 52, 68, 131. Allert actually equates the *consciousness* of canon with datable lists. "If, as some argue, the early church consciously created and closed a New Testament canon at the end of the second century, why does the proliferation of canon lists begin to appear only in the fourth century?" (131).

[98] Ibid., 76.

[99] *Contra Adimantum* 3.4 (PL 42, 134). In fairness, though, David F. Wright, who cites this passage in Saebo, *HB/OT* 1.1:714, points out that Augustine revised this to read "almost nothing" in his *Retractationes*.

[100] I had completed my initial analysis of Allert, a version of which was presented to the "Canonical Approaches to the Bible" group in the European Association of Biblical Studies (in Lincoln, England, 28 July 2009), before reading Seitz's discussion of Allert and Childs in *Goodly Fellowship*. The accounts overlap in places (see 20–23), although they obviously serve different purposes. Seitz also questions the adequacy of "canon as list," making the point, *pace* Barton, that "order and association precede lists, and they are accomplishments of a deeply theological nature to begin with" (45). He cautiously joins those who speak of an "open canon"

Like Allert, John Webster worries about the *mis*-location of canon by some Protestants as "a relatively isolated piece of epistemological teaching."[101] But from a dogmatic standpoint Webster better arbitrates the oft-emphasized correlation of canon and community. Is ecclesiology the base on which doctrines of canon and scripture build? What then of revelation, of the triune God's saving action and self-communication? "The question … is whether it is more appropriate to speak of the people of the book or the book of the people."[102] Evidence that Allert lacks a satisfactory answer to this question, in theological *and* historical terms, can be seen in the trouble he has connecting second and fourth century definitions of canon. Tellingly, his argument pivots midway through when he backs away from the narrow "canon as list" definition posited at the outset. "Even though we have here predominantly been using the word with reference to a list of texts," Allert explains,

> its initial use has nothing to do with texts… [I]n the latter half of the second century, "canon" for Irenaeus meant the Rule of Faith, the content of essential Christian belief. This was also true of other church fathers… Soon the word "canon" moved from this more fluid usage to refer to concrete things, such as conciliar decisions, monastic rules, clergy, and finally to a list, index, or table — something with which a person can orient oneself.[103]

From here the discussion vacillates between apparently contradictory senses of the key term, from the plural canons of the early church to the one canon that arrives late. Allert's conclusion merely reiterates the tension, and thus falters where it might have approached a more coherent doctrine of scripture than the thin one he deconstructs.

> The second century has rightly been identified as very important in the canonical process… The four Gospels rose to preeminence and a Pauline collection was circulating and received as authoritative in most congregations throughout the empire. Indeed, there was a core collection of Christian documents. But we must measure this statement and not read a later concept of written canon into the second century. It is quite likely that the formation of a closed collection of Christian writings was not paramount in the mind of the second-century church. This is indicated especially by its reaction to … heresies: they were countered not with a written canon, but rather with the canon of truth. If the written canon was paramount, we should expect to see a preponderance of lists following these great heresies, but this is precisely what we do not see — until the fourth century.[104]

---

to emphasize the difference between authority and closure (see 64, 79). Others who incline similarly include Edward Ellis, Iain Provan, Stephen Chapman and Karel van der Toorn.

[101] Webster, Dogmatic Location, 9.

[102] Ibid., 17–25, here 24. In places Allert seems to favor the latter and certainly emphasizes it strongly. For instance, "The Bible must be viewed as a product of the community because traditions of the community provide the context in which Scripture was produced" (Allert, *High View?*, 145, cf. 84–86).

[103] Allert, *High View?*, 78–79. Is the second century's more abstract canon of truth *not* something with which a person could orient oneself?

[104] Ibid., 129–130.

There is no reason to doubt that the meaning of "canon" (or rule) shifts in the passage of time from Irenaeus and Tertullian in the second and third centuries to Eusebius and Athanasius in the fourth. What is open to question is whether "a preponderance of lists" is the terminus with which the final significance of canon is to be identified. Canon is a fourth century phenomenon by definition, and it has only incidental links with earlier phenomena by the same name. Allert therefore laments "the unfortunate claim that the Bible itself is the Rule of Faith, or that when the Bible came into existence (second century), it *became* the Rule of Faith."[105] If there have been naive attempts to collapse the difference here — Allert finds examples among evangelical scholars — it does not follow that more informed attempts to span the gap are also unproductive. To the contrary, it is altogether unlikely that the church's two testament canon should have no relation whatsoever to its *canon et regula fidei* in the period before questions of the New Testament's scope were settled. Allert's hiatus between two ancient canons, paralleling the modern hiatus between scripture and canon, is almost the *reductio ad absurdum* of a widespread definition.

In chapter seven I will say more about the relation of Childs' understanding of canon to church fathers like Irenaeus. Without being too repetitive, let me anticipate that discussion by setting forth a major point of contrast between Childs and Allert here. Instead of maintaining a distinction, Childs actively exploits the polyvalence of the word canon, which for him is an expansive cipher. For instance, in a response to reviewers of his 1979 introduction he speaks of "a rule of faith called canon."[106] And already in *BTh in Crisis* he observes, "In its original sense, canon does not simply perform the formal function of separating the books that are authoritative from others that are not, but is the *rule* that delineates the area in which the church hears the word of God. The fundamental theological issue at stake is not the extent of the canon, which has remained in some flux within Christianity, but the claim for a normative body of tradition contained in a set of books."[107] Childs draws this insight from a few theologians and church historians. Karl Barth is one. Another is Hans von Campenhausen, whose *Die Entstehung der christlichen Bibel* (1968) had been praised by Childs in 1970 and is known to Allert in English translation (1972):

> The one rule and guideline, the only "canon" which Irenaeus explicitly acknowledges, is the "canon of truth," that is to say: the content of the faith itself, which the Church received from Christ, to which she remains faithful, and by which she lives. By this is meant neither a Summa of dogmatic propositions nor an unchangeable confessional formula nor even the sacred Scripture as such, however certain it may be that the latter teaches and contains this truth.[108]

---

[105] Ibid., 83.

[106] Response to Reviewers, 52.

[107] *BTh in Crisis*, 99, my emphasis.

[108] Campenhausen, *Formation*, 182.

Yet another is Bengt Hägglund, who draws the following conclusion in a 1958 study of *regula fidei* in the patristic period: "Es ist nicht von ungefähr, dass das griechische Wort für 'regula,' κανών, mehr und mehr zu einer festen Bezeichnung für die heilige Schrift wurde. Das ursprüngliche Zeugnis ist nicht nur deshalb 'kanonisch,' weil es mit der Authorität der Propheten und Apostel ausgestattet ist, sondern auch weil es Träger der Offenbarung, Vermittler der Heilswirklichkeit ist."[109] Or to quote Webster again on a point that I think Childs would appreciate, "a canon which is *only* a useful accident, *only* tradition, cannot *rule*."[110] In terms of Allert's discussion, the second century sense of canon as a rule of truth or faith dominates in Childs' thought, but this contains rather than rivals fourth century and other subsequent senses of canon.

To sum up, let me file three observations about the importance of seeing canon as *regula fidei* in Childs' last book, on Paul. First, contra Allert: "The Christian church was never without a canon."[111] Because canon is broad rather than narrow Childs can make tenable historical claims that avoid underestimating the role of what came to be known as the Old Testament. (Interestingly, in the midst of a discussion of how Paul reasoned about Christ, von Campenhausen's work on the OT in the early church is called on for support again.) Second, the semantic exchange between canon and *regula* operates in the background in *Pauline Corpus* — it is taken for granted on the basis of earlier work — and yet without it the task of outlining the contours of the Pauline corpus falls to pieces. Sketching Paul's canonical profile is a way of getting more specific about how the parts of the corpus interrelate, and how, together with the whole company of prophets and apostles, the corpus functions in and constrains the church's christologically ordered life. Third, however, canon's dogma is no less basic than canon's history. Childs' increased specificity about the role of both parts of the Christian Bible as one *Christuszeugnis* troubled some reviewers of his Biblical Theology, though the category that grows to prominence in his final book is not christology but pneumatology. A lengthy treatment of the life of the Spirit in Paul sets the stage for this claim about how Christianity's authoritative tradition is actualized in each generation of the saints: "it is the church's confession of the role of the Holy Spirit as the divine presence at work that continues to enliven and transform the written Word of

[109] Hägglund, Die Bedeutung, 39.

[110] Webster, Dogmatic Location, 18, cf. 15–16. Further on he argues, "Unless it is set in the larger structure of divine action and its creation of human response which we call revelation, 'canon' can become *simply* 'rule'; its normative status becomes its own property, rather than a consequence of its place in the divine economy. Above all, reference to divine action falls away… But as a function of revelation, the canon is not merely a list or code; it is a specification of those instruments where the church may reliably expect to encounter God's communicative presence, God's self-attestation" (28–29).

[111] Childs, *Pauline Corpus*, 61, cf. 4n4 and 253–254.

Scripture into the living Word for today."[112] Plainly, this is dogmatic language. It arises out of a particular Christian confession. Yet if there is just one point to underscore in view of many scholars' unease about canon as a dogmatic concept, it should be Childs' frank recognition that canon is unavoidably a dogmatic concept. What would it mean to treat it "merely" as history? Historians have a right to banish erroneous dogma from the biblical period. If canon attaches to scripture, on the other hand, it should with the proper qualifications be allowed to stay. Is there, as some have seen, a *Kanonbewußtsein* deep in the formation of the literature itself? That depends on what a person means by canon. But in all probability church teaching and academic research on canon alike will be better served by those who start with plausibly robust dogmatic conceptions than by those who shy away from scant ones and risk letting bad dogma distort their history.

C. Outline and Prospect

The time has come for a fresh look at Childs' approach. His own canon of writing is now closed, and it includes a phase beyond the one that culminates in *Biblical Theology*, in which the last major accounts of Childsian hermeneutics drew their conclusions. It is possible now, for the first time, to look back at the library he has left, to attend to all its contours. Patterns do emerge, and, contrary the powerful assertions of Barr but with dissenting voices like Harrisville and Sundberg, I contend that they have a discernible kind of logic.

The following study falls into three parts. Part one situates Childs' work as it has been received in English- and German-speaking academic contexts while at the same time registering Barr's wide influence in denouncing Childs' approach as a thing that falls apart into conflicting ideas. Chapter two surveys the large body of secondary literature pertaining to Childs' approach. This is treated with as much economy as the argument allows, but since I counter the predominantly negative assessment of Childs a degree of thoroughness is required. This chapter will be less crucial to readers who have no reason to doubt that a governing approach to scripture will be different than a particular method or technique of biblical criticism, and who also do not have strong preconceptions about the canonical approach's illogic. In chapter three, Barr's and Childs' senses of the desirability of *gesamtbiblische* theology are contrasted as a possible illustration of an English/German language gap. Here Rendtorff (among others) sides with Childs on at least one programmatic issue, which grounds the very definition of biblical theology.

---

[112] Ibid., 128, cf. 62–63, 77, 97, 112–138, 167, 255. There is also much discussion of the gifts of the Spirit.

Part two takes up the development of Childs' approach, and its integrity on its own terms. The "inner logic of scripture's textual authority," which relates to *Kanonbewußtsein* and the argument for canonical shaping, is introduced as something with a larger interiority — that is, as neither a form of biblicism, nor a text-immanent reading strategy cut off from questions of reference and truth. First, chapter four sets the stage for Childs' turn from form to final form. As mentioned above, this is the first major shift in Childs' thought, one that is in place by 1970. Hermann Gunkel especially underscores a forgotten aspect of research into the genres of biblical literature — namely, the canon — while establishing an important point of contrast for Childs' radical inversion of tradition history. The discussion also touches on the history of religions as ersatz biblical theology, and on Childs' relationship to von Rad. Second, chapter five comes to the heart of the matter, or the *res*, by exploring Childs' handling of biblical reference. He concludes, on expressly Christian grounds, that biblical reference, and hence biblical intertextuality, is not midrashic but deictic. In other words, the text of scripture points to its subject matter (*res*), which is the one God known in the face of Christ. Then, in chapter six, Childs' early study of midrash is put in the context of his reconsideration of midrash as a uniquely Jewish operation in the 1980s. This is the second major shift in his thought, and it helps explain the nature of his eventual move away from midrash and toward allegory as a Christian figural mode.

Part three sets the "mystery of Israel," an awareness of which spans Childs' work from early on, in the framework of his pursuit of the "mystery of Christ." Since for his own reasons Barr also warms to allegory at about the same time, Barr and Childs are again contrasted in chapter seven. They have different rules for allegory (one geared to the canons of criticism, the other to a rule of faith called canon), and their rules impinge on their doctrines of the Trinity, belief in which each attempts to affirm. Chapter eight then looks at Psalm 102 in Childs' work and in other recent research, setting both against an important Christian theologian and exegete of the psalm in the history of its reception, St Augustine. Here some of Childs' ambivalence about allegory emerges. Does the scope of the psalm encompass the church present as well as past? If so, as a canonical approach maintains, the way Christians articulate this today has consequences for Jewish-Christian dialogue and calls for a careful negotiation of the fault line between parts two and three. Chapter nine, an epilogue, steps toward an assessment of Childs' contribution, although this is necessarily limited. For one thing, the task at hand is primarily to give a credible account of his project in terms of his influences, his critics, and his own incremental decisions. This has not been done before. For another, it is in many respects too early to describe the long range impact of his work. The canonical approach as Childs formulates it has shortcomings — at the end of chapter eight I specify what to my mind is one of the most obvious — and also seems, to some at any rate, to have much to offer. But how it will affect use of scripture in the church or the academy remains to be seen. It will be for others to say.

Lastly, and along the same lines, let me add a word about this study's prospect. As at so many other points it seems appropriate to borrow Childs' language. His foreword to Marion Taylor's study of the OT in the old Princeton school begins as follows:

> Modern biblical scholarship can be characterized by its search for new approaches to the study of the Bible. During this process periods of methodological uncertainty arise when the older ways are abandoned and the newer ones have not yet gained support. Often at such critical moments scholars have turned their attention to the past in an effort to find new paths into the future. One thinks, for example, of how the Reformers found much aid in their struggle from their reapplication of St. Augustine, or how in the period following World War I, many theologians found an entry into the Bible through a rediscovery of the exegesis of Luther and Calvin.[113]

The suggestion is that Taylor's study helps do this at another point. He pays a similar complement at the front of Gerald Sheppard's reissuing of William Perkins' commentary on Galatians. "There can be no simple repristination of the past" for him,[114] and so it is right to press forward. I aim to perform a like service with Childs' own work. Throughout his career, the scholar's specifically Christian profile comes into sharper and sharper relief, and it is instructive to consider how he negotiates the challenges this raises. I think this book can be read with profit by any number of biblical specialists, whether by Jews or Christians, by believers, agnostics or atheists, by those who are sympathetic to what Childs attempts and by those who are not. For practicing Christians who are sympathetic, such as myself, the present situation can feel not altogether different from the one Childs faced. It is different. Ultimately, my hope is that a more complete account of his struggle to hear the total witness of Christian scripture in his own particular time will, in some small way, aid and inform the judgments of theological exegetes in this next generation.

---

[113] In Taylor, *OT in Old Princeton*, ix.

[114] In Sheppard, *A Commentary on Galatians, William Perkins*, xv.

PART I

Reading Childs in English and German

CHAPTER 2

Reading Childs in English and German

An important aspect of biblical interpretation which has often been neglected is the transmission and reception of a writer's work into a foreign language.

— Brevard Childs

Attention has sometimes been paid to the way biblical and theological research is (or is not) transmitted into another language. Take one example each from systematics, New Testament studies and Old Testament studies. First, in an impressive survey Bruce McCormack traces the way German kenotic christologies (those of the nineteenth-century theologians G. Thomasius and W. Gess) were taken up in Britain (in the works of P. T. Forsyth and H. R. Mackintosh), but he notes that I. A. Dorner's powerful criticism of Thomasius and Gess did not immediately follow them across the North Sea. British theologians adopted German kenoticism only after a sharp challenge to it had been mounted in its native Lutheran setting, remaining ignorant of the critique for a good while.[1] Second, Markus Bockmuehl laments the increased parochialism he sees in current NT scholarship, a result of declining linguistic competence.

A generation ago, lip service was still paid to "keeping up" with scholarship in other languages, even if it was already a custom more honored in the breach than in the observance. For anyone inclined to the old-fashioned view (still widely held in the natural sciences) that serious scholarly inquiry is at least in principle a global enterprise, it can only be disheartening to observe how often footnotes in English remain remarkably untouched by directly pertinent recent publications in German, French, or Spanish — and vice versa. Rare is the scholar who bothers comprehensively with the key international publications.[2]

Positive exceptions only prove the rule. Third, Hans-Joachim Kraus concludes the third edition of his history of historical-critical research (1982) by urging his European colleagues to take a more global view, and in particular to heed important new developments in Anglo-Saxon OT and biblical theology.

Es ist erschreckend, wie stark der historisch-verobjektivierende Distanzierungseffekt einer der Phänomene registrierenden "Theologie" die alttestamentliche Wissenschaft isoliert und sie im

[1] McCormack, Passibility, forthcoming in McCormack, *Humility*.

[2] Bockmuehl, *Seeing*, 35. Bockmuehl finds some comfort in the fact "that at least an Anglophone dialogue continues despite the accelerating continental drift separating Europe and America in religious, cultural and geopolitical respects" (36).

> Gefüge theologischer Forschungs- und Lehrinstitutionen zu einer unwirksamen historischen Disziplin prägt. Diese Bemerkung sei verstanden als ein weiterer Beitrag zu der von B.S. Childs und R.E. Clements ins Gespräch geworfenen Behauptung einer *Krise der Biblischen Theologie*.[3]

Kraus calls for a broadened receptivity to foreign input that will aid scholars in overcoming a crisis made worse by institutional and linguistic isolation.

All three of these examples point to the challenge different language contexts pose to an international biblical theology. From a variety of perspectives they corroborate this chapter's epigraph.[4] Further, the difficulty pertains to Brevard Childs' own work in two important respects. First, attention to the transmission and reception of OT scholarship in different languages, especially the exchange between German and English, is a significant minor theme in Childs' publications. (Not only these two languages, though they will be my focus: in his Isaiah commentary, for instance, Childs interacts quite extensively with W. A. M. Beuken's four volume commentary on Isaiah 40–66, which is only in Dutch.[5]) Second, the linguistic borders separating academies has led to a bifurcated reading of Childs himself. Kraus' appeal for international dialogue stands at a turning tide in Childs' reception, as I will illustrate below. Just as Anglophones begin to tune the "canonical approach" out, a handful of German-speaking OT specialists increasingly take notice.

To demonstrate both points, this chapter will overview Childs' tracking of international trends, then look at the way his work has been read in English, and finally characterize the rather different way it has been appropriated in German. It will continue to address a complicating factor introduced in the first chapter, one that influences Childs' reception on both sides of the Atlantic and that stems from the post-*Introduction to the OT* criticism of James Barr.

A. Orientation — Between Europe and America

Childs has been called provincial. In 1979 James Smart criticizes *Biblical Theology in Crisis* for focusing exclusively on the American setting of the crisis. He senses a "failure to set the American crisis in its full international context

[3] Kraus, *Geschichte*[3], 559, cf. 557. See Rendtorff, Bedeutung, 3 (= *Canon and Theology*, 46).

[4] Childs, Wellhausen, 83.

[5] See Childs, *Isaiah*, xii. Childs' sister, Anne Hummel, reports that he began learning Dutch while at Michigan, after Word War II, from a Dutch reformed pastor named Verdine who had taken an interest in his education. Childs studied German in high school and was proficient enough to serve as a translator for the US Army in the War (personal communication, 22 November 2008). These details are corroborated by the late Childs' wife, now Ann Keck, who adds that he began learning French during the War, from the boyfriend of a woman he met in a bookshop in a French village. For all this, she states that Childs often claimed to have struggled with languages (personal communication, 23 November 2009).

which prevents Childs from recognizing the full character and dimensions of the problem."[6] For Smart the problem is international and the solution has to be so too. If one thing stands out in retrospect, however, it is the ease with which Childs moves between Continental, British and American academic contexts. Already in 1970 Childs marks the *difference* between Europe and North America, highlighting contours of the crisis unique to the American scene. Smart was mistaken, and his timing was bad. *Introduction to the OT*, which also appeared in 1979, exhibits an uncommonly broad and international range of engagement. Yet the idea that Childs is somehow cut off from European scholarship has had other iterations. John Barton, surveying method in biblical scholarship, introduces a "Professor B. S. Childs of Yale, whose antecedents are purely Anglo-Saxon," as if the fact that Childs conducted his doctoral studies in Switzerland and Germany in the heyday of the European biblical theology movement left little to no mark on his subsequent research.[7] Barton was at best shortsighted to write, "It is not surprising that Childs has had little following in Germany."[8] That circumstance had begun to change even before Barton's *Reading the Old Testament* (1984) went to press, and it had changed altogether by the time that book was reissued with additional chapters in 1996, at which point Childs' massive Biblical Theology had already been *translated* into German.

Surely where Childs trained matters as much as where he taught. To judge by the prefaces to his books, the period spent at Basel with an interlude for Ancient Near Eastern studies at Heidelberg was highly formative. Eichrodt and Baumgartner guided his doctorate, but Childs counts many other notables among his "unforgettable teachers," including von Rad, Zimmerli, Cullmann, Bornkamm and Barth.[9] Looking back from Yale, Childs felt fortunate to have studied in Europe at a time when "the iron curtain which separates the two Testaments in American universities had not yet fallen"[10] — or conversely, his training made him "painfully aware that an iron curtain separated Bible from

---

[6] Smart, *Biblical Theology*, 29. Cf. Childs, Review of Smart. Barr appears to favor Childs' account of the biblical theology movement to Smart's: *Concept of BTh*, 646n26.

[7] Barton, *Reading*, 2. Barton handles Childs' antecedents in a very strange way. He alleges *logical* antecedents in structuralist thought (104; structuralism has strong Continental roots, of course!) and New Criticism (141, 153), but he ignores more probable *historical* antecedents, such as those Childs encountered personally at Basel and Heidelberg in the early 1950s. (Barth is the lone exception.) The situation is made still more strange by Barton's attempt "to give some idea of [Childs'] programme without for the moment going into its antecedents" (80). Barton spends several pages foregoing the (to him) logical antecedents, with the effect of severing Childs' approach from *all* influences, real or imagined. See further below, page 44.

[8] Ibid., 95. Cf. Seitz, Theological Interpretation, 84.

[9] See the prefaces to Childs' titles, including *Myth and Reality*, *Memory and Tradition*, *Exodus* and especially *Introduction to the OT*, *NT Introduction*, *OT Theology* and *Biblical Theology*. See above for a limited overview of Childs' education and biography, pages 5, 12–13.

[10] *NT Introduction*, xv.

theology, not just at Yale, but throughout most of the English-speaking world."[11] The Cold War metaphor is a reminder of Childs' moment, although curiously the ideological boundary is felt to keep siblings apart in America, or in the English-speaking world, rather than in mainland Europe. There can be no doubt that four years on the Continent impressed Childs greatly, staying with him after his return to America in 1954 and long into his tenure at Yale.[12]

Childs' research shows a pronounced interest in the transmission and reception of biblical scholarship between languages, particularly from German to English. Several examples exist, starting with *BTh in Crisis*. It purposes "to describe the emergence of a distinctive American way of understanding theology in its relation to the Bible." The biblical theology movement there "arose largely in response to certain European influences and continued to reflect a close relationship to the various theological currents abroad," but, contra Smart, "its peculiar American stamp gave the movement a significant shape that distinguished it from its foreign counterparts."[13] The term "Anglo-Saxon" appears at least once in all five chapters of the first half of *BTh in Crisis*, and contrasts with the European situation are noted throughout. For instance, discussing Bultmann and the hermeneutical turn, Childs comments on the German situation, then the American. He sums, "Again, [the debate] is dominated by German theologians whose philosophical concepts are rendered into English often with tortuous results."[14] The broader pattern, on Childs' account, is partial understanding and delayed uptake of German-language trends by American scholars.

Similarly, the article "Wellhausen in English" begins with the sentence that stands atop this chapter. A neglected aspect of Wellhausen's work is the way it was mediated in the late nineteenth century by W. R. Smith, whose controversial career helps explain the initial mistrust of the *Prolegomena* in Britain, and in different ways in America. Six years later, with S. R. Driver's *Introduction* (1891), Wellhausen's reception in English started to change for the better.[15] In an ironical twist, however, at the same time Wellhausen was gaining ground abroad, he was coming under heavy attack at home. W. F. Albright later helped bring this critique into English, laying distinctive emphasis on the idea that Wellhausen was a Hegelian. Yet this assessment too has often been "passed on uncritically," in ignorance of the fact that L. Perlitt challenges and at a least seriously qualifies the Hegelian charge.[16]

---

[11] *Biblical Theology*, xvi.

[12] Childs and his wife, Ann, met at Basel and later kept a second home in Cambridge, where they eventually spent a semester each year (I interviewed them at their Cambridge home in April 2006). They also made regular visits to the European mainland.

[13] *BTh in Crisis*, 13.

[14] Ibid., 81.

[15] Childs, Wellhausen, 84–85.

[16] Ibid., 86. See Perlitt, *Vatke und Wellhausen*, and cf. Childs, Review of Perlitt.

Another piece from the 1980s, "Gerhard von Rad in American Dress," makes the argument that some, especially in North America, take von Rad's dynamic traditioning process as a warrant for their "theological liberalism." Partly "there is a flaw in von Rad's theology which has functioned ... to blur the Christological center of his theology," and partly the Anglo-Saxon readers blatantly disregard this "center" of von Rad's work.[17] Again, an article in 1994 makes the point that, between the world wars, "theological debate concerning the Old Testament was confined largely to the Protestant German-speaking world, and was generally ignored or misunderstood in the English-speaking world."[18] And to take a final example, in his penultimate essay (2005) Childs reflects on the era of the canon debate.[19] The entire piece is *built* around the contrast between English and German scholarship. An earlier German consensus is first briefly summarized. Focus then turns to ways the debate unfolded "within the English-speaking world" in "a period of virtual silence" on canon in Germany.[20] Next, Childs sketches the more recent German scene which, despite a few reservations, he evaluates more favorably.

There is an obvious gap in this late retrospective, however, in that Childs does not plot his own research. If at one level the omission is tactful, it raises a pertinent question: where does his contribution to the canon debate fit? Childs hints that his is a minority view in the American academy,[21] and he is evidently happier about trends back in Europe. What is more, he places the work of one of his American advocates, Stephen Chapman, in the *German*-language section of his overview: "although written in English, it arises more out of the German context."[22] If nothing else, this unexpected taxonomical decision gives us a clue about where Childs feels his own scholarship belongs. Seemingly, Chapman's title is set amidst the German debate for conceptual reasons, because it rejects the disjunction between scripture and canon (Sundberg), and so "the focus did not fall exclusively on the historical forces at work in the process, which dominated the English-speaking debate."[23] A biblical theological dimension was acknowledged as ingredient to the discussion. If Childs had named his own work in 2005, one might suppose that he would have placed it on the German side of the ledger. To a far greater extent than Chapman, whose

---

[17] Childs, Von Rad, 85, 82.

[18] Childs, OT in Germany, 233.

[19] Childs, Reflections on an Era. Interestingly enough, it is an era he judges to have drawn to a close.

[20] Ibid., 36.

[21] Ibid., 32.

[22] Ibid., 35, cf. 36, 38 and 40. Chapman does have ties in Germany, though his theological education occurred at Yale. Christopher Seitz supervised his dissertation (1998), published in 2000 as Chapman, *Law and Prophets*. Chapman readied the title for publication (in FAT) during a fellowship at Tübingen.

[23] Childs, Reflections on an Era, 38. Chapman, *Law and Prophets*, 106–110, makes a strong case for the overlap of "canon" and "scripture."

work is probably a good indicator of the sort of associations "Old Testament at Yale" in Childs' day ought to evoke, it can truly be said of Childs' scholarship that, although written in English — excepting the first draft of his dissertation and a handful of articles in the 1980s and early 1990s — it arises more out of a German context.[24]

My hypothesis is that Childs' work on canon actually inaugurates, at least in part, the new course that the canon debate took in German-speaking contexts

---

[24] At least some of these articles were translated into German by others. If any English *Vorlagen* survive they have not been made available (I once asked Childs for them and was told that the translations were better, since the originals had been written on yellow paper, in pencil). The reason Childs' dissertation went through two versions, in two languages, has been partially told by G. T. Sheppard, who must have been relating information learned from his former supervisor. "At the University of Basel Childs completed his dissertation on the problem of myth in the opening chapters of Genesis just at the time when Walter Baumgartner replaced Eichrodt as the senior Old Testament scholar. Creating consternation at the time, Baumgartner informally refused to accept the methodology of Child's [sic] dissertation, so Childs had to change his plans in order to undertake a full revision... The revised dissertation, *Der Mythos als theologische Problem im Alten Testament* (1953), was never published, though Childs circulated major portions of it under the title *A Study of Myth in Genesis 1–11* (1955) among his wide network of English-speaking scholarly friends" (Sheppard, Childs, 576).

It is difficult to confirm such details now, but at least one is mistaken. Through family members I learned that because Childs' father had died, his widowed mother joined him in Basel for nine months while he finished his thesis. (Childs' first books are dedicated to his wife, Ann, but *Exodus* is "to my mother and to the memory of my father.") In late 1953 Childs seemed about to get through, and he and his mother made plans to return to New York by Christmas. Conflict between Eichrodt and Baumgartner complicated their departure. The family has kindly supplied me with a copy of the letter Brevard Childs' mother sent to "Mrs. Wylie J. Childs," her daughter-in-law, about their trauma. It is dated November 1st, 1953. "So much has happened since yesterday I hardly know where to begin to write. Bard took his exams in the morning, and came through well, Magna Cum Lauda [sic]. He was greatly relieved ... but said he had appointments with Prof. Eichrodt and Prof. Baumgardner [sic] (also O. T.) at 4:30 and 5:30 to talk about his thesis. He had been officially notified that the Faculty had accepted it with corrections. We had a dinner engagement with some American friends at 6:30 then were going to an opera. They all came to the hotel, and no Bard. I got terribly nervous (I don't seem to be able to stand strains any more), and at 8 o'clock the boys phoned Prof. Baumgardner's home, and Bard had just left. Of course, I knew that something was wrong, but I never dreamed how bad it was. There is a terrible conflict between Prof. Eichrodt and Prof. Baumgardner. They hardly speak, and have entirely different views. Bard was supposedly writing for Prof. Eichrodt, but Prof. Baumgardner is co-O. T. Prof. and has as much authority as Prof. Eichrodt. Although Prof. Eichrodt approved the thesis (wants to use it in his seminar), Prof. Baumgardner, who has only recently read it, does not like a lot of things in it. We are coming home as planned, but Bard will have to come back to make the corrections. He can't get the books in America. It just makes me sick. Bard is taking it wonderfully. He will probably return in Feb. The whole trouble was caused by Prof. Eichrodt. Bard and Baumgardner feel the subject was too big, but Prof. Eichrodt insisted upon it. He now realizes his mistake and apologized to Bard, and even invited him to come back as his guest and live in his home. Both Profs. think Bard has done splendid work. It will probably take six months for him to make the corrections."

just as lines of debate were hardening in Britain and North America. (Kraus, quoted in this chapter's introduction, is prescient.) Taking a slightly expanded international view, Childs becomes a middle term in the canon debate. In its influence, his work exists somewhere between English and German, or more precisely between phases of the academic work on canon conducted in these languages. In the two major divisions below — "Reading Childs in English" and "Reading Childs in German" — I will not follow Childs in distinguishing German from English on conceptual grounds but will differentiate simply by language of composition.

B. Reading Childs in English

James Barr has mounted numerous attacks on canonical hermeneutics. He was not always so negatively disposed, but as he states in an appendix to *Holy Scripture: Canon, Authority, Criticism* (1983), the first extended assessment of Childs' proposals, *Introduction to the OT* proved a tipping point. Barr explains in "autobiographical style" that his response to Childs through most of the 1970s was sympathetic. Everything changed in 1979. "The effect of Childs's *Introduction* was to convince me that the programme of canonical criticism [sic] was essentially confused and self-contradictory in its conceptual formulation."[25] Barr's evaluation of the canonical approach in 1983 raises this charge of incoherence at a variety of points. For one thing, Childs' broad use of the key term "canon" masks underlying incompatibilities.[26] Another issue concerns the status of Karl Barth's theology, about which Barr is not very sanguine.[27] A third involves the relationship of Christian theology to scripture. Childs quite

---

Sheppard wrongly supposes the 1953 German title to be the revised title, whereas it appears to be the title formally accepted by the faculty but rejected by Baumgartner. As a concession, Childs was permitted to make his revisions in English. This 1955 version is the one that he circulated, a copy of which is now kept in the archives at Princeton (see page 13) and at Yale. It is also the version catalogued in the libraries of the Universität Basel. Apparently, Karl Barth felt so badly about the whole affair that he called Childs into his office, apologized, and presented him with a set of his books, which he inscribed to Childs. In about 2006 Childs sold some 30,000 volumes of his personal library, including this inscribed set.

[25] Barr, *Holy Scripture*, 132, cf. 133. For a similar narrative compare Barr, *Concept of BTh*, 234–235, 393.

[26] Barr, *Holy Scripture*, 147: "the new 'broad' use of the term has a very simple value: its meaning is identical with the position 'Childs is right.'" The usage should be rejected because "the term is a result of confusion in Childs's thinking... Thus terminology is no accidental factor in the question. The endless repetition of the word 'canon' in canonical criticism is not accident, but necessity: for, as seen from without, the continual reuse of this word is necessary in order to hold together sets of arguments which would otherwise fall apart."

[27] Childs does not understand Barth, Barr alleges, but he is quite like Barth in wanting to make his method "sovereign" (ibid., 146).

ably describes the "cracking of the walls" in the biblical theology movement, but he is wrong to think that the edifice should be rebuilt. Canon delivers "the Grail for which the American Biblical Theology Movement had been the Quest," and so Childs' method "continues the older tradition in that it believes in biblical theology at all."[28] Compounding this, the canon principle is about the form of scripture and not its content, according to Barr. It therefore abandons the task of theology, which must "say something about God, about his works, about Christ and salvation. But in order to do this it must take up just that which Childs forbids, a 'vantage point outside the text'; for only so is it in a position to make estimative judgements, to make decisions about truth."[29] Fundamentally, this is why privileging a canonical context makes the Bible into "a separate cognitive zone," "a closed system" and "an intellectual ghetto separated from all other truth by the walls of relevance."[30] If theology restricts itself to the Bible, it surrenders its claim to truth. Fourth, to Barr's mind Childs' argument depends upon that which it rejects. Childs "contradicts his own deep dependence upon the tradition of critical scholarship… In this respect his work gives the impression of a fulfilment of an inner death-wish of liberal criticism."[31] Fifth, by emphasizing the Bible's final form he moves in a direction that resembles New Critical formalism or structuralism even though he insists, contradictorily, that his outlook is historical.[32] The list could go on.

There are many reasons to begin by profiling Barr's case against Childs. For one thing, some of his indictments have an air of plausibility. Can Childs really climb the ladder of higher criticism and then pull it up behind him? Or can he use "canon" as a cipher for his entire approach without admitting imprecision? These are important questions.[33] Then again, as chapter one illustrates, Barr's voice can obstruct a fair and balanced assessment of the canonical approach. He is known for a critical style as incendiary as it is incisive, and some find this to have tarnished his account of Childs. So Jon Levenson, in a penetrating review of *The Concept of Biblical Theology* (1999), observes that "Barr is harshest on the scholar to whom he refers as 'my friend Professor Brevard Childs,'" and that "Barr vitiates his own potentially formidable case against Childs by continually allowing himself to be diverted from the great hermeneutical issues to attack Childs for this or that comment, some of them mere obiter dic-

---

[28] Ibid., 136, cf. 171.

[29] Ibid., 137.

[30] Ibid., 168. Hence "canonical criticism … is simplistic. Basically it has only one idea: the controlling place of the canon." A fuller quotation is given in chapter one.

[31] Ibid., 148, cf. 132–133. There are later versions of this in *Concept of BTh* (e.g., 48–49, 193, 203, 252n21, 310, 393, 399, 411–412, 433–434) and anticipations in Barr, Childs' Introduction (esp. 14–15, 23).

[32] Ibid., 163, 169.

[33] I explore these and other plausible points raised by Barr throughout this study.

ta."[34] Levenson might as well have been reviewing *Holy Scripture* sixteen years earlier. But even those who prefer a more "fair-minded" account of canonical hermeneutics, such as that of Paul Noble, still tend to buy into Barr's sense that Childs does not know his own mind, and so changes it at whim.[35] To take Childs at his word when he speaks of the *logic* of scripture's textual authority is thus not something many of his readers are prepared to do. Some ground-clearing proves necessary.[36] The primary reason for introducing Barr's critique now, though, is its wide influence on a particular trajectory in Childs' reception, mostly in English but also in German. Barr's strong negative reaction to *Introduction to the OT* lies at the root of a specific and abnormal way of handling Childs' thought, which is to reconstruct it.

In other words, I begin with Barr partly to cast a shadow of doubt upon his notion of Childs as an addled method monger whose thought is not just in development, but incoherent. I begin here all the more because that caricature has travelled well, helping to establish a trend for critical reconstructions that turn Childs' proposals into a putatively more coherent method. Is there really no other kind of logic to the framework as it stands, on its own terms? Barr reached his verdict about Childs long before all the evidence was in (*Concept of BTh* did not really re-open the case, and anyway there are now three books beyond the three that stand between *Holy Scripture* and *Concept of BTh*). His powerful opinion has done much to establish a bizarre precedent even in more generous courts of appeal.

I. Critical Reconstructions of Childsian Hermeneutics

Few treatments of canonical hermeneutics are as ad hominem as Barr's. Childs' so-called method, on the other hand, often emerges as thoroughly muddled. Following Barr's demolition there is a long line of people who offer their hermeneutical services to Childs, unsolicited, by reconstructing a less confused canonical *method* on Childs' behalf — nevermind that Childs claims to

[34] Levenson, Negative Theology, 61–62. He illustrates: "what point does James Barr score against the canonical method by telling us (in the text, not the notes) that Childs' indices are so poor that 'the name of Karl Barth (or, indeed, my own) is cited in the text at numerous places which have been overlooked in the index'?"

[35] Esler, *NT Theology*, here 263, and cf. 309n28–29, is one recent example. Barr frequently suggests that Childs is labile (e.g., *Holy Scripture*, 152–153) and eventually wonders if Childs, in changing from a supposedly "canonical" outline in *Introduction to the OT* to a thematic one in *OT Theology*, has not abandoned a canonical approach altogether (*Concept of BTh*, 397, 422). Contrast Childs' explanation for change in *OT Theology* (15) or *Biblical Theology* (101).

[36] Undoubtedly Ernest Nicholson will not be the only scholar who continues to share Barr's distaste for "the strong zealotic legalism" in Childs' perceived wish to make the final form of the biblical text absolute and thereby to ignore or reject the history of the text's development (Nicholson, *Pentateuch*, 267, citing Barr, *Holy Scripture*, 92). Then again, James Kugel finds this remark and its citation by Nicholson "odd" (*Guide*, 768n36). Kugel may point to a broadening of the more favorable (though qualified) reception of Childs' work in English. See chapter six.

offer neither a criticism nor a method but an *approach*. Alarmingly, there have been no fewer than four monograph-length rehabilitations of Childs in English, and one in German. I will briefly look at each one, taking the English titles in sequence before setting the German one in a broader context.

John Barton: The Prototype for Reconstructing Method

The prototype for critically reconstructing Childsian hermeneutics, which appeared the year after *Holy Scripture*, is a direct extension of Barr's ideas. John Barton's *Reading the Old Testament: Method in Biblical Study* recommends "that the 'canonical approach' of B. S. Childs *ought logically* to be seen as a form of structuralism."[37] The suggestion is made in full awareness that Childs presents his development in other terms.

> There is not the slightest doubt that the route which brought Childs to canon criticism [sic] was as he states it. But this still leaves room, so far as I can see, for all the speculations in chapters 6, 7 and 10 about his literary antecedents. The demise of biblical theology is the reason why Childs looked for something new. It does not explain, except in the most general way, the character of what he eventually found.[38]

Childs cannot be trusted to describe the character of the canonical approach, Barton implies. One is compelled to look elsewhere to understand the logic of his proposal. Even the outline of Barton's book follows out this assumption. Chapter eight, on structuralism, begins, "We have arrived at structuralism *via* canon criticism, but it should be said at once that this is a very winding route, a route possibly never taken before." Structuralism clearly antedates Childs, and Childs himself denies any connection with structuralist theory. The link between them has to be defended solely in terms of logic: "the order of presentation is *not historical, but logical* — and logical within the terms of my own argument, not in a way accepted by the wider scholarly community."[39]

Actually, logic is not a suitable word for the canonical approach left to its own devices, Barton thinks. He finds the method "personally attractive," but "the valid insights that went into its making [must] be salvaged from the

---

[37] Barton, *Reading*, 133, my emphasis.

[38] Ibid., 211. This quotation does not appear in the second edition. The revised edition of *Reading* (Louisville: Westminster John Knox, 1996) is in most respects identical to the first edition up through Chapter 12, after which two chapters are added to bring the survey more up to date. Pagination differences affect only the conclusion and end notes. My interest is in the 1984 edition because of its place in the sequence I am tracing. Even so, the removal of the appendix just quoted has nothing to do with Barton's reading of Childs, as if he recanted of "all the speculations." It was removed in response to James Barr's review, which pointed out flaws in Barton's reading of the demise of biblical theology (xi, foreword to revised edition).

On the habit of calling Childs' program "canon criticism" against his wishes, see especially Barton, *Reading*, 221n3 = ^{2}256n3: the phrase "canon criticism" is "hard to resist" as, seemingly, an emblem of Childs' continuity with method-mongers past and present.

[39] Ibid., 104.

ruins." Barr's influence on Barton at this point is undeniable but not straightforward. *Holy Scripture* "should be regarded as the definitive demolition of canonical criticism in its present form." There is "overlap" with the critique in *Reading.*[40] However, these acknowledgments (deleted in the second edition) appear in a footnote explaining that Barr's book appeared too late to be incorporated into the body of Barton's argument.[41] Strictly speaking, a direct lineage from *Holy Scripture* to *Reading* is not warranted. On the other hand, Barton states at the outset that his "debt to [Barr] will be apparent in practically every chapter,"[42] and this is quite true. Barton and Barr had been colleagues at Oxford for several years at that point, and a number of Barr's riffs on Childs appear to have been picked up by Barton in some way or other.

For instance, Barr and Barton share more than an aversion to fundamentalism. They share a fear that Childs, while not a fundamentalist himself, is liable for aiding and abetting the fundamentalist cause. Possibly the most telling statement occurs in one of Barton's footnotes: the re-establishment of what the Bible traditionally meant, as against what it originally meant, "is why Childs's 'canonical' approach causes such anger, especially to those coping with fundamentalism: it seems designed to take the Christian, so recently liberated from the bonds of 'the tradition,' 'the canon,' 'the *ecclesia docens*,' straight back to the Egypt from which he has come. To such critics Childs seems to be undoing both the Reformation and the Enlightenment; small wonder that they treat him harshly!"[43] Elsewhere, of Barr's "strongly worded suggestion" (in 1980) that Childs will "be quoted by conservative polemicists for the next hundred years,"[44] Barton comments that the charge is overly speculative. "Whether fundamentalists will indeed draw comfort from Childs I am not qualified to judge," he admits. "But the structure of his arguments bears an interesting *analogy* to those used by fundamentalists," he continues.[45] And, damningly: "Canon criticism has many formal similarities with fundamentalism."[46]

---

[40] Ibid., 225.

[41] The comment is deleted in the 1996 edition, but the discussion of the canonical approach has not been revised. See above, note 38.

[42] Ibid., xi.

[43] Ibid., 230n15 = ²265n15. Cf. Barr, Childs' Introduction, 23 and idem, *Holy Scripture*, 148.

[44] Barton, *Reading*, 224n7 = ²259n7, citing Barr, Childs' Introduction, 15. For a response, see Childs, Response to Reviewers, especially 58.

[45] Barton, *Reading*, 98.

[46] Ibid., 99. In Barton's treatment of redaction criticism it becomes clear that comforting fundamentalists could be one of the canonical approach's "hazards" (49). Childs' discussion of P and J accounts of creation in Genesis 1 and 2 prepares the way for the Disappearing Redactor (49–51; cf. *Introduction to the OT*, 145–150). The case is later adduced to show the danger, "a biblical critic's conjuring trick," inherent in redaction criticism (and "canon criticism" to the extent that it is like it): "the redactor of Genesis has so cleverly integrated the two accounts of creation, 'J' and 'P,' by inserting Genesis 2:4a, that they no longer read roughly and awkwardly, and so he has achieved (what one could barely have believed possible) a text

The payoff for this comparison is also drawn from Barr, who asserts in 1983 that Childs' argument reflects an "inner death-wish." The same appraisal is visible *in nuce* in Barr's review of *Introduction to the OT*. In lieu of argument, Barr feels, the case is built upon "the contrast between the weaknesses and antinomies of historical criticism on the one hand and the virtues of the canonical reading on the other." More than that, the "picture painted of [historical criticism] is in fact very close to the conservative/fundamentalist one."[47] Lurking beneath Childs' polemic, however, is an ironic dependence upon the results of critical research. Thus "Childs' actual operation ... is bipolar."[48] Barton adapts just this line of attack in 1984. Like fundamentalists, Childs claims to stand in continuity with pre-critical exegetes. But a major distinction between moderns and pre-moderns needs to be observed. Those in the pre-critical era took the Bible at face value because another option had not yet been considered. It was simply the way everyone read the Bible then. In sharp contrast, fundamentalism and "canon criticism" are oppositional in essence. In both, a polemical bearing is actually the one defining characteristic. "Neither could survive the demise of historical criticism, for they draw all their strength from being able to wage war on it. It is the enemy they love to hate. In both cases the claim to be recapturing a pre-critical approach is attractive but specious."[49] By this logic, both are parasites on criticism, although for Childs the situation might be still more problematic. The fundamentalist wants to shut the door on historical critical research, but Childs has left the door ajar.[50]

---

which the reader is *deceived* into thinking both smooth and consistent" (56–57, my emphasis). Further, this "conjuring trick" gives the fundamentalists the magic they most desire: "it is not difficult to imagine that the trick we have just described is particularly dear to the hearts of fundamentalist opponents of non-conservative biblical criticism, and in their hands it can well become a convenient means of showing that the critics are hoist with their own petard, or (to give our analogy its last run) that when the magic box that contained the redactor is opened, not only is the redactor gone, but Moses himself has stepped into his shoes: *a very frightening prospect indeed for a higher critic of any kind*" (57, my emphasis.). Barr's influence in linking the fear of fundamentalism to a danger latent in Childs' proposals manifests itself on several occasions in *Reading*, not least with the Disappearing Redactor.

[47] Barr, Childs' Introduction, 14.

[48] Ibid., 15.

[49] Barton, *Reading*, 99.

[50] The last point is implicit (ibid., 99): "the canon critic is asking whether the Bible may not have a unity *after all*, just as the fundamentalist is asking whether it might not be right *after all*; and it is the 'after all' that defines the gulf — widest very often when it looks least daunting — which separates the modern critic of whatever persuasion from even the greatest of the pre-critical commentators." A parallel statement can only apply to Childs. "It is only after we have seen how varied and inconsistent the Old Testament really is that we can begin to ask whether it can *nonetheless* be read as forming a unity." Unlike Childs, the fundamentalist actually thinks the canon is a perfect unity. Source theory does not come into it. On this point, according to Barton's reasoning, the fundamentalist position might actually be more logical.

Central to *Reading* is the view that genre competence is a (if not the) central occupation of critical inquiry. It is a question of "reading as."[51] Childs, by brooking source criticism in the first place, makes a mess of the genre competence criterion:

> One could almost formulate the interpretative principle here as follows: Read all these texts as if they were written by one author (say, God) at a single sitting; set out what he must have meant by each of them if he also wrote all the others, and had a consistent purpose in doing so; then delete all references to the author from your final statement of their meaning. We know (from historical criticism) that the biblical texts did not in fact have a single author; but the meaning they have as a canon is the meaning they *would* have if they *had* had a single author.[52]

"Reading as" becomes reading "as *if*." Barton's language for Childs drifts subtly from literary competence to the realm of wishful thinking. Here the intrusion of a unitary canon into a critical paradigm is more illusion than method.

Like Barr, Barton uses a bipolar Childs to deconstruct the canonical approach in other ways. Childs' method wants to be old, but it is actually completely new.[53] It wants to bring pre-critical exegesis back into play, but it refuses to allow "all the old abuses — allegory, harmonization, typology, even downright falsification of the text" — which he would be "far more consistent" to accept.[54] Or again, a prime example occurs in the conclusion, where Barton borrows M. H. Abrams' well-known diagram of four poles of interpretation. Post-structuralism is reader-centric. Structuralism and New Criticism are text-centric. Redaction criticism is author-centric. But "canon criticism" cannot make up its mind. It looks like redaction criticism sometimes, but its main principles are text-centric. "Canon criticism is, as we saw, superficially like redaction criticism, ... [but] in reality most canon-critical suggestions do not depend on historical investigation at all... Here for the first time in Old Testament criticism we have a concentration on *the text itself* [the central node in

---

To anticipate, Barr and Barton also believe that the advent of historical criticism (or just "criticism") is a true Copernican revolution. See chapter seven. As Barton writes here: "All historical-critical work in biblical studies, it is not too much to say, depends on [authorial intention]. The great, and liberating, achievement of biblical criticism has been to establish, for a large number of texts, what the original author(s) meant *as against* what the text had traditionally been taken to mean by the Church, the synagogue or individual pre-critical interpreters" (184, cf. 95). This is why Childs threatens to carry us back in to slavery in Egypt.

[51] Ibid., 8–29, and esp. 134, 199.

[52] Ibid., 102.

[53] Ibid., 100. Cf. 221n3 = ²256n3.

[54] Ibid., 84–85, cf. 97. Does he really exclude these things (allowing for a moment that they are not always abuses)? Barton charges that "Childs's position would be far more consistent if he were to follow [de Lubac's] line of thinking, but his loyalty to Reformation principles about the 'literal' sense of Scripture holds him back, producing incoherence" (223n6 = ²258n6). In fact Childs' increased openness to figuration later in his career is perfectly compatible with, and even anticipated by, his early piece on the *sensus literalis*, which appeared in 1977.

Abrams' diagram], rather than on its relation to other things." Hence Childs' "move from redaction criticism is seen in its true light."[55] Childs is conscious that he is making a radical proposal; he is but dimly aware how unlike all critical Biblical scholars before him he becomes. Taking all his proposals at once, his method cannot even be placed at a node on Abrams' diagram!

The upshot of all this perceived methodological confusion is that Childs must be "salvaged from the ruins." Barton is somehow attracted to the canonical approach — possibly the biggest difference with Barr — but he cannot accept it on its own terms. In the interest of logical consistency, the kindest thing to do is to shore up Childs' inadequacies on his behalf. He asks, "Is there any way of *modifying the method*, perhaps giving it a *narrower and less ambitious scope*, that would nevertheless do justice to our sense that its innovations are sometimes fruitful, not always perverse?"[56] In a sense this has become a mantra among certain of Childs' readers. Barton's own answer is to marry Childs to the New Critics (among his supposed Anglo-Saxon antecedents, and with Yale ties), although the dowry becomes yet another way of problematizing canonical hermeneutics.[57] Here too one suspects that in the background lies a suggestion first made by Barr, who writes,

> canonical criticism would gain in theoretical strength and consistency by such a move [toward critical theory]. Any of these movements — modern literary theory, structuralism, Ricoeur's hermeneutics — is based on a *far sounder philosophical foundation* than the often *muddled conceptual incoherence* of canonical criticism. A really non-historical, literary study of the Bible on the basis of its shapes, styles and motifs could be very interesting... The *logic* of canonical criticism, and especially of its antipathy to older criticism and its historical interest, seems clearly to go in that direction.[58]

Separated by just a year, *Holy Scripture* and *Reading* delivered a quick one-two punch to the allegedly puzzled face of "canon criticism." The combined effect was to make a way for several more critical reconstructions of Childs' logic. Barton and Barr made it possible to take for granted that Childs had no coherent method to hand.

---

[55] Ibid., 202 = ^{2}241.

[56] Ibid., 100, my emphasis.

[57] Ibid., 158: "New Criticism and canon criticism stand or fall together: they are children of the same literary culture, even if they have never met. In this chapter I shall suggest that they should probably fall — encouraged in this by the knowledge that one of them has already fallen." Of course it could be that a Yale-style New Criticism lies somewhere beneath Childs' so-called method — Cleanth Brooks taught in New Haven from 1947 to 1975 — but that would not be the first or most likely place to look for antecedents to the canonical approach.

[58] Barr, *Holy Scripture*, 161–162, my emphasis; cf. idem, Childs' Introduction, 23.

Mark Brett: A Charitable Reconstruction?

Mark Brett's "charitable reconstruction" of Childs, *Biblical Theology in Crisis?*, is subtly written and raises a handful of salient concerns. A discussion of the theological nature of Childs' disagreement with representatives of the tradition-historical school is perceptive, if underdeveloped.[59] Nuance is evident in his treatment of the relationship of historical particularity to contemporary appropriation, and again in a section on synchronic interpretation.[60] Sometimes he defends Childs against unjustified criticisms, including from Barr and Barton.[61] Yet the book rests uncritically on the premise that Childs' work is methodologically inoperable as it stands. Brett follows "Barton's balanced account," differing seriously only on the score of Childs and New Criticism. There are obvious affinities between them, he finds, but "there is a much wider range of literary theories that might be fruitfully compared."[62] (Actually, this departure is something of a necessity since New Criticism serves Barton as another means by which to discredit the method.) Brett explains,

> Our discussion, as with Barton's, is not simply an account of Childs's scholarly intentions. Nor is it an attempt to evaluate a biblical scholar by "external" criteria provided by the philosophy of interpretation. Rather, there are certain weaknesses in Childs's methodological reflections which can be *charitably reconstructed* by comparisons with the influential works of Hans-Robert Jauss, Karl Popper and Hans-Georg Gadamer. Childs has received some unjustified criticism, and I aim to show how the canonical approach can become a coherent mode of biblical interpretation.[63]

What exactly makes the endeavor charitable is not clear. Brett simply assumes that the logic of the canonical approach is flawed, and so can be detached from Childs. "I have drawn from the work of Childs in a highly selective way, and this *ad hoc* method of reconstruction finds its justification in the fact that Childs himself has failed to provide a coherent exegetical theory."[64] His whole evaluation of Childs builds upon this somehow self-evident fact.

Brett likewise redraws the portrait of a bipolar Childs. He separates that which is distinctive about Childs, in his judgment, from that which is confused or confusing. At times we almost have several people in our hands. One Childs is adamant about the priority of the final form. Another Childs is interested in

---

[59] Brett, *Crisis?*, 96–100. His failure to recognize the extent of Childs' debt to this tradition shows an under-appreciation of the German context for Childs' work, and this despite attention to some of the relevant literature, by von Rad and Oeming (78, 168n4). *Why* does von Rad seem to anticipate Childs?

[60] Both of these themes feature in his fourth chapter, "Has Childs fallen into Gabler's ditch?," to which his answer seems to be: not necessarily (114).

[61] Ibid., 117, 145. For a response to the former see Barr, Crisis?, 139.

[62] Brett, *Crisis?*, 5.

[63] Ibid., 5, original emphasis.

[64] Ibid., 27. Making an appeal to *Holy Scripture*, he continues, "This lack of a coherent theory has turned out to be one of the major obstacles to a balanced appreciation of his work."

the history of interpretation. Yet another wants to talk about the prehistory of collective meanings (streams of tradition, perhaps). But "in these cases he speaks as an historical critic (usually a sceptical one) and not as an advocate of a distinctive canonical approach."[65] The resulting picture is one of "exegetical schizophrenia," for "Childs is constantly switching hermeneutical hats."[66] Again, Childs can argue like a "totalitarian," hermeneutical monist, but in his better moments the pluralist Childs prevails. Obviously "the second Childs is to be preferred."[67] This is also the thrust of the interrogative recasting of Childs' 1970 title. Is biblical theology in crisis? A fragmentary discipline is not a crisis but a state consistent pluralists ought to embrace.[68]

This strategy has the weird result of severing Childs from his argument for the final form in order to provide him with one. With respect to Childs' claims for a canonical shaping by the tradents of the Hebrew text, Brett — who neither uses the phrase "canon consciousness" nor refers to the formative article of I. L. Seeligmann — tries to show that an interest in the text's prehistory cannot coexist with the subsequent use of scripture in the church or synagogue, and feels that "in this respect some of Childs's methodological statements are just misleading. However, this recognition in no way damages Childs's overall argument [!], since his exegetical interest does not rest on a reconstruction of the canonical or textual processes. The main lines of his argument rest rather on a theory of continuous textual usage." The truly significant interest pertains to "that golden thread of continuous usage which extends to the present."[69] Neither does Childs need, however much he might want, to invest heavily in the history of exegesis, a "logically separable interest."[70] All he really needs is a solid theory of continuous usage (Brett turns to Gadamer's notion of a classic text) and, to escape the confusions of "canonical intentionality," a "theory of relatively autonomous texts."[71] With these components in place the method will be freed to be its distinctive, formalist self and can get on with the business of generating new and interesting readings of biblical material. This is the basic shape of Brett's "charitable reconstruction of the canonical process."[72]

In summary, Brett makes no effort to see why Childs might have coherent interests in the final form, its prehistory and its reception history all at once.

---

[65] Ibid., 172n20, cf. 66–67.

[66] Ibid., 68. In 1999 Barr quotes the latter phrase approvingly (*Concept of BTh*, 392).

[67] Ibid., 11, cf. 42, 68, 71.

[68] The book's parting shot is a conscious echo of Barton's closing sentiment in 1984. Brett says, "Childs wants to put all our theological eggs in one basket — the canonical approach. It would be more responsible, on the pluralist argument, to distribute them widely" (167). Compare Barton, *Reading*, 211.

[69] Brett, *Crisis?*, 64.

[70] Ibid., 7, cf. 52–57.

[71] Ibid., 26.

[72] Ibid., 133.

His justification for isolating different nodes of interest, in an *ad hoc* fashion, derives solely from the authority of Barr and Barton, and his suggestion for salvaging Childs' method follows Barton's prototype. The *logical* Childs, the Childs we all want but must reconstruct, is the text-immanent Childs. Thus "Childs *qua* historical critic" analyzes one thing, but then the essential Childs forgets this and "focuses on the communicative intention of *text itself* without correlating this intention with a particular historical period, social group or author."[73] By now it should be plain that Brett offers just a variation on Barton, who had suggested that "'canonical method' logically implies that the biblical text, or indeed any other text, can be read without paying any heed to the intentions of authors, compilers or even canonizers. It is not a sub-type of redaction criticism; it is an attempt to read 'the text itself.'"[74] And as has also been seen, the idea that Childs would do better with a purely "non-historical," text-immanent reading strategy comes from Barr in the first instance.

It is with considerable irony, therefore, that Barr's review of *Crisis?* chides Brett because "he fails to read Childs's mind rightly."[75] Probably "Childs himself will reject this charitable approach," writes Barr, and "the book will not have served Childs very well."[76] Barr makes another very apropos observation. Brett has not considered why Childs does not himself take his approach in a pluralist or formalist direction more like, say, James Sanders. "Thus, though Brett has done very well in analysing many particular exegetical statements and arguments of Childs, he does not seem to have explained what lies behind them."[77] But if it seems odd that Barr should take an interest in Childs' mind and his antecedents — historical as opposed to logical antecedents, contra Barton — the explanation relates to one thing Barr seems fairly pleased about, that *Crisis?* "adds to the total impression of incoherence." To Barr, what actually lies behind Childs' ideas explains the confusion. "Most obvious … is the failure of the book to provide any study in depth of the influence of Karl Barth… For Barth is not only an influence but is very likely the source of the antinomies and peculiarities which Brett has so well identified."[78] Barth's dogma combined with critical biblical scholarship "could not fail to produce contradictions." So again, repeating an earlier allegation, "there is nothing *difficult* in the canonical approach: it is easy to enter into, indeed simplicity itself, but its incoherences are equally easy to see."[79] Barr can hardly value a reconstruction of logic he

---

[73] Ibid., 68–69.

[74] Barton, *Reading*, 102.

[75] Barr, Crisis?, 139. Cf. also Moberly, Review of Brett.

[76] Barr, Crisis?, 137. He changes his tune in 1999. Having then seen Noble's reconstruction (below), which is more generous to Childs, Barr declares Brett's account "the best discussion published" (*Concept of BTh*, 392).

[77] Ibid., 137.

[78] Ibid., 139.

[79] Ibid., 140, original emphasis.

does not find compelling in the first place, but he does not recognize the extent to which he made it possible to disregard Childs' mind in the first place.

Barr introduces an important consideration into the assessment of Childs' work. What are his influences? How do his ideas stand in relation to theirs? Barr's hunch about the matter raises one possibility but it seems clear to me that "Barthian dogma" is insufficient as a total answer. I will try to give a fuller one in the next chapter, since a still-outstanding question is whether Childs' antecedents — let them be real, and let them not be restricted to Barth nor glossed as shorthand for failure — can be treated in a way that accords Childs' conception of his approach at least a degree of plausibility.

Paul Noble: Another Reconstruction of Canonical Hermeneutics

Paul Noble's 1995 reconstruction improves upon Brett's in many respects. To start with, it stands this side of Childs' magnum opus, and so is able to deal with the christological telos in Childs' work. (Brett's timing could not have been worse. *Biblical Theology* appeared the next year, rendering parts of *Crisis?* almost immediately obsolete.[80]) Noble also sees that Barr's *Holy Scripture* "shows little comprehension of the structure and goals of Childs' programme." Barton, too, "gives an unbalanced construal of Childs' work."[81] And "Brett has not really grasped what Childs' distinctive 'interpretative interests' actually are"; his account is "an over-hasty dismembering of Childs' work."[82] Noble appreciates that the major treatments of Childs before him are inadequate, and he sets the record straight on some counts. Yet for all this he does not escape Barr's theory of a bipolar Childs. As in Brett the premise is asserted with remarkably little argument, and it becomes determinative for the entire account:

> One important theme that keeps recurring throughout the secondary literature, however, is that Childs' own methodological foundations are insufficient for the superstructure he wishes to build upon them; and this has naturally led to various thinkers and schools of thought being suggested as providing the theoretical underpinning which Childs' work needs. In my view this is a potentially valuable way of trying to rectify what is, I believe, a significant defect in Childs' own presentations of his work. Much of the present book, therefore, will also adopt this strategy.[83]

Noble wants to proceed more cautiously than those before him so as not to create another distorted analysis of the essentials of Childs' program, which should be permitted "to explain itself *on its own terms*." Only after that has been done will he suggest methodological improvements. Despite his caution, the reconstructive aspiration is affirmed — he finds many tensions in method,

[80] See especially Brett, *Crisis?*, 60–61.
[81] Noble, *Canonical Approach*, 3.
[82] Ibid., 6, 175.
[83] Ibid., 7.

and "these tensions have continued to haunt his later work, and are significant factors in [*Biblical Theology*] falling some way short of Childs' goals."[84] Childs' vision as Noble understands it needs to be "recast."[85]

Noble's account remains useful in a qualified sense. For example, it offers a competent discussion of the literature on Gadamer and Childs. The links between these thinkers are explored in much greater depth than previously.[86] Second, Noble provides a measured orientation to the descriptive task and the differences between Stendahl and Childs. "Childs' purpose," he qualifies, "is not to *deny* that a distinction can be drawn between the descriptive and the normative but to *relativize* it."[87] Third, the handling of intentionality in Childs is more generous and comprehensive. Noble finds "Childs' work has received a seriously one-sided presentation in this respect from John Barton, who focuses almost exclusively upon the anti-intentionalist strand."[88] Even though the language of intentionalist and anti-intentionalist strands serves a parsing of Childs' thought to accommodate other ends — Noble prefers to have an exclusively intentionalist Childs — the study correctly draws out both.

Still, the book is not as successful at representing Childs' interests as one would hope. Regarding authorial intent, Noble concludes that "Childs ought therefore to maintain a consistently intentionalist stance."[89] Noble argues for an objectivist hermeneutic, which must be moored in intentionalism lest it drift into indeterminacy, and for him this is a danger that needs correcting in Childs and Gadamer alike. Childs is misguided not to take sides in debates about the author. In this basic sense Noble agrees with Barton and Brett. (Like Noble, Barton is more of an intentionalist. He thinks Childs would have been more consistent to go in a direction like Brett's, but this is not really a course he recommends. That is, against Brett, Noble and Barton seem to agree about the priority of authorial intent, but Noble choses a "strand" to reconstruct that he actually thinks will work. Barton's reduction of Childs' method to an anti-

[84] Ibid., 7.

[85] Ibid., 369.

[86] Ibid., 235–253, 254–271, 282–289, 328. In addition to Brett, earlier discussions include those of Scalise, Theological Basis and Fowl, Childs (more indirectly, see Oeming, *Gesamtbiblische*, which treats Gadamer and von Rad and also makes reference to Childs — though see section C, below). Further analysis of Childs and Gadamer could be illuminating but is not integral to this study.

[87] Noble, *Canonical Approach*, 23, cf. 30. Noble cannot see any difference between Stendahl and Childs in practice, though one wonders whether he has reckoned adequately with Childs' purpose in not making Stendahl's two questions *paradigmatic* (e.g., in Noble's summary, "(i) What did the biblical writers believe?; and, (ii) What ought we to believe?" [336, cf. 369]). Barr fails even to acknowledge Noble's discussion of Childs and Stendahl (*BTh in Crisis*, 189–190, 202 [cf. Levenson's review], 206, 379–380, 414), but others have been fully persuaded by it (Esler, *NT Theology*, 263–265).

[88] Noble, *Canonical Approach*, 50.

[89] Ibid., 328.

intentionalist "strand" is ironic and deconstructive.) The methodological outcomes for Barton, Brett and Noble are all different, but despite Noble's more cautious beginning he follows his predecessors in the belief that reconstruction is necessary. Could Childs' approach have its own kind of logic? Like others, Noble does not entertain this possibility long enough.

In this way Noble's reconstruction yields its share of implausibility. The notion of a labile Childs creates very tortuous pictures of his development. In one case, Childs has "fluctuated considerably" on the place of historical criticism in his program. In an early article ("Interpretation in Faith," 1964) Noble finds strong statements for the place of historical research in a faith perspective. There are hints of the same in *BTh in Crisis*, only "now more muted." Surprisingly, in *Introduction to the OT* "all such reservations seem to have disappeared." But then *NT Introduction* "reintroduces doubts about the inherent soundness of critical tools."[90] Such extreme dithering from publication to publication is far-fetched, evocative of the caricatures drawn by Barr and Barton, and built on a dubious use of the evidence. Sometimes a narrative like this justifies Noble's methodological intervention on Childs' behalf.[91] At other times it leads to a premature dismissal of Childs' work. *Biblical Theology* is a case in point. From the start we are told that the volume "falls a long way short" of Childs' goals.[92] But how does he know this? Disappointment is taken as given, though it is pretty clearly Noble's and not Childs'.

In addition to the idea that tensions of method "haunt" all of Childs' work, Noble perceives a failure to inaugurate the Old Testament as a witness to Christ, one of Childs' basic goals for a Biblical Theology. His culminating work "still seems to have made little progress towards setting the reading of the Old Testament as Christian Scripture on a methodologically sound basis. And likewise, therefore, he has made little progress towards hearing the two Testaments as co-witnesses to the one divine reality."[93] It is doubtful that Noble gets to the heart of the "pan-canonical" problem, however.[94] Discussion of the OT in the NT stalls out in a fairly superficial question of whether Paul's "midrashic" exegesis amounts to more than eisegesis.[95] Noble's own recommendation merely trivializes the challenge of hearing Christ in the OT. "Of course, the human authors could not, of themselves, have written proleptically of Christ; but positing God as the ultimate author of the canonical books provides the necessary epistemological underpinnings."[96] Very briefly this is attempted with Isai-

[90] Noble, *Canonical Approach*, 58.

[91] Ibid., 35–36, 37.

[92] Ibid., 76, cf. 7.

[93] Ibid., 73, and see all of 65–76. On the face of it these claims constitute a *non sequitur*.

[94] Ibid., 302. Cf. Barr's adaptation of the German term "gesamtbiblische" a few years later.

[95] E.g., see ibid., 305 (did Paul hear the intent of the OT or not?) and 158 (if midrash is not legitimate for us, why is it acceptable for the Chronicler or for Paul?).

[96] Ibid., 345.

ah 53, in which Noble seems to need "genuine foreknowledge of the future," specifically Christ's passion, rather than merely "a general presentiment of a coming Messiah," entailing a much stronger account of inspired divine authorship than Childs gives — though for Noble exegetical details are of secondary importance "since we are concerned with methodological principles rather than with the actual interpretation of Isaiah 53."[97] Lacking the full sense of how much Childs struggles with exactly this question in subsequent works (2001 and 2004), with its taxing hermeneutical *and* exegetical aspects, for which Noble in 1995 cannot really be faulted, one can still judge that his alternative to what Childs offers in 1992 is just a little too convenient.[98]

Another deficiency is the absence of any account of the scholarly context for Childs' work. No mention is made of the tradition out of which *Biblical Theology* arises. Barr's point about *Crisis?* remains unaddressed. In addition to a few scattered references to von Rad, one slight exception is an adjudication between Childs, Barr, Pannenberg and von Rad on the interrelation of "fact" and "interpretation." The shaping of the traditioning process is also mentioned in passing, but it simply does not suffice to dismiss Childs' critique of von Rad in a few lines.[99] Further, though Noble (contra Brett) rightly affirms Childs' interest in the motives behind the canonizing process, he cannot offer an accurate critique when he shows no awareness of where and how Childs develops the argument for the final form's shaping.[100] How can Noble suggest that Childs become "more flexible in his account of the tradition-process" lest, entering as he would need to "contemporary debates about the traditions behind the canonical text," he should find himself with "a daunting historical-critical mountain to climb," as if no engagement with this very debate had ever been attempted?[101] Still most disappointing are Noble's occasional attempts to improve Childs with Childs' own resources. An effort to connect the Testaments typologically calls on Hans Frei.[102] And Barth is praised as a more exemplary exegete of the OT as Christian scripture (strangely, not because of his exegesis per se, but because of the methodological issues Barth raises).[103] Noble is aware that Childs interacts with these figures, but the impression left by his treatment is of the thinnest contact.

---

[97] Ibid., 205–206. Again: "Only *divine* authorship could account for the meanings Childs wishes to find in the Bible" (206).

[98] Childs' eventual conclusions about Isaiah 53 will be discussed in chapter seven.

[99] As before, the felt need is for "some kind of doctrine of 'inspiration.'" Ibid., 140, 143.

[100] Ibid., 179–180, 183 (cf. 146–7, 152–155). Is Childs' argument for the priority of the final form really "transcendental"? Tellingly, I. L. Seeligmann is referenced nowhere.

[101] Ibid., 186–187. Contrast *Introduction to the OT.*

[102] Ibid., 306–327. "Clearly there are a number of ideas [in Frei's *Eclipse*] which are potentially of some value for a canonical approach to biblical interpretation" (309).

[103] Ibid., 76–80, cf. 345–347. Childs takes almost the opposite view. See the next chapter.

The Childs who emerges, in short, is a great assembler of proposals — the canonical principle above all — who desperately needs a methodology. *BTh in Crisis* was beset by problems of method. These went underground during a phase of descriptive work (1979, 1984) but resurfaced when Childs returned to writing theologies:

> The full range of issues, however, is taken up again in the canonical Theologies; moreover, their nature is such that the argument has to be carried mainly by the exegetical studies of the biblical texts rather than by the methodological discussions. As we have now seen, however, this quickly leads to the previously unresolved methodological problems resurfacing again. In view of this, therefore, it is not going too far to say that Childs' programme is currently in a state of crisis: It has long-standing methodological problems that greatly hinder its implementation, and which it has made little progress towards resolving.[104]

Despite a variety of advances in some particulars, Noble's reconstruction is still of a piece with Brett's and Barton's. Childs' most important antecedents are ignored or discounted. The logic of his program, taken in the abstract, is quickly judged inoperable. The canonical approach is an approach and not a brand of criticism (at last!), but it lacks a method as much as ever before.

In a way, Noble is right that Childs does not have a method. While Childs often speaks of the methodological, or more commonly, the hermeneutical issues at stake, he explains his preference clearly in the preface to his New Testament Introduction. "In the end I would rather speak of a new vision of the text rather than in terms of method."[105] In chapter one we began to see how canon implies a rule of faith for Childs, as early as 1970, and we will further explore what this means for his approach in chapter seven. The point for now is simply this: lacking a formal methodology is not the same as lacking a coherent and workable approach. Nor does it automatically entail a lack of hermeneutical sophistication. Terminological distinctions between criticism and approach, between method and vision, turn out to matter quite a bit in the case at hand. The assumption that they do not participates in an old and tired bias that Childs does not know his own mind.

William Lyons: Childs in Perspectival Perspective

For the sake of completeness we can include W. J. Lyons' *Canon and Exegesis*, which makes few advances in the evaluation of Childs' corpus. Lyons declines to comment on *Isaiah*, so it is not much more up to date than Noble's study.[106]

---

[104] Ibid., 77, cf. 174, 313, and passim. Or as he sums up later, "As a methodological investigation, this book has been primarily concerned with the *genuineness* of Childs' programme" — genuineness for Noble being a question of whether "it is methodologically equipped to do all that a theology ought to do" (361–362). The enterprise is, with modification, "on the whole, methodologically defensible" (359).

[105] *NT Introduction*, xvii.

[106] Lyons, *Canon*, 32.

Positively, the rule of faith comes into the mix,[107] and comments on the *sensus literalis* and referentiality go a little way beyond Brett by holding ostensive reference and historical background in tension.[108] An effort is made to redefine biblical theology in terms more favorable to Childs, interacting with Barr's *Concept of BTh*. Some recourse is made to German scholarship. This, however, has little impact on how Lyons locates Childs' contribution. Ebeling's call for a biblical theology of both OT and NT is rightly seen as relevant, though it almost appears as if Ebeling were the only impetus behind *Biblical Theology*.[109] There is an account of Childs' *Ausbildung*,[110] yet for some reason the figures in Europe under whom Childs learned a profound interest in problems of biblical theology play almost no role in Lyons' discussion. Finally, Lyons shows that his book belongs with the other reconstructions: "like many others, I have tended to pick and choose among Childs's many fruitful suggestions, discarding those that I have deemed unhelpful."[111]

Sometimes it seems as if Lyons does not feel another reconstruction is necessary. When detailing several aspects of "canon" Lyons defends Childs against an "appearance of weakness" left by previous treatments.[112] "Although the interplay between these … elements has caused considerable confusion for both Childs and his critics, it may also be responsible for much of the strength of Childs's canonical approach."[113] Later he tries to show how the fact that Childs' hermeneutics have "virtually always been regarded as requiring reconstruction" is not a setback: "this lack of development to Childs's hermeneutics does not necessarily mean that his approach is thereby rendered indefensible or in need of severe reconstruction if it is to survive. The question is, can Childs's language and concerns be explained and justified by a particular hermeneutical approach *without any substantive change in its self-conception or praxis*?"[114] Implicit, however, is the standard view that Childs lacks a mature hermeneutical framework. Lyons thinks he can "leave the essential contours of Childs's work intact"[115] by rejecting the "objectivist" approach of Noble in favor of the "perspectival hermeneutics" of Stanley Fish. "The final consequence of accepting a Fishian hermeneutic for the canonical approach is that Childs's set-one terminology — that relating to 'objectivity' — must be recast in terms sensible to the kind of language which can be used to describe a con-

---

[107] Ibid., 8, 28. Not too surprisingly, he finds that "a confusion exists in Childs's work as to the correct usage of this term."

[108] Ibid., 69.

[109] Ibid., 34. See the discussion of Childs and Ebeling above, in chapter one.

[110] Ibid., 25–26. The year of Childs' birth (1923) is incorrectly given.

[111] Ibid., 32.

[112] Ibid., 45.

[113] Ibid., 42.

[114] Ibid., 82, original emphasis.

[115] Ibid., 85.

sistent set-two formulation of the canonical approach, to dress the canonical approach in 'perspectival' clothes."[116] Like the rest, Lyons takes what he likes and leaves the rest.

For Lyons the technique has an extremely subjective outcome. Frequently he speaks of "my" canonical reading. This plays out exegetically in a bizarre intrusion of "my 'feminist' problem" in the Sodom narrative, and in a psychologization of Abraham in Genesis 18.[117] Coupled with his praise of perspectivalism, results like these leave this reader in serious doubt about whether Lyons has done justice to the "self-conception" of Childs, as professed. Lyons is almost aware of this limitation. Surprised at his exegesis, he writes: "Perhaps it is a case of being too close to one's own work, of liking its results too much." And his final comment on Childs begins: "In many ways I like what I have found exegetically in the canonical approach of Brevard Childs."[118] He also reveals how he finds himself "in the rather embarrassing position of offering a new reading based upon a canonical approach to the biblical texts."[119] Thankfully, it is not necessary to ascribe the embarrassment to Childs.

II. Conclusion: Pro-bono Psychotherapy is No Charitable Reading

Barton, based on a sense that Childs' "innovations are sometimes fruitful, not always perverse," once wondered how Childs' method could be made less ambitious, recommending (with Barr) a route that he himself was not much inclined to follow. He thus sent many of those interested in canonical hermeneutics off searching for a method to the madness.[120] Barr asserted meanwhile that it was mostly just madness and reinforced the pattern of reading Childs against Childs. Their combined efforts in 1984 and 1983 spawned a persona whose mind is indeed divided, even fractured. But the Childs who needs treatment for an affective disorder, schizophrenia, or some other psychic malfunction lives in an ungainly body of secondary literature. And that Childs, I suggest, is largely a work of fiction, a Frankenstein hatched in an unhappy dream that lingers in daylight much longer than it should. The four major English reconstructions of Childsian hermeneutics all share in the view that something in the canonical approach *is* perverse, even when they do not use Barton's exact language, because they proceed to excise whatever in Childs' approach does not suit the desired method. None of these readings qualify as

---

[116] Ibid., 122, cf. 95. But see also Noble, *Canonical Approach*, 57, 206–218.

[117] Lyons, *Canon*, 266, 208, cf. 272–273. As he explains, "The strongest justification for my rejecting the coherence of Abraham was not originally its obviousness as a reading of the text, but rather my personal discomfort with the implications of the readings of Ben Zvi and von Rad for subsequent texts, for the whole canonical text itself" (273).

[118] Ibid., 275.

[119] Ibid., 269.

[120] Examples could be multiplied. For one of the first, see Morgan, Madness?, 92.

charitable in the usual sense of the word. What happens if Childs' work proves to have a logic of its own, even if it is a logic one finally chooses not to enter? If so, all of these readings stand upon the same fatal flaw. As readings of Childs, they fail. To adapt Barr's language, if there is logic in what Childs does, they fail "to read Childs's mind rightly" and have "not have served Childs very well."

Naturally there are readers who do not see the need to offer their charity. (Some may feel rather in Childs' debt.) One of these is Stephen Chapman, who makes an important suggestion in his review of Noble's reconstruction. We see that a major issue in deciding what to do with Childs has been to determine for or against intentionalist and anti-intentionalist "strands," on the belief that these are logically separable interests. For Childs they are not. As Chapman has it, "What Noble fails to realize is how these claims fit together in a distinctive manner within Childs's hermeneutics — i.e. that for historical reasons both kinds of claims must be made."[121] As I try to put it in chapter one, above, more than usual counts as "history" for Childs. This is seen in (for example) his handling of the final form of the crossing of the sea in the Sprunt Lectures and in his Exodus commentary, *in addition* to his incorporated source-critical discussion from a 1952 seminar with Baumgartner. History does not evanesce in the final form. Instead, it takes on more dimension. Conversely, when Barr says that a canon-oriented approach falls short of "a really non-historical, literary study of the Bible," he limits the scope of history in a way that makes it hard to appreciate what Childs is about. In terms of Abrams' diagram, one cannot do justice to Childs' thought if movement between different historical nodes (production, reception, the text as we have it) is not allowed.

Childs has other Anglophone readers, to be sure. It will be obvious that the work of scholars more sympathetic to Childs' articulation of his approach also informs this study. Harrisville and Sundberg surface in chapter one, and we have heard from a handful of Childs' former students, such as Chapman, Seitz and Sheppard. Other obvious North American scholars include Ellen Davis, Robert Wall and Kavin Rowe, and from Great Britain one thinks of Nathan MacDonald, Neil MacDonald and Walter Moberly. Nor is this the limit, since the extent of Childs' more positive reception cannot be restricted to a catalog of those who might be counted among his natural allies. If work like this is less conspicuous, it is not because it has been excluded from consideration. Rather, my main purpose in this section has been to denude the structure that has helped establish and reinforce the predominantly dismissive way Childs is read in English. Barr's initial demolition and the subsequent reconstructions of Barton, Brett, Noble and Lyons warrant special attention because, taken together,

[121] Chapman, Reclaiming Inspiration, 173n28. Is it really the case, as Noble maintains (*Canonical Approach*, 352), that one must choose between intentionalist objectivism or fideism? On the closely related theological issue of inspiration, Noble's presentation of Childs' position (208, 219–253 [esp. 299], 340–353) has likewise been surpassed by Chapman's.

they have made Childs harder to understand and not the reverse. Some of their readings have had an influence on the European mainland as well, but in very general terms Childs' work has enjoyed a more patient reception there.

C. Reading Childs in German

Childs' reception in German is no more uniform than his reception in English. Something of the range can be seen in two installments of *Wissen*, C. H. Beck's slender paperback series, both of which appeared in revised 3rd editions in 2006. Christoph Dohmen's introduction to the Bible and its exegesis builds upon the view that, for an appreciation of "der literarischen Eigenart biblischer Literatur ist das ... Thema des *Kanons* von entscheidender Bedeutung."[122] In contrast, Christoph Levin's short introduction to the Old Testament illustrates the durability of the old project of reconfiguring the biblical literature according to its historical development. Though it has unquestionably always been received as Holy Scripture, "real" history rather than canon more nearly captures its true significance. "Man entdeckte und *entdeckt immer neu* die Differenz zwischen biblischer Geschichtsdarstellung und tatsächlich geschehener Geschichte."[123] In a particularly striking counterpoint, Dohmen's and Levin's treatments of the canonical formulae in Ecclesiastes 12:9f highlight the extent of their disagreement. Dohmen gives evidence that a centuries-long process of growth is drawing to a close. Instead of the "Ergänzungen und Fortschreibungen" typically found in "Traditionsliteratur," a postscript (or to be precise, a pair of postscripts) indicates an awareness of the canon's border and function. "Die Intention dieses Nachwortes ist deutlich. Der kritische Querdenker Kohelet soll in die klassische biblische Weisheitsliteratur eingeordnet werden."[124] Levin also cites Ecclesiastes, selecting from 12:12 a slogan for his evaluation of canon: "Of the making of many books, there is no end." Standing atop his book's final chapter, "Die Unabgeschlossenheit des Alten Testament," the verse introduces a retort to the topic surveyed in the previous chapter, "Der Abschluß des Kanons." Not surprisingly, he rejects dogmatic understandings of scripture's authority. The Christian "Inspirationslehre" constitutes a tendentious falsification of the meaning of the literature's growth and has been among "der größten Hindernisse der historischen Bibelkritik."[125]

---

[122] Dohmen, *Auslegung*, 15.

[123] Levin, *AT*, 123–124, my emphasis; cf. 21. Levin continues, "Die Bibel ist aber kein absolutes, sondern ein historisches Buch" (124). Why these must be stark alternatives is not wholly clear. The threat of fundamentalism may necessitate an ongoing "Streit um das Alte Testament" for Levin.

[124] Dohmen, *Auslegung*, 14. For Dohmen's distinction between *Traditionsliteratur* and *Autorenliteratur* see 11–12.

[125] Levin, *AT*, 121.

Dohmen's argument — it is more than a simple survey of options available to exegetes — begins with a consideration of how the Bible, a book made of books, came to be regarded as the book of books. Essential to this theme is the question of canon. When defining the term, Dohmen recognizes that canon was not used in unambiguous conjunction with the collection of Holy Scripture until at least the 4th century CE. Yet he observes that the first appearance of this usage postdates the concept it came to signify; "vielmehr hebt der Begriff auf die Funktion ab, Maßstab oder Norm der Bücher und Buchsammlungen zu sein, die schon vorliegen und mit wechselnden Begriffen wie *Schrift, Heilige Schriften/Bücher, Miqra, Gesetz, Tora, Propheten* bezeichnet werden."[126] On his reading the late appearance of the term itself explains why, in critical research, "die Frage nach dem Kanon über lange Zeit als mehr oder weniger ausschließlich historische Fragestellung behandelt worden ist." Dohmen continues: "Erst in den vergangenen vier Jahrzehnten sind die Fragen des Kanons aufgesprengt und durch die nordamerikanische Kanonforschung aus ihrer Eingrenzung auf das Feld des Historischen befreit worden, so daß heute allgemein anerkannt wird, daß die Probleme des biblischen Kanons nur noch im Gespräch zwischen biblischer, historischer und systematisch-theologischer Forschung zu behandeln sind."[127] Doubtful as this statement may be as a characterization of the general outlook, it is noteworthy in a couple of respects. The implicit recognition that the North American debate outpaced the German discussion is remarkable in itself. Also, though the analysis can in no wise qualify as a consensus, Dohmen points to the reopening of a question strict historical study was supposed to have closed. History was not rejected in itself, however; a later dogmatic term has, for Dohmen, plausibly been shown not to be anachronistic, but to suit its subject matter it describes.

Childs and Sanders are the only people named in the context of the North American discussion. That Childs' work is more formative for Dohmen, suggested already by his use of "canonical approach" instead of "canonical criticism," becomes undeniable in his enumeration of the most important two aspects of canon. First, canon pertains to the growth of the literature. Second, canon pertains to the closure and final contours of the literature. Both aspects are closely related, and in fact Sanders is criticized for emphasizing "Form" — the Bible's production — to the exclusion of its "Funktion für eine Gemeinschaft."[128] Plainly, the claim that study of the Bible's production belongs together with the product itself is a hallmark of Childs' work.

---

126 Dohmen, *Auslegung*, 20.

127 Ibid., 21.

128 Ibid., 23. Dohmen explains, "denn das, was uns als Kanon begegnet, ist ja nicht zu lösen vom Gedanken des Maßgeblichen und Richtungsweisenden, was der Aspekt des Kanons als *normative Sammlung von Schriften* und *Sammlung normativer Schriften* zum Ausdruck bringt." Dohmen's equation of form with formation, and function with reception, recalls, but should not be identified with Childs' appropriation of form-critical terminology. See chapter four.

B. S. Childs kommt in seinen Arbeiten zu der Einsicht, daß der Kanonbegriff nicht auf die späten Festlegungen des Umfangs der normativen Schriften begrenzt werden kann, sondern daß es sich beim Kanon letztendlich um etwas handelt, das *in den Schriften selbst* angelegt ist und nicht von außen herangetragen wird. Was Childs hierbei in den Blick genommen hat, ist das, was Traditionsliteratur ausmacht, nämlich die Haltung der Tradenten, die die Literatur sammeln, fortschreiben und weitergeben. Da dies konstitutiv für einen späteren Kanon ist, schlägt Childs eine Terminologie vor, die den Begriff des Kanonischen auf das Gesamte anwendet und dabei zwischen zwei Aspekten unterscheitet: Der Verschriftung und Tradierung auf der einen Seite — bezeichnet als "kanonischer Prozeß" — und dem Abschluß dieses Prozesses auf der anderen Seite — bezeichnet als "Kanonisierung."[129]

As much as anything to be found in the literature thus far, this summarizes well the core of Childs' argument for canonical shaping. Canon is not an extrinsic concept because one finds the judgments that gave rise to the term *in the writings themselves*. (This is a far cry from reading the Torah "as if" it had been written by Moses.) Dohmen, for one, is persuaded that this offers a more comprehensive explanation of the formation of biblical literature than those arising from strict historicist models.

Wissen's format permits no footnotes and few references, which apart from making the series palatable to non-specialist readers also forces authors to select only the most essential literature. For one Old Testament professor, Childs' recovery of canon orients the entire discussion. For another, Childs' work is not even on the map. In Levin's case the historical-critical paradigm endures as the best explanation of the received text, largely a jumbled product of historical accident. The literature's growth "lief meist ohne Regeln ab."[130] With surprising transparency his analysis operates according to an archaeological metaphor, often tried: "Weil die gegebene Überlieferung im Grundsatz unantastbar war" — that is, until the critical era — "ist der Ausleger in der glücklichen Lage, wie ein Test-Archäologe arbeiten zu können. Wenn er jün-

[129] Ibid., 22, my emphasis. Compare the earlier, more detailed comments in Dohmen and Oeming, *Kanontheologie*, 19–25.

[130] Levin, *AT*, 25. The process is compared to a snowball. "Einmal ins Rollen gebracht, gewinnt der Schneeball mit jeder Umdrehung eine neue Schicht" (25). And why does the process stop? "Der Schneeball mußte irgendwann zur Ruhe kommen" (26). Levin studied with William McKane in St Andrews for a semester, in the early 1970s, and his description of the canonical process recalls McKane's idea of a "rolling corpus." The direction of influence is unclear, however. In McKane's view Jeremianic kernels or poetic reservoirs trigger local expansions and commentary. "Such triggering or generation necessarily has a piecemeal character: the pre-existing Hebrew text, as represented by the Sept., has generated a kind of expansion which does not serve the ends of a thoughtful, all-embracing redaction or a superintending, theological tendency" (*Jeremiah*, I:lxxxi–lxxxii). Levin had gone to print with similar formulations a year before, in 1985, in which the whole OT canon seems to reflect Jeremiah's situation writ large (*Verheißung*, 67; Schmid, *Innnerbiblische*, 16 and Levinson, *Legal Revision*, 126 also note a link between Levin and McKane at this point). If this is the situation in Jeremiah, though, it is not easily squared with recent characterizations of unity across the Psalms, or the entirety of Isaiah, or the Book of the Twelve.

gere Schichten abträgt, darf er erwarten, jeweils auf ein älteres, intaktes Textbild zu stoßen."[131] Hence he unravels original threads from secondary developments (variously termed "artificial," "tendentious," "embarrassing," and on at least half a dozen occasions "fictitious"), frequently pointing out underlying ANE parallels as though the hermeneutical payoff were self-evident.[132] At one point the Exodus decalogue is cited, but *truncated according to a possible ur-form.*[133] Levin should not be faulted too much for neglecting to register counter-positions like this one articulated in 1974:

> Ultimately the use of source and form criticism is exegetically deficient if these tools do not illuminate the canonical text. Gressmann likened literary criticism to an archaological excavation in which no responsibility is felt by the scientist for rebuilding the mound. The analogy is inappropriate and highly misleading. The text under study is not only a record of history, but — even at its minimal formulation — a piece of literature with its own integrity.[134]

His remit here hardly permits it. Still, his general introduction demonstrates the remarkable extent to which a major critique of the long-dominant devaluation of canon — which in Dohmen's words has recently "zu einem der wichtigsten Themen der Bibelwissenschaft avancierte"[135] — has fallen on deaf ears. Levin remains utterly unpersuaded.

Dohmen's and Levin's overviews mark two poles in reception of the "North American" canon debate now mirrored in German-language scholarship. Dohmen may be right to say that the canonical approach is acquiring "Raum und Bedeutung,"[136] but the space it has won is partial at best. No consensus is forthcoming; one still finds business as usual in other quarters. Below I will sketch the way Childs' work has crossed back over the Atlantic to an environment in which he once studied (much changed since 1950, needless to say). Before proceeding, a final point of Levin's is worth unpacking. He writes, "Die

---

[131] Ibid., 26.

[132] Ibid., e.g. 23, 35, 45, 52, 56, 58, 75–6, 104. Discussion of a psalmic theme culminates in a telling phrase: it "ist religionsgeschichtlich keineswegs originell" (39).

[133] Ibid., 66. Hence the "decalogue" is reduced to Exodus 20:2–3, 5a, 13–17a. Such possibilities are often hazarded.

[134] Childs, *Exodus*, 149.

[135] Dohmen, *Auslegung*, 88. Dohmen's rebuttal of the usual criticism of the canonical approach is on target, in my view: "Von hierher ist auch ersichtlich, daß einer der häufigsten Kritikpunkte an diesem Ansatz der kanonischen Schriftauslegung, er sei ahistorische oder gar fundamentalistisch, weil er bei der vorliegenden Endform des Bibeltextes einsetze, völlig fehlgeht. Der Ansatz kanonischer Schriftauslegung ist der Versuch, die literarhistorischen Besonderheiten der biblischen Literatur mit ihren theologiegeschichtlichen in Verbindung zu bringen" (91). That Levin appears to accept the standard critique, on the other hand, is suggested by his closing comments (Levin, *AT*, 123–124). Honoring the "Aufklärung" as the decisive shift for biblical exegesis, and taking up the cause against fundamentalism, are themes James Barr addresses often, including in works which appear either exclusively in German (Barr, Bibelkritik) or in translation (Barr, *Fundamentalismus*).

[136] Dohmen, *Auslegung*, 88.

Bewahrung der Schrift geschah ja *nicht* um ihrer selbst willen."[137] But this is precisely the issue at stake in the canon debate. What, to continue the anthropomorphism, does the text want? Is the Bible's preservation as scripture intrinsic to the biblical text itself, at least in part, or is it an arbitrary outcome or perverse imposition? Anachronism cuts more ways than one, and it is hardly by accident that Levin, like Gunkel and others before him, finds within the Old Testament "die *Anfänge der Wissenschaft*."[138] Does the OT pressure us in *this* direction instead? Surely it is fair to doubt whether the rise of *Wissenschaft* is the text's inherent "will" more than any of the other possibilities.

I. Catching Up with North America

One periodization of biblical interpretation declares that until it "came of age" in the 1980s, North American biblical scholarship was characterized by a "connoisseurship of premier German criticism."[139] The characterization seems accurate enough through the post-war period. Exactly when and how North America went its own way, and whether this turn was salutary, would be difficult to establish. Did the direction of influence ever reverse? That scholarship on the Continent should play catch-up with scholarship across the Atlantic by no means follows, and probably has not been the rule — if anything, one could perhaps speak of a period of international dialogue led by a few.[140] But Childs' work is one place, as H.-J. Kraus' 1982 appeal to his colleagues to pay heed to developments in the English-speaking world anticipates, where a good case can be made that German-speaking biblical scholars were for once beholden to North America. So it happened that the editors of a fledgling *Jahrbuch für Biblische Theologie* dedicated an entire volume to the topic of canon in 1988, to apprise its readership of developments abroad. Introducing the volume, G. Stemberger and I. Baldermann explain: "Wir nehmen die im deutschsprachigen Raum kontrovers geführte Diskussion zum Anlaß, unsere Leser auch mit der Diskussion dieses Problems in den USA vertraut zu machen. Sie hat sich dort insbesondere an den Thesen von *Brevard S. Childs* entzündet," above all over his thesis "daß die Kanonbildung nicht eine späte kirchliche Setzung ist, sondern 'a consciousness deep within the literature itself.'"[141] On this occasion and on this specific topic, the direction of influence reversed.

---

[137] Levin, *AT*, 24, my emphasis.

[138] Ibid., 31, original emphasis.

[139] Olbricht, 20th Century, 556.

[140] Transatlantically, Rendtorff has been an important figure. More recently and from the other side, Christine Helmer's efforts deserve special mention. In addition to translations, a recent bilingual volume stands out: Helmer and Petrey, eds., *Interpretation*. Cf. Helmer and Landmesser, eds., *One or Many?*; also with an interest in canon, Levinson, *Legal Revision* stands out, though his interest is for interdisciplinarity in the humanities more broadly.

[141] Baldermann et al., eds., *Biblischen Kanons*, 5.

Rolf Rendtorff Spots a Genuine Alternative

"As far as I can see, German-speaking discussion has yet to take up the theological problem of the canon."[142] Rendtorff's judgement — correct for the time being, in 1982 (the date in the foreword) — was overtaken almost immediately, not least by his own work. The same *Introduction* which contains this remark makes tentative steps toward its undoing, for as he said in a guest lecture at Yale around the same time, in reading Childs' 1979 Introduction "it was as though the scales fell from my eyes."[143] Rendtorff is the first to seriously advocate canonical hermeneutics in Germany.

From a later perspective one can appreciate just how formative his encounter with *Introduction to the OT* was. In his farewell address at Heidelberg, delivered 19 July 1990, Rendtorff reflects on his four decades at the university since his arrival as von Rad's first doctoral student, in 1950. Each decade has a corresponding focal point. In the 1950s "history" was the watchword. In the 1960s key historical hypotheses began to crumble, but Rendtorff's attention had been pulled elsewhere by — this is his language — a decisive encounter with Judaism. During the 1970s he participated actively in the demolition of the old history-centric consensus, though in retrospect he views that "splendid era" with "a degree of nostalgic melancholy."[144] The 1980s, finally, saw the importation of canon to Germany:

> In the 1970s a debate had developed in the United States about the question of the Old Testament canon. At first it hardly attracted any notice in Germany. I myself came across it in the final phase of my work on an introduction to the Old Testament, to which I had at last addressed myself. (It had already been planned in the 1960s but had continually fallen victim to the circumstances and needs of the times.) The most important book in this debate was Brevard Childs's *Introduction to the Old Testament as Scripture* (1979), which drew me inescapably into the discussion. I very soon had the impression that in methodological approach what this book offered was not merely a variant of previous treatments of the Bible; it was a genuine alternative.[145]

These four foci summarize well the shape of Rendtorff's career. His early historical work is transformed by a "decisive event: my encounter with Judaism."[146] Then, into a period of dissolution, came *Introduction to the OT*, which brought a new orientation to the theological problem of canon. Rendtorff's next remarks in the Heidelberg farewell problematize the relationship of

---

[142] Rendtorff, *Introduction*, 291. I was unable to acquire a German copy (Neukirchen-Vluyn: Neukirchener, 1983) for comparison.

[143] Seitz, Theological Interpretation, 84. Seitz remembers that Rendtorff actually had Childs translate this remark for the audience, to Childs' own embarrassment.

[144] Rendtorff, *Canon and Theology*, 216.

[145] Ibid., 217. The paragraph's conclusion: "The debate about [canon] is now being vigorously pursued in the United States, and among us in Germany too the contributions of people who have come alive to it are increasing."

[146] Ibid., 116. For a sampling of early work see Rendtorff, *Gesammelte*.

these two eye-opening insights, however. Canon must square with the hope for a common Jewish-Christian theology. He explains, "I sometimes think that this could perhaps be the most important task for the years remaining to me: to make a contribution to this discussion, and to help free the Hebrew Bible from the captivity into which it was brought when it came to be labeled merely a preliminary step, now superseded and overcome, on the way to the Christian Bible."[147] By the time he completes his canonical OT Theology it is clear that canon, as perceived in Childs' work at any rate, is not quite compatible with the "discovery" of Judaism.[148]

Three questions arise. How does Childs transform Rendtorff's perspective initially? Why and how does Rendtorff eventually distance his vision of canon from that of Childs? And what understanding of canon does Rendtorff develop for his own enterprise? I will address the first question immediately but hold back the other two for later.

The justly famous *Das überlieferungsgeschichtliche Problem des Pentateuch* begins with a crystal-clear statement of its thesis. Wellhausen's literary-critical method and Gunkel's form-critical, transmission-historical method, customarily supposed to be complements, are in fact opposed from the outset. The former separates the sources that make up the Pentateuch. The latter "takes its point of departure not from the final form of the written text of the Pentateuch, but from the smallest, originally independent, individual units, and traces the process of their development right up to their final written form."[149] Von Rad and Noth undertake major studies of the last stages of the process, with different results; but while both agree that the task is to analyze the entire course of the tradition, neither one has carried this out in practice. Gunkel on the other hand investigated the smallest "units" but neglected to trace their incorporation into the entire Pentateuch. Thus Rendtorff aims to "close the gap in the study of the history of the origin and growth of the Pentateuch."[150] He performs a "crosscheck" of the reigning documentary hypothesis and finds grounds to reject it. If one starts where Gunkel does and then traces the growth of the tradition from small units all the way through to the final form, "one does not encounter the 'sources' in the sense of the documentary hypothesis."[151] Literary-critical analysis as such is still valid, even necessary, but the result it was believed to have won stands no longer.

---

[147] Rendtorff, *Canon and Theology*, 218. Compare "Toward a Common Jewish-Christian Reading of the Hebrew Bible," 31–45 in the same collection.

[148] "Discovery" is his word. "Das wichtigste theologische Ereignis der zweiten Hälfte dieses Jahrhunderts ist die Entdeckung des Judentums für die christliche Theologie" (Rendtorff, Bibel Israels, 97).

[149] Rendtorff, *Transmission*, 11 = *ügP*, 1.

[150] Ibid., 32 = *ügP*, 19.

[151] Ibid., 179 = *ügP*, 148.

Given the way Wellhausen's method is measured against Gunkel's, it comes as something of a surprise that Rendtorff's *Introduction* calls for a fresh analysis that starts with the "texts themselves." True, officially it still "follows the approach founded by Hermann Gunkel."[152] But a new emphasis on the final form surfaces occasionally which, just a few years prior, is simply nowhere to be found. Occasionally it looks as if Rendtorff's aspiration is still to write a history of the tradition.[153] Elsewhere, with nods to Childs, he notes that the Bible has functioned authoritatively in its received form, as a canon. He lodges a complaint that "the final form of the individual books as they now are, and of the Old Testament as a whole, are hardly taken into account."[154] There is also an acknowledgment that a theological understanding of canon is not entirely congruent with tradition-history as typically practiced: "opposition" with a canonical approach "could and must" be overcome.[155] That various perspectives are to be held together can be seen in the very structure of the book. Part one canvases the history of Israel (the OT as a "source"), part two the *Sitz im Leben* of the OT literature, part three the biblical books in their final shape. At various points a dawning recognition begins to go beyond the knowledge "that the form-critical approach is not enough to explain the origin of the books of the Old Testament" (i.e., that material lost its connection with the traditional *Sitzen* in Israelite society as it was theologically shaped).[156] In a clearer formulation a decade later, Rendtorff explains: canon "means first of all a *change of direction in the line of sight.*" Canonical interpretation centers "on the text in its now existing form, the wider complexes take on greater importance"[157] — as opposed to the small original units (Gunkel), or to all detectable phases from the tradition's beginning to its end (Rendtorff in 1977).

That said, it is not hard to see why *Introduction to the OT* so immediately struck a chord. A few remarks near the end of *Das überlieferungsgeschichtliche Problem* point to the study's theological implications. Rendtorff concludes "that clearly defined theological intentions were at work in the arrangement of these larger units." Moreover, "the theological intentions of the preliminary stages of the Pentateuch as a whole are most clearly grasped in these larger units."[158] There are successive layers of intentionality, so one would probably want to speak of theologies in the plural. Yet a late layer is uncovered that intends to transmit the Pentateuch as a single, intact unit. A "deuteronomically stamped layer of reworking is the first and, according to our examination so

---

152 Rendtorff, *Introduction*, ix. See chapter four, below.

153 Ibid., 80: "The exegete must now be concerned to trace developments from the beginning of the formation of the tradition to the final form of the text as we have it today."

154 Ibid., 129.

155 Ibid., 130.

156 Ibid., 127, and see all of Section 7 there.

157 Rendtorff, *Canon and Theology*, 143, my emphasis; cf. 27–28.

158 Rendtorff, *Transmission*, 189 = *ügP*, 157–158.

far, the only one which unambiguously views the Pentateuch as a whole and will have it understood as *one* great coherent complex."[159] An intentionalist hermeneutic, in other words, is compelled to reckon with the Pentateuch as a whole at some point. In a sense, then, the step to Rendtorff's position after *Introduction to the OT* is not enormous. His *Introduction*'s final chapter, on canon, summarizes: "One of the most important insights here is that the shaping of the biblical books in their present form is usually not the result of chance or of thoughtless and uncomprehending redaction, as was often supposed by earlier historical-critical exegesis, but that quite deliberate forces of shaping were at work which were often guided by a specific and often very pointed theological purpose."[160] Pages earlier Childs is commended in the strongest terms for stressing this point in conjunction with the further point that the canonical form of the books "have become the normative basis of the religious life of the Jewish — and later also the Christian — community." (Rendtorff's phrasing is notable in light of the distance he will later put between himself and Childs.) In short, Childs' "demand" in *Introduction to the OT* entails an adjustment across the entire field: "The final form of the Old Testament books and the theological intentions expressed in them must be taken seriously in quite a different way from what has so far been the norm in Old Testament scholarship."[161] This judgment reaches even to Rendtorff's earlier views in 1977.

We will pick up other aspects of Rendtorff's contribution to canonical theology in chapters three and six. The point for now is simply that *Introduction to the OT* catches Rendtorff's attention in a major way in the early 1980s, provoking "a change of direction in the line of sight." Rendtorff thus represents Childs' first significant inroad in the German scene.

Manfred Oeming: An Early Account in German

Excluding a few reviews of *Introduction to the OT*, such as those by Smend and Zimmerli,[162] Manfred Oeming attempts the first account of Childs' hermeneutics from within the German-language context as part of his Bonn dissertation, first published in 1985 with the title *Gesamtbiblische Theologien der Gegenwart: Das Verhältnis von AT und NT in der hermeneutischen Diskussion seit Gerhard von Rad*. An epilogue to the second edition (1987) adds a cautionary note on the challenge of reading scholarship across national and linguistic borders, which in Oeming's case applies above all to Childs. "Wer sich mit ausländi-

---

[159] Ibid., 196 = *ügP*, 164; original emphasis. Rendtorff is unwilling to state whether this deuteronomic layer is responsible for the basic shape of the Pentateuch or is a reworking of a received unit.

[160] Rendtorff, *Introduction*, 290.

[161] Ibid., 129–130.

[162] Smend, Questions and Zimmerli, Rez. Childs.

schen Beiträgen beschäftigt, muß in seiner Beurteilung sehr vorsichtig sein, da er die Kontexte häufig nicht gut genug überblickt, in denen diese Arbeiten stehen."[163] He (rightly) proceeds to make judgments as best he can despite this hurdle, but his conclusion about Childs is incautiously sharp.

Oeming relies heavily on the review volumes of 1980, and his critique mostly just rehearses the English-language discussion of Childs up to that point.[164] He tells the familiar story of a turn from history to dogmatism, which amounts to a dereliction of the biblical scholar's duty.

> Aus der Sorge um die theologische Verantwortung der historischen Exegese und dem Versuch, die historische Kritik gleichsam von innen her zu heilen, wird mehr und mehr eine Geringschätzung der historischen Arbeit. Gleichzeitig nimmt der Dogmatismus zu, mit dem der Kanon als die Lösung aller gegenwärtigen Probleme behauptet wird… Es handelt sich bei der zweiten Phase des canonical approach um eine *dogmatische Flucht aus den Schwierigkeiten des historischen Geschäfts* in einen in seiner Bedeutung maßlos überschätzten positiven Kanon.[165]

Further, one hears that Childs has inadvertently given arch-conservatives and fundamentalists an alibi, that "canon" is being used in far too many different senses to be useful, that as a solution to all problems an appeal to the final form is too simple, and that "canonical intentionality" is a "mystic phrase" (so Barr). Oeming also has doubts about how well-suited a canonical approach is to the contemporary, pluralist world. Here he ventures one of his least careful judgments, against Childs' prioritization of the MT as the *vehicle* to Jewish scripture and the Christian OT: at the root of this, he thinks, could be "einer gut amerikanischen Hochschätzung des Positivismus. Nur was man Schwarz auf Weiß in Händen hält, der empirisch vorliegende Endtext, ist von sicherem Wert…"[166] Childs' response to the whole account is therefore not surprising: "Meiner Meinung nach verfehlt M. Oemings jüngste Analyse meines kanonischen Zuganges … völlig den Sinn meiner Darlegungen."[167]

On the other hand, Oeming and his wife Christiane carried out the translation of *Biblical Theology* into German shortly after it appeared in English.[168] M. Oeming has invested further research into the problem of the Christian

---

[163] Oeming, *Gesamtbiblische*, 269.

[164] Cf. *HBT* 2 and *JSOT* 16. *Holy Scripture* is not cited in Oeming's first two editions, but Barr's 1980 review, and Smend's and Knight's which have some similarities, set the tone. Smart, *Biblical Theology* also features in the discussion.

[165] Oeming, *Gesamtbiblische*, 195–196 (= ^{3}204–205), my emphasis. The phrase with "dogmatische Flucht" is repeated in closing (209 = ^{3}216) and is picked up by others (e.g., Barr, *Concept of BTh*, 505 and especially Brunert, *Psalm 102*, 72, on which see chapter seven).

[166] Oeming, *Gesamtbiblische*, 208 (= ^{3}215). Oeming fails to appreciate what "vehicle" suggests for the MT; the Hebrew text preserved by a Jewish community is a starting point, not a destination in the name of positivism. See *Introduction to the OT*, 97.

[167] Childs, Endform, 248n6.

[168] Childs, *Einen Bibel* (1994, 1996), n.b. the foreword in 2:9–12. Most of the work would have been undertaken while M. Oeming taught at the University of Osnabrück. Others there

Bible's unity despite its two parts, too. Yet a third edition of Oeming's dissertation (*Das AT als Teil?*, 2001), which is accompanied by later essays, merely updates references in some footnotes and is otherwise identical to the initial account of Childs' approach. A few newer presentations of canonical hermeneutics, including Noble's, are listed in an expanded bibliography, but neither these, nor Childs' own mature statements in *Biblical Theology*, have been integrated into the discussion. Regrettably, a dated account plagued by the misunderstandings of Childs which came of age in the early 1980s has been freshly bound and propagated.

Others Move in a New Direction

An excellent, recent survey of German discussions of canonical hermeneutics makes it unnecessary to provide another here. Jörg Barthel (2007) frames his topic this way: "Kanonhermeneutik … ist die Reflexion der besonderen Verstehensbedingungen und -probleme, die dadurch gegeben sind, daß die biblischen Schriften die Gestalt und Funktion eines Kanons, d.h. einer (relativ) abgeschlossenen Schriftensammlung mit normativer und / oder formativer Funktion für die Glaubensgemeinschaft(en), haben."[169] That the author can define a field of shared interest this way suggests developments rather different to those in the English-speaking world, and indeed, he indicates that Childs rather than Sanders has left a bigger impression in the German reception of American studies of canon.[170] Though there are of course dissenting voices in German, a significant trend to emphasize the constructive exegetical and theological implications of canon surfaces in a debate alive to concerns that seem marginal in the English-speaking world. It is also noteworthy that Barthel numbers among the few anywhere who recognize the advantage to Childs in pursuing a canonical *approach* rather than a criticism or a method, and that his broad definition of canon actually serves him at precisely this point.[171]

Less well documented is the way Childs gained an audience in Europe just as interest in his research was cooling in Britain and North America. *Introduction to the OT* received the attention of no less that two review volumes in 1980 and some sixty reviews in total.[172] By comparison *Biblical Theology* was almost not reviewed at all in English (undoubtedly the most substantial response

at some time or other had more minor involvement in the project: G. Steins translated the chapter on Genesis 22 as a sample for the publisher, and C. Dohmen provided the foreword to the first volume.

[169] Barthel, Kanonhermeneutische Debatte, 5. In the same volume cf. esp. Janowski, Kontrastive Einheit. I discuss one problem with Barthel's taxonomy at the end of chapter four.

[170] Ibid., 11. In contrast, Childs, Reflections on an Era, 36 senses that Sanders quickly became the theological spokesperson for most in the English-speaking debate.

[171] Barthel, Kanonhermeneutische Debatte, 10, 14.

[172] *JSOT* 16 and *HBT* 2. The tally of sixty is Childs': *Pauline Corpus*, 1.

came off Rendtorff's desk).[173] Then, in a 2002 volume containing about thirty essays under the title *The Canon Debate*, Childs' position went almost completely unrepresented.[174] As was seen in a preliminary discussion of the canon or rule of faith, above, that tome's editors ask, "With such a long delay in the church's use of the term 'canon' to describe a closed body of Christian scriptures, one may well ask why there was an emergence of 'canon consciousness' in the church of the *fourth* century C.E. and *little evidence of it before*?"[175] It is as if the authors are ignorant of what by that point had almost become a truism in the German literature on canon, picking up on an argument made preeminently in *Introduction to the OT*, that a consciousness of canon lay deep within the formation of the literature.[176] Instead, most contributors share the will to impose a moratorium on all talk of "canon" in the biblical period, because of the term's anachronism. A very different impression is given by a 2007 collection of more than twenty German essays on canon. *Der Bibelkanon in der Bibelauslegung: Methodenreflexionen und Beispielexegesen* does not once defend the Sanders/McDonald position. One of its editors even argues for an early application of canon *despite* its apparent anachronism.[177]

So if 1980 is the high water mark of Childs' reception in English, the tide in German discussions was then only beginning to rise. Throughout the 1980s Childs repeatedly wrote or had translated pieces that only ever appeared in German, oftentimes alongside other essays exploring the value of canon from sympathetic perspectives. The first was a short overview of differences in biblical theology on the American scene (1981).[178] Then there were two "catch up" volumes, in 1987 and 1988, the latter of which included a report on the state of the question in North America by P. D. Miller.[179] Both lead off with pieces by Childs. Another is included in the important 1995 collection *Eine Bibel — zwei Testamente*, edited by C. Dohmen and T. Söding. Gradually, Childs' work began to exert a *Wirkung* on a slice of Continental biblical scholarship. Broadly

[173] Most are only a few pages in length. Three exceptions in English are Brueggemann, Against the Stream, Bauckham, Biblical Theology and Seitz, Not Prophets. On the most significant German review see Rendtorff, Rezension Childs, the reply in Childs, Witness to Christ?, and my discussion of both in chapters three and six, below.

[174] The editors explain that minority voices were invited but could not participate (McDonald and Sanders, eds., *Canon Debate*, 17), but their title remains sadly ironic.

[175] Ibid., 13, my emphasis. Recall the discussion of this quotation in conjunction with Craig Allert and second and forth century definitions of the canon of faith, in chapter one.

[176] See Dohmen and Oeming, *Kanontheologie*, 23, Janowski, Kontrastive Einheit, 45 (citing Steins, Kanonisch Lesen, 53) and a host of other places, though contrast Frankemölle, *Frühjudentum*, 74–75.

[177] See Steins' representative discussion in Ballhorn and Steins, eds., *Bibelkanon*, especially 114–117. For an overview of the whole collection see Driver, Review of Bibelkanon.

[178] Childs, Differenzen.

[179] *ThQ* 167/4 and *JBTh* 3, in which note Miller, Amerikanischen Diskussion.

speaking the trend seems there to have been the inverse of patterns in Britain and Childs' home country, even when questions of canon stayed at the fore.

A number of those writing in German with an interest in the hermeneutics of canon have internalized and extended some of Childs' arguments — above all, that canonization proper is not (wholly) an extrinsic imposition on the biblical literature. These efforts have pursued their own agendas, which no doubt is much as it should be. Dohmen, for instance, who was instrumental at Osnabrück for a time and was among the first in Germany to read Childs in earnest, now has an Exodus commentary (2004) with only a faintly discernible relation to Childs' of 1974.[180] And Georg Steins, another scholar affiliated with Osnabrück, has been particularly successful at galvanizing another generation of interest in canon — a generation which did not need to work quite so hard to bring (a minority voice in) the North American canon debate into German. Without detracting from Steins' achievement, the next section aims to show how a pattern established at a handful of British institutions, that of reconstructing Childs' allegedly incoherent method, also makes its way to Germany. Barthel terms it the "*Methodisierung* des kanonhermeneutischen Ansatzes."[181]

Georg Steins: A Reconstruction and a Second Wave

Reconstructions of canonical hermeneutics typically split over how to "fix" what lies behind Childs' troubling turn of phrase "canonical intentionality." Barton and Brett make Childs into an anti-intentionalist, whereas Noble contends that he would do better as an intentionalist. With Steins, the pendulum swings back in the formalist direction of the first two studies, by which Childs' intentionalism is remedied with literary theory. Steins welcomes the fact that in the North American discussion canon "ist also nicht ein primär historisch-deskriptiver Terminus, sondern wird zur *hermeneutischen Zentralkategorie*."[182] In outlining his distinctive canonical-intertextual reading, though, he winds up arguing with the other reconstructors, against Childs, that it is hermeneutically irresponsible to leave the matter of authorial intent open.[183]

---

[180] Thus far only Dohmen's second volume is in print. Childs' commentary is referenced occasionally, though it may anticipate Dohmen's more in its structure, its attention to *Wirkungsgeschichte* or its appreciative use of Benno Jacob than in exegetical particulars. (Childs recounts how in 1964 he found a rare copy of Jacob's Exodus commentary in Jerusalem, secured a microfilm copy, and brought it back to Yale, where he used it extensively in his own commentary of 1974 — decades before Jacob's was published in English translation [1992] or its German original [1997]. See Childs, Benno Jacob, and the section on Jacob in chapter six, below.) Still, cf. Dohmen, *Exodus 19–40*, 87–88, 130, 214, 217, 347.

[181] Barthel, Kanonhermeneutische Debatte, 15, cf. 24.

[182] Steins, *Bindung*, 10. Cf. now Steins, Kanonisch Lesen and Steins, Anamnese.

[183] Chapman, Reclaiming Inspiration, points out that restricting exegesis to authorial intent, as Noble does, would "fully undermine Childs's approach" (173). The same is true for the inverse move, here. In Childs' approach both poles are needed.

By 1999, the year in which *Die "Bindung Isaaks" im Kanon (Gen 22): Grundlagen und Programm einer kanonisch-intertextuellen Lektüre* went to press, it was easy to defend hermeneutical amendments to the canonical approach on Childs' behalf based on the widespread indictment that no canonical method exists. Steins begins with what may be the first essay to spell out the implications of Barr in 1983 combined with Barton in 1984: "There is little if any *methodological* clarity concerning how one is to study the Bible canonically."[184] He then cites German literature to the same effect. Some of the most important input in the latter category comes from Norbert Lohfink, whose title essay in *Eine Bibel — zwei Testamente* suggests that the need to keep the Old Testament alongside the New "fordert, um verstanden zu werden, gesamtbiblische Intertextualität."[185] Intertextuality is lifted up as a fresh way of approaching the unity of a pluriform Bible.

> Entstanden sind beide [Testamente] selbstverständlich aus vielen Büchern. Doch die Frage ist, ob es dabei geblieben ist. Es gibt in beiden Büchergruppen eine bei allen Variationen doch so stabile Anordnung und darüberhinaus so viele literarische Verstrebungen, daß man mit mehr rechnen muß als nur einer Reihe von in sich selbständigen Büchern. Beide Kanones bilden in sich geschlossene Sinngefüge. Das wird erst in unseren Jahren durch die Forschung nachgewiesen, scheint aber schon genügend gesichert zu sein. Damit entsteht innerhalb der beiden Büchergruppen eine neue, intensivere Art von Intertextualität. Das hat beträchtliche Folgen für den Sinn der einzelnen Bücher, ja der einzelnen Aussagen in ihnen. Die Konsequenzen sind kaum schon gezogen.[186]

Sound method is urgently required, evidently.[187] Steins' *Habilitation* attempts to tease out what consequences such a "neue, intensivere Art von Intertextualität" could have for biblical interpretation. If not yet at the "gesamtbiblische" level, Steins' use of terminology from Lohfink's essay is clearly an appreciative expansion of it applied to an important test case in the Pentateuch: Lohfink's "*konturierte Intertextualität*" becomes a key phrase in the proposed canonical

---

[184] Steins, *Bindung*, 11, Steins' emphasis, citing Morgan, Madness?, 84.

[185] Lohfink, Eine Bibel, 75. Further confirmation of this link is found in Steins, Bibelkanon. It begins with a nod to Childs for putting canon on the agenda and then quotes almost two pages from Lohfink's essay before outlining the proposed canonical-intertextual method in fourteen theses. For background on the Roman Catholic scene, especially at the University of Münster, see Steins' retrospective, Kanonisch-intertextuelle Bibellektüre — My Way (2007). On this account there was a strong preoccupation with method in the wake of the Second Vatican Council. Canon and Childs came later for Steins, at Osnabrück in 1990, though he felt a lack earlier that must have made the soil fertile: "In der katholischen Exegese gab es zwar eine elaborierte Methodenreflexion, aber keine in gleicher Intensität betriebene Bemühung um eine *theologische Methodologie*" (57, original emphasis).

[186] Lohfink, Eine Bibel, 79.

[187] Ibid., 80: "Die Entwicklung einer differenzierteren Theorie wäre sowohl für den 'systematischen' (an Sachfragen orientierten) als auch für den 'exegetischen' (Texte entlanggehenden) Teil der Theologie dringend erfordert." In German Roman Catholic circles the quest for method seems to have had its own distinctive impetus. E.g., see Steins, My Way.

intertextuality.[188] Thus even some of Childs' most sympathetic German readers are persuaded about the unworkability or nonexistence of his so-called method, and are committed to supplying the lack.[189]

Steins is careful enough to recognize that Childs declines to work out an exact method. In words italicized as they are cited in *Bindung*, Childs says, "In the end, I would rather speak of *a new vision of the text rather than in terms of method*."[190] Like Noble and others, however, Steins, who comments that this statement "verrät eine Ambivalenz; die 'Vision' beschreibt das faszinierend Neue, aber auch das (noch) Schemenhafte,"[191] concludes that Childs' *approach*, as such, is inadequate. Familiar concerns are raised about intentionality and unity versus diversity, but on the whole a supposition reinforced by literature in two languages permits Steins to say that while Childs brokers insights about the hermeneutical value of canon, his work must be leveraged with a suitable theory of canon before it will yield dividends.[192] In order to render the "apparitional," Steins augments canon with *Intertextualität*, in dialogue with M. Bakhtin and J. Kristeva, and *Lektüre*, with U. Eco and W. Iser. In this manner Childs is once again reproved for unclear thinking about authorial intent. For Steins he is stuck between a production-oriented and a reception-oriented approach. (Opposite poles of Abrams' diagram come to mind again.) If canon stays in the first camp, how is it more than a mere shifting of emphasis within traditional historical-critical concerns? If in the second, how can the dynamic process of its reception ever truly get off the ground? "Allein im zweiten Fall kommt der Kanon als normative Vorgabe für einen offenen Rezeptionsprozeß zur Geltung."[193]

But the tension is not so easily resolved, as a close reading of *Bindung* itself demonstrates. Reception theory should make the best sense of what transpires in reading,[194] and yet even though "das Maß des Gebens ist nicht das Maß des Nehmens,"[195] it would still appear to align with the production of the biblical text since, in redactional activity, "der Fokus nicht die Vergangenheit, sondern die Gegenwart und die Öffnung für zukünftige Rezeption ist."[196] Accordingly, Steins' method has two initial steps. First, identify and describe the presence/

[188] Ibid., 79; cited Steins, *Bindung*, 23, Steins' italics, and cf. 232–233. Lohfink, following Braulik, Bahnlesung, favors a reform in the Catholic liturgy that (re)introduces a first reading from the Torah before a second OT reading outside the Pentateuch. Liturgy would thus commence with Torah, as in Jewish liturgy, and culminate in Gospel, as in Christian liturgy.

[189] Cf. also Dohmen's remarks in Dohmen and Stemberger, *Hermeneutik*, 175.

[190] *NT Introduction*, xvii. Cf. Steins, My Way, 60.

[191] Steins, *Bindung*, 12.

[192] This reconstructive maneuver lies at the heart of the proposed canonical-intertextual reading: ibid., 2, 11, 16, 27–31, 36, 73–75, 130–132.

[193] Ibid., 27.

[194] Ibid., 45–83. See also Steins, Bibelkanon, 188.

[195] H. Blummenberg's aphorism, cited Steins, *Bindung*, 215.

[196] Steins, Bibelkanon, 192.

attendance ("Anwesenheit") of each *hypotext* (e.g., Gen. 12, 21; Ex. 19-24; Dt. 8; Lv. 8f/Ex. 29; Dt. 12; Ex. 3-4) in the *hypertext* (Gen 22). Second, assess how the hypotexts illuminate the meaning of the hypertext.[197] Yet Steins limits the text-text links permitted in a competent reading of Gen 22 in revealing ways. To begin with, he constrains hypotexts to the Pentateuch.[198] Beyond that, abstract thematic links are also excluded. For example, Jon Levenson's discussion of child sacrifice in connection with Ex. 22:28b is disallowed because it shows insufficient "lexematische Übereinstimmungen" with Genesis 22.[199] As a rule, unless explicit parallels can be shown, candidates for thematic intertextual *Anwesenheit* in the hypertext are rejected.[200]

Theoretical considerations push Steins to forego problems of authorship and diachronic textual dependencies, and yet they seem to reenter through a back door. After carefully delimiting intertextual constellations surrounding the Akedah, Steins ponders how his results interface with text-genetic concerns. "Von einer kanonisch-intertextuellen Lektüre eines Textes, wie sie im vorangehenden Abschnitt in acht Einzelstudien dargelegt wurde, führt kein direkter Weg zu Einsichten in die Genese des Textes."[201] But then it may still be possible to detect something of the intertextualizing of the author in the intertextualizing of the reader. Steins writes:

> Am plausibelsten lassen sich meines Erachtens die in den kanonisch-intertextuellen Lektüren entdeckten Übereinstimmungen damit erklären, daß der Autor von Gen 22 *bewußt* auf diese Texte angespielt hat. Die aufgewiesenen Text-Text-Relationen sind, zumindest größtenteils, *auch vom Autor intendierte Relationen*. Gen 22 ist geradezu ein Paradebeispiel für einen *intertextuell arbeitenden Autor*, der seinen Text gewissermaßen herausentwickelt aus einem schon groß ausgebauten Pentateuch.[202]

Although Steins aims to be more methodologically consistent than Childs by stepping fully into a reception oriented paradigm, he may not be quite so fully in this arena as he supposes.

---

[197] Steins, *Bindung*, 100. On 233 Steins suggests a third step: "Frage nach der Sinnkomplexion für den Hypertext." This involves Lohfink's contoured intertextuality, seemingly a kind of canonical tectonics in which geographic plates or zones contextualize intertextuality. Cf. 102.

[198] Space is a constraint (ibid., 134), yet little direction is given about how one extend the Akedah's intertextuality beyond the Pentateuch.

[199] Ibid., 184; cf. Levenson, *Death and Resurrection*, 142.

[200] Cf. the heavy qualifications on Gen. 21's *Anwesenheit* in Gen. 22, Steins, *Bindung*, 147–163, esp. 162. A few thematic links do sound through (210), but the restrictions tend to undermine expansive claims made in theory, e.g.: "Im Aufbau stets neuer Text-Text-Relationen wird der Hypertext immer wieder neu unter dem Einfluß der verschiedener Hypotexte beleuchtet" (226).

[201] Ibid., 214. If one only permits text-links that an author introduced, one ceases to be a reader and becomes instead a "Quellenforscher" (215).

[202] Ibid., 217, my emphasis. Given the number of intertextual links, he deduces, Genesis 22 was probably one of the last elements of the Pentateuch to be composed.

Then again, Steins' work on Chronicles shows him fluent in author-oriented source analysis in a way that sets him apart from the other reconstructors of Childsian hermeneutics. The legitimacy of text-genetic approaches, as partial accounts anyway, comes through in some methodological formulations. "Die historische Analyse wird also nicht ausgeklammert, aber neu ausgerichtet; es geht nicht mehr darum, einen Punkt hinter dem Text 'anzuzielen,' um dort der Wahrheit des Textes ansichtig zu werden. Mit dem Konzept Kanon verbindet sich eine Aufwertung des Textes in seiner spezifischen Gestalt, die er in der Bibel gefunden hat."[203] It is possible to see, too, that Steins wants a method for sympathetic reasons. Adding an "Operationalisierungskonzept" could make the method more "lehrbar und lernbar."[204] And alongside the hunger for method is a strong interest in the theological dimensions of canon, a crucial element Childs finds absent in "North American" discussions. One of the few unambiguous signs of this in the method itself is Steins' restriction of hypo-texts in a biblical hyper-text to other *canonical* texts. The method is not nearly as radical as it might have been.

Steins' reconstruction is also the only one to which Childs troubled to respond. Childs begins by affirming some points of agreement, and though he goes on to push back on a number of issues, ultimately deciding that *Bindung* lacks a theological corrective to its borrowing of theory — "how does the sacred canonical text of a community of faith relate to Steins' general theory of reception?"[205] — he seems to have taken this treatment more seriously than previous ones. There are indications that Steins has worked to sharpen the theological aspect of his proposals, too, perhaps in response to Childs' remarks, though he remains committed to the refinements of method. A re-description of canonical-intertextual reading as anamnesis, reminiscent of *lectio divina*, aims to clarify the function of reading in a community of faith.[206] Even more significantly, there appears to be a second wave of scholarly interest in canon in the German-speaking world, if one that can seem equally preoccupied with methodological controversies. Steins' programmatic *Bindung* is cited in well over half of the twenty essays in the 2007 volume *Bibelkanon*, which makes the work look like a harbinger of another generation of hermeneutical reflection on and exegetical application of insights deriving from canon.

---

203 Steins, My Way, 62.

204 Ibid., 67.

205 Childs, Critique, 176.

206 Steins, Anamnese, 129: "einer kanonisch-intertextuellen Lektüre wäre missverstanden, wenn es als Spielart einer werkimmanenten oder holistischen Auslegung begriffen würde." I will still contrast Steins' text-text relations with Childs' text-*res* relations in chapter five.

II. Conclusion: Intertextuality and the Pressure of the Sensus Literalis

What is at stake in authorial intent for Childs? On numerous occasions he has been told to discard the notion, but he has not done so. Resisting the suggestion in *Bindung*, Childs writes, "When Steins' theory of intertextuality eliminates the privileged status of the canonical context and removes all hermeneutical value from any form of authorial intent, an interpretive style emerges that runs directly contrary to the function of an authoritative canon which continues to serve a confessing community of faith and practice."[207] But then neither can Childs take the thoroughgoing intentionalist advice of Paul Noble. Canonical intentionality includes the concept of canonical *loosening*, by which biblical texts are sometimes intentionally re-addressed to wider audiences and future generations. Hosea is a good example. Pronouncements in the North are enlarged to include Judah (Hosea 6:11), and the marriage to Gomer is rendered metaphorically so as to be applicable to a future generation (Hosea 4:15, 12:11). "But a generation later, to a different people and situation, Hosea's realistic language was understood metaphorically."[208] Future communities of faith have a biblical precedent for reading the prophecy in light of their present, or better, for reading their present in light of Hosea. The biblical text is time conditioned, but it is not *intended* to be a prisoner of the past. Just the opposite. In this way Childs consistently remains in the thicket of authorial intent.

Eventually Childs is happy to refer to the text's in-built actualizing dynamic as a form of "intertextuality" or "figuration" — the language is interchanged — though not if the historic dimension of canonical shaping is erased:

> The role of intertextuality served as a means by which the coherence of the developing canonical corpus was sustained. By intentionally signaling a linguistic affinity between the past, present, and future, a substantive coherence was developed. This shaping of the text by the community was deemed constitutive for its authority. Of course, once the canonical corpus reached its relative stability, the text as religious Scripture continued to generate new intertextual relationships, but the distinction between text and figuration was maintained, at least in principle.[209]

Perhaps the best thing to call this bedrock intentionality is the *sensus literalis*. According to Childs, "both synagogue and church assigned a unique value to the text's plain or literal sense. Implicit thereby was the concern to maintain some form of authorial intent" (he qualifies that this "is not an apology for authorial historicity, but for the hermeneutical significance of the designated writer"). Thus "Torah was assigned to Moses; the Gospel in its four-fold form to designated Evangelists. Figurative meanings were not rejected, but subor-

---

[207] Childs, Critique, 177.
[208] Childs, *Introduction to the OT*, 379.
[209] Childs, Critique, 177.

dinated to the literal sense."[210] The canonical approach cannot be reduced to a Schleiermacherian quest for the mind of biblical authors, but neither does it discard all forms of intentionality. The recontextualization of individual traditions into a larger corpus introduces meaning that may not have been intended at every step along the way. Yet the transformation of meaning that occurred as the canon approached its final form did not wholly sublimate text into meta-text, or letter into spirit.

The figurative cast of all this is quite important and should be distinguished from other ways of framing the matter. Childs' use of "intertextuality" is best understood as part of a figural register rather than as diction gleaned from a close study of Julia Kristeva. Similarly, recall how Rendtorff once spoke of a "deuteronomically stamped layer of reworking ... which unambiguously views the Pentateuch as a whole and will have it understood as *one* great coherent complex." It is one thing to extend this to the "will" of the entire canon, so to speak, and Rendtorff soon moves in this direction. It takes another step to view the intentional constraints of the canon's final form as a literal sense upon which figuration builds, to which it must answer. Strikingly, for Childs it is also the sense to which *theory* must answer. To use other language of his, the force driving the process of canon formation is the same force that makes itself felt on modern hermeneuts. If things work as they should, this literal/textual/authorial pressure alters the conceptualities that readers inevitably bring to bear. Theory has enriched biblical interpretation in the past, but it needs a "theological corrective," something it gets this from scripture's plain sense. Thomas Aquinas is an instructive example, as *Biblical Theology* explains:

> It is unlikely that any modern biblical scholar would be tempted to imitate Thomas' appropriation of Aristotle. Yet the basic hermeneutical issue at stake turns on the fact that no modern biblical theologian can function without some other conceptual framework. Much of the modern search for the recovery of only internal biblical categories has been extremely naive. Rather the crucial hermeneutical issue turns on how well one can hear and understand the biblical witness even through the time-conditioned human categories which each interpreter has inherited or adopted. A study of Thomas is invaluable in seeing to what extent the author was able to adjust his philosophical perspective to the uniquely biblical message and in the process, cause his own alien categories actually to serve toward the illumination of the biblical text.[211]

As Childs puts it in 2003, addressing Steins, in best cases like Thomas' "new theories were constantly being altered and radically transformed in the light of the powerful theological coercion exerted from the biblical text itself."[212] Or so goes Childs' theory of theory. The deeper issue, Childs' "vision," concerns the integrity of the Christian Bible as a vital and abiding witness in the church. It is

---

210 Ibid., 177. Steins puts a Hans Frei-esque gloss on the literal sense (My Way, 57), which is a rare thing to find in the German literature. The concept is simply pivotal for Childs.

211 *Biblical Theology*, 41–42.

212 Childs, Critique, 175. Compare the very fine discussion in Rowe, Biblical Pressure.

not so much that there is no method to the madness (no formal methodology, granted, but these are not the same thing), far less that Childs retreats into some (American?) form of biblicist positivism. Instead, Childs' first port of call is the church and its rule of faith in Christ. When he invokes concepts like canonical intentionality, plain sense or the *sensus literalis*, scripture's inherent intertextuality, pressure, or its figurative capacity, he is above all trying to give fresh expression to orienting Christian theological realities, and he takes most of his cues from a long history of theological discourse and reflection. Everything else finds its place within this profoundly Christian vision.

Many will remain dissatisfied with Childs' handling of theory and method. Reviewers of *Struggle* have judged the chapter on postmodern interpretation to be a disappointment (rightly in my view), and the 2003 critique of canonical intertextuality (against Moberly and Frei as well as Steins) should raise the eyebrows of anyone who has dabbled in literary theory. Does this weakness with theory detract from Childs' vision? Probably yes, but then again perhaps not very much. The task of holding to a form of intent while yet recognizing that texts acquire new significance as they cross temporal and communal contexts requires a good measure of hermeneutical sophistication. There may be ways to negotiate difficulties of the Bible's authorship and reception without having a highly technical theory of reading. Nor is methodological refinement a self-sufficient good. In a word, Childs' vision would not have been well-served by a hermeneutic that was overly *raffiniert*. And lastly, amongst those with an interest in writing a Theology of the entire Christian Bible, one finds wide agreement that the project, if not altogether impossible, demands a pretty exacting set of special considerations — coordinated operations more on the order of calculus than algebra. We turn now to some of these, and to the way different conceptions of biblical theology have played out in English and German.

CHAPTER 3

What is Biblical Theology? (Does it Matter Where a Scholar was Trained?)

The term "biblical theology" can be used in a wide variety of different ways... Barr distinguishes between biblical theology and other theologies, such as "doctrinal" or "philosophical theology" ... but if a theology is meant that comprises both the Old and New Testaments, Barr likes to speak of "pan-biblical theology," with which he picks up on the title of Oeming's book (1985). In German discussion, however, the term Biblische Theologie *is used primarily in precisely this sense as theology of the whole Bible.*
— Rolf Rendtorff

On the narrow topic of text criticism Childs once expressed his hope to reviewers of *Introduction to the OT* that "discussion would take seriously the full force of the canonical argument which has been mounted rather than simply to assume the validity of the older critical model in which we have all been trained."[1] Barr, one of the reviewers, took the latter part of this statement as emblematic of Childs' attitude to historical-critical method more generally, and he objected. Childs "must speak for himself. I would not say that I was so 'trained.' What many or most of my generation were trained in was the atmosphere of the biblical theology movement, which Childs has described and analysed so well."[2] Barr's remarks tell us as much about Barr as they do about Childs. They raise a question, too, about what difference it might make where a scholar was trained. Can that really matter?

Childs trained at Basel and Heidelberg under a stout generation of Old Testament scholars who sought to capitalize theologically on tradition-historical research. Later he strove to overcome limitations he eventually perceived in their work, appreciating their theological brilliance while criticizing the method to which their theology had been fused. Childs' perspective changed after his return to America, and his most distinctive work is at once a critique and an extension of the insights of those who trained him.[3] Barr, on the other

[1] Childs, Response to Reviewers, 59, cf. *Introduction to the OT*, 84–106.

[2] Barr, *Holy Scripture*, 130.

[3] "As a young student who had fallen under the spell of von Rad, I shared with many others the conviction that his brilliant method held the key to a proper understanding of the OT... Yet [in the next generation] much of the excitement which his early post-war lectures evoked had died... Slowly I began to realize that what made von Rad's work so illuminating was not

hand, born in Glasgow in 1924, took a first degree in classics at the University of Edinburgh (his studies were delayed by service as a pilot in the Royal Navy) and then a B.D. in the Old Testament in 1951. Having been ordained in the Church of Scotland, he ministered for two years in Tiberias, Israel, where he learned Arabic and modern Hebrew, before taking an academic post in the New Testament at The Presbyterian College at McGill University, in Montreal. He returned to Edinburgh in 1955 and was Professor of Old Testament there until 1961. He taught at a number of other institutions subsequently, including at Oxford from 1976–1989 (he was Regius Professor of Hebrew from 1978 and received a D.D. in 1981). He spent much of the next decade at Vanderbilt University, retiring there in 1998, and moved to Claremont, California, where he died in 2006, aged 82.[4] Barr is less forthcoming than Childs about who his mentors were. The case will be made that one formative influence on Barr was his Edinburgh colleague T. F. Torrance, Professor of Church History from 1950–1952 and of Christian Dogmatics from 1952–1979. Torrance, who among other things worked to bring Karl Barth into English, had a strongly negative impact on Barr.

Circumstances of training appear to affect Barr's understanding of Childs and perhaps to account for one gap between English-language and German-language scholarship. As another test case for the last chapter's theme, that the reception of an author's work in another language is a neglected aspect of biblical interpretation, I will now look at how Barr and Childs understand biblical theology, and what these have to do with conceptions of the same in German literature. As the epigraph to the present chapter anticipates, the argument will be that Barr is out of touch with a dominant current in the German discussion of biblical theology in a way that Childs is not. I do not for a moment suggest that Barr has no contact with German debates — Barr's *Old and New* (1966) was translated into German the next year, and *Fundamentalism* (1977) within five years; Barr also read widely. Rather, Barr misunderstands Childs in large part because he is dismissive of the context out of which Childs' biblical theological efforts arise, whereas Rendtorff points to a more natural home for Childs' work. To present its case this chapter makes a focused comparison of three large volumes: Childs' *Biblical Theology of the Old and New Testaments* (1992), Barr's *Concept of Biblical Theology* (1999) and Rendtorff's *Canonical Hebrew Bible* (ET 2005).[5] In keeping with the title of part one, a governing purpose is to locate *Biblical Theology* internationally.

---

his method as such, but the theological profundity of von Rad himself. The same observation holds true for Wolff and Zimmerli. I am convinced that no amount of methodological refinement will produce a quality of interpretation which that generation achieved whose faith in the God of Israel was hammered out in the challenge to meet the Nazi threat against the life of the church" (Childs, A Response [Mays], 208).

[4] For a fuller biography see Knight, James Barr.

[5] *Theologie des AT* originally appeared as two volumes in 1998 and 2001.

A. Coming to Terms

From one perspective Childs' *Biblical Theology* is a pioneering book. Some have even gone so far as to call it *sui generis*. Rendtorff, despite disagreements on other fronts, can say, "Es gibt bisher nur eine einzige wirklich ausgearbeitete 'Biblische Theologie,' nämlich die 1992 erschienene von Brevard Childs."[6] The culmination of some twenty-two years' labor on Childs' part, *Biblical Theology* is the first answer to a call long sounded within the German-speaking academy. Eichrodt set about his Old Testament Theology with an awareness of a "unitive fact," that something "binds together indivisibly the two realms of the Old and New Testaments — different in externals though they may be."[7] For him a further step is required to examine the "essential coherence" of Old and New.[8] With still more clarity, von Rad appended these lines to the end of the fourth edition of his *Theologie des AT*:

> [Es] zeichnet sich aber ein noch ferneres Ziel unseres Bemühens ab, nämlich das einer 'Biblischen Theologie,' in der der Dualismus je einer sich eigensinnig abgrenzenden Theologie des Alten und des Neuen Testaments überwunden wäre. Wie sich eine solche biblische Theologie dann darzustellen hätte, ist noch schwer vorstellbar. Es ist aber ermutigend, daß sie heute immer lauter gefordert wird.[9]

Quoting part of this same passage, H.-J. Kraus concludes the second edition of his history of critical research (1969) by asking, "Wird ein Weg gefunden werden, auf dem die Spaltung überwunden werden kann? Das ist jetzt die Frage."[10] For his part, interestingly, Kraus would shortly abandon the project. In 1983 he presents a revision of earlier work under the title *Systematische Theologie im Kontext biblischer Geschichte und Eschatologie*. Also writing at about this time, H. G. Reventlow voices doubts of his own. "A 'biblical theology' has yet to be written. The way towards it is not only one of high hopes; it is also beset by a good deal of scepticism."[11] Yet as Rendtorff so neatly articulates, in 1992 Childs rendered statements like these "überholt" — obsolete.[12]

Barr, though, challenges the notion that biblical theology can be a *gesamtbiblische* undertaking in the first place. Again, despite a variety of differences, von Rad, Kraus, Reventlow, and Rendtorff agree with Childs at a very basic level: "Biblical Theology is by definition theological reflection on both the Old and New Testament."[13] Weirdly, Barr contests Childs' definition here on the

[6] Rendtorff, Bibel Israels, 102.
[7] Eichrodt, *Theology*, 1:26.
[8] Ibid., 1:31.
[9] Von Rad, *Theologie*^{4}, 2:447. See below for a discussion of text-critical issues.
[10] Kraus, *Geschichte*^{2}, 509.
[11] Reventlow, *Biblical Theology*, vii.
[12] Rendtorff, Bibel Israels, 102n25: Reventlow's claim specifically is "überholt."
[13] *Biblical Theology*, 55.

grounds that it does not "accord with most modern usage *in English*."[14] He allows that the phrase has tended to have a more restricted meaning in German usage, for what he prefers to call "pan-biblical theology," a phrase drawn from the title of Manfred Oeming's *Gesamtbiblische Theologien der Gegenwart*.[15] Defining terms this way might have its place in an overview of distinctively American or British views on biblical theology. But because Barr does not adequately reckon with the international thrust of Childs' life work, his terminological restriction of biblical theology to its English usage impinges rather severely on his evaluation of *Biblical Theology*.

To be sure, there are differences in German understandings. It is just that from the outset, Barr's analysis of the concept of biblical theology relativizes, and even inclines against, the one context where Childs' contribution most naturally fits. Barr calls the closing paragraph of von Rad's second volume "pathetic," supposing it to contain "words of apparent desperation."[16] Which paragraph does he mean? D. M. G. Stalker's translation (Edinburgh, 1962–1965) has a text critical problem of some complexity here. Based on the second edition of von Rad's *Theologie des AT* (Munich, 1957–1960), it adds a postscript that looks forward to — but does not match — the updated fourth German edition (Munich, 1962–1965). Recensionally, the translation is just slightly prior to the revision, and as others have observed, the fourth edition introduces substantial changes not reflected in the English. Although Stalker's translation includes a new postscript which von Rad must have supplied, and though a preface to the translation anticipates the changes of the fourth edition (2:ix), the concluding lines of Stalker's edition (2:428–429) reflect a different *Vorlage* than what I have quoted in German, above. Barr responds to the English version, where the final sentiment concerns the need to differentiate biblical theology proper from mere history of Old Testament religion.[17] He thus neglects something that will become more central in the revision. Even so, the need for *gesamtbibliche* theology is also emphasized at the end of the English version: "only when Old Testament theology takes this final step to the threshold of the New Testament, only when it makes the link with the witness of the Gospels and the Apostles perfectly openly, and when it is able to make men believe that the two Testaments belong together, will it have the right to term itself a theological undertaking, and therefore 'Biblical theology.'"[18] Once

---

[14] Barr, *Concept of BTh*, 1, my emphasis; cf. 180. He appears to misjudge Rendtorff somewhat on a related point, too (444).

[15] Ibid., 641n3, 497.

[16] Ibid., 510, 427.

[17] In addition to pages 510 and 427 in *Concept of BTh*, see especially 111. Cf. also Rendtorff, Lohfink, Barton, Albertz and others in *JBTh* 10. The relationship between history of religions and the biblical witness has a long and thorny history which extends back to Gunkel, as Werner Klatt illustrates. See Klatt, *Gunkel*, especially 77, 80, 189.

[18] Von Rad, *Theology*, 2:428–429 (Stalker's translation).

again a project equal to *Biblical Theology* in scope and ambition is being called for and anticipated.

Barr's reading of von Rad thus mirrors his dismissal of Childs. He is as well read in German OT scholarship as anyone in the Anglo-Saxon world, probably better than most. He is aware that "writing a biblical theology" has a fairly technical meaning on the Continent that is not always shared elsewhere and he discusses such differences from the first page of *Concept of BTh*. "To avoid confusion," he explains, "in this book the enterprise of writing a Theology of the entire Bible will be called *pan-biblical theology*... The work that most fully seeks to realize the pan-biblical ideal thus far is Brevard Childs' *Biblical Theology*... But the whole idea of 'writing a biblical theology' (i.e. a pan-biblical theology) in this sense has had a lively discussion in the last twenty years, especially within German scholarship."[19] Despite this recognition Barr stands far enough outside that context that Childs' typically German usage of biblical theology is of minimal importance to him, except insofar as it contributes to his panorama of biblical theology's many incongruous faces. By contrast, the definition according to which *Biblical Theology* is written is so naturally assumed by Rendtorff that he can say, "Es gibt bisher nur eine einzige wirklich ausgearbeitete 'Biblische Theologie.'" Not only does Childs tend to inhabit a different scholarly context than Barr; Childs' work has been *received* differently on that basis. Rendtorff accepts *Biblical Theology* as a Biblical Theology on its own basic terms. Barr does not. Again, Barr supposes that Childs' work reveals a "failure to converse with the past development of biblical theology itself."[20] But that all depends on how one conceives of the development of biblical theology. Ironically, a move that was meant to bring terminological clarity has obscured the degree to which Childs is dependent upon, and responding to, a well-established tradition of what biblical theology is thought to mean.

The contrast between Barr and Childs can profitably be taken further. Barr is highly skeptical about the very possibility of "pan-biblical" theology. For him, "'biblical theology' has clarity *only* when it is understood to mean theology as it existed or was thought or believed within the time, languages and cultures of the Bible itself. Only so can its difference from doctrinal theology, from later interpretation, and from later views about the Bible be maintained."[21] "Theology exists only in the minds of persons," he continues, and establishing the sequence and development of people's theologies is an historical task.[22] Barr grants that texts can *express* theology, but only when they do so

[19] Barr, *Concept of BTh*, 14. In his review Jon Levenson calls the English turn of phrase "pan-biblical theology" an "unfortunate neologism" (Negative Theology, 59).

[20] Barr, *Concept of BTh*, 426.

[21] Ibid., 4, my emphasis.

[22] Ibid., 214.

explicitly, and in this sense most of the Bible does not itself contain theology.[23] Drawing out theological aspects of biblical texts is a legitimate, perhaps a necessary, undertaking. But quite apart from whether it is advisable or possible to seek out a holistic picture of the theology of the New or Old Testaments on their own, it is simply inconceivable to expect a coherent presentation of the theology of the entire Christian Bible. "When taken as wholes" the two individual Testaments "are not congruent, nor even closely analogical." Hence Barr feels that between OT and NT scholarship is an "intrinsic separateness"; he recommends "that this should be accepted, rather than that vast amounts of further energy be poured into a task that has proved to be neither necessary nor salutary."[24]

Little wonder that Childs' Biblical Theology is "a fundamentally biblicistic illusion" on Barr's reading.[25] The terminological relativization of "pan-biblical theology" has the effect of ruling Childs' project out *by definition*. If this sort of thing were ever allowed, it would have to fall under the domain of dogmatics, not biblical theology.[26] "Thus the striving of biblical theology to establish coherence and unity, even if it is viable up to the level of the entire Old Testament or the entire New Testament, involves *essentially doctrinal questioning* if it is to be carried up to the level of the entire Bible, and the effect of this is to put into question the existence of biblical theology as an operation independent of doctrinal theology."[27] Briefly put, Barr has a pair of commitments that make it almost impossible for him to take *Biblical Theology* seriously. One is to the complete restriction of exegesis to what was thought by individuals in biblical times. The other is to a strict separation of the disciplines — Old Testament from New Testament, exegesis from dogmatics, historical theology from normative theology. Both relate to what Barr takes theology itself to be, and to why scripture has only a very indirect bearing upon it.

Childs on the other hand pursues a holistic account. The formation of the canon participates in the function of the final form. Canon proper is integral to the life of the church and, *mutatis mutandis*, the synagogue. Modern critical disciplines illuminate aspects of how the canon came together, how it functioned and continues to function as authoritative scripture. Dogmaticians study the same subject matter, tackling related problems in parallel as their

---

[23] Ibid., 248, 251; cf. 226–227, 242, 244–252, 376. This appears to be one of the places "Barr momentarily defines his subject out of existence" (Levenson, Negative Theology, 59).

[24] Barr, *Concept of BTh*, 186–187.

[25] Ibid., 252. That Childs is in view is made explicit in the footnote, 668n21.

[26] As Barr explains, it is not a question of whether theologians should take an interest in the Bible. Obviously they do. "The question is whether there is, or should be, a 'biblical theology' which seeks to bring together the entire biblical witness, or large portions of it, as a sort of intermediate activity between normal exegesis of individual texts and the regulative decision-making of doctrinal theology. That is quite a different question" (ibid., 242).

[27] Ibid., 376, my emphasis.

specialization allows, in a "division of labour."[28] For its part, biblical theology attends to the discrete witnesses of the one Christian Bible such that the various canonical voices are not obscured:

> The basic hermeneutical problem of the Bible, therefore, is not adequately formulated by using the terminology of unity and diversity. The oneness of scripture's scope is not a rival to the multiple voices within the canon, but a constant pointer, much like a ship's compass, fixing on a single goal, in spite of the many and various ways of God (Heb. 1.1), toward which the believer is drawn... The recognition of the one scope of scripture, which is Jesus Christ, does not function to restrict the full range of the biblical voices. It does not abstract the message, or seek to replace a coat of many colors with a seamless garment of grey.[29]

As with von Rad on Childs' reading, there is a christological center which focuses the unity. A similar sentiment is found in Eichrodt as well: "*That which binds together indivisibly the two realms of the Old and New Testaments — different in externals though they may be — is the irruption of the Kingship of God into this world and its establishment here.* This is the unitive fact because it rests on the action of one and the same God in each case."[30] Despite an array of differences, and there are many, Childs shares with his teachers a commitment to a christological core that unifies biblical theology. It is a unity of the subject matter to which study is directed, God in Christ, that finally makes reflection on the entire Christian Bible centripetal.

The move to Christ can be alarming. I will revisit challenges associated with this formulation of the biblical witness later in this chapter and further below. Meanwhile, we can tap on an obvious twentieth century source for christological claims on the Old Testament by contrasting the relationships Barr and Childs have to the work of Karl Barth.

I. The Barth Connection: Barr at Edinburgh

Barr celebrates the idea that Karl Barth has no theory of biblical theology. As a dogmatician Barth had no need of it, according to Barr, and positively rejects efforts to "induce the totality of the biblical witness." Barr quotes from *Church Dogmatics*:

> Therefore a biblical theology can never consist in more than a series of attempted approximations, a collection of individual exegeses. There can never be any question of a system in the

---

[28] *Biblical Theology*, 370: "those scholars trained in dogmatic theology are often better equipped to pursue in detail the nature of God's being, especially in light of the modern challenges to the biblical witness from various forms of philosophy. Yet it is an equally important responsibility of Biblical Theology to assure that the reflection on the being of God remains integrally related to his redemptive action within human history for the sake of Israel, the church, and the world." On the same page Childs criticizes Barr's aptly titled essay "The Theological Case against Biblical Theology," which appears in the first FS for Childs.

[29] *Biblical Theology*, 725.

[30] Eichrodt, *Theology*, 1:26, original emphasis.

> sense of Platonic, Aristotelian or Hegelian philosophy... How can we expound it except by surrendering ourselves to the recollection...? Biblical theology (and self-evidently dogmatics too) can consist only in an exercise in this surrender, not in an attempt to induce the totality of the biblical witness.[31]

Barr then quotes N. Wolterstorff on Barth for support: "The unity of the Bible does not consist in a unified theology or world-view. There is ... 'no Christian view of things,' 'no biblical theology.' The unity of the Bible consists — so Barth insists — in the unity of its content, in the fact that all its parts point, in one way or another, to Jesus Christ."[32] Barr's conclusion is that these lines prove Barth "clearly does not provide a basis for biblical theology."[33] Dogmatics is something totally different. Childs "upholds what he thinks to be Barth's viewpoint" but is blind to "Barth's *rejection* of biblical theology as a mode of procedure."[34] Yet this is a dubious reading of Barth and Childs alike. It is hard to imagine how Barr fails to see that concern for "the unity of Holy Scripture" drives the entire section from which he quotes, where Barth states that biblical "exposition is trustworthy to the extent that it not only expounds the text in front of it, but implicitly at least *expounds all the other texts*, to the extent that it at any rate clears the way for the exposition of all other texts."[35] Thus "the on the whole irreversible distinction between the two witnesses is again completely relativised by the unity of its object."[36] Childs and Barth do not subscribe to the same agendas — in many ways Childs is closer to von Rad — but somehow Barr's lengthy treatment of biblical theology completely skirts the fact that for Eichrodt, for von Rad, for Childs, and indeed also for Barth, the common reason for positing a unity between the testaments is christological. This is no minor oversight. Furthermore, for several of these *gesamtbiblische Theologien*, and especially for Childs, a strict separation between dogmatics and exegesis is therefore untenable. Any division of labor arises from other exigencies.

---

[31] *CD* 1/2, 483–484; as quoted in *Concept of BTh*, 244 (cf. 414). Would Barth thus reject dogmatics, too? What is elided in the penultimate sentence is suspect. The full question reads, "How can we expound it except by surrendering ourselves *with them* to the recollection, their recollection, and to the expectation, their expectation?" (my emphasis). This is actually a statement in favor of the unity of the two testaments in their witness to Christ. One witness looks ahead ("their expectation"), the other back ("their recollection").

[32] *Divine Discourse*, 68, quoted in *Concept of BTh*, 244.

[33] *Concept of BTh*, 244–245.

[34] Ibid., 245.

[35] *CD* 1/2, 485, my emphasis.

[36] *CD* 1/2, 482. Nearby one finds a clear analog to Childs: "When we have to do with Scripture, i.e., canonical Scripture, the Scripture which the Church has defined and we in and with the Church have recognised as canonical, when we have to do with Holy Scripture as witness, in fact the witness of divine revelation, we have to do with the witness of Moses and the prophets, the Evangelists and the apostles... The Old and the New Testament both have as their distinctive feature to attest in the one case the Messiah who is to come, and in the other the Messiah who has already come" (481).

It is not altogether clear how much all this has to do with Barr's "training," or his formative influences. It seems likely that Barr's time at Edinburgh left its stamp, and one cannot but wonder how much his interaction with Torrance shaped his overwhelmingly negative view of Barth.[37] Torrance is punished time and again in *The Semantics of Biblical Language*, at least as much as T. Boman, J. Pedersen or N. H. Snaith, and yet he also emerges there as one about whom Barr once felt quite differently. Amazingly enough Barr collaborated with Torrance on the Church of Scotland's special commission on baptism, which drafted an interim report (1955) that was corporately revised by Barr among others and forwarded to the General Assembly (1958).[38] Somehow, by 1961 the interim report had become a parade example of the abuses of linguistic evidence in theological argumentation.[39] In a footnote Barr distances himself from the committee. "I myself was associated with the production of this document ... but would now disagree with much in its approach, which in my opinion does not sufficiently depart from the methods of the *Interim Report*. This latter report contains numerous examples of the kind of misinterpretation of language which is criticized in this book."[40] Indeed, it is as if an experience of the Church of Scotland commission precipitated Barr's devastating analysis.

What is more, Barr seems to lay the ultimate blame for exegetical abuses at the feet of Karl Barth,[41] with whom Torrance studied in Basel, and whose own pamphlet on baptism a decade before (ET 1948) was undoubtedly part of the impetus behind Torrance's inquiry through the Church of Scotland from 1953.[42] Yet in 1961 Barr reacts not so much to Barth's well-known study, but to Torrance's provincial reworking of it in Edinburgh, in and for the church in which Barr himself was an ordained minister. Only this personal dimension explains how a denomination's relatively minor in-house report on baptism acquired such a high profile in *Semantics*, especially given that related material existed by Barth himself. Barth was not the first target.

Childs raises questions about Barr's reading of Barth, as we will soon see. Interestingly, he also raises questions about Torrance's. "It is a little frightening when you see some of Barth's students trying his method and coming up with

---

[37] I am told that T. F. Torrance's brother, J. B. Torrance, led the young Barr to Christ at a bus stop, and later officiated at Barr's wedding (personal communication with Alan Torrance, 21 May 2008). I have had less success finding clues about the nature of Barr's relationship to Norman Porteous, who held the Chair of Hebrew and Semitic Languages in Edinburgh from 1937–1968, and who was perhaps the first Anglophone student of Barth. Porteous simply does not appear in *Semantics*, so far as I can see. His place in *Concept*, too, is very minor.

[38] Torrance, *Interim Report* and see the introductory note in Torrance, *Study Document*.

[39] Barr, *Semantics*, 5–6, 140–144, 262, 279. To this can be added a long list of Torrance's missteps: 106, 120, 129–136, 149–156, 161, 171–175, 198, 204, 254, 259, 264, 277–279.

[40] Ibid., 141.

[41] Ibid., 156, 188, 277–279. Barr posits a close identification between Torrance and Barth.

[42] Barth, *Taufe* (ET Barth, *Baptism*); cf. M. Barth, *Sakrament?*.

something else. After reading a few of Torrance's exegeses, there were problems in Barth that I have never seen before."[43] It is obviously beyond the scope of this thesis to trace the ways Barth has been brought into the English-speaking world, but Childs, who knew Torrance at Basel, suggests that once again in the transmission of scholarship distorting factors come into play.

The main point is that Barr's treatment of biblical theology in *Concept of BTh* cuts him off from an important aspect of the venture where it has most often been taken up. For this reason one should be suspicious of his claim that "Childs comes closer to the conservative Barthian tradition which has been powerful in certain circles in the Anglo-Saxon world."[44] Undoubtedly this is the Barthian tradition Barr knows best, and distrusts most. We can be equally certain that it is not the tradition which mediated Barth to Childs. Barth may not call himself a "biblical theologian," and it is obvious that, strictly speaking, the terminology is anachronistic when applied to Calvin or Luther. But when Childs claims "Barth's exegesis is an exercise in Biblical Theology,"[45] or something similar for pre-critical exegetes, is he really just "reading his own concepts into their minds,"[46] as Barr insists? To defend a reading of that sort, one would first want an accurate picture of Childs' concept of biblical theology and its development. And this should probably include an account of Childs' years in Basel where, among other things, under the guidance of Baumgartner in the summer semester of 1952, he conscientiously divided J/E strands from P in Exodus 14.[47] Whatever Barr means by telling us that his generation "trained" in "the atmosphere of the biblical theology movement," he speaks of a radically different background. As he admits in the very same paragraph, "I do not know that I ever detected a gloss, identified a source, proposed an emendation or assigned a date."[48] For Childs it was otherwise.

II. The Barth Connection: Childs after Basel

Much has been made of the link between Childs and Barth, not just by Barr. Too often this has been colored by a distaste for Barth, such that Childs becomes guilty by association. The one extended study of Childs and Barth to date, by Charles Scalise, was never published, and unfortunately it is not as illuminating as it might have been.[49] Scalise does point to a probable source for Childs' idea that canon ≈ rule. Barth writes:

---

[43] Childs, Barth as Interpreter, 35; cf. 32 concerning Barr on Barth.

[44] *Concept of BTh*, 408–409.

[45] *Biblical Theology*, 589.

[46] *Concept of BTh*, 414.

[47] See section B.I in chapter one, above.

[48] *Holy Scripture*, 130.

[49] Scalise, Theological Basis, argues with almost no qualification that Childs' canonical approach "is in large measure an extension of the theological hermeneutics of Karl Barth. For

"Canon" means "rule," i.e., the "rule of truth," and most significantly this conception was originally connected with the dogma as well as the constitution of the texts which are recognized to be holy. The Church cannot "form" it, as historians have occasionally said without being aware of the theological implications.[50]

Scalise also draws attention to a Yale colloquium on Barth convened in January 1969, a month after Barth's death. Childs contributed, as did Hans Frei. A recording of that session was transcribed, a handful of hard copies circulated.[51] Following Scalise, there has been a tendency to treat Childs' remarks more formally than the setting suggests, as though they constitute a proper academic article. Given the sudden timing one could hardly expect polish. In fact Childs' paper at the colloquium has a conversational tone, and it brims with personal reminiscences of his student days.

Childs tells a simple narrative. He came to Basel to study Hebrew with Baumgartner, not to hear Barth, although he and the other "Bible men" listened to Barth. They formed a sort of "Biblical phalanx" and sat in the back when he lectured: "we came well-equipped with our Hebrew and Greek. And we would check his references and coach each other and sort of make fun of Barth's exegesis. Barth occasionally, when he got to the section, would look over at this phalanx and say, 'Not that I don't know all about J, E, D, and P,' and then would go on as if he couldn't care less."[52] Barth's personal charisma, and his facility with languages, won no converts from the Bible students, but he disrupted some of their prejudices about dogmatics as a second-class field. And yet, Childs says, "perhaps what I'm saying is a confession of the sins of my youth. Because I do have a change of heart, for various reasons."[53] Barth's work is not perfect, but it survives. It has something still to teach.

For Childs, looking back, Barth's work survives despite the many working in a supposedly Barthian way who have become "hopelessly outdated."[54] There

---

Childs the historical critical meaning of Scripture is subordinated to its theological meaning as discerned from the pattern of its theological shape. Childs' theological strategy, like that of Barth, enables the recovery of continuity with precritical interpretation, while incorporating the results of modern historical study" (197). Three main themes in common are: emphasis on the Bible as witness; opposition to existentialist hermeneutics (rendered in analogy shorthand, Barth : Bultmann : : Childs : Sanders); and rejection of anthropocentric theology (122). For a more readily available condensation see Scalise, Childs and Barth.

[50] *KD*, I/2, 524; *CD*, I/2, 473. Cited ibid., 66 (cf. Scalise, Theological Basis, 81; for an earlier discussion of canon and the *regula fidei* see *KD*, I/1, 103; *CD*, I/1, 113), though in fact Childs himself cites this passage in *CD* with his first use of the phrase "rule of faith" (*BTh in Crisis*, 105n7). This important connection will occupy us more in chapter seven.

[51] There are copies at Yale and Princeton; none made it to public libraries in the United Kingdom, however. My thanks go to Christopher Seitz for supplying me with a photocopy.

[52] Childs, Barth as Interpreter, 30.

[53] Ibid., 31.

[54] Ibid., 31. Childs names "Wright and Anderson and Rowley, or Richardson or Hunter or Cullmann and Filson."

are still big problems in Barth's work, but somehow he never went in for things like *Heilsgeschichte* or a Hebrew mentality, things that made others vulnerable. Some of what Barth got right in Childs' view sounds remarkably like a description of the canonical approach: "Barth always complained that one could not get behind the text, that one could not come at Scripture from a context other than the Canonical context as it had been received by the Church, that there was no neutral position from which one could start and then somehow make a bridge from neutrality to commitment."[55] Or again: "Barth allows you to read the text from different contexts. It seems to me that he is always interested in different ways of studying it. But he continues to insist that ultimately the context from which theology has to be done is the context of Scripture — Old and New Testament — in the Canonical context."[56] Barth's exegesis may be suspicious. Sometimes it seems to be.

And yet it seems to me it's the fact that Barth wants to go through the text, to the reality, that the text becomes a transparency, that the walls that separate the Apostle from the reader are dissolved, and one then begins to confront the reality itself — and for Barth there can be no antiquarian interest. And that means that Barth has the tendency always to move down, to move through, and talk about the transparency. Very soon one is wrestling with the realities of Grace, and Judgment, and Nature and Grace — all the rest of these things — and that remains a problem. It seems to me this may be somewhat of an overstatement, but it is true that the kind of work he does is of such a different genre that for one who has been trained in the traditional critical way, it does seem that wherever Barth starts, he ends up in these massive theological statements and most of us have trouble following him.[57]

Problems like these remain, yet to Childs in early 1969 it seems "we still have much to learn from this word he leaves," namely, "that dogmatics continues to be corrected by exegesis. So, exegete."[58]

Also noteworthy in the present discussion are a few off-hand remarks about Barr's criticisms of Barth. "James Barr's recent book on interpretation Old and New says it's one of the most chilling things in the whole Dogmatics to read that Barth says in 1948, Perhaps a time will one day come when dogmaticians will be able to depend on Biblical scholars. Then he says, Already we had Kittel, already we had Hoskyns on John. How could he possibly say that?"[59] Childs does not go into detail but he muses, "I wonder again whether Barr really understood what Barth was doing."[60] Time would seem to bear this out.

---

[55] Ibid., 32.

[56] Ibid., 33. Capitalization here follows the transcriptionist's decision.

[57] Ibid., 33–34.

[58] Ibid., 35.

[59] Ibid., 32. Childs paraphrases Barr, *Old and New*, 96n1 (which is citing *KD*, III/2, vii; *CD*, III/2, ix), cf. 12, 90–96, 102, 181–182.

[60] Childs, Barth as Interpreter, 34.

Another factor with Childs and Barth is the work of Hans Frei. This of course refracts Barth's thought in its own way,[61] but it is also no accident that Childs and Frei, colleagues at Yale for so many years, have been connected in the literature. So far, however, the most relevant primary source has been entirely overlooked. The Yale colloquium ended with a discussion period. The panelists speak off the cuff, and Childs' and Frei's remarks address several pivotal issues with delicious clarity. Frei advances his idea of the biblical text as a narrative universe (in line with the later Barth, he suggests), whereas Childs counters that the text needs to be read as a transparency. In church history, perhaps in Barth, in exegesis today, Childs states, "I don't see how you can avoid a dialectic between text and reality, in some sort."[62] (Frei's Barth is hardly more Childs' than Torrance's is.) Yet at this early date, five years before *Eclipse*, still on the eve of *BTh in Crisis*, what stands out today is the strong agreement between Childs and Frei on the problem of the literal sense. In view of the long chain of disagreements between Childs and Barr, particularly over the letter and the spirit (chapter seven), part of the dialogue merits quotation at a little length. A student asks the panel whether it would be possible to access Barth's genius in a more exegetically controlled way. Childs speaks up first.

CHILDS: Well it seems to me for the last twenty or thirty years people have been trying to combine the orthodoxy of Barth with the historical-critical approach. It seems to me that this enterprise has now come to an end and has proven unfruitful — that you are now at the turn of the road, you have to go either right or left; that the type of move that said Barth is right in seeing theological dimension, but now we have to take history more seriously and bring in the whole baggage — I don't think this can —

In other words, I'm suggesting that the problem is far deeper than this. It's a problem that certainly didn't just arise with Barth. (And much of what I've learned about this has come from talking with Hans Frei.) But it has often bothered and puzzled me. You see, when you read Calvin, he fights against the whole medieval tradition by saying it's the *sensus literalis* that counts — it's the literal sense — and you have page after page against the whole church dogma. But then you read Calvin on the Old Testament, and here's Jesus Christ and Jesus Christ. How could it possibly be? And everybody just says that Calvin is just inconsistent.

It seems to me that this doesn't at all touch the heart of the problem: that for Calvin, the *sensus literalis* IS Jesus Christ. And it was only when you have the eighteenth century identification of the literal sense with the historical sense that you're just hopelessly lost. And it seems to me that it's something along that line — that we've just been unable to understand what Barth is doing.

FREI: That's right.

[Julian] HARTT: Would you mind repeating that?

CHILDS: It sounds better in German, though.

---

[61] Two good studies of Frei are Dawson, *Christian Figural Reading* and Higton, *Public Theology*.

[62] Childs, Barth as Interpreter, 56.

STUDENT: Is it something we can do today?[63]

This is a pregnant exchange. By January 1969 Childs sees that theological compromise with the historical-critical approach fails (e.g., in the work of his teachers). He knows this partly because of a contrast between traditional exegesis and modern critical exegesis that can be captured in a sound-bite: for the Reformers, the literal sense of the Old Testament was Christ. Frei's account of the shift ("That's right") — that in the Enlightenment the literal sense came to be identified with the historical sense, and thus to exclude Christ — will soon be argued in detail in the first three chapters of *Eclipse*, but already Childs has bought into the thesis. Attaching the letter of the Old Testament to Christ sounds strange today, even to a trained professional (Hartt), and the challenge of this will continue to animate Childs through the final phases of his career. Although biblical theology is not mentioned, one can easily extrapolate to Childs' later mandate that a theology of the entire Christian Bible must have a christological center (one place von Rad, Barth and Childs all agree). Finally, while one can only guess at what exactly sounds better to Childs' ear in German, the cryptic aside highlights how deeply his thinking about such matters is informed by wide reading in that language.

From clues like these one gathers that Barr and Childs each had a change of heart about Barth somewhere early in their academic careers but subsequent to their studies at Edinburgh and Basel, respectively. Their turns are not quite mirror images. Barr firmly rejected an ethos associated most immediately for him with T. F. Torrance. This appears to have transpired after his student days, perhaps during his first appointment in Old Testament in which time he served on a special Church of Scotland commission on baptism and wrote his discipline-transforming *Semantics*. Childs knew Barth firsthand at Basel but sat with a hectoring "biblical phalanx" when Barth lectured. Back in America, having experienced and studied the end of the biblical theology movement, he reconsidered. He concluded that Barth, despite some lasting problems, kept an important traditional perspective intact — essentially, a keen awareness of One who grounds the church's very access to its scriptures. Childs also perceived that others who worked in Barth's name were not so free of Barr's searching critique of 1961. Suffice it to say that Barr and Childs have very different Barths in mind when it comes to the unitive scope of biblical exegesis, and that Barr's has more to do with Torrance's mediation of Barth into English and to Barr in particular at Edinburgh. Odd as it may seem, geography and training do surface as factors in the gap that opens up between one bleak conception of Biblical Theology and the first real attempt of it.

---

[63] Ibid., 52–53. Frei says "Sure" and then steers the conversation in another direction.

B. Rendtorff's Input

Chapter two showed how Rolf Rendtorff's focus on the process of transmission in 1977 became a focus on the final form sometime after 1979 due to an encounter with Childs' *Introduction to the OT*. In his own language, it was as if the book made the scales fall from his eyes; or, by elevating the final form, it changed the direction of his line of sight. I also suggested that Rendtorff's interest in Judaism, which stems from the 1960s, conflicts at some level with Childs' biblical theological deployment of canon. I left two issues to address here, in the context of a discussion of biblical theology's definition. First, why and how does Rendtorff eventually distance his vision of canon from that of Childs? And second, what understanding of canon does Rendtorff develop for his own enterprise? Before turning to these interrelated questions, it may help to briefly illustrate the way he came to feel about Childs in time.

Those who attended Rendtorff's special session at the international meeting of SBL in Edinburgh (2006) may recall the question and answer period that followed.[64] Rendtorff was asked whether the death of the Yahwist (whom he had supposedly killed thirty years prior) would have negative pedagogical consequences. The questioner explained his worry that, if Childs' canonical perspective won the day, students would lose all the sharp tools honed by critical research. Would not the demise of literary-critical analysis have this result?[65] Instead of responding directly, Rendtorff distanced himself from Childs, his "close friend." In his early days Childs was far too invested in source analysis, Rendtorff opined. Throughout his Exodus commentary, for example, we find him identifying J and E and P. Later, he left source analysis behind and took a dogmatic turn for the worse, patterned on Karl Barth. This last remark brought forth a round of applause that effectively ended Rendtorff's answer. Noteworthy about this episode is not so much what it reveals about how many in the field view Childs' proposals, but rather what it suggests about Rendtorff's later work, which *equally* relies on the vitality of canon as an exegetical and theological category. For one thing, it shows a Rendtorff only partly attuned to the Childs who, as we have seen, consistently invests in diachronic analysis. (Since Childs' presumed departure from source criticism is an apt summary of Barr's portrait in 1999, one might suppose this influence to hover in the background.[66]) More puzzling is the reaction against a putative dogmatism, since

[64] The paper Rendtorff gave on 4 July 2006, "What Happened to the 'Yahwist'?: Reflections After Thirty Years," is online at http://www.sbl-site.org/Article.aspx?ArticleId=553 (accessed 14 December 2009). Its content is incidental to the anecdote that follows.

[65] I confirmed J. H. Ellens' question in personal communications, 18 and 31 July 2006.

[66] In Childs' Exodus commentary, Barr says it is "surprising to find that the analysis into J, E and P, in great detail down to half-verses and quarter-verses, is still there" (*Concept of BTh*, 391). In later work, however, "the importance of canon is beginning to fade and the importance of doctrinal rectitude is beginning to increase" (396). In point of fact, Childs still

theological aspects of canon were central to the appeal of Childs' proposal when Rendtorff encountered it in the first place. Still more, Rendtorff had gone on to write his own massive canonical theology of the HB/OT. What, then, is the cause of his late neuralgia?

Rendtorff's comments in Edinburgh cover two main aspects of his eventual differentiation from Childs, both of which are evident in the final pages of *Canonical HB*. On the one hand, Rendtorff worries that Childs is so invested in source criticism that he barely manages to give a "canonical" reading of the text at all. In *Biblical Theology* more words are spent on a description of P and J accounts of creation than on "the effect of the joining of the sources into a continuous narrative."[67] Childs is still not canonical enough! (Note how long this is after 1974.) On the other, Childs is believed to have inappropriately yielded to dogmatic considerations. Early on, in the 1980s, Barr's invective against Childs is noted but not much regarded. Rendtorff occasionally says that the attack has the character of "a religious war." Though voicing misgivings about "some dogmatic-sounding formulations," he indicates that his "sympathies are on the side of Childs."[68] By *Canonical HB* Barr's attacks have clearly received more attention. A final and very oblique comment on the link Childs wants to forge with dogmatic theology simply refers the reader to three chapters in Barr's *Concept of BTh* which problematize that effort, the second by tracing Childs' alleged dogmatism back to Barth. *Introduction to the OT* may have opened Rendtorff's eyes to the importance of canon, but *Biblical Theology* leads into an impasse. A core conviction of the latter volume is "diametrically opposed" to what Rendtorff envisions.[69] Why? "It is of crucial significance that the church maintained Israel's Bible *unchanged*," Rendtorff explains.[70] That the point is actually directed against Childs, who makes a similar seeming claim, unfolds only later, when Childs is criticized for writing of an Old Testament "transformed" by the New. "For the maintenance of the 'Scriptures' in the form in which it was transmitted in the Jewish faith community is precisely an essential element of continuity between the Old and the New Testaments."[71] But such comments are little developed in *Canonical HB*.

---

speaks of layers in his Isaiah commentary of 2001 — perhaps surprisingly, depending on a person's preconception of what canonical reading entails.

[67] *Biblical Theology*, 113, cited by Rendtorff, *Canonical HB*, 722. A "dependence on the dominant literary-critical classification stands in the way of the express interest in a 'canonical' overview" (723). This is true to a point. What Rendtorff overlooks is the subtle hermeneutical point that "[t]he J material functions on the level of figurative language, once-removed now from its original literal sense" (*Biblical Theology*, 113).

[68] Rendtorff, *Canon and Theology*, 195, cf. 171.

[69] Rendtorff, *Canonical HB*, 755.

[70] Ibid., 749, my emphasis.

[71] Ibid., 755.

Fortunately, Rendtorff's article-length review of *Biblical Theology* offers a more complete explanation. Beginning with an acknowledgment of the book's uniqueness,[72] the review is often appreciative. At the same time, Childs is "eher konservativ" for his treatment of creation in Genesis 1–2.[73] More crucially, Rendtorff objects to *Biblical Theology* because of its understanding of Judaism. It builds on "bestimmten dogmatischen Voraussetzungen" — christology above all, as the strategy for broaching the Christian Bible's unity — that divide it from Jewish understanding.[74] Here Rendtorff interjects. "An dieser Stelle muß ich die Rolle des Berichterstatters aufgeben, denn ich habe Schwierigkeiten, Childs' Position zu verstehen." His explanation is telling:

> Über die Frage der "Arbeitsteilung" zwischen den theologischen Disziplinen kann man verschiedener Meinungen sein; ich stimme Childs zu, wenn er sagt, dies sei eher eine Frage der Strategie als eine Grundsatzfrage, wenn ich auch selbst die Aufgaben anders bestimmen würde. Was ich nicht verstehen und nicht akzeptieren kann, ist der Vorbau dogmatischer Entscheidungen vor die exegetische Analyse. Vor allem verstehe ich auch inhaltlich nicht, was es heißt, daß das Alte Testament Zeugnis von Christus ablegt. Ich bestreite überhaupt nicht, daß es theologisch legitime Weisen gibt, das Alte Testament mit dem Neuen zusammen als christliche Bibel zu lesen und dabei die christliche Bibel als Ganze vom Christusereignis her zu deuten. Aber dadurch wird doch das Alte Testament selbst nicht zum Christuszeugnis.[75]

When Rentdorff resumes this theme at the close of his review, it becomes clear just how closely bound his objection to dogmatic (= christologizing) readings of the OT is to his work for a *rapprochement* with Judaism. He names two ways in which he simply cannot follow *Biblical Theology*. First is its prioritization of dogmatic over biblical theology. The second issue is ostensibly historical. "Daß das Alte Testament Christus bezeugt (nicht einen kommenden Messias, sondern Jesus Christus), verstehe ich nicht. Eine Hermeneutik, die grundlegende historiche Sachverhalte ignoriert, ist mir nicht nachvollziehbar."[76] In truth the second objection is not straightforwardly historical, and it seems to give the first objection its teeth. Childs thinks biblical theology is "ausschließlich eine christliche Disziplin." But what about the possibility of Jewish biblical theology? "Für mich ist dies ein ganz entscheidender Punkt. Ich bemühe mich, niemals Aussagen über das Alte Testament zu machen, die von einem Juden nicht nachvollzogen werden könnten." Christians inevitably come to the text with different questions than Jews. "Aber meine Antworten, d.h. meine Auslegung des Textes müßte für ein Juden verständlich und akzeptabel sein."[77] I submit, therefore, that Rendtorff's late reaction against Childs' so-called

---

[72] Cf. Rendtorff, Bibel Israels, 102, cited above.

[73] Rendtorff, Rezension Childs, 362. Again, Rendtorff has not seen to the bottom of the potential "figurative" reading being suggested. See further chapter seven.

[74] Ibid., 364.

[75] Ibid., 365.

[76] Ibid., 367.

[77] Ibid., 368.

Barthian dogmatism stems from his commitment to a certain *theology* of the church's relationship to Jewish scripture. Not "history," not "theology" per se, but the affirmation of a *Christuszeugnis* in *Biblical Theology* is at the core of why he feels it threatens the "Integretät" of the Old Testament.

Backing up a decade or so we can also ask about the development of canon in Rendtorff's own work. From the start he reads Childs against a distinctive set of concerns, the most important being his transformative encounter with Judaism. Rendtorff proceeds to marry these theological insights. For example, in a paper delivered in Jerusalem in August 1981, three elements are all merely juxtaposed: critique of the usual historical-critical procedure, a concern that Christian exegetes recover the Jewish exegetical tradition, and "the extremely exciting discussion" sparked by Childs.[78] For some while no conflict between these interests is seen. Rendtorff does not draw on Childs much beyond this point in time, however, which helps explain why *Biblical Theology* catches him by surprise. What steps does he take instead?

One is to reassess the work of Gerhard von Rad. Rendtorff's 1989 essay "Old Testament Theology: Some Ideas for a New Approach" attests a muted displacement of Childs as the progenitor of his interest in canon. Its tour of models prior to von Rad reveals that OT Theologies typically followed outlines derived from dogmatic or systematic considerations. Von Rad's *Theology* broke the trend. In von Rad's own words, "we must submit ourselves to the sequence of events as the faith of Israel saw them."[79] So von Rad begins with creation despite his view that it was neither old nor the primary saving event in Israel's history. According to Rendtorff, for the very first time "we can talk about a 'canon-related' survey." Yet as a significant footnote qualifies, the scare quotes flag "an anachronism inasmuch as the discussion about the theological significance of 'the canon' only started very much later, and since von Rad himself was not thinking here about the 'final canonical form' of the texts, as is the case in the most recent discussion."[80] He must then explain why von Rad deviates from this template with the prophets. Still, in this way von Rad's input on things "canon-related" takes priority.

Rendtorff's reasons for transferring his newfound interest in the final form to von Rad are not altogether clear to me. He would easily have recognized Childs' debts to von Rad. Perhaps he felt he had a greater claim to being von Rad's student and follower in matters canonical. Hermeneutically, Rendtorff in the 1980s is attracted to R. Smend's defense of "Theologie *im* Alten Testament," which is to say, to the OT's theological meaning understood principally as the conscious intent of biblical authors and editors.[81] Rendtorff and Smend agree,

---

[78] Rendtorff, Rabbinic, 30 (= Rendtorff, *Canon and Theology*, 18).

[79] Von Rad, *Theology*, 1:120 (= ^{4}1:134), cited in Rendtorff, *Canon and Theology*, 9.

[80] Rendtorff, *Canon and Theology*, 9.

[81] Ibid., 143–144; cf. ibid., 12.

against von Rad, that OT theology is not a later extrapolation based on the "facts" of the credo. The collective overview itself is a late, deuronomic/deuteronomistic phenomenon. Theology *in* the OT surfaces only at secondary or tertiary levels. Theology, Smend emphasizes, is "historisch ein verhältnismäßig spätes Produkt."[82] This brand of intentionalism suits Rendtorff's detection of a "deuteronomically stamped layer" that "unambiguously views the Pentateuch as a whole" in 1977,[83] a memory of which may survive through to *Canonical HB*: "Deuteronomy is perhaps the most theological book in the Hebrew Bible."[84] Circumscribed this way even "theology" puts some distance between Rendtorff and Childs, for whom *biblical* theology "is not confined simply to a historical description of the original author's intention."[85] In other words, talk of a "transformed" OT has another, more basic sense for Childs than the one Rendtorff cannot comprehend in 1992. In addition to the transformation of sense wrought by the gospel and the canonical addition of the NT, which are at root christological, the pre-Christian scriptures of Israel take shape through a transformation of earlier material. Childs outlines his reading of this process in 1979. Some elements of canonical shaping are intentional while others are largely fortuitous. Either way, the *effect* of the process is the same, which is "to render the tradition accessible to the future generation by means of a 'canonical intentionality,' which is *coextensive with the meaning of the biblical text*."[86] A prior transformation establishes the literal sense as such before that sense is known (transformed) to deliver Christ.[87] What is more, Childs sometimes even cites von Rad to support this more basic sense of the OT's transformation. For these reasons I doubt whether Rendtorff's commitments on the meaning of theology "in" the Bible necessarily push him away from Childs and toward von Rad. Maybe the best one can say is that Rendtorff and Childs alike lay claim to von Rad's legacy but revise it differently.

Again, to what use does Rendtorff put canon, on whatever precedent? His exegetical insights are often rich, and I do not wish to minimize them. Yet his hermeneutical program is striking in its simplicity. His canonical retooling of

---

[82] Smend, Theologie im AT, 116, cf. 111–112.

[83] Rendtorff, *Transmission*, 196 = *ügP*, 164; see section C in chapter two, above.

[84] Rendtorff, *Canonical HB*, 74.

[85] *Biblical Theology*, 7–8; see the discussion in section A of chapter one. Childs' stance toward Ebeling's classic essay on biblical theology is opposed to Smend's sense of biblical theology in the narrowest sense — "was das Alte Testament enthält" — using Ebeling's very words (Smend, Theologie im AT, 116, citing Ebeling, *Wort*, 86 [= Ebeling, Meaning, 94]). Rendtorff, too, knows that Smend's interest in canon, such as can be found in the opening pages of Smend, *Entstehung*, is quite different to that of Childs (Rendtorff, *Introduction*, 129). See further Smend, Questions.

[86] *Introduction to the OT*, 79, my emphasis.

[87] *Biblical Theology* shows Childs daring to affirm Christ in the literal sense of the OT, and struggling to discover what that means. In 1979 he has clarity about a more basic implication of literal sense OT exegesis, namely, about the theological status of the "final form."

von Rad in 1989 is precisely the one that drives his OT Theology, *Canonical Hebrew Bible*: von Rad's "new approach" is named on page one, and the ensuing account sees itself as "an effort in *running through the canon from its first to its last verse* to allow the texts to speak in their present form."[88] Nevermind that if this is the method von Rad is *at least* as problematic a canonical reader as Childs. What does a "canonical" Biblical Theology look like? Can one judge by the table of contents? Rendtorff puzzles over Childs' historically chronological treatment of the NT in 1992 — Paul before the Gospels — and it may be fair to call that section of *Biblical Theology* "eine Art theologische Literaturgeschichte des Urchristentums."[89] One could try to answer how the move might serve a Biblical Theology, in what senses (if any) it qualifies as canonical reading. Alas, Rendtorff merely begs the question by saying that he attempts "viel konsequenter 'kanonisch' zu arbeiten, als Childs in diesem Buch tut."[90] What exactly does it mean to work canonically? Is it simply, from all appearances *pace* Childs and von Rad, to read from first verse to last?

Rendtorff gleans one other insight from the initial orientation to canon provoked by Childs, viz., the canon's vital function in living communities of faith. (Not by chance is the Festschrift for Rendtorff called *Die hebräische Bibel und ihre zweifache Nachgeschichte.*[91]) With this comes an increased regard for the history of exegesis, though this too has a distinctive flavor. *Wirkungsgeschichte* for Rendtorff is far more exclusively concerned with the history of Jewish exegesis.[92] Surely a major advance in Christian biblical theology, in OT theology especially, has been its awakening to the church's fraternity with the synagogue. Is this also the sum of its *Ziel*?

---

[88] Rendtorff, *Canonical HB*, 413, my emphasis.

[89] Rendtorff, Rezension Childs, 360–363, here 363.

[90] Ibid., 369.

[91] It is also not by chance that Rendtorff hesitates at Smend's acceptance of Wellhausen's distinction between Israel and Judaism (*Canon and Theology*, 144).

[92] Rendtorff's labor for Jewish-Christian dialog merits study. He has invested a career in Leviticus (above all see his *Leviticus*) and has posed forceful theological questions, i.e.: "Does the interpreter consider the pre-Christian (i.e., Jewish) meaning of the text to be theologically relevant or not?" (*Canon and Theology*, 14). He insists that "a clear distinction must be made between the *interpretation* of the Old Testament in its canonical framework — that is, under the presuppositions and conditions of its development up to the close of the canon — and its *appropriation* by the Christian church, especially since that church has become an exclusively Gentile one" (ibid., 117). Sometimes interpretation and appropriation are difficult to separate. At other times appropriation does not easily follow interpretation. The latter may be a more serious problem for Rendtorff. It may be self-evident to him what the contemporary relevance of Pentateuchal legal material is, for example (*Canonical HB*, 650), but I doubt whether others in the church are as confident. Similarly, Gerstenberger, Review of Rendtorff, asks why so little use is made of the "Ziel" rubric in the Leviticus commentary.

C. Interim Conclusion

We come to the close of this study's first part. I have attempted to give some introduction to Childs' thought and the ways it has been received. I have also raised questions, both about its significance and the adequacy of its representation up to now. Later, at the end of part two, I will revisit the question just asked of Rendtorff, above, by addressing Childs' own complicated relationship with what he calls the "mystery of Israel." The question is particularly fraught. For now let me just say that, in Rendtorff's reading of the matter, insufficient attention has been paid to how the literal sense functions for Childs, to how it can be extended through figuration, and to what all this has to do with his provocative claim that the unifying referent of both testaments is Jesus Christ. What is biblical theology? The *sensus literalis* is the hub of canonical (ruled) biblical theology for Childs, and it calls for a complex form of intentionality "coextensive with the meaning of the biblical text." This is not simple. Moreover, in terms of the precedent for this sort of biblical theology, one can find reason to doubt how well Rendtorff represents the work of his mentor. Von Rad concludes his seminal essay on typology by stepping back from his earlier harsh review of W. Vischer's controversial book, *Das Christuszeugnis des Alten Testaments*: "So muß also — um endlich das umstrittene Wort zu nennen — wirklich von einem Christuszeugnis des AT gesprochen werden."[93] At issue is how the Old Testament can retain its distinctive pre-Christian voice and at the same time function as the first witness to someone who in time would be heralded "the lamb slain before the foundation of the world."[94]

Then again, it is fitting to conclude this discussion of contexts for biblical theology in the late twentieth century by reminding ourselves that Rendtorff, despite increasing disagreement with Childs and perhaps a greater regard for Barr's caricature of Childs the Barthian, still recognizes Childs' basic definition of biblical theology as sound (i.e., that it is "theological reflection on both the Old and New Testament"[95]). "Barr distinguishes between biblical theology and other theologies, such as 'doctrinal' or 'philosophical theology' … but if a theology is meant that comprises both the Old and New Testaments, Barr likes to speak of 'pan-biblical theology,'" Rendtorff notes. "In German discussion, however, the term *Biblische Theologie* is used primarily in precisely this sense as theology of the whole Bible… *And this is how the term is being used here*."[96]

---

[93] Von Rad, Typologische, 33 (= Rad, Typological, 39). On this question compare Rendtorff's "Christological Interpretation as a Way of 'Salvaging' the Old Testament? Wilhelm Vischer and Gerhard von Rad," 76–91 in Rendtorff, *Canon and Theology*.

[94] Revelation 13:8; see section C of chapter seven, below.

[95] Childs, *Biblical Theology*, 55.

[96] Rendtorff, *Canonical HB*, 751, my emphasis.

This represents a strong current in the German discussion.[97] Disagreement notwithstanding about how best to articulate the status of "Old Testament" vis-à-vis its parallel scriptural status as Tanakh or Miqra, for Rendtorff the domain of biblical theology is much as Childs understands it.

More immediately in part two we turn to the development of Childs' fundamental argument for scripture's canonical shaping. In its most groundbreaking and thorough iteration the argument sought to found an understanding of the formation of Christian and Jewish scripture more or less equally, though it was titled an *Introduction to the Old Testament as Scripture.* Childs clearly wrote as a Christian who saw the MT as the proper "vehicle" of the OT. I will show that Childs' understanding of what Judaism and Christianity share in the Hebrew Bible shifts crucially in the 1980s, but that the essence of his argument for canonical shaping remains a constant. Hence the title of part two comes from an important essay Childs wrote in 1996, on the way to his Isaiah commentary. In it he argues that biblical intertextuality arises as a forward looking extension of a text or as a retrospective enrichment of traditional language and that it rests in either case "on the same inner logic of Scripture's textual authority."[98] To understand what Childs means here is to understand his entire project. Exploration of the inner logic of scripture's textual authority impels *Exodus, Introduction to the OT, NT Introduction, Isaiah, Pauline Corpus,* and a number of less monumental efforts beside.

To pick up another thread of argument from these first chapters, there is indeed a kind of logic to this thinking despite a large body of secondary literature committed to the illogic of canon in Childs' operation. This will be seen in Childs posture as one working for reform within a specialized field. Gunkel proves an unexpectedly important antecedent for Childs (chapter four). It can also be seen in what I call the heart of the matter — the centering function of the *res* (chapter five). Finally, in qualified senses inner logic emerges from Childs' long *Auseinandersetzung* with inner-biblical midrash, or the dynamics of intertextuality in canon formation (chapter six). Behind the allegorical "mystery of Christ" (part three) lies a deep "mystery of Israel."

[97] As Ebeling's 1955 essay attests (ET Ebeling, Meaning), there have long been two main currents in the definition of "biblical theology." If Smend, followed by Barr and Barton, represents one, Janowski, One God, shows that the other is alive too. Rendtorff may actually have feet in both streams.

[98] Childs, Retrospective Reading, 376.

PART II

"The Inner Logic of Scripture's Textual Authority"

CHAPTER 4

Form — Final Form: Canon after Gunkel

Ursprünglich haben die ältesten [Gattungen] ... eine ganz bestimmte Stelle im israelitischen Volksleben besessen, von dem sie einen wichtigen Teil darstellen, und eben deshalb, weil sie nicht auf dem Papier, sondern im Leben bestanden haben, sind auch ihre ältesten Einheiten so kurz gewesen, entsprechend der geringen Aufnahmefähigkeit der alten Hörer. — Hermann Gunkel

Beginning in the pre-exilic period, but increasing in significance in the post-exilic era, a force was unleashed by Israel's religious use of her traditions which exerted an influence on the shaping of the literature... Israel defined itself in terms of a book! The canon formed the decisive Sitz im Leben for the Jewish community's life, thus blurring the sociological evidence most sought after by the modern historian.
— Brevard Childs

Taking a long view, Gunkel provides a dramatic counterpoint to Childs on the dispensability of the canonical text. Gunkel believes the essential genres of the Old Testament have a provenance "nicht auf dem Papier, sondern im Leben."[1] Juxtapose the view of Childs, who consciously *inverts* Gunkel's method, contradicting the usual form critical account in form critical terms: the canon itself became the setting for the life of the people, the community of faith.[2] The decisive question for Childs is whether or not the biblical literature is more than an artifact of Israel's religious history. Does canonical scripture transcend the circumstances of its creation and provide the *Sitz* for a community's life of faith and practice? Gunkel asserts nearly the opposite, that scriptural codification became the very barrier to Israel's primitive strength and life.

Then again, the opposition between Gunkel and Childs should not be overdrawn. They invite comparison as innovators, for one. Pieter G. R. de Villiers, in an article commemorating the 75th anniversary of Gunkel's death, describes "the remarkable self-confidence of an innovative thinker who had explored the

---

[1] *RGG*², 3:1679.

[2] *Introduction to the OT*, 78, cf. 61–62. I am aware that Gunkel ought not be identified with the "form" or "tradition criticism" of his successors. On these terminological difficulties see Blum, Formgeschichte, 32–33, esp. 33n2, 37n15; Berger, *Formgeschichte*, 19–27. Also see section C of this chapter.

widely used exegetical method of his time and found it seriously lacking. At the same time he knows of viable alternatives. He thus writes with an authority and outspokenness of someone with a vision of important new ways of interpretation."[3] Gunkel was not always thanked for this, either (Wellhausen found "more chaos than creation"). Like Gunkel, Childs seeks to turn critical biblical scholarship upside down (or right-side up, depending). For another thing, in methodological terms Childs all but asks to be compared to Gunkel and those who follow him since, in Childs' words, "In one sense, I have simply extended the insights of the form critical method which called for an exact description of the material's literary genre."[4] The use of form criticism to talk about the final form speaks of reform, of adjustment made from *within* a discipline. And Childs actualizes more than one impulse of Gunkel, including his privileging of Israel's life which is a move traditionally bound up with scripture. As de Villiers points out, "Gunkel's historical work must be qualified carefully, because his criticism of dogmatic exegesis did not mean that he distanced himself from theology." In a curious way "the Biblical message remains the point of departure and the point of return in his research."[5] This is true despite Gunkel's profound interest in new, extra-Biblical sources, and in de Villiers' assessment it calls for "more debate":

> Gunkel insisted on a close link between historical and theological investigation. The one did not exclude the other. He also understood that a mythological thought pattern need not be less truthful than a historical way of thinking. When it comes to prophetic and apocalyptic texts, this is of great significance. While he did not develop hermeneutical observations about the relationship between history and theology, the unfortunate manner in which his research was later conducted in an almost exclusively historical and descriptive interpretation of the Bible, neglects Gunkel's other passion — that is, to understand the Bible theologically and, furthermore, to ask how the mythological and the theological relate to each other. There are many signs that theological issues are moving to the centre of Biblical studies once again — something that will hopefully do more justice to Gunkel's legacy.[6]

While Childs does not say much about mythological truth in apocalyptic thought, he does return attention to the crucial link between historical and theological investigation. In this way he picks up a neglected aspect of Gunkel's legacy.

In the pages that follow I will argue that a residual memory of the canon's function in Christian theological discourse pervades Gunkel's work, and that Childs' work addresses this quite directly. Despite first appearances Gunkel and Childs share a little methodological and theological common ground, if not enough to establish a truce. After first setting out Gunkel's "religion" in the context of his equivocal devaluation of the final form, I will take a retrospec-

---

[3] De Villiers, Gunkel as Innovator, 336.

[4] Childs, Response to Reviewers, 52.

[5] De Villiers, Gunkel as Innovator, 345.

[6] Ibid., 349.

tive glance at the project he believed would one day supplant biblical theology. I will then outline the return to canon after Gunkel. Primarily Childs' 1979 Introduction is in view, though it is appropriate to include his earlier work and the tradition-historical theology of Gerhard von Rad.

A. Hermann Gunkel's Religion

"Much of nineteenth-century biblical criticism was not an adventure in impiety but turned on assumptions about the nature of revelation and its (tenuous) relationship to the canon (as a literarily shaped and coherent theological product)."[7] However well this statement captures the spirit of nineteenth century biblical scholarship in general, it suits Gunkel (1862–1932) eminently. Piety marks his complex attitude to canon, even through his relativizing of it. He is also a believer in providence and revelation, albeit of a highly naturalistic order (his criticism of supernaturalistic exegesis is sharp). It should not surprise that personal commitments like these intertwine with Gunkel's method, and yet it has been more usual to treat, or in an earlier day to adopt, Gunkel's methodological innovations as if they had little connection to his religion. Hence one purpose in discussing Gunkel's religion, which includes his attitude to religious culture, is to show the way it infuses his method. Often enough religious conviction appears to drive his method and not the reverse. It is certainly so in his thinking about the canon's (in)significance. Subsection II will address Gunkel's tacit canon. Before turning there, however, consider Gunkel's appraisal of the formation of biblical literature across the Old Testament, in the Pentateuch (mostly Genesis), the Prophets and the Psalms.

I. On the Formation of Biblical Literature

For Gunkel the literary history of Israel falls into three general stages: the preliterary age of folk-tales (through ca. 750); the literary age which culminates in the great literary personalities ("die großen Schriftstellerpersönlichkeiten," ca. 750–540); and subsequently the epigones.[8] Israel's literary history consists in the history of genres (*Gattungen*), several instances of which "haben eine ähnliche oder dieselbe Geschichte erlebt."[9] Simple, short, "pure" genres originate in the lives of the people. They existed "nicht auf dem Papier, sondern im Leben," and were attached to highly specific situations. At this primitive stage the Israelite had developed neither a strong sense of his individuality nor yet

[7] Seitz, *Figured Out*, 28–29.

[8] Klatt, *Gunkel*, 180; cf. *RGG*², 3:1679.

[9] *RGG*², 3:1678–1679. The first edition of the entry contains many of the same statements, but in less compressed form. See *RGG*¹, 1:1193.

much ability to comprehend long units of narration.[10] Eventually, however, a strong impulse to record creative achievements arose in Israel, and thus "literature" in the proper sense was born. This facilitated the development of longer units, such as the Joseph saga. "Without a doubt, this drift towards length indicates that the times had grown more literary."[11] At the same time collections of smaller units were compiled. The noteworthy persons here are "die großen Schriftsteller, die sich der altertümlichen Gattungen bemächtigen," but who also through the mixing and transformation of older genres achieved "höchst individuelle Worte."[12] The author of Job and above all the great literary prophets deserve to be named in this context. Ultimately the "Erforschung dieser großen Schriftsteller ist die Krone der Literaturgeschichte Israels."[13] Thereafter decay settled in. The third and final age belongs to the epigones, who "counterfeit the masters [*die Meister nachahmen*]."[14] In this period styles and genres are still being mixed, though more than before, and collections are being extended, but the crowning spirit has departed. (In another place Gunkel calls this development "the tragedy of Israelite literature."[15]) At long last "die Sammlung der Sammlungen, der Kanon, entsteht."[16]

Within this broad arc of achievement and then decline are smaller peaks and valleys. The advance of writing technology wrests an oracle or story from life itself, depositing it on paper. As compositional skill increased, longer and longer narratives could be compiled, sometimes with pleasing results. Occasionally an individual author stepped forward to make his creative spirit felt. So although the road to the final form is beset by ineptitude, complications in detail set Gunkel apart from the unmitigated atavist. His belief in progress is as strong as his love of the original.

As an outworking of this, in method Gunkel is driven to two perspectives that resist integration. On the one hand, he emphatically affirms the full histo-

---

[10] Cf. "Israel's Literary History," Gunkel, *Water*, 34: "Just as we see the development of our children's minds in the gradually increasing amount that they can take in at one time, so we can trace one feature of the growth of civilization in the gradual increase of the literary units in Israel." The essay originally appeared as "Die Grundprobleme der israelitischen Literaturgeschichte," *Deutsche Literaturzeitung* 27 (1906): 1797–1800, 1861–1866, was reprinted in *Reden und Aufsätze*, 29–38, and also appears in English translation in *What Remains of the Old Testament and Other Essays*, 150–186.

[11] Gunkel, *Water*, 35.

[12] *RGG*², 3:1679.

[13] *RGG*², 3:1679.

[14] *RGG*², 3:1679.

[15] Gunkel, *Water*, 36. The full quotation parallels the the *RGG* article well: "Finally we come to the tragedy of Israelite literature. The spirit loses power. The genres are exhausted; imitations begin to abound. Redactions take the place of original creations. Hebrew ceases to be the living language of the people. By this time the collections are grouped together into larger collections. Finally, the canon took shape."

[16] *RGG*², 3:1679.

ry of tradition, stating in his seminal *Schöpfung und Chaos* (1895, ET 2006): "I hold it to be methodologically objectionable to investigate only the beginning of a thing and to ignore the subsequent, often more important and more valuable, history of the same."[17] This is the first of his "controlling principles." His inquiry goes well beyond a sourcing of biblical material in its putative Babylonian birthplace. Instead, he writes, "I have also explained the particular ways by which these materials were taken into Israel and re-formed." Hence

> the creation narrative, although of Babylonian origin, nevertheless first gained its particular meaning in Israel. Thus, I believe myself to be protected against misunderstanding, as if perhaps by proving that Israel did not lie outside the realm of world culture, I deny the particularity of Israelite religion and, in turn, lead to the destruction of the belief that in this history God has revealed himself in a special way.[18]

Is Israel's religion truly unique in the ANE, or is Gunkel merely paying his dues to a conservative orthodoxy? An element of the latter may be present, but Gunkel's personal piety rests on a genuine if awkward conviction about the revelatory value of the Old Testament. Further, while he is most interested in the state of a tale just after Israel adapted it, his first principle still requires him to trace the growth of Israel's tradition throughout its entire history.

A second principle finds clear expression in *Creation and Chaos*, too. Contending with the view that the history of a thing can be more important than its origin is the idea that as material changes hands its original significance is forgotten, or willfully suppressed. In a word, it is the problem of *darkening*. Genesis 1, for instance, is "a faded [*abgeblasster*] myth."[19] Israel transformed the struggle of Marduk against Tiâmat, to be sure, but a polytheistic ring from the original still comes through.[20] Similarly within Israel, later generations lose touch with a story's vital meaning in earlier times.

> It is in the very nature of oral tradition, when passing oh-so-tenaciously from generation to generation, that it is subjected to certain fluctuations. Such omissions, additions, displacements, which later generations have imposed on the ancient materials, are revealed in the present codification of the tradition. They are revealed by the fact that the continuity of the narrative, which formerly had been uninterrupted, currently exhibits some obscurities or pe-

[17] Gunkel, *Creation and Chaos*, xxxix = vi. Henceforth I will give the page numbers for *Schöpfung und Chaos* after the = sign. Regrettably, the English translation is problematic at many points. See de Villiers' exposé in RBL, Review of Hermann Gunkel. I use the recent edition for convenience but indicate some corrections in favor of the German original.

[18] Ibid., xl = vi.

[19] Ibid., 80 = 117.

[20] Gunkel wonders about the superiority of Genesis 1 over the Marduk myth: "do *we* have the right to value Genesis 1 totally differently than we value any other ancient myth? ... Might even the Judaistic-supernaturalistic piety understanding of God which is assumed in Genesis 1 appear to our piety not to be the highest thing? Notwithstanding that, it does continue to exist! In Genesis 1 we are able to discover again the God in whom *we* believe! All other cosmogonies are, to us, only interesting antiquities" (ibid., 80 = 118; translator's emphasis and exclamation).

culiarities. Or they are revealed by the fact that certain features, features which had a proper meaning at the time of their origins, are nether intelligible from the present context nor are they able to be considered as generally intelligible. They are, therefore, viewed as strangely brief and incomprehensible. Just as the age of a painting may be recognized by the darkening [*Nachdunkelung*], so too is the antiquity of the tradition recognized by such "darkenings" [*Verdunkelungen*]. In any examination of a tradition this darkening has to be brought into play. The ultimate object of the investigation, however, is to reconstruct the original context and to indicate the basis of its alteration, i.e., to write the history of the tradition. [*Bei jeder Untersuchung einer Überlieferung ist bei diesen Verdunkelungen einzusetzen; das letzte Ziel der Forschung aber ist, den ursprünglichen Zusammenhang zu reconstruieren und die Gründe seiner Veränderung anzugeben, dh die Geschichte der Tradition zu schreiben.*][21]

Because the tradition as it has been preserved shows evidence of darkening, the historian must restore single traditions to their original vibrancy. Unlike the art restorationist, however, "the present codification of the tradition" (i.e., the unhappy state of the canon) puts some serious reconstruction work at the historian's feet. Many small units with aesthetic integrity are encased in later, larger blocks. To extend Gunkel's metaphor slightly, the first small images grew dim naturally with the passing of time but were disfigured most by primitive artists who puttied them into a rude mural.

One principle leads Gunkel to investigate positive developments in traditions; the other urges an inquiry that runs *against* time, that seeks actively to unwork it. Supposing these two concerns are not mutually exclusive, and quite possibly they are not, the tension in method calls for resolution in a set of decisions about where one finds the stuff of tradition intact — if not in the final form, then trapped within or lurking beneath — and how. Ostensibly Gunkel adjudicates the tension with "history," but on closer inspection religious and cultural values play a vital part in his decision-making process. In the next three subsections the particulars of this truism will be shown in Gunkel's position on the collection and development of Genesis legends (at the head of the Pentateuch), the prophetic literature, and the Psalter. Along the way it should be possible to get a good sense of his take on the religious significance of canon formation.

Genesis

The lengthy introduction to Gunkel's Genesis commentary (1901, ET 1997) gives an overview of pentateuchal literary history.[22] As in *Creation and Chaos* he affirms the biblical material's full history, starting outside Israel. The foreign

---

[21] Ibid., 163–164 = 256. I have corrected the translation at a few points and have removed gratuitous punctuation. The translator rightly terms this "a classic statement of traditio-historical methodology" (xxxiv).

[22] As above, when citing Gunkel's Genesis commentary I generally give the English first, with page numbers for the German original following the = sign. For another account of Gunkel on the Pentateuch's literary history see Nicholson, *Pentateuch*, 41–43.

origin of a legend must be observed, yet it can be even more important to attend "to what Israel made of it, or to the history it underwent in Israel."[23] In *Genesis* too the history of Israel's religion is not always a tale of progress. Darkening, compounded by the changing spirits of later times, occurs as legends and sagas are handed along. This circumstance alone mandates research into a story's original setting. Legends can be appreciated even in their present state, yet "only one who holds them up to the light of their original understanding can perceive their brilliant colors. To him, they appear as small glittering and shimmering works of art."[24] Here again we see Gunkel's ambivalence about the growth of the tradition: pre-literary jewels have to a considerable extent been ruined, or at least buried under the text, yet tracing the historical development of a textualized tradition is equally part of the critic's task.

Gunkel's notion of cultural progress, governed almost entirely by the metaphor of a child's development into mature adulthood, complicates matters further. Early masterpieces are short because early Israelites lacked the mental powers to compose or consume longer narratives. Yet even as cognition improved, facilitated by the advent of writing, the people tended to lose their grasp of tradition. "We often have the feeling that we are, indeed, in a position to reproduce the attitudes of the old legends to a degree, but that the current narrators did not correctly perceive these attitudes."[25] Gunkel speaks as an adult with full, scientific knowledge. He speaks as an individual, a "man" who approves when *Männer* (though in Genesis not yet *Einzelpersönlichkeiten*) rise above the undifferentiated primal collective.[26] He speaks as a poetical aesthete with the sensibilities to know when the standard achieved is "relatively closer to modern art."[27] But, intriguingly, he also speaks as one who yearns for a lost spirit of childhood. "We join them" — not the adults recounting Israel's old stories by firelight so much as the children gathered at their feet — "and listen along."[28] In this connection a footnote in Werner Klatt's admirable biography of Gunkel comes to mind, in which is related an anecdote told by H.-J. Kraus. According to Kraus, during Gunkel's last Christmas dinner with students at Halle (1931), Gunkel said "er habe sein ganzes Leben nach seinem verlorenen Kinderglauben gesucht."[29]

---

[23] Gunkel, *Genesis*, lviii = lxviii.

[24] Ibid., xlii = xlix.

[25] Gunkel, *Genesis*, lvii = lxvii.

[26] At the earliest times narrators were faithful to the tale because "ancients, quite in contrast to moderns, do not need to exercise their personalities by altering and innovating" (ibid., lvi = lxv). The view aligns with his position, contra Wellhausesn, that Genesis 1 is not a free construction of the author.

[27] Ibid., xliv = li. The Joseph cycle, which merits the distinction "novella," is his parade example.

[28] Gunkel, *Genesis*, xxvii = xxxi.

[29] Klatt, *Gunkel*, 99n51.

Weirdly, almost as often as he mentions the culturally underdeveloped but bright-eyed children of Israel Gunkel refers to "our children." Typically the direction of analogy runs from present to past. "Like our children," for example, the ancients were content to hear the same stories over and over.[30] Or:

> The child looks wide-eyed at the world and asks, "Why?" The answer it gives itself and which initially satisfies it may be very childish, very incorrect, and yet, if it is a spirited child, captivating and touching, even for adults. Ancient peoples also raise such questions and answer them as well as they can. These questions are also usually the same we ask ourselves and seek to answer in our scientific [*wissenschaftlichen*] disciplines. What we find here, then, are the beginnings of human knowledge, of course only minor beginnings, but as beginnings still worthy of respect. At the same time, however, they are especially touching and charming to us, for in these answers ancient Israel expressed its most intimate attitudes, clothing them in the colorful garment of poetry.[31]

"We" is to Israel as parent to child. The analogy can reverse temporal direction, too. At one point Gunkel remarks that "our peasants [*unsern Bauern*]" reflect the ancient situation still today.[32] Gunkel's paternalism ranges from the ancient people (*Volk*) of Israel to his own *Volk*. It is in this mode that he appeals to the "evangelical church and its commissioned representatives" to handle their new awareness of Genesis' legendary character with tact. "Genesis reports many things that contradict our advanced knowledge."[33] Distressing as it may be "for the child who cannot yet distinguish between reality and poetry if one tells him that his beautiful narratives are 'not true,'" the news should not be hidden. Anyway, a childish comportment "would be unseemly for a modern theologian," and it would make true, "historical understanding of Genesis impossible. This awareness has already become common among the historically trained such that it cannot be suppressed. It will surely — it is inevitable — reach our people [*unser Volk*]. We are concerned, however, that it be offered to them in the proper spirit."[34] Gunkel's motives can be taken at face value. The piety here is no feint, and it blends with powerful senses of history present and past to form an intoxicating draught of *Kulturprotestantismus*.

---

[30] Ibid., xxix = xxxiv: "the ancient period was satisfied with very minor creations which hardly filled a quarter hour. When the account had ended then, the imagination of the hearer is sated and his powers of comprehension are exhausted. At most, we may imagine that when the story ends, the hearers, like our children, may have wanted the same account once more." Cf. Gunkel, *Water*, 12, 34.

[31] Gunkel, *Genesis*, xviii = xx.

[32] Ibid., xxxvii = xliii.

[33] Ibid., ix = x. Unlike William Robertson Smith a few decades before, in a different setting, the orthodoxy Gunkel countered was more in line with Wellhausen than not. He also stood at some remove from the "Babel-Bibel" controversy (Berlin, January 1902), which had a different tenor than the circumstances surrounding Smith's dismissal from Aberdeen in 1881, though no doubt the ethos leading up to it hangs in the background. See Klatt, *Gunkel*, 70–74, 99–103.

[34] Gunkel, *Genesis*, xi = xii–xiii, cf. xxvi = xxx. I have modified Biddle's translation, which renders "unser Volk" as "the people."

Prophetic Literature

A negative evaluation of canonization proper sounds out loudest with the prophets (men, not books). For Gunkel, as for many in his day, these great figures attest the triumph of individual personality over the style-bound custom that dominated the ancient world. "Here in Israel something characteristic took place that was unknown elsewhere in the Near East: the individual came to the fore. Powerful personalities arose, grasped by the storms of the age, trembling with passion, who, touched by the deity in secret hours, attained the sublime courage to proclaim the thoughts that they — they completely alone — perceived within themselves."[35] In order to fully appreciate the individuality of the prophets, it is necessary to get a picture of the styles and genres they used, to restore prophetic discourse to its original life setting.

The prophets were not originally writers but speakers. Anyone who thinks of ink and paper while reading their writings is in error from the outset. "Hear!" is the way they begin their works, not "Read!" Above all, however, if contemporary readers wish to understand the prophets, they must *entirely forget that the writings were collected in a sacred book centuries after the prophets' work. The contemporary reader must not read their words as portions of the Bible* but must attempt to place them in the context of the life of the people of Israel in which they were first spoken.[36]

Gunkel then obeys his first principle, sketching the development of prophecy. The earliest prophets, such as Elijah or Elisha, did not write at all. Later figures including Isaiah and Amos did not write at first, but "these men increasingly resorted to writing [because] times had changed."[37] Fragments werc gradually assembled, by the prophets or their students, though no thought was given to the possible long-term significance of such "primitive collections": "they thought only of momentary results and not at all of later generations. They were convinced that their prophecies were not related to a distant future but that they would soon be fulfilled."[38] Mixed as these collections were with anonymous oracles, and guided only by a concern for the immediate, one can understand how for Gunkel the textualization of prophecy obscured both the prophet — Isaiah the man — and the original setting (*Sitz*) of his speech. "Not until Ezekiel are things different: this man, accustomed as priest and jurist to scrupulous order, and convinced that his prophecies about Israel would be ful-

---

[35] Gunkel, *Water*, 86. On the emergence of the prophetic personality cf. 118–119, 128–130. This essay first appeared as "Die Propheten als Schriftsteller und Dichter," in *Die Propheten* (Göttingen: Vandenhoeck & Ruprecht, 1923) 34–70. An earlier English translation is found in David L. Petersen, ed., *Prophecy in Israel* (Philadelphia: Fortress Press, 1987) 22–73.

[36] Ibid., 87, my emphasis.

[37] Ibid., 89.

[38] Ibid., 90.

filled only after centuries, wrote what was the *first book* of prophecy."[39] Generally speaking, however, Gunkel feels we must reckon with "the deplorable condition in which our prophetic books are found."[40]

The Psalms

Gunkel's zeal for poetry finds natural expression in his study of the Psalms.[41] As an anthology the Psalter also turns a mirror on vital Israel. It contains remarkable declarations of thanksgiving and praise, which though known elsewhere in the ANE come to unique expression in Israel.[42] As in Genesis, some psalms reflect Israel's gradual turn from myth to legend. Prophetic influence can also be seen: "The heart of the pious Israelite thrills when he thinks of the time that is to come."[43] Finally, the law is in evidence. Its arrival is hardly a welcome development, and it seems a relief to Gunkel that "only very rarely and not till a late period that enthusiasm for the Law found its voice in the hymns."[44] Then again, late stages saw a turn from corporate worship to personal devotion. Thus the Psalms represent the entire range of Israel's uneven life.

At times one hears pleas "of a people that refused at all costs to bow to the fate that providence had laid upon it" and simply asked "Why?"[45] At others, one senses that the mantle of the prophets themselves has been put on. In the Psalter at large, "Israelite piety thus oscillates between two extremes: … the lament of the people and the hope of the prophets."[46] Gunkel comments less positively about the royal psalms. They show an unbecoming "extravagance" and exaggeration in view of their humble setting in the court of a petty king. Still, the type is borrowed from Israelite neighbors, and it improved considerably under Israelite care: "On the whole, judged by our standards, the reli-

---

[39] Ibid., 91, my emphasis. See now Seitz, On Letting a Text, reprinted in Seitz, *Prophecy and Hermeneutics*.

[40] Gunkel, *Water*, 91. Eventually the prophetic spirit departed. Gunkel, *Creation and Chaos*, writes of the "author of Daniel," that "undistinguished successor who venerates the old even when he does not understand it" in a manner "typical of the decadent spirit of his time [*für den Geist der Epigononzeit*]." Though an author, the "man is no prophet" (213–214 = 335).

[41] Gunkel wrote poetry, and it is not by accident that he makes poetry central to true religious feeling. Klatt includes a lament for the forgotten book 4 Ezra. Gunkel praises the book's "Menschheit," thinks on the profound "Volkes Schmerz" that inspired it, and concludes with a plea addressed to the apocryphal book to whisper to human hearts once more: "Nun hebe wieder an die alte Weise, / Und wo do Herzen findest, rede leise" (Klatt, *Gunkel*, 38–39).

[42] Gunkel, *Water*, 137: "The Israelite hymn has borne the fairest of blossoms. The Babylonian and Egyptian hymns consist mainly of a lifeless enumeration of divine attributes. Even some of the hymns in the Bible are trite enough, but there are many majestic hymns that throb with power and life." This essay first appeared serially in *Die Christliche Welt* 36 (1922).

[43] Ibid., 139.

[44] Ibid., 140.

[45] Ibid., 142.

[46] Ibid., 144–145.

gion of the court is largely 'Byzantine'; but when compared with the court songs of all the other ancient kingdoms of the ancient Near East, it is much more moderate and sane."[47] Gunkel keeps his highest praise for the individual expression attained in some psalms. "The gravest error made by students of the Psalms is that they have completely misunderstood this personal poetry and have taken the living 'I,' meaning the poet himself, as a mere figure of speech meaning the people."[48] In actual fact, he maintains, it is the religion of the individual that undergirds the psalter and infuses the communal religion there with its life. "These personal songs are more precious to us than the songs of public worship. We have to excise and omit a great deal from the songs of public worship before we can use them for our own needs. Many of these personal songs — though not all — we can make our own as they stand. They are 'the Psalter within the Psalter.'"[49] At times a psalm even "transcends itself." In the penitent's prayer for a pure heart, Psalm 51:10, "the idea emerges that goodness in humanity must be the work of God. This is the culmination of the religion of the Psalms."[50]

In Gunkel's present the Psalter serves "us" best where the expression of religion and piety is highest. In contrast to Genesis this most admirable phase is fairly late. Yet even here the individualist spirit eventually yields. "Especially in the later period, when the poetic genres became more and more literary, a great deal of mixture took place and the structure became more complicated... Ultimately, naive religion was invaded by a rational reflection that finally destroyed it. That is what we have in Psalm 119 and in the noncanonical *Psalms of Solomon*."[51] Impurity (ironically) and calcification take hold. What all this implies about the Psalter as a canonically ordered entity seems clear enough. Gunkel concludes by making the result transparent.

On the one hand, it is utterly impossible for us to use the entire Psalter in Christian worship, although earlier times may have so used it. The modern mind has found in it so much that is alien and even repellent that we have long been compelled to make selections for use in church and school and home. On the other hand, we should be careful not to go too far in this direction. We must remember that the Psalter is not a contemporary book and therefore cannot possibly voice modern thoughts and feelings... Whoever earnestly studies these poems will not fail to find many passages that give perfect expression to true religion, and generations still to come will humbly bend the knee on this holy ground and learn from the Israelite psalmists how to pray.[52]

[47] Ibid., 148.
[48] Ibid., 149. Mowinckel, *Psalms*, 1:46, counters this point.
[49] Gunkel, *Water*, 150.
[50] Ibid., 157.
[51] Ibid., 161.
[52] Ibid., 161–162.

As with the legends of Genesis, as with the prophetic literature, Gunkel's most basic principle of selection here is whatever inspires "true religion." Piety of a certain style finds its canon within the canon.

II. Gunkel's Tacit Canon

Religion, conservative by nature, is particularly conservative in worship, according to Gunkel. "Practices are much more tenacious than concepts." Thus the cult is prone to keeping practices alive which dimly reflect their original significance. "In many cases, we too, whose worship withstood a powerful purification in the Reformation and again in Rationalism, do not, or only partially, understand the original meaning of what we see and hear in our churches."[53] This comment is at once revealing and enigmatic. What does true worship consist in for Gunkel? An indirect answer can be read off his description of cultural progress in ancient Israel's literary history, where a purification of understanding shows through some etiological legends. Gunkel's explanation for this in *Genesis* gives the child-adult trope another turn: "Ancient Israel considered the origin of many such cultic practices. Although adults, deadened by familiarity, no longer note the unusual and incomprehensible, they will be stirred from their rest by the children's questions. If children see their father performing all manner of unusual practices at the Passover feast, and — this is expressly indicated (cf. Exod 12:26; 13:14) — ask, 'What does that mean?' one should tell them the Passover story."[54] In like manner legends were developed to explain religious customs, ancient landmarks and sites of worship (e.g., Genesis 19:1, 16:7, 28:10, 32:33). Etiology marks the beginning of historiography, which is central to the purification of dead religion. "Wir haben in diesen Sagen *die Anfänge der Religionsgeschichte*."[55]

True science and true religion are two sides of a coin. On one side Gunkel finds the concepts of God encapsulated in the legends of Genesis to be "naive." On the other, his analysis is offered in a spirit of "piety and love."[56] The fusion of these perspectives is evidenced in Gunkel's professesion, in the third person, of belief in transcendent providence: "We believe God works in the world as the quiet, hidden, basis of all things. Sometimes, his efficacy can almost be apprehended in particularly momentous and impressive events and persons. We sense his reign in the wondrous interrelationship of all things. But he never appears to us as an active agent alongside others, but always as the ultimate cause of all." The God of Genesis often appears as a physical presence. He is encountered not as the prophets encounter him, "in ecstasy," but in physical speech and action. Presented with such crude views "we hesitate to believe

[53] Gunkel, *Genesis*, xx = xxiii.

[54] Ibid.

[55] Ibid., xxi = xxiv, my emphasis.

[56] Ibid., xi = xii. The word here is "Pietät" rather than "Frömmigkeit."

them."[57] But then Israel stands out among her neighbors in the ancient Near East. Whereas other religions remained polytheistic, Israel, despite having polytheism just beneath the surface of its official narrative, inclined to monotheism almost from the beginning. And Israel rapidly progressed toward more elevated, fitting conceptions of providence, toward a doctrine "we" would be much less reluctant to affirm. "Thus, through many intermediate states, Genesis moves from a crass mythology to a belief in providence very attractive to us moderns."[58] In this and other respects "Genesis reflects the struggle higher religion fought for Israel's soul."[59]

The purification in concepts of God is a clear marker of E being later than J, for example. Neither J nor E attains the distinction of literary personality (*Schriftstellerpersönlichkeit*), or even of intentional personality. They are mere "Sammlern." The sheer "variety [of material adapted] demonstrates that the legends of E, and even more so of J, do not bear the characteristic of a specific period, let alone of an individual personality, but that the collectors essentially took them as they found them."[60] In a sense these schools are the first epigones; they "are not masters but servants of their material."[61] But there is more to the story. J and E also exhibit "fidelity." "They infused the legends with their spirit." From the "unified diction" which they impart to their collections we sense a "spiritualization of the legend material" that contributes to a "higher religious and ethical superiority" when contrasted with the "other ancient peoples": "Thus we may imagine the collectors, towering above their people [*Volk*], with the intention of elevating them by their ideals through the collection of legends in a great work."[62] Small, bright lights from the pre-literary era have darkened but nonetheless shine through the work of these collectors. They are perhaps kindred with the precocious children who ask what Passover means. Through them higher religion wins a battle.

By all rights P, who clearly does bear the characteristic of a specific period, ought to come off even better. J and E "only loosely heaped up the received building stones; P, however, erected a unified structure according to his tastes."[63] But P of course is seriously downgraded in Gunkel's total calculation. Why? P appears to descend from the father blindly administering Passover rites to his children. P's "is the spirit of an orthodoxy ambivalent to history."[64]

---

[57] Ibid., x = xi.

[58] Ibid., lix = lxix.

[59] Ibid., lxi = lxxi.

[60] Ibid., lxxi = lxxxii–lxxxiii.

[61] Ibid., lxxiii = lxxxv.

[62] Ibid., lxxiii–lxxiv = lxxxv. "So dürfen wir uns die Sammler denken, als ihr Volk weit überragend, mit der Absicht, es durch die Sammlung der Sagen in einem großen Werke zu den Idealen emporzuheben, die ihnen selber vorschwebten."

[63] Ibid., lxxxii = xcvii.

[64] Ibid., lxxxii = xcvi.

He "has the tone of *prosaic learning*, indeed, often in the style of legal documents." And he is "painfully precise and exemplarily orderly, but he, like many other scholars, was not gifted with a feeling for *poetry*."[65] He is far too fond of structure. "This order-loving man encased the colorful legends of the ancient period in his gray schemata." At his touch the legends of old "lost all their poetic fragrance."[66] What is lost, in the final equation, is genuine personal piety. P's poetic failure, concomitantly a failure to understand the true historical nature of his material, stems from a religious failure. Hence this "author's religion is characterized by the fact that he says almost nothing about the personal piety of the fathers [*die persönliche Frömmigkeit der Väter*]... The religion he knows consists of regulation of practices."[67] J and E clung to "vital legend" as best they could, but by P's time, Gunkel reasons, "a massive spiritual revolution must have occurred in the meanwhile, a revolution that created something entirely new in the place of the old folk tradition recorded in the legends."[68] This had its perks. "P's concept of God is higher, more developed than in the ancient legends. Nevertheless, P stands far below these ancients who, although they did not yet know the 'ecclesiology' of Jerusalem, knew what piety is."[69]

In "our churches" too Gunkel feels called to the double tasks of purging ignorance and restoring the youthful piety it masks. Rationalism and Reformation each play a part in the necessary purifications, but since religious practice breeds tenacious habits, the best hope may be to make praxis more conceptual. In short, "a vital, truly historical understanding of the history of Israel's religion" is indispensable for Gunkel,[70] and the cultural project which strives for this understanding could become nothing less than true religion itself. The closing remarks of Gunkel's introduction to *Genesis* illustrate the possibility. "Israel produced great religious reformers who created a comprehensive unity in religious spirit from the dispersed traditions of their people. But it did not produce a Homer. This is fortunate for our scholarship," and thus, "because there was no great poetic whole and the passages were left in an essentially

---

[65] Ibid., lxxx = xciii, my emphasis.

[66] Ibid., lxxxi = xciv, cf. lxxiv = lxxxvi.

[67] Ibid., lxxxii = xcv.

[68] Ibid., lxxxiv = xcvii. For Gunkel the sea change must have been provoked by the exile. See lxxxiv = xcviii: P is credited with "the beginnings of 'world history'" but criticized for falsifying it. Gunkel then contrasts the "piety of the patriarchs" with the less desirable "piety of the Babylonian Exile."

[69] Ibid., lxxxiii = xcvi. Gunkel thinks P's history of the turn to a higher concept of God is "childish," however (lxxxii = xcv): "Nor may we fail to mention that this viewpoint of P — that Yahweh first revealed himself very generally as 'God,' then somewhat more specifically as *El shaddai*, and only at the end by his proper name — is still very childish. The actual history of religion [*Geschichte der Religion*] does not begin with the general and develop toward the concrete, but, to the contrary, it begins with the most concrete and only slowly and gradually do people learn to comprehend the abstract."

[70] Ibid., lxxx = xciii.

unfused state, we are able to discern the history of the whole process."[71] Genesis lacks formal and poetic unity, and yet it rivals "the greatest creations of the human spirit." It participates in the "inner unity that unifies all the variety" of other great creations, such as cathedrals, the state, or *Faust*. All of course are human creations. "One will be unable, however, to prevent the pious observer who has reached this conclusion from recognizing this *unity in the variety of the history of Israel's religion as the providence of God* who once spoke childishly to children and then maturely to adults [*zu Männern männlich*]."[72] Thus stands Gunkel, with this bizarre fusion of 1 Corinthians 13 and turn of the century German protestant liberalism, ready as one of the prophets of old for the service of his people and his God.

There is a vast divide running through the canon for Gunkel: a darkening of sagas removed from life and collected on paper, a massive revolution in religion between J/E and P, an invasion of rationalism between the spirit of individual poets and the epigones who praised the law, a deplorable textual tangle that separates the fiery prophets from the books that wrongly carry their names. Enter the mature Protestant scholar. Proper piety jettisons the false adulthood of Israelite legalism, and it rediscovers the childlike, pre-textual, naive but pure religion of the ancients. The canon must be unmade *for the sake of true religion*. Somehow it must also be reconstituted. Gunkel feels compelled to refashion the canon, or at least its spiritual equivalent, in his own day. How so? Unreconciled with his indifference to the final form is his thoroughgoing preference for Israelite religion over all other religions of the ancient Near East. Almost without exception Israel's reworking of ANE material is "much more moderate and sane." But what if the modern biblical critic is not one of the tradition's master distillers? Or what happens when the wheels fall off the cultural/religious project in which the unity of Israel, cathedral domes, Goethe, humanity's collective spirit, and the state, can all be earnestly invoked in the same breath? Though Gunkel's profound ambivalence to canon has been noticed before, it is not widely recognized (at least not in English). I will therefore conclude this section by developing the point in a little detail.

Gunkel was adamant that *Religionsgeschichte* did not mean the history of all religion, but of the *biblical* religion. He strove against the "Schranken des Kanons" maintained by church dogma, to be sure. And he wanted to rescue pseudepigraphal books (such as 4 Esra) from disrepute. The one who could bring a wider history into daylight could, he hoped, at last conceive of "die gesamte Geschichte der israelitisch-jüdisch-urchristlichen Religion als Einheit." Yet Gunkel was anxious when some pushed further than he intended: "zugleich aber tat man im Geiste Tür und Tor auf, um alles Ausländische, woraus sich irgend etwas für das Verständnis der Bibel ergäbe, mit Freuden

[71] Ibid., lxxxvi = xcix.

[72] Ibid., lxxxvi = c, my emphasis.

einzulassen: auch dies in starkem Gegensatz gegen die Vergangenheit, die gegen das Nicht-Biblische vielfach gleichgültig oder gar voreingenommen gewesen war."[73] The conceptual unity offered in history not a unity of world religion; rather the unity sought is of the "Israelite-Jewish-Christian" trajectory. The point is made with perfect clarity in 1922. "Wenn wir also damals 'Religionsgeschichte' auf unser Banner schrieben, so dachten wir nicht an eine 'Geschichte der Religionen,' sondern an eine Geschichte der *biblischen* Religion."[74] If one speaks of a *Religionsgeschichtliche* "school," it should be born in mind that Gunkel was an uncomfortable member.

Hence the first methodological principle in *Creation and Chaos*, that the full history of a thing must be pursued because subsequent developments can be as or more important than origins, has a strong proviso in it. Gunkel may feel the need "to be protected against misunderstanding" given the way he challenges the traditional dogmas; yet he certainly does not "deny the particularity of Israelite religion," and he does in fact support, in his own way, "the belief that *in this history* God has *revealed* himself in a special way."[75] Klatt describes the situation well. "Die babylonische Religion erscheint in *Schöpfung und Chaos* nur in einer negativen Beleuchtung, und Gott scheint mit Israel doch eine besondere Geschichte gehabt zu haben." He also rightly discerns that, although Gunkel would seem to affirm truth in all religion, "liegt hier ein Problem, für dessen Lösung … Gunkel auch in den folgenden Jahren und Jahrzehnten nicht genügend systematische Kraft besaß."[76] We will soon consider how the problem fared among biblical scholars after Gunkel.

Finally, by removing a vital function of the canon to a pious history Gunkel only exacerbates the problem of the biblical tradition's unity. A more traditional doctrine of providence would affirm God's activity in the whole of human history, but Gunkel insists on "biblical" theology in a history-of-religions mode. "Theologisch gesehen, fordert Gunkel hier eine religionsgeschichtlich ausgerichtete Theologie, die Offenbarung Gottes nicht versteht als ein isoliertes Handeln Gottes an einem bestimmten Volk oder einzelnen Personen in diesem Volk, sondern die das Handeln Gottes in der gesamten Menschheitsgeschichte als Offenbarung, d. h. die Menschheitsgeschichte als Offenbarungsgeschichte begreift."[77] Are there torches of light in Babylon and Egypt? Yes. And yet the brightest lights of the ANE burn in Israel, and are picked up, one way or another, in Christianity.[78] The history attested in the Christian canon,

[73] Gunkel, Christliche Welt, 153–154.

[74] Gunkel, Richtungen, 66; cited in Klatt, *Gunkel*, 27 (cf. all of 26–28).

[75] Gunkel, *Creation and Chaos*, xl = vi, my emphasis.

[76] Klatt, *Gunkel*, 77.

[77] Ibid., 80.

[78] Gunkel was not particularly clear about the relation of Israel to the Church, or to Judeo-Christian culture in the West. Klatt thinks Gunkel's approach to Christ amounts to a flight into mysticism (ibid., 99).

though it must be reordered, and though it continues beyond the established borders into apocryphal texts, is the *one* history into which all other ancient history runs. To use Klatt's word, Gunkel copes with the disconnect between canonical and ostensive history by setting history on a "gradient" (*Gefälle*) that slopes toward canon.[79] Gunkel never arrives at the final form since for him the spirit it attests lives in history, not on paper. One has to wonder about the viability of a move away from "paper" toward Israel's "life," though. Klatt:

> Indem Gunkel eine ... literaturgeschichtliche und religionsgeschichtliche Untersuchung der Heiligen Schrift fordert mit dem Ziel einer geschichtlichen Darstellung, ist einmal der Gefahr gewehrt, daß durch die kritische Analyse der Kanon von innen her aufgelöst und eine Einheit der biblischen Bücher nicht mehr auszumachen ist, sondern nur noch eine Vielfalt von Quellen und religiösen Anschauungen. *Die Einheit der Heiligen Schrift wird zurückgeführt auf die hinter ihr liegende Geschichte.* Damit kommt aber nun ... die Frage in Sicht, worin diese Geschichte ihre Einheit hat, m. a. W. es wird die Frage nach dem Gefälle dieser Geschichte virulent.[80]

Where indeed does the history behind the biblical text find its unity? How does one know which history is canonical? Why not that of Egypt, Assyria, Babylon, or Ugarit? And anyway, in keeping with Gunkel's first core principle, what of the subsequent, often more important history in which the "paper" exercised its influence over later generations of Jews and Christians? Is this not also, for a text and its people, a kind of life?

B. Ersatz Biblical Theology? Religious History in Four Editions

Mindful of the question posed in chapter three (what is biblical theology?), I have begun to suggest that Gunkel's piously spirited history is a kind of surrogate for biblical theology as well as for the traditional biblical canon. Gunkel's biographer sees that for him "kommt die gesamtbiblische theologische Problematik hier überhaupt nicht in Sicht."[81] In point of fact he hoped that biblical history of religions would take the place of biblical theology. This did not quite happen. In this section, as a way of tracing the afterlife of this aspect of Gunkel's work, I will drill down through four editions of a single article as it appears across the four editions of the standard reference work *Religion in Geschichte und Gegenwart* (*RGG*), in 1909, 1927, 1957 and 1998.[82] When Gunkel had it, in the second edition, it bore the singular title "Biblische The-

[79] Ibid., 80: "Betrachtet man das 'Gefälle' der Geschichte nur recht, so fällt die Unvergleichbarkeit der Offenbarung Gottes im Volke Israel mit etwa in Babylonien oder Ägypten; so sehr auch dort wahre Gotteserkenntnis vorhanden gewesen ist, erst recht sinnenfällig ins Auge."

[80] Ibid., 189, my emphasis.

[81] Ibid., 192.

[82] These are the publication dates only of the four volumes in question.

ologie und biblische Religionsgeschichte, I. des AT." The exercise is a shorthand way of probing how, in twentieth century Old Testament scholarship, the relationship between these two very different pursuits has shifted.

We may begin with Gunkel. In 1927 he writes of the inability of the traditional, dogmatically ordered biblical theology to bring the "lebendige, aus dem Herzen kommende Religion" of the Old Testament to expression. Among the "großen religiösen Personen" the prophets above all have been neglected, not through the fault of the researchers themselves but due to a flaw in the very nature of the old approach. The dogma of inspiration flattened the collected biblical material, shoehorning it into a unified systematic account which good scholarship has increasingly shown to be incompatible with the history of biblical religion. "Die Erscheinung, die unser Geschlecht erlebt hat, wonach die B. Th. durch die 'Religionsgeschichte Israels' ersetzt wird, erklärt sich also daraus, daß an Stelle der Inspirationslehre jetzt der Geist der Geschichtsforschung zu treten beginnt."[83] Gunkel predicts that study of the history of Israelite religion will replace biblical theology in the foreseeable future, and he believes that the term "Religionsgeschichte," despite occasional misuse, encompasses far more appropriately the outlook of biblical research. He concludes by washing his hands of a challenge raised for dogmatic theology: "In welchem Sinne auch bei dieser religionsgeschichtlichen Betrachtung der biblischen Religionen von Offenbarung zu reden ist, wird die Dogmatik zu handeln haben."[84]

Accordingly, the tasks of biblical research are oriented to religion *instead* of literature. OT *Bibelwissenschaft* is obligated to discover the meaning of the collected scriptures ("der in der Bibel gesammelten Schriften"). Because the present text includes errata, a preliminary task is basic text-criticism. Second, scholars must compare, evaluate and array the biblical material. This, in a word, is the domain of "Bibelkritik." Third, the terminal aim of biblical scholarship is to write "eine Geschichte des Volkes Israel auf allen seinen Lebensäußerungen."[85] Israel's history can be further divided into history of culture, or of politics, but ultimately, one should aspire to history of religion. "Seine höchste Aufgabe findet der Forscher sodann in einer Geschichte der Religion und Sittlichkeit Israels, dem Ersatz der früheren 'Biblischen Theologie.'" But again, for Gunkel it is not just any history, but the "biblische Religionsgeschichte" which must replace biblical theology. The history of religion unites

[83] *RGG*², 1:1090–1091. Childs actually quotes the last sentence in *Biblical Theology*, 6. His translation misconstrues the tense: "The recently experienced phenomenon of Biblical Theology's being replaced by the history of Israelite religion is to be explained from the fact that the spirit of historical investigation has now taken the place of a traditional doctrine of inspiration."

[84] *RGG*², 1:1091.

[85] *RGG*², 1:1073.

the Old Testament.[86] A further but peripheral task involves the "Schrifttum Israels." This has been treated as literary-history, often in the genre of Introduction, though the history of the various literary genres might, Gunkel suggests, be a more fruitful approach in future. Yet Israel's religious life — life as opposed to literature — remains the proper focal point.

In the first edition of *RGG* (1909), for which Gunkel's editorial input was preeminent,[87] Bruno Baentsch wrote the equivalent article. It got filed under "Bibelwissenschaft: I. AT, D. Biblische Theologie,"[88] and it might as well have been written by Gunkel. The "großen religiösen Persönlichkeiten" of the OT are "die eigentlichen Träger der israelitischen Religion."[89] The old biblical theology is criticized (better to speak of Israelite religious history), dogma's exclusion of apocryphal and pseudepigraphical texts lamented, revelation set right as a gradual historical process, systematics ruled out of bounds.

> Nur so gewinnen wir ein wirklich geschichtliches und lebendiges Verständnis von den einzelnen religiös-sittlichen Anschauungen und Ideen, die uns immer als Glieder eines geistigen Organismus entgegentreten, wie von den einzelnen Perioden des religiösen Lebens in Israel und der Entwicklung der israelitischen Religion überhaupt. Darum ist an die Stelle der "Biblischen Theologie" mit Recht die "Religionsgeschichte Israel" getreten.[90]

Religious history is even named the "Krone" of all OT sub-specialties. Baentsch had died in 1908, and Gunkel borrows (plagiarizes?) a fair bit of the article's language in the second edition. Apart from the addition of a few distinctives, Gunkel's most important change was in amending the title to reflect how biblical theology was not really the subject matter, that the history of Israelite religion was being championed as its surrogate.

Three decades on, in *RGG*³ (1957), Gunkel's title was kept verbatim, but the content of the entry was entirely rewritten by Johannes Hempel. The piece reflects a new awareness that *biblische Theologie* had not in fact died, and that it did not easily coexist with *biblische Religionsgeschichte*. In Hempel's view "hat der Umschwung der theologischen Lage seit 1918, insonderheit die Betonung der Verwurzelung der ganzen Schrift in der Offenbarung des *einen* Gottes in Jesus Christus (W. Vischer) und die Erkenntnis der Unmöglichkeit, Wahrheitsfragen durch rein geschichtliche Forschung zu lösen, zur Forderung

[86] *RGG*², 1:1074. "Alle andern alttestamentlichen Disziplinen sollen dieser Aufgabe dienen: eine Forderung, die aus der Natur des AT, in dem die Religion der eigentliche Mittelpunkt ist, ebenso hervorgeht, wie sie zugleich dem Bedürfnis des Glaubens entspricht."

[87] For an overview of Gunkel's involvement in *RGG*¹ and *RGG*², see Klatt, *Gunkel*, 87–90, who suggests that Gunkel's reputation was less secure during work on the first edition.

[88] *RGG*¹, 1:1194–1197. Childs interacts with Baentsch's work on Exodus (1903) in 1974, where it tends to represent the standard critical view. Later Childs remarks: "Baentsch's companion volume to Gunkel's *Genesis* has long provided a solid, if uninspiring, handling of the technical problems of the Hebrew text" (Childs, *OT Books*, 39).

[89] *RGG*¹, 1:1195.

[90] *RGG*¹, 1:1196.

einer Neubelebung der B.Th. neben der Religionsgeschichte geführt."[91] The copulative between theology and the history of religion remained, but a new generation of confessing Christians in Germany had powerfully challenged the historicist hegemony. Their offensive helped make Gunkel's prognostication about the fate of biblical theology seem much less inevitable.

By the fourth edition (1998), "Biblische Theologie" is a distinct entry again, as in 1909, but for the first time in the history of *RGG* it is discussed as a viable topic in its own right. Bernd Janowski, whose contribution addresses exegetical (rather than "Fundamentaltheologisch") aspects of the pursuit, acknowledges an as yet "ungeklärte Nebeneinander von (religions-)hist. Methodik und normativem Anspruch."[92] The history he details speaks to tortuous developments in the field after Gunkel. Continuing in the historicist spirit, some began to emphasize *commonalities* in the tradition to counteract the stress on differences (Eichrodt, Köhler). Others sought to meet somewhere between OT theology and religious history (König, Sellin, Fohrer). Only with von Rad did a bona fide "Neuorientierung der Disziplin" commence. His OT Theology cast "die Frage nach der Korrelation von Offenbarung und Gesch. zu ihrem hermeneutischen Prinzip" in a fresh light.[93] Even though the relationship between history of religions and biblical theology remains uncertain, Janowski can speak of the Christian (not necessarily Jewish) concern for the unity of scripture, the pertinence of "*Geltung* (Verbindlichkeit der Schrift)" over against "*Genese* (Entstehung der Überlieferungsvielfalt)," the significance of normative disciplines as such — all in a way unthinkable in Gunkel's time, and for that matter in Hempel's. Of the several tasks enumerated for biblical theology, one is of particular note in the present study:

> Der Entwurf einer BTh hat von der Existenz und der Anerkennung eines aus den beiden Testamenten bestehenden bibl. Kanons auszugehen. Inwieweit für eine gesamtbibl. Theol. das Faktum des Kanons relevant ist, ergibt sich aus der Tatsache, daß ein theol. bestimmtes Verhältnis beider Testamente zueinander schon für die Entstehung des christl. Kanons vorauszusetzen ist... In diesem Vorgang wird deutlich, daß das NT sich von seiner eigenen Schrifthermeneutik her gar nicht als von der Lektüre des AT unabhängiger Kanon, der additiv neben das bereits abgeschlossene AT gestellt wurde, versteht, sondern zusammen mit jenem ersten Teil — dem später und aufgrund dieses Vorganges so genannten "AT" — die *eine zweigeteilte christl. Bibel sein will.*[94]

Such an intricate affirmation of the potential unity of the entire Christian Bible, made in terms of its finished character in two parts and the will or intent of its historical development (canon consciousness, or, one is tempted to say, the "Gefälle" of the canonical process), is an index of just how intricate the historical and theological problem of the canon has become since Gunkel.

[91] *RGG*^{3}, 1:1256. See further Hempel, AT und Religionsgeschichte.

[92] *RGG*^{4}, 1:1548.

[93] *RGG*^{4}, 1:1547.

[94] *RGG*^{4}, 1:1548, my emphasis. In English translation see further Janowski, One God.

Whether this way of thinking has any promise for the future is naturally a matter of debate.[95] Janowski, for one, finds grounds for hope.

C. Canon after Gunkel

After Gunkel the form critical method won broad support. Gunkel's sweeping religious-historical aesthetic was quickly left behind, however, and as Erhard Blum explains, methodologically *Formgeschichte* underwent a "narrowing, which was to mark the disciplinary discourse for generations."[96] Dibelius and Bultmann may have been aware of the initial departure — certainly Gunkel was — but it was easily forgotten.[97] Albrecht Alt more strongly emphasizes the pre-literary oral context, and he strives to tighten up the methodological sloppiness of previous efforts. He wants to uncover the "real origins of Israelite law" and feels that the newer form- or genre-critical approach "has not yet been applied as consistently as it ought to be."[98] As Blum sees it, Gunkel's sometimes vague appeal to *Gattungen* gives way to "a downright 'mandatory' relationship between 'form or genre' and 'content.'"[99] Thus "vor allem" Alt seeks out the "ältesten und reinsten Ausprägungen nach Form und Inhalt."[100] One distinctive of Gunkel's approach that becomes muted here is the later textual history of a tradition. Another, which fades almost as a consequence, is the tacit concern for canon. Alt notes a "contradiction between the fragmentary state of the literary material and the unity demanded by the theory [of canon]," but he merely problematizes the older literary-critical handling of the issue.[101] He is thus relatively subdued on the question of the triumph of Israelite religion over rival cultures in the ANE.[102] Compared with Gunkel, in the search for the tradition's "Wurzeln im Leben" Alt operates with a more detached interest in the roots themselves.

---

[95] From the history of religions side a comparable attempt to Childs' in 1992 is that of Albertz in the same year. His much discussed history was translated from German to English with similar dispatch, and it was heralded as the hoped-for replacement of biblical theology, though the "gesamtbiblische theologische Problematik" does not fall within its purview.

[96] Blum, Formgeschichte, 37.

[97] Ibid., 36, citing Bultmann, *Synoptischen Tradition*, 4.

[98] Alt, Origins, 86 = Alt, Ursprünge, 284–285.

[99] Blum, Formgeschichte, 41. Buss, *Form Criticism*, 404, feels Alt represents an extreme.

[100] Alt, Ursprünge, 285 = Alt, Origins, 88.

[101] Alt, Origins, 81 = Alt, Ursprünge, 278–279.

[102] Still, while hardly religion's struggle for Israel's soul, casuistic law had an extra-Israelite provenance involving "secular justice" in a single tribe, whereas apodictic law was a creation *unique to Israel*, "a sacral action involving the whole nation" of confederated tribes (Alt, Origins, 125 = 324). The "clash" between secular and sacred "is typical of the whole history of Israel, which manifested for centuries a tension that is essentially due to the encounter of a young people newly come to nationhood and an ancient and alien culture" (131 = 331).

In a later day Klaus Koch comments on the theological significance of form criticism. The apology that follows sits atop a section entitled "Kanon und biblische Literaturgeschichte."

Up to this point my task has been to enquire into the principles of form-critical research, but now I shall try to tackle paths which have been so far little frequented. It concerns what we might call the keystone to the construction of form-critical exegesis, the theological consequences. Most Old and New Testament scholars working from a form-critical standpoint do not consider the points which I now put forward, and as a rule no one appears to be interested in them. However, the longer I work with form criticism, the more I feel that these additional (and perhaps final!) problems can no longer be evaded, even though *few people other than Gunkel* have touched on them.[103]

Koch realizes that Gunkel is just inconsistent on the canon's literary history. "On one side he dismisses the late period as the time of the epigones, and on the other he emphasises the theological importance of the post-biblical writings of the Apocrypha and Pseudepigrapha." Yet he "never lost sight of the fact that the Old Testament was not simply a compendium of Israelite national literature."[104] This points to a larger hermeneutical (and dogmatic) issue which requires further thought.

We must ask not only the reason for such an exhaustive investigation of individual units but quite simply the motive behind any interpretation of the sacred writings [*die schlichte Frage nach dem Ziel der Auslegung der Heiligen Schrift überhaupt*]. Is an interpreter's work finished with his study of the individual text? Is it enough, as is often said today, to extract the kerygma from biblical pericopes? Or must the interpreter seek further for a relation between the individual passages and the books, between the Old and New Testaments and the Bible as a whole?[105]

Koch believes that "a literary history along the lines of the one planned by Gunkel is urgently needed, if form criticism is to have any point at all," and from where he sits he can see a few promising steps by the likes of Noth, von Rad, Rendtorff and Lohfink.[106] That was in 1964. From the present perspective, however, Koch's most important insight here is that Gunkel's work, through a deep antinomy, raises the canon question in a way the subsequent discussion largely forgot. Apart from Klatt, who cues off Koch, few others have made the connection.[107]

---

[103] Koch, *Growth*, 100 = Koch, *Formgeschichte?*, 110, my emphasis.

[104] Ibid., 102–103 = 113–114.

[105] Ibid., 104–105 = 116.

[106] Ibid., 105 = 116.

[107] Klatt makes a few salient criticisms of Koch's discussion here (*Gunkel*, 190), yet Klatt credits Koch for introducing him to the problem that he eventually took up in his dissertation (7). Koch did not guide the dissertation, but the foreward to *Growth* thanks a Mr. Klatt for assisting with proofs and the index.

I. Childs after Gunkel

Childs, who reviewed Klatt's work on Gunkel the year it appeared (1969),[108] took up the canon question almost immediately. His sights were on a bigger target than Gunkel — indeed, they were on historical criticism as such — but he worked out his critique from within the form critical tradition associated with Gunkel. This is not to say that Gunkel would have agreed with Childs that "the concept of canon was a corollary of inspiration," or that the canon "set the boundaries within which God's voice was heard."[109] Rather, the point is that for Gunkel inspiration did have a corollary, if less obviously associated with its erstwhile companion, revelation, and it entailed distinct boundaries on the arena within which God's voice was heard. Revelation did occur, after a fashion. And yet like Koch, Childs' protest four decades later, in 2005, still has a ring of plausibility: "to suggest with some that the theological importance of the canon has recently been overemphasized is a gross misunderstanding. The opposite is nearer the truth."[110] The canon's historic purpose has proved enormously difficult to comprehend in the wake of the atomizing done by source and form critical investigations, and more recently, the mortgaging of canonical boundaries (internal and external) to tradition-historical process. The surprising thing about Gunkel's work in hindsight is how for him, despite an internal conflict between religious atavism and the progressive reforms of higher religion, canon-like borders stay vaguely intact.

To those familiar with the portrait of Childs given in the literature, it may be just as surprising to learn of the extent to which Childs' understanding of the canonical process accepts the messiness of the final form, in line with a state of affairs Gunkel emphasizes. In *Introduction to the OT* Childs hopes "to enter into a post-critical era."[111] Post-critical does not mean post-historical, though. "The term canon has both a historical and a theological dimension."[112] Childs deals with these dimensions dialectically, treating them as separate but intimately related processes in the canon's development. Literary history in ancient Israel was *broader*, canonical history *narrower*.

The former process resulted in innumerable forces such as laws of saga, the use of inherited literary patterns of prose and poetry, the social setting of diverse institutions, the changing scribal techniques etc., whereas the latter process was much more closely defined by those forces which affected the literature's evaluation, transmission, and usage. Although non-religious fac-

---

[108] Childs, Review of Klatt. His comments are brief but favorable: "Seldom has this reviewer read a more informative and thoroughly enjoyable book" (508).

[109] Childs, Speech-act, 381. Since this article is Childs' last, it shows clearly that an interest in the "form" and "function" of scripture never leaves him (cf. 384–385).

[110] Ibid., 380.

[111] *Introduction to the OT*, 16.

[112] Ibid., 58. See further the discussion in section B of chapter one.

tors (political, social, and economic) certainly entered into the canonical process, these were subordinated to the religious usage of the literature by its function within the community.[113]

For him any effort to patch the tattered authority of the canon without addressing the historical problematics is rejected as a "theological construct" because the "recognition of the complex history of the growth of the Old Testament literature did more than anything else to bring about the collapse of the older dogmatic understanding of the canon."[114] History is a necessary ingredient in the canonical dimension Childs wants at long last to address. And history teaches that the older dogmatic understandings were inadequate. "For theological reasons the biblical texts were often shaped in such a way that the original poetic forms were lost, or *a unified narrative badly shattered*. The canonical approach is concerned to understand the nature of the theological shape of the literature rather than to recover an original literary or aesthetic unity."[115] Something very like Gunkel's aesthetic in *Genesis* is implicitly affirmed — though Childs does not speak of "darkening," the original setting of a tradition is often "blurred." Here Childs' instincts are quite unlike those of Auerbach, or under his influence, Frei (Alter is just beyond the horizon). The unity of the final form is emphatically *not* an aesthetic unity in *Introduction to the OT*, or for that matter anywhere else in Childs' corpus.

One senses how very much Childs' immersion in form criticism (not some vaguer "atmosphere") affects his formulation of a canonical approach.

Why should one stage in the process be accorded special status? Were not the earlier levels of the text once regarded as canonical as well, and why should they not continue to be so regarded within the exegetical enterprise? Is not the history which one recovers in the growth of a text an important index for studying Israel's development of a self-understanding, and thus the very object of Old Testament theology? Having been trained in the form-critical method, I feel the force of these questions and am aware of the value of the approach.[116]

On what basis then can a critically informed scholar speak of the integrity of the final form? "The reason for insisting on the final form of scripture lies in the peculiar relationship between the text and the people of God which is constitutive of the canon."[117] This is both a theological and an historical judgment. The peculiar, textually-mediately relationship between God and his people begins well within the biblical period, Childs argues, in a series of decisions meant to become binding on future generations of Israel. By highlighting this process, Childs says his "Introduction attempts to offer a different model *for* the discipline from that currently represented. It seeks to describe the *form*

---

113 Ibid., 61.

114 Ibid., 60.

115 Ibid., 74, my emphasis.

116 Ibid., 75. Compare the more traditional use of form criticism in, e.g., *Memory and Tradition*, 34, 46.

117 *Introduction to the OT*, 75, cf. 41.

and function of the Hebrew Bible in its role as sacred scripture for Israel."[118] Whatever one makes of this move, there really should be no doubt that Childs writes as a well-trained *Fachmann*, in and for an established tradition.

If Childs does not feature in the histories of form criticism — Buss hardly mentions his work, and virtually never after 1970 — it is because he turns the discipline on its head. "Beginning in the pre-exilic period, but increasing in significance in the post-exilic era, a force was unleashed by Israel's religious use of her traditions which exerted an influence on the shaping of the literature... Israel defined itself in terms of a book! The canon formed the decisive *Sitz im Leben* for the Jewish community's life, thus blurring the sociological evidence most sought after by the modern historian."[119] Paper was accorded religious significance. The textualization of the tradition did not create a barrier to life; instead, it placed a text at the very heart of true religion in Israel.

Put in Hans Frei's categories, faced with a choice between canon and "true" or ostensive history, Gunkel made a pivotal error. As Childs has it, "Scripture bears witness to God's activity in history on Israel's behalf, but history *per se* is not a medium of revelation which is commensurate with canon."[120] Gunkel was right to a point. Unlike the Reformers, in the post-Enlightenment era it became impossible "to *assume* the coherence of text and historical reference" and "the biblical interpreter was forced either to be critical, anti-critical, or postcritical, but the pre-critical option has been forever lost."[121] Gunkel knew some options were finished. But by the nineteenth century "scholars who pursued historical criticism of the Old Testament no longer found a significant place for the canon. Conversely, those scholars who sought to retain a concept of canon were unable to find a significant role for historical criticism."[122] Just so in the scholarly venture "to describe the development of the Hebrew literature and to trace the earlier and later stages of this history ... there always remains an enormous hiatus between the description of the critically reconstructed literature and the actual canonical text which has been received and used as authoritative scripture by the community."[123] As I have argued above, such a hiatus exists within Gunkel's reading of the history of biblical literature. To a considerable degree it confounds his methodological formulations. The poles of biblical and "real" history have come apart, though in an odd way they are still in the same orbit. It took a while after Gunkel before the study of biblical forms (genres) seriously grappled with scripture's final form again. By then

---

[118] Ibid., 16, my emphasis.

[119] Ibid., 78, cf. 61–62.

[120] Ibid., 76.

[121] Childs, Vitringa, 98.

[122] *Introduction to the OT*, 45. Childs is addressing 'the nature of Old Testament Introduction." Gunkel had no love for the genre Introduction, but the history of it that Childs tells has wider implications.

[123] Ibid., 40.

so many other factors would have changed that one could well ask how much else Childs' approach to the matter and Gunkel's have in common.

II. Childs after von Rad

The status of canon after Gunkel becomes more complicated with von Rad, which explains why so much has been made of the relationship of Childs' work to von Rad's. There is at least one dissertation on the topic exclusively.[124] In published literature lines of continuity and discontinuity have been developed by a variety of scholars. Oeming's study of 1985 draws out some implications. Steins puts forward a comparison focused on Genesis 22.[125] With Rendtorff (see section B of chapter three), some have suggested that the new interest in canon properly begins with von Rad. Janowski asserts that he achieved a "Neuorientierung der Disziplin" (above) — undoubtedly true, though one wants to know in what sense precisely — and in a recent volume he edited on the hermeneutics of canon, Jörg Barthel even speaks of the "kanonhermeneutische Debatte seit Gerhard von Rad."[126] Others have been less quick to subsume Childs' work under that trajectory. Ernest Nicholson, for instance, points to the following classic statement of von Rad's, part of which Childs cites in *Introduction to the OT*:

> The Hexateuch in its present form arose by means of redactors who heard the peculiar testimony of faith of each document and considered it binding. There is no doubt that the present Hexateuch in its final form makes great demands on the understanding of every reader. Many ages, many men, many traditions and theologies, have constructed this massive work. Only the one who does not look superficially at the Hexateuch but reads it with a knowledge of its deep dimension will arrive at true understanding. Such a one will know that revelations and religious experiences of many ages are speaking from it. *For no stage in this work's long period of growth is really obsolete; something of each phase has been conserved and passed on as enduring until the Hexateuch attained its final form.*[127]

Thus ends Nicholson's survey of pentateuchal research in the twentieth century, which decides against Childs that "[t]o concentrate upon the final stage is to foreshorten what was a long process of reflection, debate, and not infrequently controversy in the history of the community of faith."[128] Such a judgment betrays an imprecise understanding of what *Introduction to the OT* actu-

---

[124] Hartzfeld, Two Methodologies. Von Rad's "method" is preferred (210). This work suffers from a weakness common to all studies of Childs in the 1980s and early 1990s, namely, that one of the most important pieces of "data" (*Biblical Theology*) was not available. It also restricts the definition of "canon" unhelpfully (20, 108n48).

[125] Steins, *Bindung*, 5, 122–125, 175.

[126] Barthel, Kanonhermeneutische Debatte. This needs qualification: see below, note 140.

[127] Von Rad, *Genesis [ET^1]*, 27 = von Rad, *Genesis^5*, 19–20. The italicized line is cited in *Introduction to the OT*, 157. Childs reviewed both editions of the translation (1962 and 1974).

[128] Nicholson, *Pentateuch*, 268. This take on the canonical approach has been influenced by Barr; cf. Childs' response in *Struggle*, 320–321.

ally claims about the nature of OT scripture's unity, as we have begun to see, even as it represents another common position — that in essential respects Childs does not improve upon von Rad, and may actually take a step backwards. In Britain, a more nuanced discussion of Childs with an eye to von Rad can be found in the writings of Walter Moberly.[129]

Childs himself has a bit to say about von Rad (one of his "unforgettable teachers"). Of the passage just cited, he quickly admits that von Rad is right about the "layering of tradition" in Genesis, but he criticizes him for a failure "to reckon seriously with full implications of the canonical process on the traditioning process."[130] (Incidentally, that the charge has at least some justice is immediately seen in von Rad's preference for the term *Hexateuch*.) One could go so far as to say that a major component of *Introduction to the OT* is its running critique of von Rad, inter alia, on the canonical significance of actualization (*Vergegenwärtigung*), in place of which Childs defends a once-and-for-all actualization in the final form:

> it is constitutive of the canon to seek to transmit the tradition in such a way as to prevent its being moored in the past. Actualization ... is built into the structure of the text itself... The usual critical method of biblical exegesis is, first, to seek to restore an original historical setting by stripping away those very elements which constitute the canonical shape. Little wonder that once the biblical text has been securely anchored in the historical past by "decanonizing" it, the interpreter has difficulty applying it to the modern religious context.[131]

An indirect but extensive confirmation of this point resides in a study conducted under Childs' guidance at Yale in the late 1970s. Joseph Groves' *Actualization and Interpretation in the Old Testament* gives a thorough account and critique of actualization in von Rad's work, and at several turns one senses the hand of the supervisor.[132] Outside *Introduction to the OT*, Childs' next most important title here is "Gerhard von Rad in American Dress" (1986), which commends Groves' analysis and argues that many of the complexities of von Rad's method and theology have been lost in translation. This helps explain the way his work "has been accommodated to the ideology of American theological liberalism," but then there is "a flaw in von Rad's theology which has functioned in both [sic] American, British, and European theology to blur the Christological center of his theology."[133] Von Rad rightly holds to this center; he does not recognize the extent or interpretive significance of the transformation that took place later in Israel's life in the textualization of its tradition.

Following *Biblical Theology*, a further aspect of Childs' critique of tradition history has been carried forward by Christopher Seitz, who mounts an argu-

---

[129] E.g., Moberly, *Bible, Theology, Faith*, 1 and passim.

[130] *Introduction to the OT*, 157.

[131] *Introduction to the OT*, 79; cf. the much earlier *Memory and Tradition*, 81.

[132] Yale dissertation of 1979, published in 1987 as Groves, *Actualization* (see esp. 103–163).

[133] Childs, Von Rad, 85; "both" may refer to the two languages he habitually tracks.

ment about the nature of Christian scripture in its *two* testament form that is deeply indebted to Childs, and in which the "gesamtbiblische theologische Problematik" features. One of Seitz's titles captures the problem with von Rad's work from this perspective especially well: "Two Testaments and the Failure of One Tradition-History."[134] Childs favored this critique of a tradition-historical freighting of prophecy, and little wonder since he had laid the groundwork for it.[135] Part of von Rad's brilliance was his regard for the christological center; his limitation was in fusing this center to a theory of cascading actualization. He misconstrues the unity of the Testaments because it is *not* the case that "Israel's history with God thrusts forward violently into the future," from Old to New.[136] This important departure from von Rad is a factor in why Childs begins his *Biblical Theology* by discussing two discrete witnesses. It also has something to do with why he cannot escape the word "dialectical."

Another passage that has often been invoked in this connection occurs in the sixth edition of von Rad's Genesis commentary, revised just before his death in 1971. Von Rad considers Franz Rosenzweig's suggestion that "R," the final redactor of the Pentateuch, should stand for Rabbenu, "our master." The OT theologian is drawn to this Jewish affirmation of a composite final form, with depth dimension intact, yet pushes back by insisting that for Christian readers Jesus Christ is the true master.[137] Bernhard Anderson, Barton, Moberly, Seitz and Steins have all drawn attention to this passage.[138] To my knowledge Childs does not discuss it, but Seitz hews closely to Childs' promotion of the two testament Christian Bible united by one God in Christ:

> It was unnecessary, and indeed somewhat confusing, for von Rad to speak about Jesus Christ in contrast to some other sort of "master." Indeed, one could just as easily say that the access Jesus Christ gives those outside Israel, in the Christian church, is an access to "our master" as reflected in the final form of the text, seen now from the perspective of the post-Easter faith. There need be no theological distinguishing of Jesus Christ as the bringer of the Old Testament to the Gentile Christian church and the Old Testament in its final literary form. Indeed,

---

[134] In Seitz, *Figured Out*, 35–47. Cf. also "The Historical-Critical Endeavor as Theology: The Legacy of Gerhard von Rad," in Seitz, *Word*, 28–40. Childs and Seitz differentiate the canonical approach from those following von Rad who take up tradition history as a way of uniting the testaments. H. Gese, P. Stuhlmacher and H. Hübner are recurring examples, and R. Hays is indicted with similar charges. In incipient form see Childs, Biblische Theologie, 23, and cf. *Biblical Theology*, 70–79.

[135] Seitz's piece offered at the Heidelberg symposium for von Rad, Prophecy and Tradition-History, now adds to a more comprehensive argument in Seitz, *Prophecy and Hermeneutics* (2007). Childs had just read a draft of this book when I interviewed him in Cambridge, 5 April 2006. He enthused that it was the best work on von Rad he had yet seen in English.

[136] Rad, *OT Theology*, 2:332, cited Childs, Von Rad, 83. For Seitz's discussion of "violently thrusting forward" see *Prophecy and Hermeneutics*, 21, 50–51, 73, 98, 111, 117, 248.

[137] Rad, *Genesis [ET²]*, 42–43.

[138] B. Anderson, *Contours of OT*, 28–31 (cf. idem, From Analysis, 29); Barton, Canon, 41 (cf. idem, *Reading*, 47); Moberly, *Bible, Theology, Faith*, 143; Steins, *Bindung*, 21n48.

this form preserves a composite character constrained within the final literary shape. The New Testament's hearing of the Old occurs with reference, therefore, not to a critically delineated tradition-history, but to the Old Testament's final form, a form which Rosenzweig sought to honor when he spoke of the final form of Genesis as bequeathed to us — Jew and Gentile — by Rabbenu (our Master).[139]

This analysis of von Rad's late interest in the final form recalls the course plotted by Childs in 1969, 1979, 1986 and elsewhere. Christ simply *is* the literal sense and scope of the the Old Testament, a deliverance independent of what the New Testament makes of the Old or what the Old might yearn for (thrust toward) in the New. For such reasons, in terms he calls canonical, Childs declines to follow the *gesamtbiblische* program of Gerhard von Rad, with its deep roots in the tradition-historical method once formulated by Hermann Gunkel.

III. Continuity and Change

Let me emphasize two points in conclusion. First, to the banal observation that Childs has more in common with von Rad than Gunkel, caution warns against making too direct an identification. A good case can be made against Rendtorff's anachronistic use of von Rad to displace Childsian insights about canonical, final form exegesis. To be sure, there are anticipations of Childs in von Rad, but one wants to be clear about what these are, and to leave room for departure on Childs' part, whether retrograde (so Nicholson) or innovative (so Seitz). Barthel's decision to track the "kanonhermeneutische Debatte" from von Rad has the potential to mislead.[140] Childs' approach turns Gunkel upside down, and in profound ways it inverts basic commitments of von Rad as well. What then is Childs' relationship to antecedent scholarship? As he puts it in the introduction to his *Introduction to the OT*,

> Having experienced the demise of the Biblical Theology movement in America, the dissolution of the broad European consensus in which I was trained, and a widespread confusion regarding theological reflection in general, I began to realize that there was something fundamentally wrong with the foundations of the biblical discipline. It was not a question of improving on a source analysis, of discovering some unrecognized new genre, or of bringing a redactional layer into sharper focus. Rather, the crucial issue turned on one's whole concept of the study of the Bible itself. I am now convinced that the relation between the historical critical study of the Bible and its theological use as religious literature within a community of faith

---

[139] Seitz, Prophecy and Tradition-History, 44–45 = idem, *Prophecy and Hermeneutics*, 177.

[140] Barthel, Kanonhermeneutische Debatte, 3: "wenn von Rad selbst das hermeneutische Problem des Kanons in seiner *Theologie des Alten Testaments* nicht eigens reflektiert hat und deshalb nur bedingt als Referenz für eine kanonische Theologie in Anspruch genommen werden kann, liegt eine solche Reflexion doch im Gefälle einer gesamtbiblischen Theologie." This quite rightly rejects Rendtorff's transference of canon from Childs to von Rad, and I am appreciative of von Rad's *gesamtbiblische* precedent, but *Biblical Theology* aims to break with his model precisely on how to move from OT to NT, a step von Rad never fully took.

and practice needs to be completely rethought. Minor adjustments are not only inadequate, but also conceal the extent of the dry rot.[141]

Childs goes back to the foundations of form critical research to undermine them, and only then to rebuild. In the same decade in which Koch looks about and wonders how many scholars still hold the link Gunkel held, tenuously — "that the Old Testament was not simply a compendium of Israelite national literature," that focus on individual texts is insufficient, that "the interpreter [must] seek further for a relation between the individual passages and the books, between the Old and New Testaments and the Bible as a whole" — Childs begins to rethink completely how the form and function of biblical texts relate to the Bible's received form and ongoing function in actual, living communities of faith and practice. Koch suggests that tradition history is ready made for theological application, and there are those who subscribe to a derivative model. Childs is decidedly not one of them. I have featured Gunkel as one who transfers theological aspects of canon to history to illustrate the radical nature of Childs' counter-proposal. It cuts against von Rad and others more friendly to biblical theology, too.

Second, the critique nonetheless comes from within a recognized tradition. That is, Childs was not so critical of von Rad while at Heidelberg and Basel. If he experienced a change of heart about Karl Barth after returning to America, as he says at the Barth colloquium in 1969, to some degree he must also have broken ranks with that "biblical phalanx" from his student days in Europe. This was a process. Childs recollects hearing von Rad's famous 1952 lecture on typology. "I was sitting somewhere near Barth, and it seemed to me that there were some of the most glorious lectures I'd ever heard — so crystal clear and all. When he finished, Barth turned around in a half-sleepy way to the person behind him and said, 'Ich habe ihn gar nicht verstanden,' which seemed to me appalling, and I felt like saying, 'Herr Professor, I can explain it all to you.'" But reconsidering Barth meant reconsidering von Rad, too: "in the years that have passed, the more I read over that article, the more I wonder, perhaps Barth didn't understand it because it wasn't quite as clear as I had thought."[142] Like von Rad, Childs will think hard about typology (see chapter seven); from no later than *BTh in Crisis*, though, he consciously pulls away from von Rad, in how he approaches tradition history, figuration, the *Christuszeugnis* of the OT, the unity of the canon, and in a host of lesser respects.

Again, the point is not that Childs' broke with his training altogether, but that he seeks *reform*. A gradual shift can be seen in the way Childs' early work on form modulates into a concern to describe the final form. There are clear

[141] *Introduction to the OT*, 15.

[142] Childs, Barth as Interpreter, 30. The lecture in question is Rad, Typologische. One of Childs' very first articles comes rather closer to von Rad here (Childs, Prophecy and Fulfillment, esp. 262).

echos of von Rad in Childs' form critical study of 1962. It speaks of the actualization of cultic tradition in a way that will soon become problematic for him: "The great acts of the tradition are not removed in past time, but recharged with energy they become again a present event."[143] Similarly, the relative weight of oral tradition (as against its textualized afterlife) is greater than it will be before long: "How can one accurately trace the development of a term in a living oral tradition solely on the basis of chance occurrences on the literary level?"[144] And Childs quotes von Rad, with approval, to this effect: "If we want to go a step farther, instead of working with proof texts, it is necessary to throw light on the specific cultic tradition which lies behind the single statements and to arrange them from the point of view of the history of the tradition."[145] But then other statements in 1962, seen from a post-*Introduction to the OT* vantage, presage a novel application of form criticism. "The role of actualization underwent a process of transformation."[146] At many points an old tradition inherited from the cult is given "new meaning," a "new role" in a "new context." In one case "[a]n expansion of the form away from its cultic origin" emerges.[147] In another, Childs rejects an interpretation that posits an adaptation of a hymn (Psalm 77) *for* a cultic festival. One could almost speak of a loosening of texts from their historical origins and situations. Childs also insists "that there are no avenues to the history of which the Bible speaks except through the Scripture's own testimony to these events."[148] And even more obviously counter an understanding current in Gunkel's day: "Redemptive history is not merely a reflection of Israel's piety — a *Glaubensgeschichte*."[149] Or finally, "biblical events have the dynamic characteristic of *refusing to be relegated to the past*. The quality of this reality did not remain static, but emerged with *new form and content* because it identified itself with the changing historical situations of later Israel."[150] In like manner Erhard Gerstenberger, who knew Childs in his first years at Yale and who revisited Childs' early form critical work in preparation for remarks at a memorial session in

[143] Childs, *Memory and Tradition*, 63. It is a word study, too: Childs will take Barr's criticism to heart in future work. *Memory and Tradition* also comes up for criticism in Groves, *Actualization*.

[144] Childs, *Memory and Tradition*, 34.

[145] Von Rad, Gerechtigkeit, 238, cited in Childs, *Memory and Tradition*, 34n1. The essay was shortly translated as von Rad, Righteousness (there 256).

[146] Childs, *Memory and Tradition*, 76.

[147] Ibid., 44. A more chastened appreciation of the way von Rad explores the change in function of traditional language across its history can be seen as late as 1987: Childs, Death and Dying.

[148] Childs, *Memory and Tradition*, 88.

[149] Ibid., 89.

[150] Ibid., 88, my emphasis. That Gunkel has little trouble actualizing biblical tradition could be taken as an indication of his "canonical" instincts. Then again, ample material strikes him as "utterly impossible for us to use … in Christian worship."

his honor (2007), concludes that durable threads of continuity run right back to the beginning of Childs' publishing career.[151]

All this raises the question of continuity and change in Childs' own work. There are two major turns, in my judgment, the first of which has just been outlined. Somewhere in the late 1960s Childs reorients his study of biblical forms to the final form. This entails taking steps away from Gunkel, von Rad and tradition-historical method at large. Canon becomes a hallmark of Childs' work only after this shift is complete (1970), which it remains. The second is an outworking of the first — canon, in a sense, encloses this turn also. It concerns what Childs calls the "mystery of Israel" and it will be our focus in the last chapter of part two. In the next (middle) chapter I will unpack what I take to be the heart of Childs' approach, or its "inner logic." Although it should be sufficiently clear by now that the unity of the final form is never an aesthetic unity (not in 2008, 1992, 1979, 1974, 1952, or at any other time — throughout one finds a commitment to "depth dimension"), I will try to explain more fully why Childs resists the sheer formalism of literary, narrative and intertextual approaches to the Bible despite some apparent overlap.

[151] SBL San Diego, 18 November 2007.

CHAPTER 5

The Heart of the Matter (*Res*): Against Narrative and Intertextual Readings

As the realistic narrative reading of the biblical stories broke down, literal or verbal and historical meaning were severed and literal and figural interpretation, hitherto naturally affiliated procedures, also came apart. Figural reading had been literalism extended to the whole story or the unitary canon containing it. But now figural sense came to be something like the opposite of literal sense.

— Hans Frei

The prophets and apostles spoke of things which they saw and events which they experienced as testimonies to what God was doing in the world. It is far too limiting to restrict the function of the Bible to that of rendering an agent or an identity. Rather, the nature of the biblical referent must be determined by the text itself which points referringly both to the Creator and the creation in a wide variety of different ways. — Brevard Childs

Those who place Childs in a Yale "school" associate him with a certain stripe of narrative theology. The move has proved more distracting than anything, but there is some sense in it. After all, Childs once expressed an interest in biblical narrative as a new approach to scripture. The strongest examples I can find are preserved in a minor audio magazine called *Catalyst: A Resource for Christian Leaders*. Two issues in 1979 have Childs reading work appropriate to the target demographic. The first includes "The Recovery of Biblical Narrative," a piece given at Perkins School of Theology in March of that year.[1] In it Childs calls the growth of interest in narrative "one of the most exciting areas in present biblical studies" since it has swept up not only OT and NT specialists but theologians as well. It involves a synthetic rather than an atomistic look at the text, and so enables the recovery of "holistic reading"; it is a corrective to the historicism whereby "the biblical text dissolved under *our* handling."[2] Gressmann's excavative metaphor is described and rejected.[3] Childs then offers theological reflections on the value of a narrative approach. First, "story" pushes

[1] *Catalyst* 11/8 (16 May 1979). The essay was read "two months ago," say the editors.

[2] My emphasis.

[3] Cf. *Exodus*, 149 (cited above in footnote 133 of chapter two). "It seems to me," he says here, "this is a disastrous sort of analogy for biblical interpretation. There is a responsibility to recover the … received canonical text."

history (as reference, one supposes) back from center stage. Second, in story the reader is drawn into a world — Barth's strange new world. (Parenthetically, Childs says that one has to relate all this to a doctrine of the Spirit.) Third, the story is corporate. Like family stories, it pertains to a community.[4] Fourth, Childs tries to accommodate a distinction between the testaments with a temporal barrier (which he says Luther dissolves). Fifth, narrative aids the teaching of the Bible, since professionals — again he numbers himself with them — "we render inoperative anything in the common sense of the laity by laying out contexts they could never have imagined." A recovery of biblical narrative in the guild mitigates, serving Bible study at the "grass roots."

An audio essay in the next issue illustrates a narrative approach with a close reading of the Judges 13–16, the Samson cycle.[5] What is the theological message, Childs asks in the end? "I don't think there is one message which you can extract from this story. The story as it stands in its narrative form sparkles like a diamond, and it depends on what light comes into it, what vision, what angle you look at the story." The diamond has to be picked up by the preacher. A "major task of biblical theology" is "*nacherzählen* — that is, the retelling of the story." The challenge is "to wrestle with the biblical story with skill and insight," since the preacher's "task is to proclaim the word of God to a congregation that changes mood and historical setting."[6] The Barthian impress is transparent. Emphasis on interpretation amidst cultural and temporal change is vintage Childs, too, though it is interesting to compare *Introduction to the OT*, which is more concerned to describe "the effect of the Deuteronomic redaction" on the Samson cycle than to retell it.[7] One does not find him engaging in straightforward *nacherzählen* very often: a great bulk of his scholarly output engages and tweaks historical-critical "results" that may or may not have any bearing on his actual exegesis or the exegesis he wants to sponsor.[8] Preoccupation with getting the hermeneutical framework right is at least one factor in what leads

---

[4] Here Childs digresses into an alluring family story of his own. His family moved from South Carolina to New York when he was about five. His "ancient grandfather" would visit every few years. "He was fifteen when the Civil War ended, and I always looked on him as the last Confederate." Grandpa would martial the kids in front of a family portrait and would then "recount the burning of Columbia by Sherman's troops. I always wondered how the South lost: in our stories the South was always clever." The story goes that the family silver had been stashed in a steamer trunk on the front porch. Sherman's army ransacked the house but went out the back door and left the silver.

[5] *Catalyst* 11/9 (13 June 1979).

[6] His 1977 bibliography for pastors sounds a similar note when it voices frustration with "a sterile impasse" between theological conservatives (who reject source criticism by reflex) and liberals (who do not understand what is "at stake for the life of the church") and calls for "profounder wrestling with Scripture by a broad segment of the church as part of its life of praise and service" (*OT Books*, 11). Cf. also *NT Introduction*, 546.

[7] *Introduction to the OT*, 261.

[8] See the discussion in Provan, Canons, 29–30.

Childs to curb his enthusiasm for narrative and literary approaches. When dealing with the bequest of historicism, he later says in *Biblical Theology*, "I greeted largely as an ally the growing twentieth-century appeal to narrative theology as at least a move toward recovering a holistic reading of the Bible. After all was not Karl Barth considered a great narrative theologian by some?" In the time since his first Introduction it became clear that the technique could "propogate a fully secular, non-theological reading of the Bible"[9] (Barr, Alter) or come wedded to "avowedly Jewish"[10] perspectives (Sternberg), either of which made its positive contribution to Christian biblical theology less obvious. Interestingly, the 1979 recordings herald narrative as a boon for nothing other than biblical theology. Childs will have had some idea of everything else that project entails.

All along the most decisive issue has been biblical referentiality, or the Bible's capacity to witness to its subject matter (*res*). This has *always* moved Childs to draw a distinction with his colleague Hans Frei, one of the best known narrative theologians and the one whose thought overlaps most with Childs'. "In Kings," to take an example from 1979,

> the presentation of Israel's history is particular rather than representative, common rather than confessional, archival rather than midrashic. The use of chronology to render Israel's historical particularity strains the term 'story' almost as much as it does that of modern history. Even the more flexible term of Hans Frei ... which designates the biblical material as *'history-like narrative' needs to have its content informed by the elements of chronology as much as by other analogues*. It may be that the term runs the risk, unless carefully qualified, of losing important features which are essential to Israel's witness.[11]

If there are unqualified uses of Frei's categories in Childs' writings at any point I am not aware of them. Still, some later incriminations against Frei would have been hard to anticipate. Consider one from 1992. "It is basic to Christian theology to reckon with an extra-biblical reality, namely with the resurrected Christ who evoked the New Testament witness. When H. Frei, in one of his last essays, spoke of 'midrash' as a text-creating reality, he moved in a direction, in my opinion, which for Christian theology can only end in failure."[12] One of Childs' most clarifying statements on the subject is an excursus, "The Canonical Approach and the 'New Yale Theology.'" Prompted by George Lindbeck's *The Nature of Doctrine* (1984), it appears at the back of *NT Introduction*. Childs says that if Lindbeck's three models for religion and religious doctrine are the only ones available then he is "firmly" in Lindbeck's camp, but that he

---

[9] *Biblical Theology*, 722–723.

[10] Ibid., 20. See all of 18–22.

[11] *Introduction to the OT*, 299.

[12] *Biblical Theology*, 20. He references Frei's very dense essay entitled "The 'Literal Reading' of Biblical Narrative in the Christian Tradition: Does it Stretch Or Will it Break?"

has several problems with Lindbeck's cultural-linguistic model.[13] Of the three points he develops, only the second, about the narrative theology in Lindbeck's "intratextual theological faithfulness" (Frei's *Eclipse* is also named), concerns us here.[14] A theory of "intratextuality," Childs fears, raises "serious problems when used as a positive formulation of the Bible's relation to the external world." From his explanation I pull one of this chapter's epigraphs:

> the New Testament bears witness to realities outside itself. The prophets and apostles spoke of things which they saw and events which they experienced as testimonies to what God was doing in the world. It is far too limiting to restrict the function of the Bible to that of rendering an agent or an identity. Rather, the *nature of the biblical referent* must be *determined by the text itself which points referringly* both to the Creator and the creation in a wide variety of different ways. To recognize that the Bible offers a faith-construal is not to deny that it bears witness to realities outside the text. Christians have always understood that we are saved, not by the biblical text, but by the life, death, and resurrection of Jesus Christ who entered into the world of time and space.[15]

One side of the "biblical referent" is the Triune God in Christ. God's nature is "determined by the text itself," and this text "points referringly" — as opposed to attributively, I think, as in points predicatively. On the other side, too, with a nature to be determined in a rather different sense, is creation. Christ of course is the bridge. Again, the fear is that narrative, cultural-linguistic, intra- and (soon) inter-textual theories of reference — allegedly with some connection to "midrash," too — that all these approaches participate in something that is disastrous for the church's use of its scripture.

Although it is increasingly well known that Childs comes to resist narrative approaches, the reasoning behind his decision can be opaque. In simplest terms I think he just finds traditional categories like *sensus literalis* and *regula fidei* more serviceable than "narrative," less prone to misreading. But what is the heart of the matter? This calls for further discussion. Chapter four showed that literary history and canonical history are not identical, and how within this (dialectical) separation Childs sees on *theological* grounds that the narrower canonical history did some damage in the literary history: "original poetic forms were lost, or a unified narrative badly shattered." This leaves considerable room for Gunkel. Canon has a profound, overarching unity, but it is not a "literary or aesthetic unity."[16] The present chapter will look at Childs' rejection of purely inner-biblical, non-referential hermeneutics. Something compels him to move "beyond the textual,"[17] and it bears on the canon's unity. I will proceed by looking at Frei and Georg Steins (introduced in chapter two),

[13] *NT Introduction*, 544. Tillich and Barth might both be called "neo-orthodox," Childs suggests, but the common classification could imply far more similarity than is warranted.

[14] See Lindbeck, *Nature*, 113–124.

[15] *NT Introduction*, 545, my emphasis.

[16] *Introduction to the OT*, 74.

[17] Childs, Critique, 183, see below.

whom Childs quite unexpectedly links in his penultimate essay. My argument has three stages. After further relativizing the idea of a "Yale school," it will contrast Childs' assessment of the canonical process with that of Steins. Frei drops out here because he does not address this aspect of the text's history despite documenting the importance of literary-historicism to German debate. Finally, it will broach Childs' later conclusion that intertextuality, rightly considered, is a subset of figural reading. Here it will differentiate Childs' sense of intertextuality as figuration from Steins' proposed canonical intertextual reading (*kanonisch-intertextuelle Lektüre*) and from Frei's so-called midrashic intertextualizing of the biblical narrative's literal sense, while at the same time pointing to an important lasting agreement between Childs and Frei.

A. The Notion of a Yale School — Chiefly on Biblical Reference

In the jointly authored essay "Story and Biblical Theology," Bartholomew and Goheen follow the convention of classifying theological and philosophical interest in narrative geographically — the Yale school, the Chicago school, the California school — and declare a primary interest in the Yale school associated with Frei and Lindbeck. The authors of the essay recognize that Childs personally demurs from the so-called Yale school, and they opine that it would be better to split the difference between Yale (excluding Childs) and Chicago. This permits the storied world of the Bible to attach to the "real" world, as Bartholomew and Goheen see it. Narrative theology has to plug in to ontology and history.[18]

The matter is roughly similar for Childs, for whom (with debts to Frei) an interpretive crux arises in the wake of radical change in the perception of biblical reference wherein "real" history drifts apart from the history-like world of the Bible. Once these two realities diverge — that is, with the rise of biblical criticism — all biblical interpretation enacts some form of response. People can give minimalist or maximalist accounts of biblical history, or can transpose meaning into another (idealist) register, but it becomes impossible to take the correspondence of biblical narrative and its ostensive historical referent for granted. The tale of this hermeneutical shift is told, of course, in Frei's *The Eclipse of Biblical Narrative* (1974). As was seen in chapter three, Childs shows his acceptance of Frei's account of the change to the Bible's literal sense by 1969, in the Yale colloquium for Barth. Also at that early date Childs keeps his distance from Frei's narrative remedy. In the discussion session panelist Robert

[18] Bartholomew and Goheen, Story, 146, 154, 162. The authors find Barr's early emphasis on story more helpful, but it may be doubted whether he would "wish to privilege the final form of Scripture as we have it, and … maintain that in this final form all the books, in one way or another, are closely connected to God's unfolding story" (160).

Johnson states, "So, from the point of view of what Hans is arguing, what [Barth's] really talking about is not the historical context but the literary context." Childs makes a rebuttal:

> That's where Hans and I differ somewhat. I move in a little different direction here. In other words, it seems to me that there are problems when you get — I would agree fully with Hans when he's combatting those historical critics who would want to go behind the text, but it's interesting when you begin to deal with the narrative text, as a context. One has to keep in mind that the early church, in the controversy with Judaism, took quite a different move. Where the Jews were saying, read the text! read the text!, the Christians said, there's something behind the text. It's what the text points to, namely: Jesus Christ. And there was a dialectic between the reality and the text.
>
> It seems to me, what buttresses this from getting into the kind of ontology you're talking about is the *scope of the canon*: namely, the *reality which is in dialectic with the text, defined by its canonical context*. I don't see how you can avoid a dialectic between text and reality...[19]

The discussion continues between Johnson, Frei and a student, who asks about Frei's sense of story. Childs then sides with Johnson and declares "that the new hermeneutic is not only mistaken, but is one colossal *cul de sac*."[20] Frei's diagnosis is correct, but from before *BTh in Crisis* Childs searches out medicine more effective than what he already sees as a self-contained world of biblical narrative. For him the eclipse Frei describes so well provokes a dialectic that involves the canon, its scope and the divine referent that is identified by, but not identical to, the canonical text.

As often as Childs has been harangued for a Yale affiliation with New Criticism, it is regrettable that his lucid differentiation from Frei in 1969 was not more widely known. Barr, for whom "[t]heology as a mode of understanding comes into existence only when one moves out of the plane of the text itself and begins to ask about the extrinsic realities to which the text refers," might have found a little common ground.[21] And Brett, who had the benefit of Excursus III in *NT Introduction*, still only manages a Childs who is indecisive, who vacillates between two incompatible theories of reference. One is a theory of historical background in the text's prehistory. The other is a theory of theological reference. Because he tends to privilege the latter, Brett thinks, it would be more consistent to drop the former and adopt the methodology of New Critical formalism.[22] Yet despite Childs' worry that exclusive concern for

---

[19] Childs, Barth as Interpreter, 56, my emphasis.

[20] Ibid., 57–58. Presumably he means New Criticism. Frei appears to retreat after this: "I don't know at that point [that it all coheres in story] how much I'm reading myself into Barth. But yes, I think that's it" (59, cf. 62).

[21] Barr, *Holy Scripture*, 102. This is felt to score a point *against* Childs, for whom, according to Barr, the text is a "closed system" and thus a "ghetto" (168). Cf. Barr, *Concept of BTh*, 416.

[22] Brett, *Crisis?*, 31–47. He acknowledges some separation from Frei (174n8) but waves it away it with a less than self-evident assertion: "synchronic final form readings cannot use diachronic reconstructions without lapsing into confusion" (46).

meaning as historical reference gets biblical exegesis into trouble, he knows the critical problems of positivity do not go away if they are evaded.

Anglophone readers tend to treat Childs' source-critical analysis as either a liability or a disposable interest. This in itself is symptomatic. If Frei's analysis of the situation in the eighteenth and nineteenth century is right, responses to the split between explicative meaning and historical reference took on different profiles in England and Germany. In England the main focus was on externalist accounts of reference, on raw historical fact (e.g., did geology confirm or disconfirm Noah's flood?). Germany stayed closer to "the broader hermeneutical issue of the meaning of biblical texts. Unlike the English discussion of the fact issue, which had by this time become completely mired in the external evidence question, the German scholars' procedure was therefore almost exclusively internal, i.e. literary-historical."[23] It is tempting to extrapolate, to say that these ripples in the history of ideas have not totally subsided. Certainly when considering the taxonomy of chapter two, it should be little surprise to learn that among Childs' readers it is mainly Europeans who can be brought into serious dialogue with him on the issue of canon formation. The concern falls out in Frei, too, who was born in Europe but finished his education in England and America because of the Jewish persecutions.[24] The next two sections will take up different "theories" of reference, starting with the literary-historical. Section B will contrast Childs and Steins on the genesis of the final form. There are correspondences despite Steins' recommendation to move in a formalist direction. Section C will bring Frei and this chapter's first epigraph back into the mix for an analysis of canonical intertextuality and christian figural reading. Though the last section might seem to have more to do with theological reference, my purpose throughout is to show why all biblical textuality for Childs is necessarily "deictic," viz., pointed to the *res*.

[23] Frei, *Eclipse*, 56. Cf. 218: "In Germany, in contrast to England, there was a strong, continuing interest in the Bible not only as true or false report but in addition as a large series of written sources with their own literary history, an interest augmented by the hallowed tradition of belief in the text's inspiration. In the pursuit of such matters, the narrative features of many of the biblical writings were not ignored, and interest in them was strengthened by the developing quest for a manageable view of the Bible's unity through the development of a single history traced in its pages."

[24] Born in Breslau to Jewish parents, Frei (1922–1988) was at first educated in Germany but then in 1935 was sent to a Quaker school in England, where he became an Anglican. In 1938 he was joined in exile by his parents, now in America, where he completed his education (Higton, *Public Theology*, 16–17).

B. Parsing "Canon": Is its Formation Centripetal or Centrifugal?

Critical to Childs' use of the term canon is its ability to serve as a "cipher," a shorthand expression with which "to encompass the various and diverse factors involved in the formation of the literature."[25] In *Biblical Theology* at least, looking back at his Introductions to the Old and New Testaments, this is how he claims to have used "canon" and "canonical." Childs lists several factors in the way the the biblical "material was transmitted through its various oral, literary, and redactional stages by many different groups towards a theological end," factors that, consonant with the tradents' concern "to maintain a normative function [of the traditions] for subsequent generations of believers," belong under one umbrella. As a cipher, canon

> was, above all, useful in denoting the reception and acknowledgment of certain religious traditions as authoritative writings within a community of faith. The term also included the process by which the collection arose which led up to its final stage of literary and textual stabilization, that is, canonization proper. Emphasis was placed on the process to demonstrate that the concept of canon was not a late, ecclesiastical ordering which was basically foreign to the material itself, but that canon-consciousness lay deep within the formation of the literature. The term also served to focus attention on the theological forces at work in its composition rather than seeking the process largely controlled by general laws of folklore, by socio-political factors, or by scribal conventions.

"Canonical," adds Childs, "also included ... a theological extension of its primary meaning" in that the final form of the text is normative for living communities of faith whose members affirm the canon still. They do this in line

> with the faith community of the original tradents. The modern theological function of canon lies in its affirmation that the authoritative norm lies in the literature itself as it has been treasured, transmitted and transformed — of course in constant relation to its object to which it bears witness — and not in 'objectively' reconstructed stages of the process. The term canon points to the received, collected, and interpreted material of the church and thus establishes the theological context in which the tradition continues to function authoritatively for today.[26]

Canon identifies life amidst the parameters of biblical tradition, a life in which current readers identify with "original tradents" who acknowledge, receive, and draw nourishment from an established form.

Many deny that all this constitutes one "canonical" thing. In a fairly typical move after Barr's *Holy Scripture*, Steins parses Childs' use of canon into five aspects.[27] Into a block quotation of the passage just cited he inserts the following numbers: "Canonical" refers to (1) a faith community's reception of

---

[25] *Biblical Theology*, 70; cf. Childs, On Reclaiming, 5. A similar point is made by Chapman, Canon Debate. I question whether the introduction of canon as a "cipher" in 1992 is a significant departure from Childs' earlier usage of canon — see *BTh in Crisis*, 99.

[26] *Biblical Theology*, 70–71.

[27] Barr's enumeration of canons is not the same as Steins'. Cf. *Holy Scripture*, 75.

authoritative traditions; (2a) the *process* by which the traditions were assembled along with (2b) the resulting stabilized body of literature — showing that "*canonization proper*" was not "basically foreign to the material itself, but that *canon-consciousness* lay deep within the formation of the literature"; (3) "the theological forces" driving the process; and (4) how the tradition continues to be normative today.[28] A striking thing about this way of carving up the process of canon formation is that it runs against the grain of Childs' talk of a single "cipher." By making (2a) distinct from (2b) Steins drives a wedge between two factors, the canonical process and canonization proper, in which Childs sees the closest identity. Tellingly (2b) has not been made (3). Steins is at least implicitly aware that his parsing of the process contradicts the logic of Childs' own presentation. Just how deep does a *Kanonbewußtsein* lie in the formation of the biblical literature?[29]

Childs' imprecision, Steins believes, stems from his terminology and needs mending. He summarizes his problem with *Biblical Theology* this way:

> In der bisweilen opak wirkenden "erweiterten" Verwendung von "Kanon" bei Childs lassen sich zwei grundlegende Sichtweisen unterscheiden, die ich als semiotisches Konzept und als funktionelles Konzept von "Kanon" bezeichnen und im folgenden erläutern möchte. Um alle seines Erachtens wichtigen Aspekte von "Kanon" zu integrieren, verbindet Childs eine Bedeutungstheorie des Kanons mit einer Funktionstheorie und wechselt je nach Bedarf die Ebenen ohne explizite Hinweise.[30]

A more controlled use of the term canon should differentiate between two senses of "canon," in a manner that turns out to supply its own dynamic of actualization or generation:

> Kanon (1) = *Kanon als* (der kanonisierte) *Text* (der Bibel) und
>
> Kanon (2) = *Kanon als Metatext* (Metasprach/metalinguistischer Rahmen).[31]

By way of clarification Steins calls on the semiotics of George Aichele. Every attempt to close down the meaning of a text merely results in further commentary. The unending process of expansion and deferment of meaning can be arrested, however, by the canon's closure. Canonization proper involves first identifying the accepted text, then fixing the text's wording. But these activities are *extrinsic* to the text: "Beides sind extrinsische Vorgänge, liegen nicht im Text selbst, sondern werden an den Text herangetragen." Closing the canon

---

[28] Steins, *Bindung*, 13, his emphasis. One could concede that the German translation leaves the riven sentence *slightly* more open to dissection. It reads, with Steins' numbering and italics, "(2a) Der Begriff schloß auch den *Prozeß* ein, durch den die Sammlung entstand, (2b) und der sie bis zû ihrem letzten Stadium der literarischen und textlichen Stabilität führte, was dann *Kanonisierung* im eigentlichen Sinne bedeutet."

[29] Provan, Canons, raises this very question for different purposes.

[30] Ibid., 14.

[31] Ibid.

naturally involves the work of a community, those for whom the meaning of the text is a concern, and what they attain thereby is "[eine autoritative] Begrenzung des Sinns" which frames the region within which the text's meaning may be sought. "So wird die interpretatorische Kreativität angeregt und zugleich begrenzt." Thus the extrinsic act of canonization creates a metalinguistic frame within which intertextual play occurs, enabling interpretation within boundaries. The framework metaphor ("Rahmen") brings with it a pair of pivotal concepts, border ("Grenze") and play area ("Spielraum"). The former speaks to the canon's *function* (the "Funktionstheorie"), to terminate the endless process of commentary becoming text that requires commentary, while the latter addresses canon's *meaning* (the "Bedeutungstheorie"), or the sense readers make of scripture once it becomes a closed, "selbstreferentielles System."[32]

The proposal for canonical-intertextual reading enlists other theoreticians, but their incorporation by Steins need not detain us. Does Aichele help solve the putative confusion in Childs? Quite the contrary, he worsens it. Had his definition of canon been taken on board without modification, the result would have been radically opposed to Childs.[33] Aichele holds that "the demand for commentary that is provoked in the written story is endless. The concept of canon arises from the need to end this endless demand by completing the uncompleteable story. The canonizing of a text is the final and greatest attempt to overcome utterly and even to eliminate the physical dimension of the text."[34] On this view canonization proper (2b) is not just arbitrary but antagonistic with respect to canonical process (2a). Aichele sees the canonical process as inherently centrifugal, whereas for Childs it is centripetal: the product is intrinsic to the process (though the two are not identified). With another set of interlocutors this relates to a discussion of the meaning of "canon" as against "scripture." Stephen Chapman draws attention to how the the canon's "use" by (of) religious communities undergirds its formation as an historical process. He is with those who argue "for a messier, more multiplex character to canonization as a socio-historical phenomenon." What, Chapman asks, "is the nature of the canonical process"? "Rather than defining 'canon' as essentially a matter of delimitation and 'closure' as an official, quasi-legal decision (two basic presuppositions of the majority view), the alternative view understands 'canon' as an issue of authority or communal identity and 'closure' as the con-

---

[32] Ibid., 15, summarizing Aichele, *Sign*, 127–139.

[33] Aichele's semiotics leads to a more radical sense of canon than Steins', as evidenced by the former's more thoroughgoingly Kristevan sense of the word intertextuality (Aichele, *Sign*, 14), which marginalizes the canon as a normative collection of texts. His classification of theology as a subset of ideology (15) calls into question any affirmation of the biblical canon as a distinct and normative collection of literature.

[34] Ibid., 127. On eliminating the "body" of the biblical text see Boyarin, Eye; idem, *Intertextuality*; idem, *Radical*; cf. the perceptive critique in Dawson, *Christian Figural Reading*.

sequence of tradition and use."[35] Canon, for Chapman an association of scripture (unattached inspired writings) operative since deuteronomism, is dynamic and generative as a "collection" and "range" of voices, as a "chorus." Naturally there are limits, since "without limitation there can also be no 'chorus' and therefore no 'life.'"[36] But to see canon as a composite entity of "*relative* stability"[37] with built-in generative potential is actually to see canon *as* body and not the antithesis to body. This attests quite another dynamic than a putative "need to end this endless demand [for commentary] by completing the uncompleteable story."

For Steins the disagreement about the nature of the canonical process, with Childs' position amply represented by Chapman, is less stark. In chapter two I noted Lohfink's input (that "man mit mehr rechnen muß als nur einer Reihe von in sich selbständigen Büchern"). As Steins himself puts it in an essay on Chronicles and the closing of the Hebrew canon, "Daß 'Kanonisierung' nicht nur 'Auswahl und Zusammenstellung autoritativer Schriften' bedeutet, sondern sich 'im Text' niederschlägt ... wird in der Regel nicht genügend beachtet."[38] But it is difficult to emphasize a move toward canonization within the biblical tradition and at the same to insist that canonization proper is an extrinsic, after-the-fact imposition. A recognition of this pushes Childs to keep Steins' canons (2a) and (2b) together. In form-critical terms, canon's form and function are two sides of a coin (the "Funktionstheorie" ought to have a part in the "Bedeutungstheorie"). We can refine the contrast that emerges here by comparing Childs and Steins on the Chronicler's "midrashic" technique. To what extent is Steins' emphasis on an extrinsic canonization counterbalanced by an awareness of thick, inner-biblical processes?

I. Midrash and the Chronicler

In "Torabindung und Kanonabschluß" (1996) Steins upholds internal aspects of canon formation. "Kanonisierung ist nicht *nur* ein äußerlich deklarativer Akt, mit dem Auswahl und Anordnung der normativen Schriften festgelegt werden; sie hat — wie die neuere Kanonforschung herausgearbeitet hat — auch im Text selbst einen Niederschlag gefunden."[39] The ambivalence marked by italics will become more pronounced in *Bindung* (1999); canonization is an external act, just not wholly so. For the time being Steins heralds Childs as an

[35] Chapman, Reclaiming Inspiration, 169.

[36] Idem, *Law and Prophets*, 108–109.

[37] Ibid.

[38] Steins, Torabindung, 213–256, 250n150.

[39] Ibid., 213, my emphasis. I will focus on this essay, but compare his more comprehensive study from the year before: idem, *Abschlussphänomen*.

ally in emphasizing the canonical shaping at work in the text.[40] Specific to Chronicles, Steins argues that, as with earlier tradents except on a much larger scale, the Chronicler attempted "einer Zusammenführung und Fokussierung verschiedener Traditionsstränge."[41] If at first this statement seems compatible with Childs' treatment of Chronicles in *Introduction to the OT*, a handful of parallel judgments manifest a slight departure.

For Steins the Chronicler synthesizes "der disparaten Traditionen der älteren kanonischen Bücher."[42] Similarly, the formula "law, prophets, and other writings," first found in Sirach, indicates that the third grouping (in some contrast to the first two) is "eine Sammlung formal und inhaltlich disparater Werke."[43] The observation that the writings are in a greater state of flux than the law and prophets receives special comment:

> Ist man durch die Einsichten in den Formierungsprozeß der ersten beiden Kanonteile darauf aufmerksam geworden, daß der Kanon von inner her wächst und Abschlußphänomene im Text selbst zu finden sind, sich Kanonbildung also nicht in einem äußeren deklarativen Akt vollzieht, dann drängt sich die Frage nach einem analogen Vorgang für den dritten Teil auf. Für diesen Kanonteil stellt sich das Abschlußproblem zudem in besonderer Weise: Wie sollte eine derart disparate Sammlung abgeschlossen werden?[44]

His answer is that the Chronicler attempts to draw the disparate writings together, and so begins to close down the endless-seeming proliferation of commentary. It is a recapitulation and summary of the history of Israel held in both previous mini-canons, particularly the law. Chronicles focuses and clarifies what it means to be Israel in light of Torah. "Das letzte Buch des dritten Teils bindet so diesen Teil an die beiden vorangehenden zurück und eröffnet eine torazentrierte Gesamtsicht des dreiteiligen Kanons."[45]

To retroject terminology from 1999, the *function* of Chronicles is part of canonization proper — arresting the growth of the tradition. But Chronicles associates itself closely with biblical tradition and becomes interior. Why then is the mechanism it enacts *extrinsic*? Among a few different possibilities the

---

[40] A footnote claims an allegiance that will become problematic within three years: "Der 'kanonische Prozeß' ('canonical process') als je neue Aneignung und Aktualisierung der biblischen Traditionen ist zu unterscheiden von der 'Kanonisierung,' mit der dieser innerbiblische Prozeß beendet wird. Zum 'kanonischen Prozeß' als entscheidendem Faktor der 'Schriftwerdung' vgl. B.S. Childs, Introduction (1979) 77–79" (Steins, Torabindung, 216n14). The essay anticipates other themes pursued in 1999. It is "*[m]ethodisch* wichtig" to maintain distinctions between the historical emergence of the canon and "*der Herausbildung einer Kanontheorie*," between the fact that a group collected the canon and the subsequent reception of the same, and between a stabilized selection and ordering of scripture and the fixing of the text's form (ibid., 247, my emphasis).

[41] Ibid., 246.

[42] Ibid.

[43] Ibid., 247.

[44] Ibid., 250.

[45] Ibid., 251.

main reason seems to be that the tradition to which it refers is "disparate." The Chronicler overcomes something centrifugal by fiat. Within the closed canon it is as if one observes a jostling, and against this a will to subdue the basic momentum towards disunity. The *meaning* of Chronicles is apprehended within the borders it helped frame. Its inertia toward still more commentary is what excites the reader's play in the resulting "selbstreferentielles System." The canonical metatext energizes as much as it limits ever new text-text relations.

The contrast with Childs is subtle but basic. Chronicles' contribution to canon formation ought not be called disparate or centrifugal — it is not *essentially* disharmonious — because it voices notes across the register of a choir. (Harmony needs discord, but not all music is composed by Stravinsky.) Later, most notably in *Isaiah*, this feature — we might call it the associative property of canon — is connected with "the role of intertextuality" (said to be "one of the most important recent insights" in biblical interpretation):

> The growth of the larger composition has often been shaped by the use of a conscious resonance with a previous core of oral or written texts. The great theological significance is that it reveals how the editors conceived of their task as forming a chorus of different voices and fresh interpretations, but all addressing in different ways, different issues, and different ages a part of the selfsame, truthful witness to God's salvific purpose for his people.[46]

Twenty-two years prior, *Introduction to the OT* draws much the same result from Chronicles. The Chronicler adjusts and realigns the diverse tradition before him using a kind of "midrashic method."[47] Yet he also thereby

> bears witness to the continuity of the obedient response within the history of Israel. Because God did not change his will, demanding one thing of his people earlier and something different later, there emerged a *common profile of the faithful within Israel*. There is a *family resemblance* in their praise and thanksgiving, in prayers and laments which extends throughout all ages. The Chronicler shaped his material to highlight the continuity within the community of faith.[48]

The notion of a "family resemblance" will become prominent in later work on Isaiah's formation *and* reception, and it has anticipations. Aichele leads Steins to emphasize what canonical texts bury.[49] Childs affirms instead an intrinsic continuity in scripture on the basis of vertical extra-textual reference (the profile of an "obedient response" across time). He cannot help agreeing that the

46 *Isaiah*, 4.

47 *Introduction to the OT*, 654.

48 Ibid., 655, my emphasis. The phrase "family resemblance" occurs only here in 1979, and I think not before. Cf. *Biblical Theology*, 336, 500, 655, and see B.III in chapter seven, below.

49 Aichele, *Sign*, 129: "canon functions in the same way that genre does, burying the incoherence of the text and reinforcing belief that a complete message has been received." But as Eagleton, *Theory*, 69, cautions, frequently "the plurality and open-endedness of the process of reading are permissible because they presuppose a certain kind of closed unity which always remains in place: the unity of the reading subject, which is violated and transgressed only to be returned more fully to itself."

Chronicler's material has "disparate parts," or that he labors to "reconcile the differences."[50] There is much to say about how the tradition is transformed, expanded, harmonized, omitted, and shaped. Above all, though, an alternative vision fires Childs' insight "that canon-consciousness lay deep within the formation of the literature." Of Chronicles he writes, "At times the process of harmonization is quite unconscious and appears as almost a reflex from a concept of canon." And: "It is important to notice in the process of harmonization that the Chronicler did not for a moment feel himself at liberty to change his text at will, as commentators have tended to imply. In fact, such an assumption is totally foreign to a sense of canon." He exercised "creativity only within certain boundaries."[51] His harmonization stemmed from an "aim to establish an inner harmony of all his sources."[52] Likewise his supplementation of the material shares "a canonical concern that the full extent of the normative tradition be represented" — "these expansions reflect a critical, theological process."[53] So too with typology. "The Chronicler used the method to draw out elements of *ontological* continuity within Israel's history."[54] In shaping the historical material paradigmatically, "the Chronicler's attempt to document the correspondence between action and effect is an essential part of his concept of God's revelation through the prophets which is contained in a body of authoritative scripture."[55] By searching out a "family resemblance" in this tradent's community of faith, *Childs finally aligns himself* with the theological judgment of the Chronicler — he steps into the last canon (4) of Steins' parsing. Because "the Chronicler speaks to the ontological question and faithfully testifies to the unchanging reality of the One God,"[56] God becomes the tradition's center of gravity. As scripture's true referent and scope, he brings its witness into focus without obscuring its polyvalence.

Near the top of this section we saw an affirmation that the theological function of canon rests in "the authoritative norm [that] lies in the literature itself as it has been treasured, transmitted and transformed — of course *in constant relation to its object to which it bears witness*."[57] This gets at why, broadly speaking, the Chronicler's "midrashic" activity is a point of agreement between Steins and Childs, but its programatic, hermeneutical or theological significance is not. It is only by apprehending the literal sense at a level "beyond the textual" that Childs can address the unity and diversity of scripture in terms

[50] *Introduction to the OT*, 648.
[51] Ibid.
[52] Ibid., 649.
[53] Ibid., 650.
[54] Ibid., 651, my emphasis.
[55] Ibid., 653.
[56] Ibid., 655.
[57] *Biblical Theology*, 71, my emphasis.

other than a flat "gemeinsame Nenner der verschiedenen Stimmen."[58] This is the thrust of his ubiquitous appeal to the Bible's "scope," "res," "Sache," "witness," and so on. In other words, when Steins says the "interpretatorisch relevante Bezugspunkt ist der Text,"[59] he introduces strictures on the *sensus literalis* that Childs' canonical approach cannot abide. In the end even Barton begins to mark the difference: "When Childs talks of the 'final form' of the text he does not mean the text as a unified aesthetic object, but (Barth-like) as the communication of the word of God… The question is not: what does the final form mean as a literary unity?, but: what word of God is communicated through this passage?"[60] To be still more precise, the question is: given the text's ontic pressuring of its readership, how does one trace the common profile of obedient response?

II. Isaiah is Deictic, Not Midrashic

The next chapter will look at why Childs moves away from the language of "midrash" between *Introduction to the OT* and *Isaiah* even as use of the term "intertextuality" increases.[61] The point I wish to illustrate now is that Childs' construal of what he most often calls "canonical shaping" does not change much over his career even though his terminology for the phenomenon can shift. Like the finished product, the canonical process is chiefly about pointing or witnessing. In its final shaping and its history of effects in the church,[62] the book of Isaiah has more to do with text-*res* referents than text-text referents.

Childs makes a major reaffirmation of the argument for canonical shaping in *Isaiah*, his last major exegetical work on the Old Testament. "Retrospective Reading" (1996), a dense and important expression of Childs' career thesis, anticipates the argument of the Isaiah commentary (2001) and is cited there more than any other of Childs' works. The essay concerns not just the misapplication of "midrash" to inner-biblical exegesis by modern scholars, but an "entire projection of textual expansion" which goes by other names as well.[63] As an alternative, in Isaiah Childs detects a consciousness "already deeply embedded in the earlier tradition" (citing I. L. Seeligmann for neither the first

---

[58] Steins, *Bindung*, 73.

[59] Ibid., 95. Childs thinks Steins collapses text and commentary (Critique, 176). Instead, but equally problematic for him, Steins appears to collapse text and referent.

[60] Barton, Canonical Approaches, 201.

[61] By a Google Books search, "intertextuality" (or "intertextual") registers zero hits in *Introduction to the OT* (1979), three in *NT Introduction* (1984), nine in *OT Theology* (1985), two in *Biblical Theology* (1992), and 110 in *Isaiah* (2001). *Struggle* has 14, *Pauline Corpus* 16.

[62] Too often absent from discussion of Isaiah's role in the church, he says, "is the ability to see the effect of the coercion of the text itself in faithfully *shaping* the life of the church — its doctrine, liturgy, and practice — in such a way as to leave a *family resemblance* of faith throughout the ages" (*Isaiah*, 5, my emphasis).

[63] Childs, Retrospective Reading, 370.

nor the last time).[64] In addition, he observes, "Prophetic authority is related to the function of the biblical text. The text is the tradent of authority in establishing a link with specific prophetic figures."[65] The text itself is figurative or intertextual, and in its formation it acquired and "continues to exert a coercion" on readers.[66] That the literature of the Hebrew Bible was configured around persons (Isaiah, David, Solomon, Moses) can be ignored, and often has been ignored, but in this case "it is not the Bible that is being interpreted." Put differently, "the concept of final form is closely connected with the issue of readership."[67] There are of course readers who do not identify with the community of faith in ancient Israel. There are also those who understand themselves to be included in the future generations of Israel, for whom her scriptures form a lasting testament.[68]

Turning to the Isaiah commentary itself, the first thing to note is how much the work stands in continuity with Childs' earlier ventures. It forms a coda to the arguments that culminated in *Introduction to the OT* and seriously dates criticism of that book's treatment of "loosening" in Isaiah. In 2001 one finds the same acceptance of the critically discovered layers, a similar effort to press beyond entrenched factions to the left and right, and an unshaken conviction that the many hands involved in shaping the book leave a product better characterized as "accumulated experience" than as colliding intentionalities or disparate voices.[69] Perhaps the single biggest change from 1979 to 2001 is that an interest in the textualization of oral tradition, and even with an intertextual "unity" of the book, had overtaken the field.[70]

As in the discussion of Chronicles in 1979, in *Isaiah*, midrash (or something akin) is an acknowledged dynamic in the shaping of the tradition. Yet with newfound clarity the function of inner-biblical citation in Third Isaiah is said to be *deictic*, not midrashic. The *schriftgelehrte Prophetie* he sees is not primarily oriented to the textual. Instead, it testifies to "an encounter with actual

---

64 Ibid., 373, cf. 362. On Seeligmann's influence see section B.I in the next chapter.

65 Ibid., 375.

66 Ibid., 376.

67 Ibid., 377.

68 What kind of reader is involved can make a difference to what gets interpreted, and who. For a recent New Testament perspective compare Bockmuehl, *Seeing*.

69 *Isaiah*, 228, cf. 3.

70 This is partcularly true of work on later parts of Isaiah. See Steck, *Tritojesaja*, as well as the criticism of Steck in Lau, *Schriftgelehrte Prophetie*. An important precursor of this trend is Barth, *Jesaja-Worte*, esp. 305–309. Childs himself is most energized by Beuken's four volume commentary on Isaiah 40–66 (in Dutch). On Isaiah 33, it is suggested, Beuken rivals Gunkel (*Isaiah*, 245). Sommer, *A Prophet Reads*, also deserves mention, particularly because he is so careful to distinguish intertextuality (as synchronic reading) from allusion (willful reference). That Childs blurs the difference will trouble some readers just as his willingness to move ahead "irrespective of intentionality" (*Introduction to the OT*, 79) did from 1979. See the long history of debate about intention in Childs, discussed in chapter two.

historical realities, albeit seen in the light of the divine. This dimension dare not be flattened simply into a type of learned scribal activity dealing exclusively with literary texts."[71] Intentional intertextuality in Third Isaiah "is deictic — that is, pointing, identifying — rather than midrashic."[72] Childs' interpretation of the evidence accommodates his emphasis on scripture's *res*, *Sache*, or subject matter. Canonical shaping is central to the coercive force Isaiah acquires; its text becomes the indispensable vehicle by which its message pressures the church (and synagogue, now more more mysteriously) and in each generation of faith brokers fresh encounters with the One God.

C. Canonical Intertextuality and Christian Figural Reading

Does canonical intertextuality have anything to do with figural reading? Steins evidently thinks not. Intertextuality in his proposal for *kanonisch-intertextuelle Lektüre* is a surrogate for "sehr enge traditionelle" means of connecting biblical texts such as "Analogie," "Exempel," "Typologie" and "Überbietung," old tools one should not handle again without serious methodological reflection on the hermeneutics of the canon.[73] Like the call for sophisticated theory, this displacement of figuration by intertextuality may go back to Lohfink. In the same place where the need for theory is said to be pressing Lohfink writes, "Wie eine entsprechende theoretische Hermeneutik aussehen würde, wäre erst Schritt für Schritt zu erarbeiten. Ich kenne keine vorhandenen Theorien, die diesem Ansatz entsprechen und zugleich auf exegetischer Erfahrung aufruhen würden. Im Endeffekt hatte wohl auch die Theorie vom mehrfachen Schriftsinn nicht genügend Atem."[74] These are almost off-hand remarks. To my knowledge neither Lohfink nor Steins sảy why intertextuality must now be the alternative to multiple senses in biblical exegesis, or why the traditional strategy proves to have insufficient breath.[75]

Childs differs. Astoundingly, his article-length response to *Bindung* posits two *figural* modes of intertextuality, one midrashic, the other allegorical. "The differences between the two interpretive approaches greatly affect how one understands the role of intertextuality within the Bible. My aim is to argue that much exegetical and theological confusion arises when the distinction between the two approaches is not recognized."[76] He refers briefly to Jewish scholarship showing midrash to have "a highly developed understanding of

---

[71] *Isaiah*, 462.

[72] Ibid., 445, cf. 442, 479.

[73] Steins, *Bindung*, 128.

[74] Lohfink, Eine Bibel, 80.

[75] But cf. Dohmen, Vom vielfachen Schriftsinn, 16–26, 29–30, 59, 61, 66–67. Note that Steins, then as Dohmen's assistant, compiled the bibliography.

[76] Childs, Critique, 183.

intertextual referentiality,"[77] and then contends that Christian intertextuality is a subset of allegory. Moreover, both modes trade on divergent understandings of biblical reference:

> midrash and allegory, in spite of large areas of overlap, are two very distinct and different interpretive strategies, reflecting very different hermeneutical understandings of how intertextuality functions. While midrash works at discerning meaning through the interaction of two written texts, allegory — I am using the term in its broadest sense — finds meaning by moving to another level beyond the textual. It seeks to discern meaning by relating it referentially to a substance (*res*), a rule of faith, or a hidden eschatological event. Christian exegetical use of intertextuality moves along a trajectory between promise and fulfillment within a larger christological structure.[78]

Steins' work on Genesis 22 (and with it, allegedly, the exegesis of Moberly)[79] fails to account for the unique way intertextuality operates in a Christian setting. It is not that allegory is innately superior to midrash, but that allegory has been more central in traditional Christian theology for good reason.

This is not quite the place to unpack differences in Jewish and Christian figuration on Childs' understanding — for that see chapters six and seven, respectively — although we have just seen that *Isaiah* makes room for an affirmation of proto-midrash in the post-exilic period while also charging that intertextual reference in Third Isaiah is deictic more than midrashic. Maybe to Childs the prophetic book's shaping leaves a warrant for both techniques. For now, let me address this more limited intra-Christian debate about figuration (if that is what it is), in which it is useful to turn again to Frei. On the question "is canonical intertextuality figural?" Frei stands much closer to Childs than Steins. Why, then, after Steins and Moberly in the 2003 "Critique of Recent Intertextual Canonical Interpretation," is Frei's the third name adduced of persons having "moved in a direction which for Christian theology can only end in confusion"?[80]

In his final essay (2005) Childs endorses a modification to Frei's thesis in *Eclipse*. For Neil MacDonald, Frei's characterization of the literal sense in precritical exegesis is correct, but his description of its transformation under the pressure of the Enlightenment is better described as an epistemic shift than a change in the way biblical narrative is read. Formerly basic beliefs became non-basic beliefs in the critical era.[81] But Childs' depiction of the literal sense

---

[77] Ibid., 181.

[78] Ibid., 182–183.

[79] Ironically, Moberly is the person Steins criticizes for reverting to "enge traditionelle" categories, above. Cf. Moberly, Akedah; idem, Key; and now, idem, *Bible, Theology, Faith*.

[80] Childs, Critique, 184. Compare the quote at footnote 12, above.

[81] It was a change "from a 'faith seeking understanding' paradigm to what may be termed a 'faith requiring justification' one" (MacDonald, Illocutionary, 324). The piece is referenced in Childs, Speech-act, 384. I myself am not persuaded that MacDonald's analysis of *Eclipse* does full justice to the problem, or that his emendation works as a simple overlay.

and its attenuation after the Reformation period aligns very closely with Frei's, and *Eclipse* augurs the recovery of figural extensions of the literal sense that Childs will incline toward more and more in the latter part of his career. In addition to Childs' remarks at the 1969 Barth colloquium (recall section A.II in chapter three), compare Frei's statement from 1974:

> the confusion of history-likeness (literal meaning) and history (ostensive reference), and the *hermeneutical reduction of the former to an aspect of the latter*, meant that one lacked the distinctive category and the appropriate interpretive procedure for understanding what one had actually recognized: the high significance of the literal, narrative shape of the stories for their meaning. And so, one might add, it has by and large remained ever since.[82]

with Childs' statement from 1972:

> I am convinced that when the Reformers spoke of the literal sense of the Biblical text as normative (*sensus literalis*) they had in mind the canonical sense and not a hypothetical projection of what scholars thought originally happened.[83]

and from 1977:

> The impact of the new approach which drove a wedge between the biblical text and its reference brought an immediate and profound effect on the interpretation of the *sensus literalis*. Among the Reformers the identity of the literal and historical sense had been assumed and the terms *sensus literalis* and *sensus historicus* were often interchanged. In the new approach the identity of the terms was also continued, but the historical sense now determined its content. The historical sense was construed as being the *original* meaning of the text as it emerged in its pristine situation.[84]

as well as from 2000:

> The distinction between the so-called literal sense and the figurative/allegorical cannot correctly be defined in terms of historicity... Rather, the heart of the problem of allegory turns on the nature of referentiality of the biblical text.[85]

Here again we come to the heart of the matter, where there is real overlap with Frei's critique of meaning-as-reference and of the restriction of literal meaning to ostensive reference. Frei's analysis underpins the figural proposals of Frei and Childs alike, different as these may be in theory and execution. To quote *Eclipse* again, "As the realistic narrative reading of the biblical stories broke down, literal or verbal and historical meaning were severed and literal and figural interpretation, hitherto naturally affiliated procedures, also came apart. Figural reading had been literalism extended to the whole story *or* the unitary canon containing it. But now figural sense came to be something like the opposite of literal sense."[86] It seems to me that the "or" between story and

---

[82] Frei, *Eclipse*, 12, my emphasis.
[83] Childs, OT Scripture of the Church, 721.
[84] Childs, Sensus Literalis, 89.
[85] Childs, Allegory, 6–7.
[86] Frei, *Eclipse*, 6–7, my emphasis, cf. 2.

canon permits figuration to be taken in two directions. Its renewal can be predicated either on the Bible's narrative thrust, or, with a more historical view of the text's prehistory and a distinct take on its reference, on some unitive read of the Christian canon. Both strategies restore the old alliance between literal and figural meaning.

What differences exist between these alternate proposals for figural reading in a critical or post-critical age? Three, which I will state briefly with the help of John David Dawson's impressive 2002 analysis of Boyarin, Auerbach, Frei and Origen, are of special importance. An initial difference between Childs and Frei turns on the relationship of the Testaments. For Childs the relationship between Old and New is irreducibly dialectical, in different respects all related to biblical reference, but "Frei frames the relationship between the two testaments using the comprehensive category of story rather than meaning. The image, appropriate to narrative, is *linear rather than vertical*."[87] A second difference is closely related. Christian appropriation of the literal sense is distinguished from the foundational place of the *peshat* in Jewish midrash for both Childs and Frei, though on dissimilar grounds. For Frei, instead of narrowly concentrating on individual words, the literal sense in Christian theology is caught up into a wider narratological or storied universe.[88] In that context the gospel's literal sense fitly renders Jesus Christ while yet preserving His unique identity. For Childs, Jewish exposition in midrash centers on text-text relations, whereas Christian biblical theology demands text-*res* relations. Canon has a historical, horizontal dimension, yet the vertical dimension is paramount as it gives the horizontal its distinctive profile. Third, Childs parts company with Frei on whether or not figuration is to be distinguished from allegory. Because of a close reliance on Auerbach's account of figural reading, Frei perceives allegory as "a fundamental threat to the form of figural interpretation he wants to advance."[89] Though "history" is a proximate concern to Frei, this move is a holdover from the desire to protect history that marked a short-lived movement to recover figural reading earlier in the twentieth century. Childs develops a proposal for Christian figural reading that rejects this strained distinction and in the end is happy to live with the consequences — "call it allegory" he concedes in 2004.[90] When Frei says of the *sensus literalis* that "the *descriptive* function of language and its conceptual adequacy are shown forth precisely in the kind of story that does not refer beyond itself for its meaning, as allegory does, the kind of story in which the 'signified,' the identity of the protagonist, is enacted by the signifier, the narrative sequence

---

[87] Dawson, *Christian Figural Reading*, 164, my emphasis.

[88] Ibid., 171–172. Cf. Frei, *Types*, 123–124 and idem, Literal, 73–74.

[89] Dawson, *Christian Figural Reading*, 186, cf. 183–183. Cf. Frei, *Theology*, 168–169; cf. also Auerbach, Figura and idem, *Mimesis*.

[90] *Struggle*, x. The decision is informed by research into allegory's historic deployment.

itself,"[91] Childs simply cannot agree. In precisely this sense there remains a purpose for Christian allegory.

The peace Childs eventually makes with allegory will be explored later. Meanwhile, I close with four suggestions about literal biblical reference and Christian figural reading. First, we have seen that Karl Barth is a middle term for Childs and Frei, even though they disagree early on about the hermeneutical implications of Barth's theology. It is impossible here to settle the question of where Barth comes down on literal reference — on Childs' side, or Frei's, or neither. Yet in an essay dedicated to Frei, George Hunsinger appears to suggest that Childs comes closer to Barth's conception.

> In his actual exegetical or hermeneutical practice, Barth sought to be guided by the *sensus literalis* in the sense that he did not find the meaning of the text in a subject matter accessible independently of the text. His reading of scripture led him to assume a fittingness in the relationship between signifier and signified, that is, between textual depiction and intratextual as well as extratextual subject matter. However, *intratextuality was, for Barth,* never an end in itself, but was rather *the bearer of extratextual semantic force.* Intratextuality without extratextuality would merely aestheticize the subject matter.[92]

On this reading Barth presses beyond literalism and expressivism, by means of analogy, such that scripture's reference is truthful, extratextual, and a matter of exegesis. God is utterly different from us, other, and yet mysteriously the text's witness to the divine referent is somehow not other than the meaning of the biblical sentence itself.

Second, a critical point of contact between Childs and Frei remains. It is scripture's capacity to order the lives of its readers, or in Frei's language to "fitly render" the addressee: "Through the coincidence or even identity between a world being depicted and its reality being rendered to the reader (always under the form of depiction), the reader or hearer in turn becomes part of that depicted reality and thus has to take a personal or life stance toward it."[93] Childs does not think we can make the same identification of subjects within the text's compass — historical, vertical, doctrinal, applicative — that Calvin made. (As a matter of fact he critiques Calvin for defining the *sensus literalis* too broadly, as will be seen.) But he agrees that the biblical text, in its received shape, is an instrument without which Christian faith languishes. The two testament canon properly rules the life of the church. With similar reasoning Seitz, who writes of figuration and the eclipse of biblical prophecy,[94] emphasizes the antique notion of *providence*. If the Bible addresses or even renders history ordered by a providential hand, its readership may in the end require some brand of figuration. "The challenge of our day is how to see in Jesus'

---

[91] Frei, *Theology*, 112, cited Dawson, *Christian Figural Reading*, 172.

[92] Hunsinger, Beyond Literalism, 221n8, my emphasis.

[93] Frei, *Eclipse*, 24.

[94] Seitz, *Prophecy and Hermeneutics*, 75.

death and raising actions truly in accordance with the scriptures of Israel. For that, we shall need to return to typological and figural senses once more keenly available in the church's handling of the 'literal sense,' before such a sense was conflated with the 'historical sense.'"[95] Seitz's intricate fusion of Childs and Frei serves as a reminder of all that they share.

Third, as can readily be seen, this literal sense has a christological face. How today can one see Jesus "truly in accordance with the scriptures of Israel," as Seitz has it? When Childs speaks of "a family resemblance of faith throughout the ages" in *Isaiah*, he has in mind the book's shaping *in* its effects. He senses a "coercion of the text … shaping the life of the church" that he will soon present in great detail, in *The Struggle to Understand Isaiah as Christian Scripture* (a well-chosen title). He can only anticipate in 2001: "In search of this goal, the voices of the great Christian interpreters — Chrysostom, Augustine, Thomas, Luther, Calvin — remain an enduring guide for truthfully hearing the *evangelical* witness of Isaiah in a manner seldom encountered since the Enlightenment."[96] In general terms, the underpinnings of this new direction had already been set in *Biblical Theology* (think, again, of Rendtorff's bewilderment) where we can see the most basic and provocative sense in which intertextuality is not midrashic (horizontal) but deictic (vertical) — hence allegorical — as well as the dynamic Person (choirmaster?) who makes canon generative: because "the text itself is not the generative force of truth. Rather, through the Spirit the reality to which the text points, namely to Jesus Christ, is made active in constantly fresh forms of application."[97] There is some equivocation here on what Childs claims is seen on either side of the canonical boundary that for him is quite fixed, between text and commentary, between us and the prophets and apostles. "The church's continual struggle in understanding the literal sense of the text as providing the biblical grounds for its testimony arises in large measure from its canonical consciousness." The *church's* canonical consciousness? Had not "the original tradents" sensed this in the first instance? Then again, to run analogy in reverse — if OT authors and editors respond to "the Spirit," and bear witness to "a hidden eschatological event" — some fuzziness seems inevitable. In any event, Childs makes it "a basic Christian confession that all scripture bears testimony to Jesus Christ. In this sense, there is a single, unified voice in scripture."[98] Christological unity turns on a dialectic, though, that he later says "is simply an effort to maintain the tension between the divine and human interaction essential to Scripture's function in the church."[99]

---

[95] Idem, *Figured Out*, 47.

[96] *Isaiah*, 5, my emphasis. See the first part of the quotation at footnote 62, above.

[97] *Biblical Theology*, 724.

[98] Ibid., 725. Note that the unity is not a common denominator of the voices but "is more like a ship's compass, fixing on a single goal, in spite of the many and various ways of God (Heb. 1.1), toward which the believer is drawn" (ibid.). Cf. *Pauline Corpus*, 26.

[99] *Pauline Corpus*, 16.

Finally, it will be even more obvious that this take on the literal sense, as the church's one pointer to the *res*, Christ, according to a rule of faith called canon, makes it impossible for many to accept Childs' hermeneutic — including some Christians. It seems especially to exclude Jews. Since Childs derives his insight about a *Kanonbewußtsein* deep in the Hebrew Bible's formation from a Jewish scholar, even from a meditation on the character of midrash, since he further refines his thought in dialogue with Jewish scholarship and reception history, it is necessary to say a bit more about the inner logic of scripture's textual authority. This brings us to the second major shift in Childs' thought, one that impinges on his problematically vague refrain "community of faith." What is midrash, actually?[100] Working out an answer to this question brings Childs face to face with a profound theological mystery.

[100] I am fully aware that "intertextuality" and "midrash" are problematic terms due to the great variety of ways they are understood and used. My usage of both aims to keep close to my primary subject. I do not intend to define these terms for general use; rather, I will have succeeded if I can show how they function in Childs' thought and also keep from doing great injustice to the thought of his interlocutors.

CHAPTER 6

Canon and Midrash: Confronting the "Mystery of Israel"

Könnte es nicht sein, dass das Kanonverständnis von der 'ganzen Schrift' her, deren Kanonizität die christliche Gemeinde bejaht, nicht unwesentliche Modifikationen erfährt? — Walther Zimmerli

Only within the limited area of the smaller literary and historical contexts is an ecumenical biblical theology possible, and only as awareness grows of the difference that context makes shall we understand where agreement is possible and where it is not, and why. — Jon Levenson

Long before he had begun to think in terms of biblical "intertextuality," Childs' waning confidence in the prioritization of orality over textuality in tradition-historical research led him to reconsider the status of midrash. Just to hold the textualization of oral tradition in regard was something of a breakthrough. Gunkel felt it was "to Wellhausen's undying credit" to have exposed the "character" of P,[1] and he almost certainly would have agreed that Wellhausen got the true measure of the Chronicler as well, whose midrashic activity confirms his as the age of the scribes. "Midrash," Wellhausen concludes,

> is the consequence of the conservation of all the relics of antiquity, a wholly peculiar artificial reawakening of dry bones, especially by literary means, as is shown by the preference for lists of names and numbers. Like ivy it overspreads the dead trunk with extraneous life, blending old and new in a strange combination. It is a high estimate of tradition [*Hochschätzung der Überlieferung*] that leads to its being thus modernised; but in the process it is twisted and perverted, and set off with foreign accretions in the most arbitrary way... Within this sphere, wherein all Judaism moves, Chronicles also has had its rise. Thus whether one says Chronicles or Midrash of the Book of Kings is on the whole a matter of perfect indifference; they are children of the same mother, and indistinguishable in spirit and language, while on the other hand the portions which have been retained verbatim from the canonical Book of Kings at once betray themselves in both respects.[2]

Childs' last major form critical study (in the traditional sense), *Isaiah and the Assyrian Crisis* (1967), evaluates diverse biblical accounts of the invasion of 701, including three in II Kings 18–19 (A, B^1, B^2) and the Chronicler's harmo-

---

[1] Gunkel, *Genesis*, lxxx = xciii.

[2] Wellhausen and Smith, *History of Israel*, 227 = idem, *Geschichte Israels*, 223.

nization of these traditions in II Chronicles 32. Childs finds that Wellhausen's characterization of the latter "has wrought much havoc,"[3] and he gives an alternative account of what he is content to call "the midrash of the Chronicler" on Kings.[4] Not unlike B^2, Chronicles presents an idealized piety. Hezekiah is "a model of faith in God."[5] But the designation "legend" does not adequately describe the later portrait because the text does not rework *oral* tradition:

> A basic characteristic of the account is its dependence upon *written* sources. This is not to suggest that the Chronicler's only source was Kings… Rather, the point being argued is that the compiler of II Chron. 32 had the Kings account available to him as a written source. The thesis of an alleged reference to temple records, which were independent of the book of Kings in its Dtr. redaction does not do justice to the Chronicler's text. This dependence on a written source at once distinguishes the Chronicler's account from those of Kings. Both B^1 and B^2 were dependent on *oral* tradition which they then reworked in different ways.[6]

This distinction is what makes it appropriate to speak of midrash in the Chronicler's case. "By midrash we mean a specific form of literature which is the product of an exegetical activity by a circle of scholars interpreting a sacred text. Essential to the midrash is an attempt to elucidate a written source."[7] It would not be wrong to speak of *Schriftgelehrten*, but the sphere and spirit of their activity must not be distorted. Are they really epigones? At stake is the quality and religious/theological significance of their exegetical activity.

Childs will refine this emphasis on the textualization of oral tradition with a theological point about the authoritative form in which scripture functions: he will speak of scripture's textual authority. All the work that follows *Assyrian Crisis* reinforces the historical and incipiently canon-theological analysis there. As he will write in 1990, "If in early Israel the transmission and actualization of Israel's sacred tradition occurred in the context of the cult, increasingly in the late pre-exilic and post-exilic periods Israel's tradition was given a written form and transmitted by scribal schools… There was a growing tendency toward the textualization of the tradition."[8] Once it emerges this insight always remains part of the bedrock of Childs' ruled approach.

Early in its development, however, Childs' work toward a rehabilitation of canon was more closely allied with midrash (so called) than it would be in time. Footnoted in 1967 is I. L. Seeligmann's seminal "Voraussetzungen der Midraschexegese," from which Childs will borrow the term *Kanonbewußtsein* for the "canon conscious" exegesis in scripture found in Chronicles and else-

---

[3] *Assyrian Crisis*, 107n4. The passage stayed with Childs. He mentions it in 1996 (Childs, Retrospective Reading, 370) along with a few of Wellhausen's latter-day manifestations.

[4] *Assyrian Crisis*, 121.

[5] Ibid., 106.

[6] Ibid., 106, my emphasis.

[7] Ibid., 107.

[8] Childs, Generation, 360.

where. Childs adapts the concept for his own purposes, eventually pursuing its outworking across the entire Christian Bible, OT and NT, but at first it is not clear that there will be any substantial departure from Seeligmann. In 1972 Childs defends "a form-critical understanding of midrash" and argues on that basis for significant parallels between the Tannaite and Old Testament periods.[9] He adjudicates the work on midrash first cited in 1967 — S. Sandmel fails to distinguish the direct literary dependency of parallels from material that simply shares an oral tradition (e.g., Gen 12 and 20), and so casts too broad a net for midrash; A. G. Wright, on the other hand, defines midrash so narrowly that he cannot connect a description of its known form with its function, which was to "actualize" a canonical text in a new situation (ideally the text will also exegete the present) — evidently agreeing with Seeligmann, against Sandmel and Wright, that to study inner-biblical midrash is

> to trace the forces which were exerted on the interpretation of the Bible by what has aptly been described as "the consciousness of canon." Whereas Gunkel and his school felt that such institutions as cult in early Israel were the dominant sources for the tradition-building process, it is becoming increasingly clear that the formation of a sense of authoritative Scripture unleashed another set of forces which then tended to operate according to laws quite distinct from those at work in the development of oral tradition. The study of the development of midrash should be significant in attempting to describe the nature and impact of these new factors on the composition of the Bible.[10]

Again, "midrash is, above all, an interpretation of a canonical *text* within the context and for the religious purposes of a community."[11] And in fact Seeligmann and Childs partake in a mid-twentieth century consensus about the cardinal difference between oral as versus textual stages of tradition,[12] even when language of a "set of forces" that was "unleashed" by Israel's late use of scripture distinctly anticipates Childs' more mature formulations.

Along with standard form critical assumptions in favor of orality, another once pervasive view quickly unravels in the 1970s. Wellhausen's disparagement of midrash, as ivy over a dead tree, will cease to be the default. In *BTh in Crisis* Childs assumes that "a midrashic approach ... is foreign to the present critical

---

[9] Childs, Midrash, 52. He concludes, "Although the early biblical parallels to full-blown rabbinic midrash are often only remotely connected, there is enough similarity between the two to speak of proto-midrashic forms within the Old Testament" (58). Still, Childs is leery of finding midrash too early in the Old Testament. The year before he criticizes the "tendency among some scholars to project the midrashic method back into the pre-exilic period without adequate discrimination" (Childs, Psalm Titles, 149).

[10] Childs, Midrash, 53.

[11] Ibid., 49. Chronicles' relationship to Kings is plied as a test case for both Sandmel and Wright.

[12] E.g., Genesis 12, 20 and 26 remain at an oral stage: Seeligmann, Midraschexegese, 153. The older consensus was seriously challenged by Thompson, *Historicity* and especially Van Seters, *Abraham*, in 1974 and 1975.

age,"[13] and in 1971, in another significant interaction with Seeligmann, thinks that "[o]bviously there can be no direct adaptation of the midrashic method."[14] He is interested in the hermeneutical implications of inner-biblical exegesis, wants to defend it against the likes of Wellhausen,[15] but he does not imagine that critical scholars could propose a revival of the paradigm. From 1972, however, James Sanders would make the positive value of midrash in Christian exegesis of the Old Testament contested territory for Childs.[16]

Once the possibility is suggested it will remain true for Childs that there can be no direct application of midrash today, in the modified sense that the method *ought* not be employed in Christian exegesis. Sanders helps prompt shifts in Childs' terminology, from midrash to "canonical shaping" (and from "criticism" to "approach"),[17] but this is not the major turn in Childs' understanding of the "mystery of Israel" to which I have alluded. Much like von Rad or Gese, Sanders' proposal is typically handled as part of an in-house debate about the nature of Christian scripture. In point of fact, in 1971 Childs believes his study of midrash points to an *alternative* to the tradition-historical school with respect to the relationship of OT and NT:

> midrashic interpretation offers a pattern of exegesis which differs fundamentally from the prophecy-fulfilment pattern exploited by von Rad and others. A theological analogy is directed not primarily to the typological unfolding of a future-oriented tradition, but rather to the exploring of an area which has been staked out by means of a sacred text. History has retained its importance, but in the transformed state of being canonical history.[18]

Like Gunkel, if to a lesser extent, von Rad does not reckon with the full significance of the tradition's movement away from cultic contexts to its textualized, scriptural context. It is only that after Sanders (1972), glossing the new emphasis on textuality as "midrash" becomes a bit more problematic when one wants to distinguish it from the previous generation's hermeneutical commitments to tradition-historical actualization (*Vergegenwärtigung*).

As *BTh in Crisis* labors to articulate in 1970, one year before von Rad died, Childs aims to provide a better foundation for Jewish-Christian dialogue than

---

[13] *BTh in Crisis*, 117.

[14] Childs, Psalm Titles, 149.

[15] Ibid., 149: "midrashic — or proto-midrashic — exegesis is not some post-biblical 'Jewish distortion,' but part of the biblical tradition itself, and must be taken seriously as such." As in *Assyrian Crisis*, the call is to a fair and neutral description: "Categories such as annal, legend, midrash should carry no theological bias, whether positive or negative" (124).

[16] Sanders, *Torah and Canon*, followed by idem, Adaptable.

[17] In fact "canonical shape" occurs early, too, in *Exodus*, and at least once in *BTh in Crisis*: "Historically Judaism was the bearer of the Old Testament traditions and the instrument through which the traditions received their first canonical shape" (121). This is an indication that the terminological adjustment away from "midrash" in the 1970s does not reflect a substantive change in Childs' position.

[18] Childs, Psalm Titles, 150.

tradition history, one that maintains both Christian and Jewish distinctives by holding them in tension. Recognizing that the OT has more than a Christian faith context, the Christian exegete "is made aware of the fact that the Old Testament does not 'naturally' unfold into the New Testament. It does not lean toward the New Testament, but the Christian interpretation within its new context is fully dependent on the radically new element in Jesus Christ." That Jewish interpretation often goes in a different direction reminds Christians of the extent to which the Old is transformed by the New, and yet the need for "dialogue with Judaism in relation to a common text" confronts the church with "the mystery of Israel."[19] Still the "offense" of the New Testament, which "lays claim to the Scriptures of Israel and hears in them testimony to the rejected Messiah of God,"[20] remains vital to Christian hope in the Triune God. Right from the beginning, then, Childs' study of midrash in the Old Testament challenges von Rad's belief that Israel's history and its scriptures "thrust violently forward" into the New. With respect to Jewish scripture another set of post-biblical literature appears every bit as inevitable.[21]

All these basic points — the re-prioritization of textual over oral transmission in the formation of Jewish scripture, a consequently higher regard for midrash (proper or emergent) than had been the case among critical OT scholars for most of the twentieth century, the radical and transformative newness of God's self-revelation in Christ attested in the NT — all remain stable commitments in Childs' work from 1970. After turning form criticism upside down in the late 1960s (chapter four), the second monumental shift in Childs' thought turns on the precise nature of the relationship of the two testaments of the Christian Bible, and specifically *in the bearing of this relationship on the church's relationship to the synagogue.* It has weighty implications for Jewish-Christian dialogue and is reflected in the kind of figuralism Childs embraces. It has everything to do with what he means by a "transformed" Old Testament.

---

[19] *BTh in Crisis*, 122.

[20] *BTh in Crisis*, 218. Note that sheerly as a matter of historical description in 1970, the church "employed different exegetical skills" than the synagogue in that "allegory and typology replaced midrash" (106). But now see the developments described below, in chapter six.

[21] Now compare Seitz, *Prophecy and Hermeneutics* (footnote 136 in chapter four). As Seitz puts it in another context, "It remains meaningful that the terms 'Old Testament' and 'Tanak' are *both* postbiblical terms. Both require a commitment to a subsequent theological literature. Neither goes straightforwardly back to the scriptures of Israel without argument and defense" (*Figured Out*, 43). The implications for Jewish-Christian dialog pertain to the "common text" Childs affirms in 1970. The way Seitz comes to frame the issue in 2001 also affirms a Childsian critique of von Rad: "Old is to New Testament not as Tanak is to Talmud. Instead, the concept of a literary canon, based on a covenantal relationship, is extended to a secondary, literarily distinctive deposit whose formation and rationale is developed on analogy to the first, with a new covenantal relationship at its heart. The testaments are, of course, different, and they bear witness to the one subject matter of them both, in different ways. 'Tanak to Talmud' may actually be more akin to what Gese means by 'tradition-history,' strictly speaking" (ibid.).

And it happens somewhere in the early 1980s, after he sets aside major work on the OT to devote himself to broad study of the NT, and thus is fully represented in his *Biblical Theology*. For a time Childs remains open to the idea that the NT is a kind of (proto-)midrash on the OT, granting that it will sometimes make moves very unlike midrash proper.[22] But this outlook changes. To pose the turn as starkly possible, an assumption Childs makes easily in 1970 — "the New Testament's reading of one Old Testament passage through the perspective of another text ... is a typical midrashic technique"[23] — stands in dramatic contrast to this statement from 1988: "Das Neue Testament ist kein Midrasch zum Alten Testament"![24] The burden of the present chapter is to account for this reversal. Because the decision for canon *against* midrash is controversial on many fronts, I will first air a number of major objections.

A. Why Canon over Midrash?

Despite superficial similarities between Sanders and Childs, it is proper to distinguish "canonical criticism" from a "canonical approach" already on the basis of the way each defines the relationship of the Christian Bible's two testaments. Sanders: "Canonical criticism, for the Christian, sees the Bible in terms of Scripture, not primarily in terms of testaments." The attendant view that "Scripture has its proper *Sitz im Leben* in the believing communities which are today's heirs of those who formed and shaped it in antiquity" allows scripture to have a place in the church, which allied with the paradigm seen through comparative midrash provides for the dynamic adaptation of tradition to changing social circumstances.[25] This is the inverse of Childs' position that "a force was unleashed by Israel's religious use of her traditions which exerted an influence on the shaping of the literature" with the result that "canon formed the decisive *Sitz im Leben* for the Jewish community's life."[26] Theologically speaking the community is located in the book, not the reverse.

Childs concludes a late (2005) critique of Sanders' hermeneutics this way: "I would further argue that the role of Jewish midrash which is central to Sanders' hermeneutical proposal is incompatible with the New Testament's understanding of the authoritative function of the Old Testament, which has been continually transformed by the Spirit into the law of Christ."[27] This is an

---

[22] E.g., Moses' slaying of an Egyptian in Exodus 2 is read in Acts 7 as a "pattern of unbelief." Moses becomes a type of the rejected Christ, a negative analogy "that would be unthinkable for the midrash" (*BTh in Crisis*, 175, cf. 168–171).

[23] *BTh in Crisis*, 116.

[24] Childs, Biblische Theologie, 22.

[25] Sanders, *Canon and Community*, 69.

[26] *Introduction to the OT*, 78, cf. *Biblical Theology*, 70–71. See chapter four, above.

[27] Childs, Reflections on an Era, 34.

extraordinarily complex claim, and sure to provoke disagreement. On Childs' definition of canon, as established testament rather than as flexible scripture, why should he decide for the rule of canon over the dynamics of midrash (perhaps as a monotheizing process), especially when something like proto-midrash is seen in the formation of the Hebrew Bible itself?

I. Five Objections

The following list is not meant to be exhaustive. It *is* meant to evoke Aquinas.

Objection 1

Childs does not make a reasonable decision at all but changes his mind at whim. Barr states, "I have spoken as if canonical criticism [sic] is one united position, but of course it is not: it is more like a current of opinions running in roughly the same direction and containing certain recognizable elements of agreement as well as many differences."[28] Barr is not drawing a contrast between the proposals of Childs as versus Sanders. This is Childs all on his own, and it is incoherence.

> The *Introduction*, discussing the titles or superscriptions of the Psalms, says that these remove the Psalms from their older cultic context; … they move the emphasis to the inner life of the Psalmist and give an access to his emotional life. 'Far from tying these hymns to the ancient past, they have been contemporized and individualized for every generation of suffering and persecuted Israel.' But Childs himself had published, a decade earlier, an excellent study on these same titles… But this very fine article contains very little, in its more technical and detailed analysis, that can be said to foreshadow or justify the interpretation offered in the *Introduction*.[29]

One should not bother too much with the tension between canon and midrash because, Barr suggests, Childs simply drops midrash in later work without any discernible rationale.

Objection 2

Further, canon is a poor controlling concept because its meaning is too diffuse. "The endless repetition of the word 'canon' in canonical criticism is not accident, but necessity: for, as seen from without, the continual reuse of this word is necessary in order to hold together sets of arguments which would otherwise fall apart."[30] Frankly, midrash would not likely serve any better in this respect since its usage, too, is beset with imprecision. Probably we ought to be searching for another hermeneutical paradigm altogether. Barr, joined by Barton, recommends "criticism" (see chapter seven). Criticism provides the stage

[28] Barr, *Holy Scripture*, 152–153.

[29] Ibid., 155–156, citing *Introduction to the OT*, 521 and Childs, Psalm Titles.

[30] Barr, *Holy Scripture*, 147.

from which Nicholson, in like manner, can look beyond the canon's final form to see what von Rad sees, "a long process of reflection, debate, and not infrequently controversy in the history of the community of faith."[31] One does not want to "foreshorten" this in the name of canon or anything else.

Objection 3

Alternately, we should disallow canon in Childs' sense because midrash, or the flexibility inherent in scriptural tradition, is the operative paradigm. Sanders' theology of canon is to be preferred because there is no consciousness of a *closed* canon (a "list") deep within the formation of the literature. As Sanders and Lee McDonald have it, "With such a long delay in the church's use of the term 'canon' to describe a closed body of Christian scriptures, one may well ask why there was an emergence of 'canon consciousness' in the church of the fourth century C.E. and little evidence of it before?"[32] Or in Eugene Ulrich's words, being clear about the meaning of canon is important, but "the definition of canon is a relatively minor matter. Much more important, interesting, and ripe for analysis is the canonical process — the historical development by which the oral and written literature of Israel, Judaism, and the early church was handed on, revised, and transformed into the scriptures that we have received, as well as the processes and criteria by which the various decisions were made."[33] A "consciousness of canon" is coterminous with the first appearance of lists of canonical books, well into the Common Era, and the fluid state of affairs the notion of a canon belies constitutes the proper locus of attention, scholarly or religious.

Objection 4

Even if one accepts something like Childs' notion of canon, it is an error to speak of a "transformed" Old Testament because of the theological imperative for Jewish-Christian dialogue that arises from a Christian affirmation of Jewish scripture in its canon. "It is of crucial significance that the church maintained Israel's Bible unchanged," insists Rendtorff.[34] And in this the church ought to perceive "an essential element of continuity between the Old and the New Testaments."[35] There are ways of reading both testaments as a unity, but one has to avoid making the OT a *Christuszeugnis* on its own, which is what Childs' position entails. Instead of affirming a testament "continually transformed by

---

[31] Nicholson, *Pentateuch*, 268, cited at footnote 128 in chapter four, above.

[32] McDonald and Sanders, eds., *Canon Debate*, 13, my emphasis. Childs borrows *Kanonbewußtsein* from I. L. Seeligmann but is responsible for bringing it into wider usage, especially in English.

[33] Ulrich, Canon, 33, cf. 31.

[34] Rendtorff, *Canonical HB*, 749.

[35] Ibid., 755.

the Spirit into the law of Christ," far better to strive "niemals Aussagen über das Alte Testament zu machen, die von einem Juden nicht nachvollzogen werden könnten."[36]

Advocating the history of Israelite religion rather than OT theology, Rainer Albertz takes the point further. "Je mehr es die Theologie des Alten Testaments zu ihrem Anliegen macht, das Alte Testament in Bezug auf das Neue auszulegen, um so mehr gerät sie in Gefahr, es christlich zu vereinnahmen… Die Theologie des Alten Testaments trägt somit den Keim des Antijudaismus in sich." The tendency is latent in Eichrodt or von Rad. "Die Einsicht von B.S. Childs ist wohl unausweichlich: Die Theologie des Alten Testaments ist 'essentially a Christian discipline' und darum konfessionell begrenzt. Das macht sie ungeeignet für den christlich-jüdischen Dialog."[37]

Objection 5

To identify midrash as Jewish entails, for Childs, an embrace of allegory as part of a uniquely Christian intertextual reading strategy. Allegory and not midrash is how the church addresses the unity of its two testaments. Even granting this as possibility, though, how can Childs be sure he knows the difference between allegory and midrash, and thus know what it is he banishes from Christian exegesis? For example, he faults Moberly for identifying Moriah in Genesis 22 with Jerusalem, a move made by Jewish readers.[38] To this Moberly responds, in a letter, "Is the identification really (substantively) 'midrashic,' apart from the fact that it was most fully articulated in classic rabbinic midrash? I think not, for my argument … is *not* proposing a particular strategy of reading through the interaction of particular texts, … [but] only that [the identification with Jerusalem] is conveyed implicitly in a pregnantly allusive kind of way ('let the reader understand,' 'if you have ears to hear then hear') rather than explicitly."[39] In other words, Philo knew the value of allegory, too. Is it not the case that the line between Jewish and Christian reading is fuzzy, even in sight of the very basic differences separating committed Jewish and Christian readers of the Tanak or Old Testament?

---

[36] Rendtorff, Rezension Childs, 368.

[37] Albertz, Religionsgeschichte, 13, citing *OT Theology*, 7.

[38] Childs, Critique, 183. Cf. Moberly, *Bible, Theology, Faith*, 108–116, 177–183, 225–230.

[39] Moberly continues, "I find your point about the intrinsic logic of midrash and figuration interesting and suggestive, and I will need to think about it. But whether or not it is right, it is figuration much more than midrash that my handling of the text embodies." Personal correspondence from Moberly to Childs (11 August 2003). Unfortunately Childs' reply does not address this issue (cf. Moberly, What is Theological Interpretation?, 173n37). My thanks to Professor Moberly for supplying me with a copy of this correspondence and for granting permission to cite it.

II. Sed Contra

Some of these objections are more easily addressed than others. I have already spoken at length to shortcomings in Barr's reading of Childs (objection 1). It is hard to imagine how he fails to see the overlap between Childs' early work on midrash, in 1971 and 1972, with the argument that culminates in 1979. I will follow the development closely, below; I have also already given evidence of the way proto-midrash or canonical shaping is consistently and deliberately taken by Childs as grounds for breaking with the tradition-historical approach represented by von Rad, while yet leaving room for a composite final form with "depth dimension." His canonical history is not identical to the literary history. As for criticism's better way (objection 2), more remains to be said in the next chapter.

Objection 3 downplays Childs' argument from midrash for its own reasons, authorizing variations on tradition history that are rarely concerned with the problems presented by the affirmation ("confession") of a two testament Bible. There may be sound historical rebuttals to the dominant English-language moratorium on "canon" in the biblical period.[40] It is important to realize that theology can masquerade as history even when keeping theology's nose out of history is the official concern. In chapter one (section B, "Canon and History") I suggest that the rejection of scant dogmas of canon by some (e.g., Allert) can be equally distorting. It would almost certainly help historians whose work has theological ramifications to invite the participation of active, self-described dogmaticians. The "canon debate" needs to face this problem more directly for real debate to continue, but that is another matter.

More to the point at hand, for those who affirm a version of objection 2, doubting the viability of *canon* as a cipher for an entire approach to Christian scripture, it is notable that at least one Jewish scholar had made *midrash* into a comparable umbrella term. Midrash, writes Jacob Neusner, "stands for at least three specific things, as well as a great many things in general."[41] It is a book: "a compilation of biblical exegeses, amplifications, and compositions, as in Midrash Rabbah." It is an activity: the "explaining or applying the meaning of a biblical verse (or group of verses)." It is "*hermeneutics* of a particular kind": "people use the word *midrash* to mean the reading of one thing in terms of some other. This usage is so general as to defy concrete application."[42] Mindful of these difficulties, Neusner opts not to use the term at all, or only very rarely,

---

[40] As Chapman puts it (Canon Debate, 14), "Scholars who maintain that 'canon' only properly refers to a situation in which a scriptural collection has obtained absolute literary boundaries are inevitably forced to concede at some later point in their argument that the biblical canon has never really been completely 'closed' in an absolute sense… [W]hen did the canon finally meet with universal approval and absolute consistency? The answer is: never."

[41] Neusner, *Midrash*, xvi.

[42] Ibid., xvi.

in *Midrash in Context* (1983). But if the impression given is that a word spread thin loses its meaning, this is in fact not the case here, as Neusner's title corroborates. "Since we are able to use the same word for three things, and since, moreover, the same word is made to serve by others for many more things, I shall generally avoid the word *midrash. But I shall always mean it.*"[43] For all its overexposure and potential for misunderstanding, midrash retains enough semantic force that Neusner makes it his defining category. An analogy with Childs suggests itself at once: Childs' deployment of canon is as Neusner's of midrash. On controlling terms it is as if Childs and Neusner are opposite sides of a swivel mirror — one is concave, the other convex. The major difference is whether the focal point, canon or midrash, is in front of or behind the glass.

More difficult are the objections in 4 and 5. They come from people alive to the indispensability of canon in biblical exposition and so urge a more robustly theological debate about just how the church affirms Jewish scripture in its confession of the biblical witness — unless with Albertz one decides that all vestiges of the claim are better abandoned. It is not my intent — indeed I think it beyond my ability — to "answer" such questions in quite the same way. Some responses to Childs have been tendentious, misled or careless, bordering at times on the silly. Others have rightly marked the seriousness of what one reader calls "the great hermeneutical issues." (Usually there is a mixture.) I do not wish to fall into the trap of trivializing these issues myself, as if my purpose were to foreclose on debate by defending Childs to the bitter end. It is not. Up to now I have frequently had to say that this or that reading does not rightly see what Childs is up to, perhaps because it has not been attentive enough to the context out of which his work arises or to which it is addressed, perhaps for other reasons. The argument has reached a point at which this task must give way to an account of how Childs' thought matures, where it ventures, and the sorts of questions and problems it finally addresses and raises — to later developments little discussed in the secondary literature. (This is not quite the end of the *sed contras*, but that end draws closer.) It will take the remainder of this chapter to give a full sense of Childs' puzzling move away from midrash. Quite frankly I do not know if the move is proper or not, and I purpose simply to show it for what it is.

To anticipate, Childs' considered position, subsequent to the shift I will tease out below, includes an assumption implicit in much of his work, and to which not a few Christian exegetes would give their assent. That is: "Wenn irgendeine biblische Auslegung ihre Sichtweise nicht mehr auf den biblischen Text selbst gründen kann, sondern nur auf spätere Traditionen, dann ist dies ein Zeichen einer ernsthaften Schwäche, sowohl im Judentum als auch im

---

[43] Ibid., xvii, my emphasis. In fact the three things named here are different again to the three cited above; he refers now to a sub-taxonomy within midrash as rabbinic book.

Christentum."[44] The first part sounds at least vaguely Protestant. Is it also a point of agreement with Judaism, as claimed? In what sense might canon as a theological force obtain in Judaism as well as Christianity? To what extent do these religions really share a "common text"? Is it fair to say that the church's canonical instincts (wherever these may be) are learned or inherited from the synagogue in the first instance? The rub is that Jewish and Christian traditions hearken back to the plain sense — *peshat, sensus literalis* — of (some of) the same scriptures. A peculiar challenge for Christian faith, therefore, is to know how to hear in Israel's testament to its God the One who in time raises Jesus Christ from the dead.

The following two sections will take up such questions as they occur in Childs' work, with an eye to some known objections. Section B contextualizes the early lesson Childs draws from inner-biblical exegesis (a.k.a. midrash), describing two different roads Childs associates with midrash that from the beginning (1970) he refuses to travel. Section C explores his reconsideration of midrash in the early 1980s, including how this pushes him toward a Christian affirmation of allegory in a canonical framework. I will conclude by pointing to some implications for Jewish-Christian dialogue on the basis of the shared scriptures of Israel.

B. Two Roads Not Taken

This section will look at what Childs' gleans from Seeligmann, and then at two distinct types of "modern midrash" that Childs rejects. In some respects the types are polar opposites; one is represented by Benno Jacob, the other by James Sanders. It will then comment on the intersection of proto-midrash with the study of inner-biblical exegesis (Michael Fishbane). To set the stage, we can let Childs explain the arc of his investment in the study of midrash. I asked about it in a letter and got this reply:

> In regard to the subject of midrash, let me just repeat my own experience in the field. When I returned to America in 1954, I got a teaching job in Wisconsin at a little E&R Seminary, Mission House. After a couple of years there, I started reading midrashic texts with the local Jewish rabbi. Then in 1958, when I was called to Yale, one of the requirements was that I teach a course on Judaism, about which I knew little. So I audited Judah Goldin's seminar for four years. He was reading the Mechilta on Exodus and it was very exciting since I had started writing my own Exodus commentary. Golden was a major influence and I realized that I had to train myself in a whole new field. (In his class he only wrote Hebrew on the blackboard in the

[44] Childs, Jüdischen Kanons, 281. Some Jewish scholars would seem to agree. Leiman, *Canonization*, 14: "To an observant Jew in the 20th century, not only the Hebrew Scriptures, but the Mishnah, Talmud and halakhic codes are also canonical in that they are authoritative and serve to guide him in his daily behavior… The canonicity of the Hebrew Scripture, however, differed in kind from the canonicity of extra-biblical literature."

form of the cursive script.) So I enrolled two summers in NYC Jewish Theolog Seminary to learn Modern Hebrew and this prepared me for a sabbatical to Israel in 1963–4. I worked terribly hard to gain written and spoken Hebrew but was only partially successful. I even had private instructions in reading midrash and listened to many Hebrew classes with at best only a partial understanding. Then I began to realize that I would need a decade more work if I continued down this track. I began to reconsider. When I was at the Jewish Seminary, my roommate was Jacob (Jack) Neusner. We had many talks, but his major interest at that time was trying to relate historical criticism to traditional Jewish learnings.

After I returned from Israel, I decided that I would not pursue my study of midrash actively. Actually Goldin's influence remained important for me, but by the time Jacob Neusner's book appeared [*Midrash in Context*], I was already well out of the field. Several factors seemed to support my vocational decision. I soon discovered that Jewish scholars differed widely among themselves. Goldin and Neusner were always at odds. Neusner's understanding of the relation of *halacha* to *haggadah* was the reverse of Goldin and most of the field. I learned from Alter's work but thought he knew little of OT scholarship.

I also found that the Christian scholars who were focused on midrash were not very compatible. W. D. Davies was without theological interest. E. P. Sanders had a dubious interpretation of Paul, although it was widely accepted in NT circles (Neusner was unimpressed). Then the interest in the Dead Sea Scrolls exploded (e.g. Stendahl etc), and I did not want to go down that route.

So I only returned briefly to the subject when, for example, in my *ZAW* article of 2003, I thought that W. Moberly's understanding of intertextuality was inadequate and referred him to some of the leading Jewish scholars.[45]

For about a decade, Childs undertook to become a fully competent scholar of midrash, and though he abandons the pursuit, he retains a deep appreciation for traditional Jewish exegesis. As he states in the preface to *Exodus*, during the long period of writing "I have gone through many different stages in my own thinking. Somewhere *en route* I discovered that Calvin and Drusius, Rashi and Ibn Ezra, belong among the giants. I have tried to show why these great expositors — the term 'pre-critical' is both naïve and arrogant — need to be heard in concert with Wellhausen and Gunkel."[46] The time and energy he devotes to traditional Jewish exegesis tapers off in the latter half of his career, judging by the contents of his output. It comes to be supplanted by a more rigorous study of Christian foundations in patristic, medieval and reformation exegesis. Undoubtedly, however, luminaries from both sets of traditional exegetes keep their seats among the "giants," in Childs' estimation.

---

[45] Personal correspondence with Childs (21 November 2006). (The letter also states: "Although I remain friends of James Sanders our understanding of the field differs widely.") To this compare NT Introduction, xv: "two summers at the Jewish Theological Seminary, four years of attending Judah Goldin's midrash seminars, and a year at the Hebrew University studying midrash gave me a rich background in Jewish studies."

[46] *Exodus*, x.

I. With Seeligmann for Midrash and Kanonbewußtsein?

Childs met Isac L. Seeligmann in Jerusalem in 1963, and he first cites "Voraussetzungen der Midraschexegese" (1953) after returning to Yale from that sabbatical. The essay, as has been suggested,[47] is a singularly important precursor to Childs' argument for canonical shaping. Childs' early interaction with it already begins to realign its thesis in view of other considerations. To show how Childs makes it his own, it is appropriate to first set out the argument of Seeligmann's essay, in which the word *Kanonbewußtsein* appears exactly once.

Seeligmann wants to explore the prehistory of midrash within the Bible. More specifically, he focuses on the transition from biblical thinking into midrash ("der Übergang des biblischen Denkens in das des Midrasch"). In fact there is a double goal, "das Verhältnis darlegen zwischen den Ursprüngen der Midraschexegese und der biblischen Literatur und dadurch einen Beitrag liefern zum besseren Verständnis von beiden."[48] The preliminary remarks culminate in a summary of the transition that will be described:

> Wie erwähnen zuerst die ausserordentliche Geschmeidigkeit von Erzählung und literarischem Motiv in der Bibel, dazu das Spielelement des semitischen bzw. hebräischen Geistes, sodann eine ausgeprägte Neigung sich Gedanken und Vorstellungen, die einer fremden Umgebung oder anderen Zeit entstammen, durch Umgestaltung der eigenen Atmosphäre bzw. Epoche anzupassen, und schliesslich das Aufkommen eines Kanonbewusstseins: der wandelbare Strom der Überlieferung gerinnt und wird zum heiligen Wort; speziell der Begriff Thorah wird beladen mit einem Inhalt, der Interpretation geradezu herausfordert.[49]

The changeable currents of tradition in transmission coagulate and become Holy Scripture. What starts as a free-for-all thickens gradually as a sense of the tradition's authority takes hold, until at last interpretation breaks away from the text completely, becoming commentary in its own right. The gradation is somewhat artificial, Seeligmann acknowledges; it is not always possible to separate each stage from the next. But it has heuristic value, he insists, and it undergirds the four-part structure of his discussion.

Stage one shows great fluidity (e.g., the three variants of the ancestress in danger). Conscious wordplay does sometimes occur at this level, such as in Psalm 8:5–6 and Job 7:17–18,[50] but it is marked by the freedom which an existing theme, characteristically in *oral* tradition, can be taken up and altered for a different purpose. Stage two, Seeligmann finds, has two sub-classes of "associative meanings." One encompasses "die Doppelsinn des Wortes, Gleichklang und Wortspiel,"[51] in which emerges a new concern to explore the full

---

[47] Above, and see Sheppard, Criticism, 863–864.
[48] Seeligmann, Midraschexegese, 150–151.
[49] Ibid., 152.
[50] Ibid., 153, 156.
[51] Ibid., 157.

range of a word's meaning. Considerable play is still possible.[52] The other subclass concerns proverbs, where clauses can be combined in different contexts with very different results.[53] Stage three, adaptation, is a "völlig anderer Art" because it adds "ein Element der Bewusstheit in die Vorgänge" — a consciousness of the processes.[54] "Ein späteres Geschlecht begnügt sich nicht mit der Übernahme des alten Wortes, sondern ändert den Sinn — seltener auch den Wortlaut — desselben, um es den Denken und Fühlen einer neuen Zeit an zu passen."[55] For example, Sirach 50:26–27 (37–38) directs the language of Deuteronomy 32:21 to a contemporary referent. The foolish nation called "no people" in Deuteronomy is specified as the foolish nations in Shechem. Seeligmann calls this an instance of "proper actualizing midrash" and cites rabbinic parallels. The point is that Jewish exegesis "wurzelt im Midrasch und das Ziel des Midrasch ist, den Bibeltext zu aktualisieren, d.h. zu zeigen, dass das alte Bibelwort sich bezieht auf geschichtliche Ereignisse in der Zeit des Erklärers."[56] Finally, stage four is when true commentary comes into its own. All the interpretive ventures and tendencies discussed before this initiate exegesis, "aber noch nicht als Auslegung im eigentlichen Sinne gelten können. Das Spielelement färbt die Motivabwandlung, das Zitat wird durch Adaptation transponiert, doch betreffen all' diese Erscheinungen eine sich noch im Fluss befindliche, nicht 'geronnene,' zum Abschluss gekommene Literatur."[57] Torah becomes an entire complex, not just isolated instructions, in which pious Jews immersed themselves (Sirach 24:20, cf. Proverbs 18:7). Those responsible for the New Testament searched the prophets for deeper and deeper meaning. The psalms, through the addition of psalm titles, came to be read as aggadah.[58] Importantly, the interest here is "nicht der *äussere* Prozess der Kanonisierung,

[52] In Amos 8:2, for example, "Amos sieht Obst קיץ und das genügt dazu, bei ihm die Vorstellung des Endes קץ aufsteigen zu lassen" (ibid., 157–158). Overall "das Bewusstsein von der Mehrdeutigkeit der Worte" (159) anticipates typical maneuvers in rabbinic exegesis, such as the אל תקרי formula. Cf. Fishbane, Garments, esp. "Extra-biblical Exegesis: The Sense of Not Reading in Rabbinic Midrash," 19–32.

[53] Proverbs 13:1 reads, "A wise son loves the discipline of his father, but a scoffer לא שמע גערה does not listen to rebuke." In 13:8 by contrast, "Wealth is a ransom for a man's life, but the poor לא שמע גערה does not hear threats." Seeligmann, Midraschexegese, 163–164. The same proverb is used in divergent ways in canonical proximate contexts.

[54] Ibid., 167.

[55] Ibid., 168, my emphasis.

[56] Ibid., 170. The burden to actualize scripture becomes particularly heavy in historical periods of crisis. In addition to Seeligmann's example, the targum of Pseudo-Jonathan identifies "no people" with the Babylonians. This draws attention to the fact that what might be called adaptation does not always align texts with contemporary referents. In Pseudo-Jonathan the *past* event of Babylonian captivity is in view.

[57] Ibid., 176.

[58] Ibid., 176–180.

sondern der *Wandel im Bewusstsein*, der dem alten Wort eine neue Bedeutung und Autorität beilegt."[59]

Seeligmann suggests in closing that midrash sits atop a paradox. The presuppositions (*Voraussetzungen*) which underlie it are heterogeneous. Even after midrash becomes a distinct rabbinic genre, it retains its characteristic flexibility in verbal play and actualization. "Einerseits will er einen abgeschlossenen Text erklären, der eben in dieser Gestalt die höchste Autorität besitzt, anderseits ist er bestrebt denselben ... offenzuhalten, vor Versteinerung zu behüten und mit immer neuen Leben zu erfüllen — für jede neue Situation und für jeden neuen Tag!"[60] A conflict thus arises between Seeligmann's two stated goals, to understand the biblical literature and to illuminate its relationship to later midrashic exegesis, or in short, between the dynamics of canon and midrash.

In this way Seeligmann adumbrates the two main positions in subsequent Christian debate over the hermeneutical significance of canon, both Sanders' talk of adaptability, as well as Childs' stress on the abiding significance of decisions made by canon conscious tradents. But lest midrash be seen as yet another area in which Childs, leaving the term behind after Sanders picks it up, changes his views out of sheer convenience, it is worth explicating where and when Childs parts company with Seeligmann's analysis of the formation of biblical literature. The short answer is: exactly when and where he parts with form criticism's analysis. Seeligmann is well versed in the critical views of his day and shares in much of the critical consensus that dominated in the mid-twentieth century. The contentious point has to do with the adaptation or actualization of remote tradition.[61] By way of illustration, consider the late addition of superscriptions to some psalms.

On Psalm Titles

Seeligmann feels a tension between individual and communal consciousness in the way individual psalms are brought into the life of a community. Psalm 30, he says, can be understood in no other way except as the praise of an individual who has recovered from illness — something the tradents' historical consciousness was strong enough to preserve intact. By affixing in the title a reference to the dedication of the temple, however, the psalm has been related to a historical moment in the life of Israel, and so this bit of interpretation must have been done by the generation that rebuilt the temple after the Babylonian exile. Psalm 30, then, is a prime example of "adaptive exegesis" (stage three) in the psalms in which "Midrasch liest und deutet [eine] Äusserung

[59] Ibid., 176, my emphasis.

[60] Ibid., 181.

[61] Childs mostly engages von Rad on *Vergegenwärtigung*. Although Seeligmann derives *Adaptation* from Solomon Schechter, the concepts occupy similar conceptual space.

eines Individuums als das Zeugnis der Gemeinschaft von Israel."[62] This is work of and for a *single* generation.

At first glance Childs' 1971 study "Psalm Titles and Midrashic Exegesis" upholds Seeligmann's basic picture of a fluid–solid trajectory toward canon. A preparatory form critical analysis of psalms in narrative settings finds that some psalms, such as Exodus 15 or Jonah 2, were easily incorporated into narrative frameworks. Others caused more "friction" and were less easily integrated.[63] The function of Isaiah 38:9 is noteworthy. "The poem is no longer regarded simply as a 'song' or 'word.' Again, Hezekiah is not the speaker, but the author."[64] "No attempt has been made to work the poem into the narrative of vv. 1–6. Rather, the poem is retained apart from the narrative and provided with a title as a literary piece by an author which was composed at a specific time in the historical past."[65] In fact Isaiah 38 is the only example outside the Psalter of a psalm title with the same form as the Davidic ascriptions, Childs' main focus. It "reflects a stage in the transmission of poetic tradition in which its literary fixation as an independent composition made it difficult to incorporate within a larger narrative setting. Nevertheless, the need to supply a setting resulted in the use of a stereotyped form of the superscription which offered the minimum information of author and historical referent."[66] Tradents at this stage could not adapt the psalm with the freedom that was exercised in an earlier period. On this basis Childs argues for the lateness of the additions. The Chronicler did not use the technique of superscriptions, so "it seems logical to set a *terminus a quo* after the Chronicler." And "a *terminus ad quem* for the formation of the titles is provided by the Qumran Psalm scroll." Therefore, "the titles are an extremely late post-exilic phenomenon."[67]

But something changes fundamentally in this process for Childs, something Seeligmann does not quite register. "The titles represent an early reflection on how the Psalms as a collection of sacred literature were understood. The titles established a secondary setting which became normative for the canonical tradition."[68] Childs restricts his form-critical study to psalms attached to the life of David (esp. Pss. 50–60, 68), making a direct comparison on Psalm 30 impossible, but Childs turns out to be far less committed to the the individual–communal dynamic Seeligmann employs to explain that superscription. Instead of positing a moment of historical crisis underlying the adaptation, Childs focuses on the literary/exegetical dynamic at work. He uses Sanders' work on the Qumran Psalms Scroll to support the claim that the psalm titles

---

62 Ibid., 172.
63 Childs, Psalm Titles, 139.
64 Ibid., 141.
65 Ibid., 142.
66 Ibid., 142.
67 Ibid., 148.
68 Ibid., 137.

are not historical memories "but are the result of an exegetical activity which derived its material from within the text itself."[69] For instance, the superscription on Psalm 60 seems aware of David in 2 Samuel 8 *and* of Joab in 1 Kings 11. "By introducing Joab into the passage drawn from II Samuel, the author of the title appears to be drawing attention to his other source which supplies the missing link for the Psalm. Once again a Psalm title reflects considerable study of Scripture which goes much beyond noticing obvious allusions."[70] More important than whatever crisis or event might have provoked an author to pen a superscription are the "signs … of scholarly study of the Psalms in relation to other Old Testament passages."[71] This is indeed the age of the *Schriftgelehrten*, and their exegetical activity changes the course of tradition permanently. Seeligmann sees that Psalm 30 has been attached to a contemporary event, but for Childs the Davidic superscriptions affiliate psalms with a wider body of scripture.

This is not to say that Childs ignores "history." He emphasizes an historic transformation, of various traditions into an affiliated textual corpus, with long-lasting historical consequences. For "the titles functioned in a way completely different from the 'pesher type' midrash of Qumran, and they lack any concern to actualize past traditions by means of superscription. Again, the titles which relate to David's life do not serve to legitimate any later religious institutions, which is a characteristic tendency of midrashim from Pharisaic circles." The effect is to fill out the canonical register, which ultimately suggests a new way of reading scripture. "By placing a Psalm within the setting of a particular historical incident in the life of David, the reader was suddenly given access to previously unknown information. David's inner life was now unlocked to the reader, who was allowed to hear his intimate thoughts and reflections. It therefore seems most probable that the formation of the titles stemmed from a pietistic circle of Jews whose interest was particularly focussed on the nurture of the spiritual life."[72] This descriptive observation, which Barr approves of in 1983, is redolent with theological implications.

As Childs puts it the next year (1972), "One way to reinterpret a text is to reshape it within a new composition. Another equally effective way is to change the context from that in which the text originally functioned. The text itself is not altered, but a *new framework* is provided which assigns to it a *new role*. The classic illustration of this second approach is to be found in the superscriptions of certain psalms." Thus begins a section called "Establishment of a New Context" — not quite the "canonical context," but nearly so.[73] Form

[69] Ibid., 143.
[70] Ibid., 147.
[71] Ibid., 148.
[72] Ibid., 149.
[73] Childs, Midrash, 57, my emphasis.

critically speaking, if a tradition is placed in a different form, its function will also change. Rather than reading psalms in the context of the cultus (Mowinckel), a precedent is established for attending to the textualized, canonical context. "Psalms which originally functioned within a cultic role for the community have been secondarily given a specific historical setting in the life of an individual. Lying at the base of this process of 'historization' is the conviction that Scripture can best be interpreted by Scripture (*Scriptura sui ipsius interpres*), which is a corollary derived from a consciousness of canon."[74] The terminology stems from Seeligmann, but it is being deployed for new, decidedly canonical ends.

Road One — Benno Jacob's Modern Midrash

A recurring section in *Exodus* is called the "Old Testament Context." In the introduction we are told that it "forms the heart of the commentary," that it "attempts to deal seriously with the text in its final form, which is its canonical shape, while at the same time recognizing and profiting by the variety of historical forces which were at work in producing it. In my judgment, the failure of most critical commentaries to deal with the final shape of the text without falling into modern midrash is a major deficiency."[75] One could be forgiven for thinking that "modern midrash" here means the midrash-allied hermeneutics of Sanders, whose *Torah and Canon* Childs had recently criticized in a review. In fact this is not the thing Childs rejects in 1974. He is more worried about midrash as a *conservative* instrument for the harmonization of tensions and contradictions kicked up by historical critical research. The commentators who come up most frequently in this connection are Umberto Cassuto and Benno Jacob.[76] I will now look briefly at Childs' interaction with the latter.

In 1999 Childs wrote an appreciation of Jacob, hoping to draw attention to "the enduring and genuine contributions of this largely forgotten scholar."[77] Childs says he learned of Jacob from von Rad in Heidelberg, and that he later had great difficulty locating Jacob's commentary on Genesis, even at Yale.

> Soon I discovered that among my colleagues in the academic guild the name of Benno Jacob was virtually unknown. Then in 1963 I spent a sabbatical leave in Jerusalem and learned that

[74] Ibid., 57. A related article from 1976, Modern Study of Psalms, continues to push hard against traditional form criticism — "the function of a secondary setting often seems to be more significant for exegesis than a fixation with an alleged original *Sitz*" (378) — with reference to Seeligmann: "the concept of a normative scripture unleashed a new set of forces which were different in kind from those influencing the development of the oral tradition in the pre-exilic period" (382). Psalms have been "loosened from their original cultic context" and have been given a "different function" in their canonical form (383). Seeligmann is not the only important input; Hertzberg, Nachgeschichte, from 1936, also surfaces frequently.

[75] *Exodus*, xiv.

[76] For good examples of this criticism see *Exodus*, 364 and 614, respectively.

[77] Childs, Benno Jacob, 275.

in Israel Jacob was far from unknown. Some of the older scholars, such as Professor Isaac Leo Seeligmann, had known Jacob personally, and Seeligmann regaled me with interesting stories concerning this remarkable scholar. I had gone to Jerusalem to work on an Exodus commentary and to my delight and amazement I learned that the Hebrew University possessed a rare microfilm copy of an unpublished commentary on the book of Exodus by Jacob. Seeligmann recounted that when Jacob was expelled from German in 1938, he departed with the manuscript of his Exodus commentary clutched in his arms, undoubtedly regarding it as his most precious possession. When I returned home from Israel in 1964, the librarian of the Hebrew University generously provided me with a microfilm of the Exodus commentary. I had it photocopied, bound in four large volumes, and deposited in the Yale library as a rediscovered treasure.[78]

Jacob seems a good illustration of the problems that arise for biblical interpreters in and after the critical age.[79] His effort to destroy the documentary hypothesis explains "why his work has largely been ignored by modern biblical scholars."[80] It prevents him from "[engaging] in a mutually fruitful dialogue on the larger critical issues," leaving him behind with nineteenth century interlocutors whom the critical discussion had long since surpassed. Yet other "aspects of his work remain highly impressive and uniquely worthy of careful scrutiny."[81] In 1999 Childs illustrates with Jacob's Genesis commentary, though Childs' earlier work on Exodus is the best place to get a sense of the extent of his regard for Jacob. He is referenced nearly as often as Gressmann or Noth.

Illustrations could well be given of the positive insight Childs derives from Jacob, but in keeping with my concern to understand what Childs does and does not make of midrash, the following excerpt shows what Childs typically means by "modern midrash" in the early 1970s, and why he cannot follow suit.

In recent years there have been several attempts to solve the literary problems within Ex. 16 by denying the presence of sources. Benno Jacob ... begins with a sharp polemic against critics who have "cut up the chapter without understanding its intention." But when Jacob offers his own alternative solution it very much resembles a modern midrash. He attempts to avoid the difficulties in the sequence of vv.1–12 by assuming a speech of Moses before v.4. He interprets the verb in v.11 as a pluperfect which he assigns to a period prior to v.4. Finally, he suggests that the faulty Hebrew syntax in v.8 is intentional in order to demonstrate that indeed Moses is not a good speaker and requires Aaron's help![82]

---

[78] Ibid., 273. Cf. "The Life and Works of Benno Jacob" by his son W. Jacob, in Jacob, *Exodus*, xv–xxxiii, who also translated the commentary for English publication in 1992. The German original was finally published in 1997.

[79] Again, "the pre-critical option has been forever lost" (Childs, Vitringa, 98).

[80] Childs, Benno Jacob, 274.

[81] Ibid., 275. One remark stands out in light of the fact that Childs never joined the digital revolution (he worked on a typewriter): "Long before intertextuality had become a modern fad generated by computer print-outs, Jacob listened for every possible resonance within the entire canon" (276).

[82] *Exodus*, 275.

The Basel seminar with Baumgartner made a big impression.[83] In light of the later preoccupation with midrashic hermeneutics as an emblem of liberal Protestant attitudes to canon, it is surprising to see just how long this sense of midrash as a coping strategy for those who reject the documentary hypothesis lasts in Childs' work. This understanding predominates in *Introduction to the OT* as well. For example, concerning the canonical shaping of Ezra-Nehemiah, "two pitfalls" must be avoided:

> The one approach — call it modern midrashic — would rule out *a priori* the possibility of any accidental factors at work and would evaluate the present composition consistently on the same level of intentionality throughout. The weakness of this approach is its inability to deal with the historical dimensions of the canonical process which established a *scale of intentionality*... The other extreme of the spectrum, which is characteristic of the dominant historical critical method, seeks to establish a historical sequence as normative and thus disregards any theological intent which would override the concerns of the modern historian.[84]

Still in 1979, tradition history can be an opposite category to midrash. Wellhausen casts a very long shadow, and for a good while it must have seemed unlikely that midrash could ever be seriously allied with the cause of liberalism. That would change for Childs, however, over the course of the so-called canon debate.

Road Two — James Sander's Modern Midrash

In 2005 Childs laments that Sanders became the spokes-person for the majority position on canon's hermeneutical (in)significance in English.[85] How does this relate to "modern midrash"? In a 1992 overview G. T. Sheppard identifies a line that was increasingly drawn between the ways midrash, understood as inner-biblical exegesis, had been accommodated in work on canon. Sanders and Fishbane (see below) place an emphasis on "continuity between the prebiblical interpretation of the normative traditions and the later postbiblical interpretations of scripture in Judaism and Christianity," whereas "Childs, Rendtorff and Sheppard have emphasized elements of discontinuity between the prescriptural functions of ancient traditions and the new roles they play within 'the canonical context' of Jewish and Christian Bibles."[86] How true this remains for Rendtorff is difficult to say. For Childs and those like Sheppard who follow him more closely, a new understanding of midrash fell in place alongside an established distinction between the canonical approach and tradition history. Childs resists Sanders' hermeneutics from the start, all the while crediting his insight about the canonical function of Deuteronomy at the close

[83] See section B.I in chapter one.

[84] *Introduction to the OT*, 630, my emphasis. On intentionality, see the conclusion of chapter one.

[85] Childs, Reflections on an Era, 36.

[86] Sheppard, Criticism, 863. His major contribution is Sheppard, *Wisdom*.

of the Pentateuch,[87] and yet only later identifies Sanders with "Jewish midrash." In 2005 he does not challenge Sander's assessment, that early Judaism "developed the techniques of midrash by which to exploit the fluidity of its sacred text in order to reinterpret them into new forms for regenerating its life," but contends that this paradigm "is incompatible with the New Testament's understanding of the authoritative function of the Old Testament, which has been continually transformed by the Spirit into the law of Christ."[88] Sanders eventually comes to represent another variety of "modern midrash" — almost the opposite of Jacob's — and a second road which Childs never takes.

Although Childs is highly complimentary when he reviews *Torah and Canon* in 1973, he lodges a telling objection. "Sanders and I seem to differ," he writes, "in the theological stance which one adopts when interpreting the significance of the historical factors shaping the canon." Sanders' interest lies in "the *hermeneutics* of that generation which gave the canon its basic shape. In the *process* by which the ancient Hebrews shaped their tradition, we are given a key how to transform our own tradition in the light of changing situations. It is at this point that I strongly differ in theological approach."[89] In contrast, "I believe that the witness of the Old Testament lies in the *historical shape* which the Jews gave their Scriptures, and not in the *historical processes* which gave them a shape."[90] Witness is the operative word. This is how the scriptures speak. The phrase "final form" first occurs in 1974, so it is possible to take its introduction as a clarifying step.[91] A form critical study of midrash — e.g., of Chronicles' use of Kings, or of the late addition of psalm titles — illuminates the emergence of a more final corpus. It obtains the form in which it functions in the community of faith. Later in that commentary we find him committing to the "challenge to hear the Old Testament as God's word in a concrete and *definite form* for one's own age." The church's different use of scripture from generation to generation "only demonstrates the function of the canon. Scripture is different in kind from the church's reflection upon it."[92]

Another bit of shorthand for this distinction will surface before long: we are not, Childs insists, prophets and apostles. The late post-Exilic transformation of Old Testament tradition, put into relief by Sanders and Seeligmann in their own ways, remains binding in the Christian church, where a New Testament witness was fashioned on analogy with that first authoritative corpus.

---

[87] *Introduction to the OT*, 131.

[88] Childs, Reflections on an Era, 34.

[89] Childs, Review of Sanders, 90, Childs' emphasis.

[90] Ibid., my emphasis.

[91] *Exodus*, xiv: "the historical development which lay behind the final form" seems a rather wordy, though more precise, circumlocution for what just two years prior was simply glossed as midrash. (Searchable versions of many of Childs' titles are available online.)

[92] *Exodus*, 438, my emphasis.

II. Inner-biblical Exegesis

Another scholar whose analysis of psalm titles in the 1970s led to to a much more comprehensive project is Michael Fishbane.[93] His classic study of inner-biblical exegesis, *Biblical Interpretation in Ancient Israel* (1985), remains unsurpassed in quality and extent. Unfortunately, it will be impossible here to give it the attention it deserves. Comments from Childs' review of the book serve as a fitting coda to the above discussion, however, because they neatly recapitulate themes I have been at pains to trace. After praising Fishbane for excellent research, Childs makes a trio of queries. The first upholds the textualization of oral tradition as *the* turning point in the formation of biblical literature, a point made as early as 1967.

> My first query is whether Fishbane has blurred the sharpness of the break which occurred in Israel when the traditions were transmitted in written form. In my judgment, Fishbane has been led astray at the outset by taking over the terminology and historical patterns of the traditio-historical critics, for example, in his use of D. Knight's distinction between *traditio* and *traditum*. Admittedly this vocabulary is useful for understanding and describing the early oral stages of Israel's development, but to extend these traditio-historical patterns into the later period of Israel's history, even when slightly modified, misconstrues the *very new dynamic which resulted from textualization* and which Fishbane has so brilliantly analyzed. The actualization of the Exodus traditions by Deuteronomy which von Rad, for example, studied reflects a very different process from the proto-midrashic, inner-biblical exegesis of texts of the exilic and post-exilic periods.[94]

Midrash or proto-midrash comes into play once actualization becomes an *exegetical* procedure (geared to scriptural texts) and not before. Israel defined itself in terms of a book, thereby altering the context for interpretation permanently. Second, with reference to Sandmel,[95] Childs claims that it is anachronistic to find biblical exegesis too early. "My query to Fishbane is whether he has also tended to project inner-biblical exegesis of texts back to an early stage of Israel's development in which its traditions were largely unwritten and were actualized in a variety of different ways which cannot be encompassed under the rubric of inner-biblical exegesis."[96] Related to the first point, Childs seems to want to protect an early oral phase of the tradition in which great flexibility in adaptation is possible. There is a palpable and important difference between the use of tradition in Second Isaiah and Third Isaiah, Childs says. Finally, he turns to the "theological implications."

> The third query is not a criticism, but a recognition that Fishbane has raised some important hermeneutical issues whose theological implications have not as yet been fully explored. In the

---

[93] Fishbane, Torah and Tradition. Significantly, it appears in a collection of essays dedicated to theology and tradition history: Knight, ed., *Tradition*.

[94] Childs, Review of Fishbane, 512, my emphasis.

[95] Sandmel, Haggada. Recall the critique of this in 1972: Childs, Midrash, 48–50.

[96] Childs, Review of Fishbane, 513.

past, historical criticism of the OT as practiced by Christians has frequently disparaged Jewish midrashic exegesis as a rabbinic distortion which has no genuine place in the Hebrew Bible, but appears just on the outer perimeter as a sign of decay. One recalls Wellhausen's derogatory characterization of midrash in his famous chapter on Chronicles. Fishbane has mounted an impressive case for the deep roots of an interpretive process which reflects the strongest possible analogies with later post-biblical Jewish exegesis. What are the theological implications of Fishbane's work for the modern debate over Scripture and tradition within an ecumenical context?[97]

Fishbane's study could advance religious dialogue between Protestant and Catholic, and between Christian and Jew. For Childs the first common denominator is the *historical* result of Israel's textualized tradition. Theological disagreements would have to be arbitrated on whether they "auf den biblischen Text selbst gründen kann"; when "spätere Traditionen" are the only justification to be found for an article of faith, then we have an "ernsthaften Schwäche, sowohl im Judentum als auch im Christentum." A more modest claim would restrict itself to the state of affairs in Christianity, and one sometimes finds just this — e.g., he criticizes "any theological method" that "does not feel constrained to engage in continuous exegesis of the Bible itself as the indispensable ground for all Christian theological reflection."[98] Childs is finally unwilling to surrender a "literal sense" scriptural link with Judaism, however.

But what if the status of tradition is the point of contention? If Seeligmann correctly identifies the paradox of tradition within the biblical literature, where and how should one seek a resolution? Should one seek a resolution at all? Bernard Levinson, a student of Fishbane's, has carried forward the work of his teacher in ways every bit as rigorous, every bit as challenging. He argues that canonical formulas are splendid paradoxes; there is a "vantage" from which "the canon is radically open."[99] In his work taking a hermeneutical stance behind inner-biblical exegesis tends very much to break the canon down. And almost by intuition Levinson sees the relation of his model to the one we have been studying:

The approach of a canonical reading departs from both standard source-critical or redaction-historical models and from the model of inner-biblical exegesis. It is no longer interested in attempting to demonstrate the literary dependence of one text on another, so as to show exegetical revision (the Fishbane model) or to use diachronic analysis to show how the redactional structure of a book reflects the reception and reinterpretation of earlier literary models (the Steck model). The focus shifts to a *different horizion*, presupposing the completion of the texts in their present shape, and finds strategies to make thematic, literary, and theological connections to integrate the disparate material.[100]

---

[97] Ibid., 513.

[98] *NT Introduction*, 545–546.

[99] Levinson, *Legal Revsion*, 94.

[100] Ibid., 166, my emphasis. The connections Childs finds are above all theological.

Much more could be said about this impressive work. For now it must suffice to note Childs' small place in Levinson's annotated bibliography on the history of scholarship on inner-biblical exegesis from Wellhausen to 2008.[101] Only one piece is included — the 1971 "Psalms Titles and Midrashic Exegesis" (with an essay by Childs' onetime student Alan Cooper).[102] The 1972 "Midrash and the Old Testament" might have been included, too, but this is actually about the extent of it. Even in these well-remembered essays I find Childs laying the groundwork for something else, along different lines. Later, further out from Wellhausen's shadow, he will gain clarity about just how unlike "midrash" his biblical theological frame "canon" is. To this realization we now turn.

C. The "Mystery of Israel" Reconsidered

Introduction to the OT "seeks to describe the form and function of the Hebrew Bible in its role as sacred scripture for Israel."[103] In defining historical and theological facets of his key term canon, Childs maintains, contra Sanders, that the category "witness" is far more central than the biblical tradents' self-understanding. "Because the process of forming the scriptures came to an end, canon marked off a fixed body of writings as normative for the community rather than attributing authority to the process itself. When Israel later reinterpreted its scriptures to address its changing needs, it did so in the form of the targum, that is to say, commentary, which was set apart sharply from the received sacred text of scripture."[104] Childs then adduces the following warrant for a study of the canonical process:

> Seeligmann has described a process of interpretation within scripture which he correctly derived from a consciousness of canon (*Kanonbewusstsein*). This process involved the skilful use of literary techniques, word-plays, and proto-midrashic exegesis which emerged during the final stages of the formation of the canon and continued to be developed and to flower during the post-biblical period. Although such exegetical activity grew out of a concept of the canon as an established body of sacred writings, it is a *derivative phenomenon which does not represent the constitutive force lying behind the actual canonical process*. Rather, the decisive force at work in the formation of the canon emerged in the transmission of a divine word in such a form as to lay authoritative claim upon the successive generations.[105]

Historically speaking, commentary and text do break apart at some point. The theological and hermeneutical crux is whether or not exegesis is "derivative" of

---

[101] Ibid., 95–181.

[102] More play is given to Sanders, which is to be expected, though Levinson raises doubts about whether Sanders does enough to show how "reformulated texts challenge the authority and break down the coherence of the original texts" (ibid., 15n5).

[103] *Introduction to the OT*, 16.

[104] Ibid., 59, cf. 101, 370.

[105] Ibid., 60, my emphasis.

scripture, and how one knows. As has been seen, Seeligmann is rather more ambivalent about canon (fixity) getting the upper hand on midrash (exegetical activity). For Childs the "constitutive force" that was unleashed by Israel's late, religious use of its tradition leads inexorably toward canon. Ever after text and commentary are wholly, almost ontologically distinct. Separating *literary* and *canonical* histories into overlapping but non-identical processes enables Childs to address the theological function of canon as a binding collection of literature before every last detail is locked in place (parallel to the flexibility in his "search for the Christian Bible," since across Christendom no official text *ever* emerged on par with the MT; see below). On the basis of the bond between church and synagogue that this entails, Childs argues for the MT as the *vehicle* for the recovery of the canonical text in the church, not the LXX,[106] and even "for the priority of the Jewish tripartite division — normative is now too strong a word — when dealing with the Hebrew Bible for the same theological reasons which have been outlined before, namely to confirm the role of the Jews as tradents of the canonical tradition."[107] Jews and Christians read their common scriptures in different contexts — for Jews tradition is "now codified in the midrashim, Mishnah, and Talmuds," and Christians bring "the gospel of Jesus Christ found in the New Testament" — but the difference "does not sever the common link with the scriptures of Israel."[108]

Summing up, canon identifies an historical development which well predates the advent of Christ, though in literary terms the authoritative tradition is in a certain degree of flux. As canon, Israel's scripture was (and is) received by the church from the hands of the Jews. According to its testimony early Christians articulated their encounter with the risen Lord. But the processes leading to a split between Tanak and Old Testament do not obliterate the profound historical and theological reality that connects synagogue and church. "The notion that the 'real' Old Testament is purely 'Hebrew' in character and was later distorted by Judaism is a legacy of Wellhausen which cannot be sustained either from a historical or theological perspective."[109] Neither does the construct of a single tradition history (Gese, through von Rad), which because of the prominence of the LXX in the NT must cut ties with the parallel Hebrew canon, square with the way authoritative tradition changed as oral became textual tradition in the post-exilic period.[110] In short, the historical-theological link between church and synagogue *founds* the mystery of Israel.

---

[106] Ibid., 100–103.

[107] Ibid., 667. Childs of course recognizes that Christian orderings of OT books vary, and that early Christians disregarded the tripartite version. But they "chose an order from among the variety of options which best supported the Christian claim of a different understanding of the Old in terms of the New" — i.e., they did not redact a new OT to suit their purposes.

[108] Ibid., 666.

[109] Ibid., 668.

[110] Ibid., 669.

Yet after setting variations on Wellhausen's separation between Israel and Judaism to one side, and on von Rad's to another, Childs considers a "problem of relating the Hebrew Bible to the Christian Old Testament which arises from the side of Judaism."[111] The issue is raised in a well-known article by L. B. Wolfenson (1924).[112] Wolfenson wants to separate two distinct meanings of canon, according to Childs. One is the usual "classic collection of religious writings and is synonymous in Judaism with the term Bible." The other "denotes a norm of recognized regulations for faith and practice. Wolfenson denies that the whole Hebrew canon ever had such a normative role for Judaism in this second sense of canon. Only the Torah was considered normative, that is to say, legally and morally binding, and by the term Torah was included the interpretation of the Mishnah and Gemara as well."[113] Childs finds reason to doubt if this is historically plausible. There is also a "theological problem": "if Wolfenson's description of the Jewish attitude towards the canon is correct even for later, post-Talmudic Judaism then he has indeed focused on a basic theological difference toward the use of the Bible which distinguishes Judaism from Christianity." Again, if correct, Wolfenson would signal major "elements of discontinuity between the two faiths."[114] Addressing the issue is important but beyond the scope of *Introduction to the OT*, Childs concludes.

As a matter of fact *Introduction to the OT* assumes that Wolfenson is wrong. In response to reviewers Childs writes,

> The New Testament writers took over various hermeneutical techniques current in the Judaism of the Hellenistic period (midrash, pesher). Of course, midrash focuses on one specific passage at a time — one looks in vain for broad topical summaries — but the assumption undergirding the method is that of a fixed and closed corpus of Sacred Scriptures which constituted a unity. All the various hermeneutical rules which were later articulated by the sages assumed a fixed canon. The freedom of the Jewish homilist in actualizing his texts does not undercut the concept of an established, authoritative text, but rather proves just the opposite.[115]

Is "the assumption undergirding the method" really of a closed canon? How can such a free operation testify to a fixed unity? Childs begins to sound like he protests too much. Note the acceptance of the place of midrash in the NT. Within a few short years he will issue a retraction: the NT is no midrash on the OT. When exactly, and above all, why?

In *NT Introduction* Childs observes that it has become common to characterizes the NT's use of the OT as midrashic. Of course, the NT shares "many of the formal conventions of Jewish exegesis" at that time. "Nevertheless, I have a growing conviction that the use of the term 'midrash' can be very mislead-

[111] Ibid.
[112] Wolfenson, Ruth.
[113] *Introduction to the OT*, 670.
[114] Ibid.
[115] Childs, A Response [Mays], 203.

ing."[116] As with tradition history, though not in the same way, the decisive point turns on a distinction between oral and textual tradition. "Crucial to Jewish midrash is a particular hermeneutical understanding of the biblical text which implied not only a closed corpus of canonical literature, but a dogmatic construal of the written text's relation to Jewish oral tradition." A heightened sensitivity to Oral Torah's weight in Jewish belief starts to make midrash look *constitutively* Jewish. The formal technique factors into the formation of the NT, and it remains an ally in the theological concern to take the the textual authority of scripture seriously, but there is an emerging sense of difference. "Jewish midrash is," comes the conclusion, "text-oriented in a very different manner from that of early Christianity."[117]

Childs does not say if Judaism is unlike Christianity in separating text from commentary, but it seems relevant that he insists on a "qualitative difference between apostolic tradition and subsequent church tradition which the canon sought to establish."[118] Further, in an excursus on NT text criticism, Childs points out many differences between the development of OT and NT literature despite the more recent trend to see a generally similar situation, of a gradual move from great fluidity to increasing stability. These observations impinge on his account of the separation of church and synagogue. "There are some important differences between the development of the Hebrew text within the Jewish synagogue and the Greek New Testament text within the Christian church."[119] The early church sat more loosely to the Hebrew text than did the early synagogue. The church's willingness to translate the NT "resulted in a different dynamic of textual transmission from that of the Hebrew text." And in terms of the canonical process, "the understanding ... was not identical. For the Christian church canonization was derivative of christology. The New Testament scriptures gained their unique authority in their role as the apostolic and prophetic witness to Christ's death and resurrection which was also uniquely tied to the one specific period of his earthly life."[120] Jewish interpretation was Torah-centric, whereas Christian interpretation was christocentric. Extrapolating slightly, insofar as the latter entails a certain approach to the scriptures of Israel, one can appreciate how in the course of his five-year venture into NT scholarship Childs moves away from the language of midrash and the OT, and toward the language of a christologically transformed Old Testament.

So then, what if Wolfenson was on to something after all? What if Judaism focused not exclusively on the narrower textual Torah, but equally or even pri-

[116] *NT Introduction*, 491.
[117] Ibid., 491.
[118] Ibid., 522.
[119] Ibid., 526.
[120] Ibid.

marily on Oral Torah? The historical shift from oral to textual tradition which Childs develops out of a form critical perspective, with an eye to the subsequent and ongoing theological function of scripture, is rather unlike the traditional Jewish articulation, solidified in the rabbinic period, of an oral tradition reaching back to Moses. But if one had an eye to canon in that religious context, as opposed to its Christian setting, might not the sparse historical evidence be read very differently, with a fundamentally different understanding of canon? It seems quite possible that Seeligmann was doing more with tradition history in the early 1950s than giving a neutral, religiously disinterested account of the historical origins of Jewish midrash.

I. Neusner's Always-open Canon

The 1983 book *Midrash in Context* raised this challenge in a forceful way for Childs. A look at Neusner's thesis quickly shows why. "Exegesis is not Torah. But books of exegeses became part of Torah. How come? Is the category 'canon' ever relevant to Judaism?"[121] Based on a taxonomy of rabbinic texts from 200–600 CE, including case studies of Mishnah, Talmud and Midrashim, Neusner concludes that the relationship of Talmud to Mishnah is formally identical to the relationship compilations of exegeses (the Midrashim) have to scripture. The Mishnah, therefore, becomes part of Torah. "Receiving the Mishnah meant setting it into relationship with the ancient Scriptures. Let me now, in a single sentence, report what they did. The sages totally reformed the meaning of the word *Torah*, thereby, in the literary framework, *reopening the canon of Judaism*, and, in the theological setting, redefining the meaning and limits of revelation."[122] The reform had palpable results. In literary terms, it created the Talmud. In theological terms it brought about "Judaism as we know it: a living and enduring faith of everyday encounter with God through Torah and its holy way of life."[123]

The "measure of *midrash*"[124] Neusner seeks goes beyond Seeligmann's paradox at the end of the biblical period in historical and theological respects, centering on the post-biblical revisioning of canon as such. For Neusner, the exegetical activity called midrash changes in kind when rabbinic sages reform Torah. "As we know full well, Israelite thinkers — whether lawyers and philosophers, like the heirs of the Mishnah in the Talmuds, or visionaries and prophets, like the Essenes at Qumran, or messianists and evangelists, like the members of the school of Matthew — routinely read one thing in relationship to something else, old Scripture in the setting of fresh concerns and sure

[121] Neusner, *Midrash*, xiv.
[122] Ibid., 11, my emphasis.
[123] Ibid., 12.
[124] Ibid., 110.

knowledge of new truth."[125] Midrash proper does not introduce a new technique. Neither is it in essence technique — in Seeligmann's words, associative exegesis or crisis-provoked adaptation. "What captures our attention is not the techniques of exegesis but, in particular, the place and purpose assigned to the larger labor of exegesis."[126] Neusner defends a change in consciousness of another order: midrash does not inhere in the paradoxical closing of the text it opens; rather, "the heart of the matter [is] the standing of the sage."[127] When a rabbi gave an opinion on a verse, what was the status of his judgment? His view was clearly seen as authoritative, but at the same time his view would have been easy to distinguish from the ancient words of scripture. "Did the distinction between media make a difference?"[128] There are only two options, Neusner decides. "Either there is *torah* [revelation] which is not part of the Torah, the canon of revelation. Or there is no such thing as a canon at all." For: "The entire thrust of the exegetical process is to link upon a *single plane of authority and reliability* what a rabbi now says with what the (written) Torah said, or what the Tosefta says with what the (written) Torah said."[129] His simple conclusion could not be more contrary to Childs' view. "Interpretation and what was interpreted, exegesis and text, belonged together. In so vivid a world of divine address, what place was there for the conception of canon? There was none."[130] Neusner even goes so far as to call the rabbi "the word of God ... made flesh. And out of the union of man and Torah, producing the rabbi as Torah incarnate, was born Judaism, the faith of Torah: the ever-present revelation, the always-open canon."[131]

Neusner does allow that traditional Christianity had an entirely different orientation to sacred scripture. "The contrast to the standing for Jerome's biblical commentaries" jumps out in view of his conclusions, he writes. "Jerome treated books of the canon; his commentaries were not canonical. The earliest *midrash* compilations spoke not for an individual but for the collectivity of the sages; they demanded and gained a place with the canon of rabbinical writings, thus entering the Torah. The difference is fundamental."[132] If Neusner correctly describes the standing of the Jewish sage, Childs would have to occupy Jerome's space in order to maintain the distinction between scriptural text and commentary. He would have to claim a Christian canon without analogy to the Jewish understanding, at least in Neusner's representation of it.

---

[125] Ibid., 49–50.
[126] Ibid., 50.
[127] Ibid., 127.
[128] Ibid., 126.
[129] Ibid., 135, my emphasis.
[130] Ibid., 136.
[131] Ibid., 137.
[132] Ibid., xv.

A "recht starken Angriff"

Childs confronted Neusner's position in January 1985 at a Bern symposium on "Biblische Theologie und jüdische Auslegung des Tanach." A translation of Childs' paper appears alongside other conference proceedings in the volume *Mitte der Schrift*. He begins with an address to his "Christian colleagues," and he ends with a call to serious dialogue between Jews and Christians over their common scriptures, albeit from a distinctly Christian point of view. Most remarks in the first half of the essay appear to be aimed at Christian scholars — those invested in Old Testament theology of some stripe — but they serve double duty, setting the stage for a deep contrast Childs draws between Jewish and Christian exegesis. First, it is a category error to extract theological justification for textual freedom from Jesus' or Paul's use of the Old Testament. When P. Stuhlmacher or U. Luz attempts to draw a direct analogy between modern exegesis and the New Testament's use of the Old, they overlook the essential function of the *Christian* canon (throughout Childs almost never invokes canon without the modifier "Christian"). Its function is to sharply distinguish "dem ersten apostolischen Zeugnis und jeder folgenden kirchlichen Tradition."[133] As he insists here and elsewhere, "I am neither Jesus Christ nor an apostle." Text is distinct from commentary. Second, the two-testament Christian canon provokes some form of dialectic. Canon functions as a normative witness in the received prophetic and apostolic form. It is a closed unity ("eine abgeschlossene Einheit").[134] Consequently, searches for an original sense do not do justice to the theological task. Neither do quests for a "Mitte der Schrift," whether thematic (e.g., covenant) or developmental (e.g., prophecy and fulfillment in tradition history). Rather, beginning with an affirmation of the formal arena of Christian scripture, a unitive canon requires a dialectic on at least two planes, one historical and another intertextual. Third, the theological foundation for an affirmation of Christian canon is christological. OT theology is a Christian discipline *in essence*, subsidiary but integral to the broader Christian theological enterprise.[135] Characteristically, all Old Testament theologies assume a relationship of some kind between Christ and the history of Israel. Though this is talked about in different ways — "sei es ein Wesen, ein Kerygma oder eine historische Entwicklungslinie, die oft durch ein philosophisches System (Idealismus, Existentialismus, Ontologie) mitbestimmt sind" — it inevitably confirms a basic Christian standpoint; far better when such undertones are made explicit from the start. This is an obvious departure from Judaism: "Für das Christentum, *um* [sic] *Unterschied zum Judentum, wurzelt der Kanon in der Christologie.*"[136] Fourth, the priority of the

---

[133] Childs, Jüdischen Kanons, 270.

[134] Ibid., 274.

[135] Ibid., 274.

[136] Ibid., 271, my emphasis.

literal sense in Christian exegesis is presupposed. The OT must be allowed to speak on its own terms rather than too quickly identifying its *Christuszeugnis* with Christ. The *sensus literalis* also cuts against modern schemes of salvation history as well as medieval and modern allegorizing.[137]

A previously implicit point becomes quite explicit: *canon* derives from *christology*. Canon's relation to Judaism in the *NT Introduction* is a more fraught and open question than *Introduction to the OT* leads one to expect. Not by chance are Jewish scholars little interested in biblical theology, it seems; religious adoption of the Hebrew scriptures by Jews happens in ways that do not require the christologically oriented dialectics of biblical theology.[138]

Admitting his limitation as a Christian scholar in trying to describe characteristics of Jewish exegesis, Childs nevertheless attempts a few summary points in the latter part of his Bern essay. "Erstens werden die Hebräischen Schriften nicht als geschlossene Grösse verstanden und auch nicht als in einer dialektischen Beziehung zur späten rabbinischen Tradition stehend, sondern es gibt eher eine ungebrochene Kontinuität zwischen Schrift und Tradition, die zu einem verschiedenen Verständnis von Schrift-Autorität führt."[139] Three clauses in this first point are exact opposites of the distinctives of Christian biblical theology Childs has just defended. The scriptures are not a closed unit, they are not in a dialectical relationship to later tradition; text and commentary stand in continuity. Secondly, he continues, "bewirkt das jüdische Verständnis der Rolle der *mündlichen Tradition als eines massgeblichen Kommentars zur schriftlichen Tradition* eine sehr unterschiedliche Dynamik gegenüber der des Christentums (*in Gestalt des Midrasch*)."[140] On the face of it, this is a near reversal on his position from 1967, that midrash obtains only after the oral tradition becomes a textual tradition. However, it needs to be emphasized that the theological dynamic Oral Torah introduces in a Jewish interpretive context cannot be identified with a form critical study of biblical tradition in historical development. Third and finally, the core of the Bible for Judaism is Torah rather than Christ.[141]

Only after these remarks have been made are we told what precipitates them. "Meine Position, der Gegenstand der biblischen Disziplinen seien die kanonischen Schriften der jüdischen Synagoge, gesehen aus der Perspektive christlicher Theologie, hat kürzlich einen recht starken Angriff durch *Jacob Neusners* neuestes Werk *Midrash in Context* hinnehmen müssen."[142] The book opens up a new phase in the discussion of the Bern conference theme, he sug-

[137] Ibid., 280, cf. 269.

[138] Ibid., 275. A dramatic statement of this is of course Levenson, Not Interested, though not all Jewish scholars agree (e.g., Benjamin Sommer embraces a form of "biblical theology").

[139] Childs, Jüdischen Kanons, 275.

[140] Ibid., 275, my emphasis.

[141] Ibid., 276.

[142] Ibid., 276.

gests. Without too much modification Childs may still be able to say, as he does in 1980, that with midrash "the assumption undergirding the method is that of a fixed and closed corpus of Sacred Scriptures which constituted a unity." But he has had to rethink entirely the bounds of scripture's authority in Jewish faith. Is the corpus closed? Is it textual?

That said, Childs lodges a pair of reservations about Neusner's thesis. First, the traditional history of midrash traces lines of continuity into earlier eras, including the biblical period. Neusner, however, has proposed something as revolutionary as Wellhausen's inversion of Pentateuchal sources, turning the accepted line of development upside down. Childs feels Gunkel's criticism of Wellhausen applies to Neusner. "Muss man nicht deutlicher unterscheiden zwischen der Entstehungszeit der Stoffe und der Zeit ihrer endgültigen literarischen Fixierung?"[143] Second, even granting that the rabbinic situation is as Neusner describes it, was canon not an important category in Judaism nearer the turn of the eras? Was not a distinction drawn with books that "tarnished the hands"? "Die Idee eines Kanons, d.h. einer begrenzten Sammlung autoritativer Schriften, ist nicht einfach eine christliche, sondern auch eine jüdische, auch wenn ihr Inhalt und ihre Rolle recht verschieden aussahen."[144] Intriguingly, Neusner does talk of the sages *reopening* a closed canon, though he has considerably less interest in the hermeneutical significance of *Kanonbewußtsein* among late post-exilic tradents.

The upshot is that Childs becomes more explicit about the confessionally Christian foundation of his proposed approach to scripture. From the mid-1980s he struggles to express the witness of the Old Testament not just as scripture, but more acutely as *Christian* scripture, even as *Christuszeugnis.* And yet working hard to preserve the theological tie Jews and Christians seem to have in a common scripture, Childs opposes two possibilities. On the Christian side, there is the Marcionite temptation to dissolve any connection with the Old Testament. On the Jewish side, there is the danger of completely relativizing the distinctive authority of the Hebrew Scriptures through "spätere rabbinische Tradition." "Beides führt dazu, die Möglichkeit eines ernsthaften theologischen Dialogs zwischen Juden und Christen auf der Grundlage einer gemeinsamen Schrift zu untergraben."[145] Still, Childs wants for historical and especially for theological reasons to keep from christianizing the witness of Jewish scripture to the God of Israel.[146]

---

[143] Ibid., 278. This seems to advocate a form critical approach to midrash proper, much as Childs briefly attempted with inner biblical midrash in the early 1970s.

[144] Ibid., 279.

[145] Ibid., 279.

[146] Ibid., 280.

The adjustment is in place in *OT Theology*, which incorporates a brief summary of the Bern paper.[147] As in *Introduction to the OT*, the ongoing life of the synagogue furnishes Childs' strongest theological argument for a Hebrew rather than a Greek Old Testament: "the theological issue of how Christians relate to Jewish scriptures cannot be decided biblicistically by an appeal to New Testament practice, but must be addressed theologically."[148] Only a minor point is of additional note here. In one place "midrash" is said to be an irrelevant category because the text in question is not interpreting another text.[149] It seems Childs does not rescind the form critical distinction between oral and textual tradition. Midrash remains text-centric, even if as a Jewish approach to scripture it admits an oral tradition without parallel in Christianity. Childs' mid-career reconsideration of midrash, prompted especially by Neusner, pertains more to the hermeneutical and theological measure of midrash than to the historic profile of (proto-)midrash as an exegetical technique.

II. "The Church's Ongoing Search for the Christian Bible"

Without "Die Bedeutung des Jüdischen Kanons in der Alttestamentlichen Theologie" for background, it is easy to misunderstand a number of later statements about the peculiarly Christian challenges of biblical theology. For example, the second section of *Biblical Theology*, "A Search for a New Approach," begins with a chapter titled "The Problem of the Christian Bible."[150] It is a revision of a piece that appeared in German four years earlier, preserving a number of near-verbatim parallels. Both texts suggest that the problem of the Christian canon must be addressed by "the church's ongoing *search* for the Christian Bible."[151] Childs is concerned to show why Sundberg's argument for an open canon in the first century CE is unsustainable (in part because of a *Kanonbewußtsein*[152]), and to explore the theological problem raised by the fact of the Septuagint's prevalence in the New Testament. His answers, in four interrelated theses, reflect a deepened sense of the "mystery of Israel."

---

[147] *OT Theology*, 7–8. Neusner's book is not cited. Neither is the Bern paper, though several direct parallels show that some version of that essay lies behind *OT Theology* here, or possibly is anticipated by it.

[148] *OT Theology*, 10.

[149] *OT Theology*, 193.

[150] *Biblical Theology*, 55–69.

[151] *Biblical Theology*, 67; Childs, Biblische Theologie, 27; emphasis original in each. Wagner, The Septuagint, picks the phrase up in a paper originally presented at St Andrews (14 March 2007). His lays more emphasis on the Septuagint than Childs does. Provan's earlier discussion (Canons, 12–16) has quite recently been engaged in Seitz, *Goodly Fellowship*, 47–48 (cf. 59n16). With Seitz I do not think Childs backs away from prioritizing the MT after 1979.

[152] Childs, Biblische Theologie, 14.

First, in contrast to Judaism, the church's "basic stance towards its canon was shaped by its christology."[153] *Biblical Theology* summarizes what this entails, including how Sundberg fails to recognize the difference, but "Biblische Theologie" gives a fuller explanation that makes the relation to the argument in "Jüdischen Kanons" more obvious. The early church saw in the Jewish holy scriptures not just historical background, but a living witness to Jesus Christ. Later the New Testament was juxtaposed with the Old, and while the three-part ordering of the Tanak was relativized somewhat, giving higher priority to the prophets, it is highly significant that the Old Testament was preserved as a witness in its own right.[154] An important consequence is that the New Testament concept of fulfillment does not suppose "einfache Kontinuität."[155] A complex dialectic is introduced. Similarly, a single tradition-history does violence to the shape of a two testament canon.[156] In short, as in the Bern piece, making canon about christology signals imperatives for Christian exegesis that set it apart from Judaism: discontinuity in the tradition, at least in some degree; a sharper distinction between the prophetic/apostolic eras and subsequent eras; a dialectic arising from a two testaments canon; the *Christuszeugnis* of the Old Testament.[157]

Second, the New Testament is different in kind from later rabbinic traditions, and therefore, so is the entire Christian canon. The evangelists' confrontation with Christ as the resurrected Lord produced a different dynamic altogether. "Das Neue Testament ist kein Midrasch zum Alten Testament."[158] The power driving the New derives not from the Old, but from the new encounter with Christ. Still, it must not be overlooked that New speaks with the words of the Old. "Die Identität Jesu wird mit der Begrifflichkeit des Alten Testaments gänzlich verständlich gemacht. Doch wurde die Kontinuität der einen umfassenden Erlösung Gottes *ausschließlich vom Standpunkt des Neuen Testaments aus entdeckt* und allein von ihm aus die Brücke zum Alten Bund geschlagen."[159] The one-time arrival of Christ in history divides Christianity

---

[153] *Biblical Theology*, 64.

[154] Childs, Biblische Theologie, 21.

[155] Ibid., 21.

[156] Ibid., 22, cf. *Biblical Theology*, 76. See now Seitz, *Figured Out*, 35–47.

[157] Concerning "dialectic" Childs explains, "The fact that one at times falls back on the problematic term 'dialectic' is merely a sign that there is not comprehensive philosophical or hermeneutical system available which can adequately resolve with one proposal the whole range of problems arising from the historical critical method" (*Biblical Theology*, 99).

[158] Childs, Biblische Theologie, 22. This line has a parallel in *Biblical Theology*: "Nor can one rightly envision the New Testament as a midrashic extension of the Hebrew scriptures which stands in closest analogy to rabbinic and Qumran exegesis. The canonical continuity established by the shape of the Christian Bible is of a different order" (76).

[159] Childs, Biblische Theologie, 22, my emphasis. In a sense, he adds, Bultmann was right that the Old Testament witnesses to its failure; he overlooked the fact, though, that for the evangelists this was a witness to Christ (cf. *Biblical Theology*, 77).

from the continuity sought by rabbinic sages. Yet the shape of the Christian canon also makes "radical discontinuity" inadequate. That two different testaments testify to the one will of God requires a "kunstvolle Dialektik" in biblical theology.

> Die sorgfältige Beachtung des christlichen Kanons führt zu einem theologischen Nachdenken über beide Testamente, das sich weder mit Kategorien einer ungebrochenen Kontinuität noch mit denen einer radikalen Diskontinuität zufrieden gibt; und nur die theologische Reflexion, die beide Kategorien freimütig gebraucht, stimmt mit der einen christologischen Mitte überein.[160]

Thus scripture's "Mitte" in Christ emerges out of the complex dialectic evoked by a two testament canon.[161] This dynamic in turn feeds into the dialectic of biblical witness and its subject matter (*res*), which is Christ.

Third, the christological *Sachkritik* required by the Christian Bible in no way unravels the integrity of the Old Testament as a witness to Christ in its own right.[162] Harmonizing the witnesses is therefore not an option. But neither can the *Christuszeugnis* of the Old Testament be avoided. "Der moderne Christ liest das Alte Testament genau wie die Urkirche als Hinweis auf Jesus Christus. Das Alte Testament ist Teil der Schrift der Kirche, weil es Zeugnis für den einen Herrn ablegt."[163] Obviously this distinguishes Christian from Jewish exegesis, but paradoxically it ties the church indelibly to the literal sense of Jewish scripture. Just how the Old Testament is to be a *Christuszeugnis* is an enormous problem, as Childs well knows. "Allerdings bleibt es schwer bestimmbar, was es bedeutet, im Alten Testament einen Hinweis auf Christus zu finden, und das Ringen mit diesem Problem führt ins Herz der Biblischen Theologie."[164]

The fourth thesis concerns the scope of the Bible in relationship to scripture and tradition.[165] Facing the problem of multiple Christian Bibles, Childs finds that "two different principles appear to have been at work in the history of the church."[166] One was the criterion of apostolicity. Jerome's insistence on the Hebrew scriptures is the Old Testament equivalent of this. He rightly saw "the theological argument that the Jews ... were the proper tradents of this tradi-

---

[160] Ibid., 22.

[161] Cf. *Biblical Theology*, 25, which reiterates the skepticism about Jewish biblical theology earlier expressed in *OT Theology* and "Jüdischen Kanons."

[162] Childs, Biblische Theologie, 25 addresses problems arising "aus dem kanonischen Rang des Alten Testaments als eines unabhängigen Zeugnisses Jesu Christi in eigenem Recht."

[163] Ibid., 24. Hence we have "Israel's confessional witness" (*Biblical Theology*, 100).

[164] Ibid., 24.

[165] Compare ibid., 25–26 with *Biblical Theology*, 64–66.

[166] *Biblical Theology*, 64; Childs, Biblische Theologie, 25.

tion."[167] The other criterion was "catholicity … which was expressed in an *unbroken continuity* of sacred tradition."[168] The larger canon of the Vulgate is evidence of this principle. Childs acknowledges that the question of the canon's scope has not been settled to this day, and he grants that each side (now Protestant, Roman Catholic) has strengths and limitations, which is why he ultimately speaks of "the church's ongoing *search* for the Christian Bible." But it is also conspicuous that a completely "unbroken continuity" between text and tradition is not a Christian option. I quote from the German because of an important phrase that disappears in *Biblical Theology*:

> Die Gefahr der katholischen Position, in reichlichem Maß in der Kirchengeschichte veranschaulicht, lag natürlich in der Drohung, das Wort Gottes — oft im Namen der Frömmigkeit — zum Gefangenen der kirchlichen Traditionen zu machen. Läuft nicht letztlich eine Berufung auf die Tradition an sich, ohne daß der vom Inhalt des biblischen Zeugnisses ausgeübte kritische Maßstab berücksichtigt würde, dem einzigartigen christlichen Verständnis des Kanons, *das es vom jüdischen unterscheidet*, zuwider?[169]

The italicized line demonstrates how the Christian position at which Childs arrives has yet again been sharpened by the mysterious like and unlike of church and synagogue. *Broken continuity* is an imperative for Christian biblical theology. Christ and not Torah became incarnate.

Let me summarize Childs' position by 1988. First, christology drove the church's "basic stance towards its canon." Second, we know this because the stance of the apostles to the Old Testament is different in kind to the stance of rabbinic sages to Torah. Old and New have been juxtaposed, not brought into alignment. A dialectic results. Third, though, the church did not impose a christological redaction on the Old Testament, but received a form of it from the hands of the Jews, the dialectic does not *sever* the link between church and synagogue but *binds* it. Like the early church, the modern church receives the OT as a witness to Christ according to its literal sense, and yet the ongoing life of the synagogue remains a strong theological argument for preferring the Hebrew Old Testament to the Greek or Latin, or for Jerome over Augustine. But again, fourth, the scope of the canon is very much at issue. Canon as Childs defines it does not necessarily require a resolution of the debate; it does present one imperative to all interested parties: to hold scripture distinct from

---

[167] Biblical Theology, 65. Cf. Childs, Biblische Theologie, 26. Jerome is not discussed, but: "Ein ebenso wichtiges Argument war der theologische Anlaß zur Solidarität mit den Juden, den auserwählten Tradenten dieser Tradition." In both places, Romans 9:5 is referenced. Romans 1:4 is added in *Biblical Theology*.

[168] *Biblical Theology*, 65, my emphasis.

[169] Childs, Biblische Theologie, 26. Cf. *Biblical Theology*, 67: "the danger of the Catholic position which emerged in the course of the church's history lay in the temptation to render the Word captive to more easily adaptable human traditions, often in the name of piety. Any appeal solely to tradition or praxis apart from the critical norm exercised by the content of the biblical witness eventually runs counter to the essence of a Christian theology of canon."

commentary.[170] We are not prophets or apostles; we are exegetes — or the exegeted. Scripture inscribes tradition, not the other way around.

III. Conclusion: Whither the Mystery?

In 1996 Childs gives his fullest definition of "midrash," complete with a reprise on Seeligmann, who is said to have argued that the roots of adaptive midrash in the late biblical period "assumed a quasi-stable biblical text which established fixed parameters."[171] The definition occurs in a discussion of the misapplication of midrash, especially in Wellhausen's mode.[172]

> The concept of midrash had its origins within the specific historical context of rabbinic Judaism during the Tannaite and post-Tannaite periods. In the early 19th century Jewish scholars such as Zunz and Geiger found the warrant for this approach to interpretation already present in the late books of the Hebrew Bible, especially in Chronicles, but the technical use of the term is rabbinic in origin. The midrashic approach to exegesis worked with a variety of assumptions. It assumed a *largely stable text* of the Hebrew Scriptures which formed a coherent corpus of authoritative writings. The written text was complemented by a body of *equally authoritative oral tradition*. Scripture thus provided an inexhaustible resource for the interpreter to draw from the text religious wisdom for the continuing instruction of the community in Torah. Tensions which arose in the text were to be resolved with the help of oral tradition by a form of *intertextuality* in which one passage illuminated another according to a pattern of holistic reading. In sum, the midrashic method worked within carefully articulated restraints which were grounded in certain religious precepts of orthodox Judaism and which had been shaped by careful philological and contextual rules.[173]

By emphasizing constraints and parameters on historic Jewish midrash, Childs implicitly guards against misapplications by modern liberal Christians. The *Schriftgelehrte* intertextuality seen in OT prophets (e.g., Third Isaiah) still attests the authoritative "function of the biblical text. The text is the tradent of

---

[170] Childs, Critique, 177: "Judaism distinguished sharply between text and commentary. Christianity continued this position in setting apart apostolic witness (text) from later church tradition. To retain this distinction both synagogue and church assigned a unique value to the text's plain or literal sense." With more nuance Sheppard, Criticism, emphasizes that historic Christianity and Judaism took fundamentally different approaches to a common scriptural heritage. Midrash was formative in rabbinic Judaism, but Christians tended to prioritize "a nonmidrashic, 'plain' or 'literal sense'" (864). The starkness of Childs' phrasing is harder to credit, and is one of the places he is most vulnerable to the charge of letting his theology cloud his history. His pronounced disinterest in the DSS (see the penultimate line of the letter at footnote 45, above) could be taken as indicative of this weakness. It is seriously doubtful whether the Habakkuk Pesher or the Book of Jubilees upholds such a firm distinction between text and commentary.

[171] Childs, Retrospective Reading, 362.

[172] The use of "midrash" by Clements is "an unfortunate aberration akin to Wellhausen's characterization of the Chronicler's distortion of the book of Kings" (ibid., 370). It smacks of "naïve supernaturalism or arrid [*sic*] historical rationalism" (371). (In 1967 Childs had covered some of the same ground as Clements, *Isaiah*, does in 1980.)

[173] Ibid., 369–370, my emphasis. Cf. *OT Theology*, 213.

authority in establishing a link with specific prophetic figures. The literature has no life apart from Israel's life, institutions, and offices."[174] It is simply that this authority functions differently in church and synagogue. Intertextuality (a species of figuration) will thus also be a different animal in Jewish exegesis. And yet the warrant for intertextual reading derives from the shape of the prophetic literature. "A prophetic text is specific and concrete, yet its imagery continues to reverberate within the tradition. It continues to exert a coercion on future generations of recipients and gives evidence of its force in the way in which a text is actualized to remain highly existential even in changing historical contexts." An "echoing effect arises from a widespread conviction that the authority of a single text extends to the larger story and partakes in the self-same reality." This exegetical activity was extended or retrojected in the formation of biblical prophecy; either way the "intertextuality rests on the same inner logic of Scripture's textual authority."[175] But scripture's inner logic, as chapter five shows, moves to a center beyond the textual — perhaps further inside — pulled along by a divine referent on another plane or horizion.

In this same vein flows Childs' criticism of several Christian scholars for a misguided reliance on hermeneutics of "Jewish midrash" (Sanders, Steins, Moberly, Frei). It should now be clearer why this is felt to be "incompatible with the New Testament's understanding of the authoritative function of the Old Testament."[176] I do not know that it can be entirely clear — the rejection of "midrash" (even forms of it in the NT, let alone in the largest sense) is a point where Childs is uncommonly counterintuitive, and in more senses than one hard to follow. Moberly's objection 5, above, is justifiably perplexed. It asks just how possible it is in the biblical or post-biblical period to tell midrash apart from allegory. It asks also how Childs might know that a scholar's reading of Genesis 22, for example, is insufficiently Christian — a serious charge. In an academic context, moreover, the hermeneutical point that inner-biblical exegesis (not just in Isaiah) is deictic and not midrashic,[177] seems desperately hard to prove. Actually, proof seems not to have been the goal. Even in *Exodus* we are told that the exegesis there "arises as a theological discipline and is directed toward the community of faith which lives by its confession of Jesus Christ." Childs has always been "unabashedly theological."[178] By the time Christian "allegory" gets off the ground, as there will be occasion to observe in the next chapter, it will be plainer still that "the church's spiritual reflection on scripture according to its ontic wholeness falls into the genre of praise, worship, and self-criticism rather than apologetics and polemics."[179] If so, one has to wonder

[174] Ibid., 375.

[175] Ibid., 376.

[176] Childs, Reflections on an Era, 34, quoted at footnotes 27 and 88, above.

[177] *Isaiah*, 442, 445, 462, 479. See section B.II in chapter five, above.

[178] *Exodus*, ix.

[179] *Struggle*, 125; see chapter seven.

what all the critique is about. There is a great deal of critique, often (as against Frei, Moberly and Steins in 2003) very sharp. Why? I think it significant that at Bern in 1985, facing Neusner's challenge (a "recht starken Angriff") to the very idea of canon, Childs begins by appealing to his "Christian colleagues." There is something very fitting about this. He is struggling to understand and defend the character of Christian scripture, and this is a Christian vocation.

I leave aside the question of whether such an approach belongs in the academy, fully aware that for many (Albertz's version of objection 4) it does not. It used to, for others it still does, and in Childs' life it did. This chapter seeks instead to address the ecumenical connection Childs feels, that from his lucid, early rejection of Wellhausen on midrash accords a great deal of respect to the synagogue. Is it possible for the church — through repentance, Childs will say, and a diligent searching of the scriptures — "to speak meaningfully on the faith it shares with Judaism"?[180] It is one thing to say in a Christian setting — the pages of *Pro Ecclesia* in fact — that in the NT (and Christian) view "the authoritative function of the Old Testament … has been continually transformed by the Spirit into the law of Christ." How does this play as a claim vested in "the role of Jewish midrash"?[181] Rendtorff feels the predicament as keenly as anybody. Is he right that Christians today should limit their claims for the Hebrew Bible to things that will be "verständlich und akzeptabel" to Jews? This is the harder version of objection 4.

To say that the Old Testament is christocentric whereas the Tanak is Torah-centric when configured in larger religious structures is, in a sense, banal. The claims may be mutually exclusive, but the comparison illuminates little. Is there something more to Childs' linking of these centers to figuration? For an explanation of the point made against midrash in *Pro Ecclesia* (2005) we are referred to an article in *ZAW* (2003) in which we are told why "it is not by chance that rabbinic Judaism interprets its Scriptures by means of midrash while Christianity has always found the form of allegory most compatible along with its traditional figurative subdivisions." Here, as was seen in chapter five, allegory "seeks to discern meaning by relating it referentially to a substance (*res*), a rule of faith, or a hidden eschatological event. Christian exegetical use of intertextuality moves along a trajectory between promise and fulfillment within a larger christological structure."[182] It is easy to see that Christ the divine referent does not *figure* in the usual accounts of intertextuality (Steins' canonically framed text-text relations for one example) or in the emergence of proto-midrash (always coterminous in Childs' mind with the textualization of Israel's tradition). Making Christ the hidden center helps considerably in making apprehension of the Church's one Bible a coherent enterprise, without

[180] Ibid.

[181] Childs, Reflections on an Era, 34.

[182] Childs, Critique, 182–183.

also making dubious claims about the natural slant of history (Gunkel) or tradition history (von Rad). I think it an advance in biblical theological framework and an advantage to one's neighbors to keep *Historie* and *Geschichte* in dialectical tension — history can thus run in different directions, as it is wont to do; the Tanak and Old Testament can find different fulfillments. But what of the ecumenics of Childs' theological vision? Is it the case that, as Jon Levenson once saw, "[f]ounded upon a historical particularity — the Protestant canon — Childs's method harbors a potential for respect for other historically particular traditions"?[183] Or is it an aggression that will not stand?

The "mystery of Israel," seen in those terms already in 1970, thickens considerably for Childs through the 1980s as he gears up to write his magnum opus. His response to Rendtorff's affronted review of it: "For the Christian church the continuing paradox of faith lies in its encounter through the Jewish Scriptures with the *selfsame* divine presence which it confesses to have found in the face of Jesus Christ."[184] The phrase "mystery of Israel" surfaces again in the Isaiah commentary of 2001,[185] and the concept is integral to Childs' 2004 struggle alongside the church to understand Isaiah as Christian scripture.

This wrestling is the context in which Childs' remarks on figuration and biblical intertextuality are best understood. When Steins says the "interpretatorisch relevante Bezugspunkt ist der Text,"[186] he steps in a direction that Childs (respectfully) associates with midrash, but that his christologically ordered "new vision of the text" cannot follow. The Jewish technique has a number of formal characteristics. For one, "it focuses on the surface irregularities as signaling a tension to be overcome in reaching a new coherent understanding." For another, it "is an exegesis of biblical verses, not of books, which means that each verse is in principle connected to the most distant text as much as to its adjacent neighbor." It "remains concrete in its focus in moving between two texts rather than in seeking a hidden semantic level below or above the written corpus." In Jewish reading this may be appropriate and justifiable. After all, "proto-midrashic techniques had already appeared in the post-exilic biblical period and provided a biblical warrant for seeing a strong

---

[183] Levenson, *Hebrew Bible*, 122, cited at footnote 39 of chapter one, above.

[184] Childs, Witness to Christ?, 64, my emphasis. Cf. Childs, On Reclaiming, 13: the canonical approach "initially agrees with the Enlightenment in affirming that the Old Testament should be understood in its own right. Nevertheless, it interprets this move in a very different manner. The Old Testament is to be understood in its own right because it has its own Jewish voice, which was never altered by the coming of Jesus Christ." The mystery has a little more to do with Israel present than past, although both come into play.

[185] *Isaiah*, 59, 326. For a discussion of these and related passages, see the next chapter.

[186] Steins, *Bindung*, 73. Although I am not entirely convinced Childs has the measure of Steins (see chapters one and three), Steins official focus on the text in 1999 is quite explicit. I am even less sure the criticism, insofar as it applies to Steins, can be transposed to Moberly. See his remarks under Objection 5, above.

element of continuity between the earlier and later periods."[187] As a live figural technique, however, midrashic intertextuality is either insufficiently historical (harmonizing) or insufficiently christological (decanonizing) from Childs' religiously committed perspective. Bound to the selfsame literal sense, Christian allegory "finds meaning by moving to another level beyond the textual."

Highest Common Denominator Jewish-Christian Dialogue

James Kugel has expressed gratitude for Childs' theologically minded work, and he seems well-disposed to the canonical approach.[188] Still, he asserts that "Childs does not go far enough" in defending the final form over its earlier stages.[189] Describing the transformation of biblical literature that occurred late in the biblical period does not sufficiently account for the status of scripture as such. For Kugel "it was not principally the rearranging and interpolating done by editors that turned these ancient writings into Scripture, but the whole tradition of interpretation that emerged toward the end of the biblical period." The emphasis on canon is selective, it smacks of "Protestant allegiance to the Bible alone," and it underplays the traditional rules of interpretation that in a sense also became "canonical": "It does not seem to realize that the earliest 'community of believers' canonized not only the text but their own peculiar way of reading and interpreting it."[190]

Kugel has a point, but it is difficult to reconcile his sense *in 2007* that Childs does not go far enough in owning his tradition with the sense of others that he finally goes too far. The potency of Childs' earlier formulations is more visible in hindsight, especially following the *Biblical Theology*, and it is symptomatic that Kugel neglects Childs' work after the 1979 Introduction and he leaves the secondary literature with Barton in 1984. Interestingly, though, OT theologian Walther Zimmerli makes a closely related point in his major 1981 review of *Introduction to the OT*. To him it is clear from the book's structure that the whole undertaking is meant to serve the "theologischen Interesse des Schriftverständnisses." If the section addressing "The Hebrew Scriptures and the *Christian* Bible" is justifiably short, given the constraints of the Testament being introduced, Zimmerli nevertheless pushes for an answer to the *Gesamtbiblische* question. "Man wird immerhin die Frage stellen, ob in einer so

---

[187] Childs, Critique, 182. And: "Midrash as Oral Torah is a program of preserving the old by making it constantly new."

[188] Kugel, *Guide*, v, lists Childs' name at the top of a list of former teachers and colleagues whom he wished to thank, along with Frank Cross and Isadore Twersky of Harvard. Kugel also stood up at the small memorial session for Childs in Vienna (International SBL, 25 July 2007) to offer remembrances and to praise "that wonderful piece on the literal sense" (i.e., 1977).

[189] Ibid., 768n36 (the footnote numbering is off by one; this is note 35 in the body of the text, page 678).

[190] Ibid., 679.

entschlossen vom Kanon her denkenden, theologisch abgezweckten Darstellung dieses fast völlige ... Absehen von dem Bereich, in dem für den Verf. selber sein Kanonverständnis gründet, legitim ist. *Könnte es nicht sein, dass das Kanonverständnis von der 'ganzen Schrift' her, deren Kanonizität die christliche Gemeinde bejaht, nicht unwesentliche Modifikationen erfährt?*"[191] Zimmerli's answer is plainly yes: a canonical regard for the entire Christian Bible would lead to certain modifications. Indeed, its absence puts the very theological character of the enterprise in jeopardy. "Bleibt die Frage nach dem Canonical Shape der einzelnen alttestamentlichen Bücher, wenn sie so, wie sie in der *Introduction* behandelt ist, ohne grundsätzlich auf die Frage nach dem umfassenden Kanonverständnis der Gesamtbibel einzugehen, dann nicht *doch* ein 'historisches' Unterfangen, gegen das sich abzugrenzen doch ein Hauptanliegen des Buches ist?"[192] Zimmerli's criticism must have registered, for Childs had already turned his attention to the New Testament and would shortly attempt a Biblical Theology in full. In the years between 1979 and 1992 Childs becomes no more explicit about the Christian nature of his community's "confession" of canon than he had already been through the 1970s — think of the "unabashedly theological" commentary in 1974, or revisit the constructive back half of *BTh in Crisis* if there are any doubts — but his work through the 1980s did undergo certain modifications as it progressed toward a more fully realized Christian theology of canon. That is, Kugel's remarks are on target but seriously dated since they do not keep pace with developments beyond the first Introduction. Precisely *as* a Christian, and a Protestant biblical theologian at that, Childs felt pressure to extend his account.

A consequence of this shift — the second of two — will remain a puzzle, if not an offense, to many readers, namely, that the "mystery of Israel" acquires an increasingly christological cast. "Reflections on an Era" closes by applauding the German canon debate for its focus on the central relationship of the testaments and the implications for Jewish-Christian dialogue, yet the piece voices "strong disagreement" over two issues. First, theological compromise with criticism is not an option. To strike the right balance between a "theological reading" of the Bible as a "witness to God's divine revelation in Jesus Christ" and a historical-critical reading, history and theology must be held in tension. Scripture is a "human, fully time-conditioned" witness, *and* "the Holy Spirit unlocks its truthful message to its hearers in the mystery of faith"[193] — this is *Historie* alongside *Geschichte*. Second, soft ecumenism must be avoided. "The gospel is neither simply an extension of the old covenant, nor is it merely a commentary on the Jewish Scriptures, but it is an explosion of God's good news. The theological paradox is that the radically new has already been testi-

---

[191] Zimmerli, Review of *Introduction to the OT*, 237, my emphasis.

[192] Ibid., my emphasis.

[193] Childs, Reflections on an Era, 44.

fied to by the Old (cf. Mk. 1:12; Heb 1:1)." What is more — and more controversially — "there remains a dark side of the New Testament's witness": "all Israel will be saved," but "hardening has come on part of Israel." Israel *will* be saved, Childs maintains, though not "by religious pluralism or ecumenical inclusivity, but by a divine eschatological event."[194]

Pauline Corpus further grapples with this paradox in a consequential section with the heading "Israel and the Church: Romans 9–11."[195] I must content myself with two observations (and commend the full statement to the interested reader's attention). First, Childs' last work points to a possible source for his notion of the "mystery" that has been this chapter's focus. A footnote in 2008 points to "the interesting essay of Wilhelm Vischer, 'Das Geheimnis Israels. Eine Erklärung der Kapitel 9–11 des Römerbriefs,'" which in the same issue of *Judaica* 6 (1950) is followed "by an essay of Leo Baeck, 'Das Judentum auf alten und neuen Wegen'... Baeck closes his essay with the affirmation: 'Judaism and Christianity are bound together with one another through the mystery.'"[196] Vischer and Baeck set up an interesting juxtaposition, to say the least. What space do they share? Some version of this is one of the major questions Childs' later work probes. Second, for Childs there is an "*ontological adumbration*" of Christ in the scriptures of Israel, but this can only be seen through a version of "*Paul's* dialectical approach," as in Romans 11:28.[197] That is, the dialectic Childs sometimes falls back on is not just between criticism's "neutral" history and history in the eye's of faith; it is every bit as much a tension within a faith family. And this too, as Paul himself puts it in Romans 11:25, is a "mystery."

Let me return to the hermeneutical issue Kugel raises, from a perspective of observant Judaism also steeped in critical biblical scholarship. It stands at the crossroads of scripture and tradition. In contrast to the Protestant affection for *sola scriptura*, Kugel sees that the "situation in Judaism is quite the opposite."[198] Traditional interpretation was codified alongside the Torah as Oral Torah. "Although these two bodies of writings were, and are, said to be of equal authority, in practice, the Oral Torah always wins."[199] This makes traditional Jewish belief hard to square with critical scholarship, since the latter expunges traditional interpretation from the text's original meaning. Kugel offers his own solution to the impasse, but he wants Childs to say more about the role of his respective tradition. Kugel pushes Childs to go *further* than he thinks he

---

[194] Ibid., 45. Cf. also *Struggle*, 306–308.

[195] *Pauline Corpus*, 178–193.

[196] Ibid., 193n181. This may be the only time Childs refers to Baeck, but we will have more to say about Vischer in the next chapter.

[197] Ibid., 193 and 184, my emphasis in both places. Romans 11:28 reads, "As regards the gospel they are enemies of God for your sake; but as regards election they are beloved, for the sake of their ancestors" (NRSV).

[198] Ibid., 679.

[199] Ibid., 680.

does. My basic point here, though, is that Childs goes a great deal further, starting when he canvases the New Testament's witness to Christ in the early 1980s — 1979 is not the culminating year 1992 is. (I cannot say whether the outworking of *Gesamtbiblische* issues there would have satisfied Zimmerli, though I am sure that biblical theologian would have read with great interest.) After thinking hard about midrash again, the result is this: *in a way not necessarily incompatible with Kugel's own committed position, Childs opts for highest common denominator Jewish-Christian dialogue.* Here is his best summary:

> A major point to emphasize is that Christianity can make no proper theological claim to be superior to Judaism, nor that the New Testament is of a higher moral quality than the Old Testament. Human blindness envelops the one as much as the other. Rather, the claim being made is that the divine reality made known in Jesus Christ stands as judge of both religions. This assertion means that Judaism through God's *ḥesed* has indeed grasped divine truth from the Torah, even when failing to recognize therein the manifestation of God in Jesus Christ. Conversely, Christianity, which seeks to lay claim on divine truth in the name of Christ, repeatedly fails to grasp the very reality which it confesses to name. In a word, two millennia of history have demonstrated that Jews have often been seized by the divine reality testified to by their Scriptures, but without recognizing its true name, while Christians have evoked the name, but failed to understand the reality itself.[200]

It goes without saying that this is a decidedly Christian take on the relationship of church and synagogue, and the radical christology is only slightly mitigated by the claim that Christ stands as the judge of Christianity as of Judaism. But maybe one should not expect less. Jon Levenson has written cogently on the limits of consensus in biblical scholarship. He recognizes that "Christians must ultimately aim for another sense as well, one that upholds the idea that their two-volume Bible is a meaningful whole."[201] This has more than a bit to do with why Jews are not interested in biblical theology. Consensus breaks after certain larger contexts are introduced. "Only within the limited area of the smaller literary and historical contexts is an ecumenical biblical theology possible, and only as awareness grows of the difference that context makes shall we understand where agreement is possible and where it is not, and why."[202] It is an open question how well Childs' clarity about his commitments serves inter-religious dialog. It does show some of the limits on agreement. And it seems obvious that at least in his case heightening the particularity deepens the mystery. It would be misleading, however, to say of the turn of thought just explored that the "inner logic" of scripture's textual authority comes at last to see its real "outer logic." By recognizing the church's "canonical context" we are not dealing with the triumph of tradition over scripture, as Kugel seems to

---

[200] Childs, Witness to Christ?, 63–64, cf. idem, Toward Recovering, 25–26.

[201] Levenson, *Hebrew Bible*, 103, cf. 104.

[202] Ibid., 81.

imply.[203] In terms of theological vision it would be truer to say that, after gaining a new perspective on the historically particular commitment of some Jewish biblical scholars and hence a better measure of midrash, Childs looks further into his own situation, sensing in the text another mystery.

[203] Childs is Protestant, but the canonical approach often seems to me more broadly Christian, not least on account of its appeal to a handful of Roman Catholic scholars (maybe especially in Germany, and including the current Pope). And the origins of the *regula fidei* are very catholic (small "c"). As for Catholic-Protestant dialogue Childs' most promising work is surely his last. His discussion of church offices in *Pauline Corpus* is particularly aggressive against an older generation's disparagement of *Frühkatholizismus*.

PART III

The Mystery of Christ

CHAPTER 7

Criticism and the Rule: Two Measures of Allegory

Where there is no critical interpretation of Scripture, there will be a mystical or rhetorical one. If words have more than one meaning, they may have any meaning. Instead of being a rule of life or faith, Scripture becomes the expression of the ever-changing aspect of religious opinions. — Benjamin Jowett

Without a form of allegory that at least allows for analogy, the biblical text can only be an object of archaeological interest. — Frances Young

It troubled Benjamin Jowett that scripture could be made to mean almost anything. Like the wind-vane on the belfry, scripture turns wherever the winds of dogma blow. Counteracting this, in 1860 Jowett appeals to its "plain and obvious meaning," to its "one sense." Allegory was the culprit. "For many remains of the mystical interpretation exist among ourselves; it is not the early fathers only who have read the Bible crosswise, or deciphered it as a book of symbols." It does not matter if the departure from the plain sense is slight. Frankly, any foray into the "mystical and allegorical" is treacherous. "A little more or a little less of the method does not make the difference between certainty and uncertainty in the interpretation of Scripture. In whatever degree it is practised it is equally capable of being reduced to any rule; it is the interpreter's fancy, and it is likely to be not less but more dangerous and extravagant when it adds to the charm of authority from its use in past ages."[1] Adherence to the one true meaning of a biblical text, critically arbitrated, is the only safeguard.

Rules and creeds, whether Catholic or Protestant, unitarian, binitarian or trinitarian, are forever overriding, *overruling*, the one sense of scripture. No rule is better than any other in this respect — except (of course) the rule of common sense. For Jowett this does not destroy the Bible's privileged and authoritative status, as one might suppose, but actually restores its occluded power. "When interpreted like any other book, by the same rules of evidence and the same canons of criticism, the Bible will still remain unlike any other book; its beauty will be freshly seen, as of a picture which is restored after many ages to its original state; it will create a new interest and make for itself a

[1] Jowett, Interpretation, 369.

new kind of authority by the life which is in it."[2] To get there, however, one must banish the figurative methods which sponsor established rules and canons. "Where there is no critical interpretation of Scripture, there will be a mystical or rhetorical one. If words have more than one meaning, they may have any meaning. Instead of being a rule of life or faith, Scripture becomes the expression of the ever-changing aspect of religious opinions."[3] Applicative steps may follow criticism, and should, but on the condition that they build upon the bedrock of honest, reasonable inquiry truth demands. Critical interpretation rules allegorical or figural interpretation out of bounds because the latter contrives meanings and referents foreign to scripture's native voice.

Jowett also believed that allegory was on the decline. "The mystical explanations of Origen or Philo were not seen to be mystical; the reasonings of Aquinas and Calvin were not supposed to go beyond the letter of the text." Yet in a new day these revered interpretations "are no longer tenable." (One proof is that those who uphold them resort to apologetic.) They "belong to a way of thinking and speaking which was once diffused over the world, but had now passed away."[4] Surely in just a little time multi-level readings of the Bible would be nothing more than a faint memory.

By the late twentieth century that outcome began to look much less inevitable. In 1981 Andrew Louth delivered a paper in defense of allegory, even at Oxford.[5] At the end of that decade Louth's colleague James Barr concluded that allegory had not only not been expelled from the canons of criticism, but in fact was alive and well in critical biblical scholarship. Moreover, for Barr this was not altogether lamentable. Then Childs, who discovered Louth's call slightly later than Barr, began to consider its implications from another point of view. Although Barr and Childs arrive at contrary understandings of allegory's bearing on the interpretation of scripture, in the end both will disagree with Jowett that allegory had outlived its time. Thus in this chapter, in order to refine the contrast between two almost perfect contemporaries, I will look at two modern-day measures of allegory, one by criticism, another by the rule or canon of faith. In the most general terms my thesis is that in each case, for Barr and for Childs, allegory has rules.

To begin it may help to introduce a partial definition of allegory. Allegory, for Childs and Barr in different ways, means locating the meaning of scripture at another level than the textual. For Childs, as the immediately previous chapters have shown, Christian allegory (as opposed to Jewish midrash) moves biblical interpretation to a "level beyond the textual." This is not an entirely new idea to him in 2003. As was seen in chapter three, at the Yale colloquium for

[2] Ibid., 375.

[3] Ibid., 372.

[4] Ibid., 419.

[5] See now "Return to Allegory" in Louth, *Mystery*.

Barth in 1969 he draws a similar conclusion: "Where the Jews were saying, read the text! read the text!, the Christians said, there's something behind the text. It's what the text points to, namely: Jesus Christ. And there was a dialectic between the reality and the text."[6] To claim the Old Testament as a direct witness to Christ he finds himself having to rethink the modern ban on allegory. The dialectic involved in expositing Christian scripture as a witness to Christ could well *require* allegory, or something very like it.

Barr does not actually think Childs' approach moves beyond the text and in criticizing "canon criticism" for this he reveals how important it is in his own program. Childs is literalistic because he makes the text a closed system, "an intellectual ghetto separated from all other truth by the walls of relevance."[7] This is fatal since theology "comes into existence *only when one moves out of the plane of the text itself* and begins to ask about the extrinsic realities to which the text refers." For Barr "no step in the actual operation of canonical criticism can be described as genuinely theological. It does not attempt to wrestle with the question of *truth*."[8] And truth requires that biblical interpretation move away from the text to some other level of meaning. Barr may share more with Jowett at this point than with Childs, but it is intriguing that Barr and Childs both move toward an affirmation of allegory later in their careers, that in qualified senses they accept this traditional term, and that differences between them here correspond to the ways they understand the Christian Bible and the realities to which it refers.

In the first section I will look at Barr, and in the second, at Childs. Then in a final section I will contrast the way their approaches to the OT as Christian scripture impact their doctrines of the Trinity, which correlate directly to their views on the nature of biblical reference. Before proceeding, though, a few more remarks introducing the history of their debate are in order.

A Long Chain of Disagreements: Professors Barr and Childs

The best-known exchange between Barr and Childs appears fairly one-sided. Subsequent to reviewing *Introduction to the OT*, which permanently altered his opinion of Childs' project, Barr took a different look back at Childs' piece in the 1977 Festschrift for Walther Zimmerli (both had contributed). "The Sensus Literalis of Scripture: An Ancient and Modern Problem" became the occasion for Barr's "Jowett and the Reading of the Bible 'Like Any Other Book'" (1982), in which he challenged Childs' emphasis on historicism in appraising biblical criticism. Jowett was not really a *historical* critic as alleged, although he was indeed a critic, and a (liberal) theologian. His prominent case does not fit Childs' description of criticism and thus casts doubt on his wider diagnosis. In

[6] Childs, Barth as Interpreter, 56.

[7] Barr, *Holy Scripture*, 168.

[8] Ibid., 102, my emphasis (thought the emphasis on *truth* is original).

fact, Jowett offers a salutary alternative vision to the distorting one cast by Childs. Childs never publicly responded. Barr, however, resumed the offensive in "The Literal, the Allegorical, and Modern Biblical Scholarship" (1989), quoting some of the same offending lines that he had in 1982 and widening his counter-analysis of the literal sense in biblical scholarship to include allegorical and theological senses, which on his read are far more integral to biblical criticism than typically held. Two issues later, *JSOT* featured Childs' brief, six page response (1990). Barr replied twice more. In 1993 he wrote of Wilhelm Vischer, whose name emerged as yet another "link in the (seemingly endless) chain of disagreements between the writer and Professor Childs,"[9] arguing this time that Vischer operated not in an allegorical mode, but in a literal-historical mode (or quasi-historical — Vischer seems not to have been very *critical* on Barr's reading). Finally, "Allegory and Historicism" appeared in 1996, in which Barr again took Childs to task for his devaluation of the Enlightenment and his attendant failure to come to terms with the theological challenge posed by truly critical biblical scholarship.

The backstory to this debate is that Childs actually did respond to most of Barr's articles, in low profile ways. After the 1982 piece on Jowett he sent Barr a careful letter, dated 3 September 1982. Childs specifies that his definition of *historicism* follows Frei's by including "ideal reference," which characterizes Jowett or Spinoza, as well as "W.R. Smith's strictly historically reconstructed reference." He accepts "some blame … for not distinguishing more sharply between" these types of historicism and says that the failure to distinguish them is what he takes Lightfoot's criticism of Jowett to be about. Childs stands by his "major point," though — "to point out the increasing separation of text from referent which 19th century scholarship engendered" — and pushes back on what "historical reference" denotes after this historic split:

> One of my criticisms of your article is that you have overinterpreted my use of the term historical reference. You appear to understand this only in its strict sense (like W.R. Smith) and rule out the ideal reference from inclusion. I had thought it obvious that Jowett was not a historical critic in the sense of Baur, nor was he ever concerned with the modern issue of the layering of tradition upon the biblical text.

Barr's 1989 article is in part a response to this challenge. Childs reply to that in *JSOT* the next year, "Critical Reflections on James Barr's Understanding of the Literal and the Allegorical," continues to defend the diagnosis of historicism, arguing that Barr's discovery of allegory in modern scholarship only blurs the extent to which "biblical scholars of the Enlightenment broke with tradition." That is, "the major element which separates ancient or medieval allegory from that of the modern era has not been adequately assessed. The dominant characteristic of biblical scholarship following the Enlightenment is the different understanding of the Bible's function as a medium of revelation. In modern

[9] Barr, Vischer, 38.

terminology, it is the issue of *referentiality*."[10] I do not know how Childs reacted when Barr published again in 1993, on Vischer, but "Allegory and Historicism" got another prompt letter, dated 21 March 1996. It returns to the long-standing issues of historicism and the nature of biblical reference:

> In respect to your argument, the initial problem is that we do not share in common one definition of historicism. You define it as "the idea that, in order to understand something, the essential mode is to get at its origins" (p. 106). My understanding is a very different one. It has been been shaped by the European debate and is largely compatible, say, with the entries in the *RGG*, 2nd and 3rd editions. In a word, historicism is an approach to the critical study of history which assumes that historical reality has been formed solely from forces with the phenomenological world — to use Kant's terminology, or must conform to the rules of analogy or uniformity common to human experience — to use Troeltsch's language.

The letter is cordial, but also promises to drop the long chain of disagreements. "I am happy that you have had the chance to express in detail your position on these matters. For my part, I shall not pursue the matter, but let this debate lapse. I fear that we are like two ships passing in the night." Childs did take one further step, though. In 1995 he had selected a handful of letters and papers for deposit in the Princeton Seminary archives. He later sent a supplement. A handwritten note the the archivist (1 April 1996) states: "May I request that you file these enclosed copies of two unpublished letters in my archival storage box. I think that the material may be of interest to anyone in time who is pursuing the long debate between J. Barr and me." Indeed.[11]

Childs did respond in print to this front of Barr's attack on other occasions, such as in a few pages of *OT Theology* and his review of Barr's *Holy Scripture*. Inferences can be drawn, too, about the Festschrift items each wrote for the other. Barr sketched what he supposed to be the theologian's case *against* biblical theology,[12] whereas Childs recalled an almost forgotten era whose biblical scholars, despite their reputation for polemics, achieved a surprisingly broad "interconfessional and international range" of engagement, possible in part because of a shared language (Latin), but also, significantly, because of a commitment to an agreed literal sense.[13] Multi-level readings of scripture were permissible in the seventeenth century but clearly to be distinguished from scripture's plain sense. Consensus like this was destroyed by loss of this in the rise of historical criticism, not enabled by it.[14] But Childs largely turned away

[10] Childs, Barr's Understanding, 4, my emphasis. To anticipate, the major difference between Barr and Childs turns on the directness of biblical reference, which actually confirms the idea of a major hermeneutical rupture at the Enlightenment in matters allegorical.

[11] Both letters are reproduced in full in the appendix, below.

[12] Barr, Against Biblical Theology.

[13] Childs, Seventeenth Century, 326; cf. 333: "the literal sense was considered by all to have the greatest authority and not to be abused when moving to a different level of interpretation."

[14] Ibid., 333: "Few would wish to deprecate the enormous gains in understanding which emerged from the new historical methods. Yet perhaps one of its greatest ill effects was that it

from the long chain of disagreements with Barr to spend his energy on other pursuits.[15] Barr sought twice to discount the story told in "Sensus Literalis," an anticipatory stand-in for the thesis across *Introduction to the OT* and one that required less digging to undermine,[16] and he got a single public reply. He probed that response twice again, but the improbable provocation with which his fourth rebuke closed — "What else did I say?" — finally went unanswered.

Perhaps because of Childs' relative silence, which is even more conspicuous following *Concept of BTh*, Paul Noble once attempted to referee. "The *Sensus Literalis*: Jowett, Childs, and Barr" (1993) surveys the debate up to that stage,[17] examines Jowett again, and on most counts sides with Childs. Noble points to precarious foundations underlying Barr's treatment of Jowett and then argues positively that Childs' focus on Jowett's interest in the original meaning, as one index of how history somehow acquired prominence in the critical era, is justified. Barr introduces an important qualification or two, but "interpreting the Bible 'like any other book' was a rubric that had strong anti-canonical, pro-original connotations."[18]

I do not intend to re-open the question of Jowett's significance for trends in biblical scholarship, except insofar as it is a link in the chain under consideration. I do wish to revisit this exchange, however, for two main reasons. First, it fills out the comparison of Barr and Childs begun in this book's first chapters. I hope to sharpen the theological and hermeneutical contrasts between these scholars, both giants in their time. Second, Barr serves well to put into relief Childs' thought on the *sensus literalis*, allegory, the rule of faith, the value of traditional exegesis in contemporary scholarship and theology — all crucial ingredients in what I gloss as Childs' sourcing of the tradition. In this respect Noble offers a better reading of Childs than does Barr, but he too overlooks the full, programatic significance of traditional discourse for Childs.

---

initially nourished and exacerbated the disharmony between Catholics and Protestants which has only recently begun to heal." Contrast Barr, Bibelkritik, 37–38, or *Holy Scripture*, 150.

[15] It is worth pointing out that Childs always remembered some of Barr's contributions favorably. For instance, after reviewing *Semantics* in 1961 (where he expresses appreciation and "frequent disagreement" [377]), he invariably affirms the core of that book's critique. Childs' criticism of Moberly for the fallacy of "totality transfer" in 2003 is a dramatic instance of this, and it is not an isolated one.

[16] Barr, Allegory, 109–110: "I make no pretense of having done the extensive study of past exegesis that Childs has done. I only say that, at various points where I have made soundings, my impression has been a very different one." Barr's refusal to credit Childs' wide reading is bewildering. Has Childs really "forfeited the right to instruct us about history"?

[17] Barr acknowledges the piece in 1996 but seems not to have been affected by its argument, unless it prompted him to declare Mark Brett's *earlier* account "the best discussion published" in 1999 (*Concept of BTh*, 392).

[18] Noble, Sensus Literalis, 7. Barr's argument about Jowett has been invoked recently by Barton, *Nature*, 40, 69–71, who unfortunately shows no awareness of Noble's challenge to it.

Finally, a word of caution. The danger of terminological slippage between Barr and Childs can be severe. I have argued that Barr is not a reliable guide to Childs' thought in general — frequently because Barr operates with narrower definitions, e.g. of canon (a list of books) or of history (the truth about what really happened) — and this is no less true when they conflict over traditional categories like spirit and letter. I fully agree with Noble "that Barr has largely missed the point that Childs is making" in 1977,[19] as with his identification of the reason for Barr's misunderstanding of Childs on the *sensus literalis*. After comparing Barr and Childs on creation in Genesis, Noble summarizes,

> Barr is here using "literal" in a quite different sense from Childs. Childs' use of "literal," when characterizing critical studies, affirms that Gen. 2 f. was interpreted as evidence for a positivity behind the text. But whether, when interpreted literally in *this* sense, it informed one of specific (purported) facts about a historical Adam and Eve — i.e. whether it is also "literal" in Barr's sense — or whether it is a witness to general truths about man's creaturely status — i.e. is "allegorical" in Barr's sense — is a different question entirely.[20]

Thus in what follows I will concentrate less on Barr's complaints against Childs and more on each scholar's distinct understanding of letter in relation to spirit. Barr sets himself as Childs' foil on things literal and allegorical, thus making allegory a suitable way of exploring their differences. The next step in that task is to look at Barr on his own terms.

A. Barr and the (Allegorical) Nature of Biblical Criticism

If a statement equivalent to Childs' seminal "Sensus Literalis" exists for Barr, it is probably his "Bibelkritik als theologische Aufklärung," an essay presented in 1981 at a Vienna conference on the Enlightenment's theological legacy. In it the impact of the then-recent *Introduction to the OT* is muted but palpable. One senses that Barr is still swimming in the wake of that argument but that he has found his bearings and plotted a course. He sets forth a bracing revision of biblical criticism. As a theology of biblical authority, it was almost certainly honed as an alternative to the one associated with canon. "Bibelkritik" grounds what he will eventually say about the canonical approach in 1983 and beyond. Themes in the essay recall Barr's earlier work, too, but have been marshalled to a new, clearer purpose. At its core, Barr now claims, criticism is not a method, nor a mode of historical inquiry, but rather a world-view in its own right: biblical criticism is "auch eine Weltanschauung, die in genau demselben vielseitigen Verhältnis zur Philosophie, zur Literaturanalyse, und besonders zur Geschichte der Theologie steht."[21] *Freedom* is its most essential characteristic;

---

[19] Noble, Sensus Literalis, 9, cf. 12.

[20] Ibid., 13.

[21] Barr, Bibelkritik, 30.

its most important task, to liberate God's people from dogmatic systems that threaten powerfully to imprison their minds.[22]

John Barton, in a 2007 book dedicated to Barr's memory, signals the importance of "Bibelkritik" by citing the essay as one of two core stimuli to his own thinking over decades (the other: Barr's *Holy Scripture*). *The Nature of Biblical Criticism* dovetails again and again with themes to be discussed below, even as Barton's earlier work echos Barr at many points (see chapter two). Since Barr's foundations remain my primary concern I will reference *Nature* only as necessary. Yet its title, adapted for the present section heading, serves well as an epithet for the Barr/Barton counter-offensive. I choose it aware that Barton selects for a similar purpose *Reclaiming the Bible for the Church*, a collected volume parallel in name to Childs' title essay.[23] Barton's declaration that "[t]here is a battle going on at the moment between those who believe that biblical criticism is too much in the grip of a secular and skeptical spirit and those who think it has still not managed to escape the hand of ecclesiastical and religious authority" is a touch dramatic, and his report on the munitions of theological exegetes lacks precision,[24] yet he underlines and extends the line Barr begins to draw in the sand in 1981. For Barton as for Barr, the stakes of war are nothing less than religious and intellectual freedom.

The hallmarks of Barr's proposal, then, are as follows. It begins with a semantic shift. Rather than the typical designation "historical-critical method," current among its advocates and opponents, the older designation "biblical criticism" is much to be preferred. Advocates should welcome the shift as a move to territory less vulnerable to the sniping of those who resist. Yet not so much a retreat from the embattled term "history," it recognizes the properly basic characteristics of biblical criticism, especially "Literaturverständnis."[25] (Hence the allergy to Introduction — the genre focuses too exclusively on historical matters which, although possessing real importance, are ancillary to the critical enterprise.) Theology is a basic ingredient as well, of which the essence, again, is freedom. Barr struggles a bit to identify the theological heritage of criticism, vacillating from Luther's reformation ideals, where a congruence with Paul is considered, to the Renaissance, where Aristotle or John Dryden

---

[22] Webster, *Holy Scripture*, spots in Barr a "collapsing together of Luther's understanding of Christian liberty and Kant's understanding of free inquiry" (104). And Topping, *Revelation, Scripture and Church*, 23, adds that classically reformed accounts of freedom, such as Barth's, emphasize freedom as a property of God.

[23] Childs, On Reclaiming, cf. Barton, *Nature*, 142.

[24] Ibid., 185. For an extensive review see Moberly, Biblical Criticism. Moberly finds much to commend, but he observes "that Barton, despite his professed concern not to distort the case for 'theological reading,' has in fact patently distorted it. For some reason, when he comes to theological issues, Barton loses both the nuance and the eirenic spirit of the preceding discussion" (76).

[25] Barr, Bibelkritik, 31. Or in Barton's formulation of 1984: genre competence.

might be named, to the Enlightenment, when critical ideals first blossomed.[26] Yet there can be no doubt that criticism is a theological category:

> Kritik ist kein neutraler Begriff, auch keine Methode, auch kein Forschungsbereich wie die Einleitungswissenschaft. Die Idee Kritik verweist auf die Freiheit. Sie ist *keine Methode*, sondern die *Freiheit*, die Ergebnisse der Methode anzunehmen. Man kann sogenannte "moderne Methoden" anwenden, ohne im geringsten vom Geiste der Kritik berührt zu werden. Kritik bedeutet die Bereitschaft, nicht nur Methoden anzuwenden, sondern ihnen zu folgen, wohin immer sie führen mögen. Auf die Bibel angewandt, bedeutet das besonders: die Freiheit, zu exegetischen Ergebnissen zu kommen, die von der früheren theologischen Exegese abweichen. In diesem Sinne ist die Kritik ein Kind der Aufklärung; aber zugleich auch ein Kind der Reformation, denn die Theologie der Reformation war in diesem Sinne ausgesprochen "kritisch." Die theologische Tradition war nicht mehr imstande, die Möglichkeiten der Interpretation vollkommen zu bestimmen.[27]

Thus Barr asserts Christian grounds for an ideal that long predates freedom's secular pedigree, that has first-order consequences for any understanding of the Bible's place in religious discourse, and that impacts directly (positively, though often by negation) on the well-being of believing communities.

But there clearly is something pivotal about post-traditional scholarship. Barr's title already indicates the centrality of the Enlightenment in his critical paradigm. As he worries in his review of *Introduction to the OT*, Childs seems not to see that "critical study" makes "a quite *decisive* difference to our understanding of scripture."[28] Over time Barr only becomes more adamant about our need to hearken the sea change. As in "Bibelkritik," so in 1999 one finds the belief that criticism emerged to counterbalance the weight of tradition, a burden which threatens to overwhelm scripture's essential meaning to this very day.

> Theological interpretation is already there in the mind of the student before any exegetical courses are undertaken. Theology has priority. It comes from the religious tradition and is inculcated *as the essential meaning of scripture* before any academic exegesis is done. Exegesis therefore does not work by *initiating*, in the absence of theology, a move which should eventually lead to some sort of theological interpretation. On the contrary, it operates as a *critical* force, questioning the theology that is already there, asking whether it really has a biblical basis, enriching it with new information and perspectives.[29]

---

[26] Ibid., see 33, 32 and 34, respectively.

[27] Ibid., 32, my emphasis. To say one can wield critical tools without having the critical spirit is likely a dig at Childs, and it may contextualize Barr's intransigent use of the phrase "canon criticism" over and against Childs' express preference for "canonical approach."

[28] Barr, Childs' Introduction, 17, original emphasis. Cf. *Concept of BTh*, 553, where Barr has Childs compete with Walter Brueggemann for the obviously undesirable "prize" title "greater hater of the Enlightenment." It is awarded to Brueggemann on a technicality.

[29] Barr, *Concept of BTh*, 79, original emphasis. For an early rendition of the same theme, see Barr, *Old and New*, 170. As an aside, Barton's allegation in 1984 that "canon criticism" is parasitic, that without criticism proper it would cease to exist appears to be internally inconsistent. For Barr, too, biblical theology "depends for its existence upon that with which it

Against pre-critical retrenchment on the one hand (Childs on Barr's read), and post-critical revolt on the other (Brueggemann), Barr insists that a critical paradigm remains the best option. In the history of ideas, the Enlightenment first secured a vantage from which to evaluate scriptural truth — to interrogate what we might now call theological exegesis — and the hard lesson taught in that Age has still not been properly learned.

So Barr shows a certain ambivalence about the tradition. He claims for his model a kinship with the greatest successes of the American experiment. He also owns biblical texts like Galatians 5. Since tension can arise between secular and religious warrants, Barr seems to recognize that Joseph II's edict of religious tolerance in 1781 supplies one of his best precedents, an event of religious moment with a firm setting in the Age of Enlightenment. Yet if it ever comes to a serious contest between the received religious understanding of a text and that text's native meaning — which happens only rarely, Barr assures us, criticism as a rule having upheld traditional beliefs in practice — but when such a conflict arises, the critical impulse plays trump. Every conceivable secular investigation of the Bible should be welcomed as potentially enriching — but again, such openness is manifestly for the health *of the church*.[30] The energy Barr spends thinking about the good of faith communities, especially (as a minister ordained in the Church of Scotland) Christian ones, points to an unfeigned theological motivation to his theory, and to a conflicted one.

I. Ambiguities

To better appreciate the distance that opens between Barr and Childs after *Introduction to the OT*, it is worth teasing out some of the ambiguities arising from Barr's dual commitment to the church and the academy.

The Church's Book?

Barr's first interaction with *Introduction to the OT* carries the not entirely ironic title "The Bible as a Document of Believing Communities." The companion keynote to Gerhard Ebeling's "The Bible as a Document of the University," it was delivered at the University of Chicago in 1979. The liminality of Barr's position emerges in statements like this: "The effectiveness of the Bible as a document of the believing community is related to the extent to which the

is contrasted" (*Concept of BTh*, 5). Is the watchdog criticism any less dependent on the intruders whom he warns with his bark? Without a collar and an estate, even a pit-bull is just a stray. As Barton puts it, "One of the most basic functions of criticism is to criticize, not the Bible itself, but people's understanding of the Bible. And one aspect of this is by showing that texts do not mean what they have commonly been taken to mean" (*Nature*, 102). Without misunderstanding, criticism, or at least one of its most basic functions, would cease to exist.

[30] One good example of this concern is an in-depth discussion of criticism's practical use to preachers (*Old and New*, 188–200; cf. *Holy Scripture*, 92).

study of it is shared by the believing community with the academic world."[31] From one perspective the Bible *is* the church's book — except the only way to keep the book is by giving it away. Barr reflects on how the church's misuse of scripture hinders its life so that he can commend its health. But he is also aware that Ebeling's title captures the spirit of his argument better than the one he was presumably assigned.[32] "It was a major aspect of the Protestant Reformation that it sought to liberate scripture from its bondage to traditional doctrine; and this was a correct insight. But of course, as manifold experience has shown, Protestantism is fully as capable as was medieval Catholicism of imprisoning the variety of the biblical message within a rigid doctrinal system."[33] Because of this very present danger, the church must forego any exclusive right to scripture and acknowledge its need for competent academic input. Short of this, "the Bible *will be imprisoned* in the categories of the present religious community and *will cease* to have *any* new message to deliver."[34] Barr himself once saw that this extreme result does not follow necessarily from the church's claim to a privileged relationship with her scriptures.[35] But henceforth the church must find by losing.

In 1981 the implication is still more overt. "Mit dem Auftreten der Bibelkritik war also eine Verlagerung der Kriterien für die Richtigkeit einer Exegese eingetreten. Denn die Antworten auf kritische Fragen erforderten als Maßstab nicht mehr die kirchliche Lehre, sondern die Forschung."[36] Once criticism came of age, the rules of arbitration changed for good. The Bible is the church's book, but then again not.

The Word of God?

An extension of this paradoxical view falls under the rough heading "Word of God," which includes aspects of inspiration and revelation. Barr's position can

---

[31] Barr, Believing Communities, 36–37.

[32] Barr cites Ebeling, whom he reads as collateral support for his own thesis, repeatedly in the chain of disagreements he forges with Childs: Bibelkritik, 32; Literal, Allegorical, 7; Allegory, 108 (cf. also Barton, *Nature*, 121). Then again so does Childs: Barr's Understanding, 4 (for a gauge of Childs' views on the relationship of church to academy see: Search).

[33] Barr, Believing Communities, 36.

[34] Ibid., 37, my emphasis. The deduction is spurious.

[35] In a slightly earlier essay on a similar theme (Barr, Biblical Study?, originally his inaugural lecture as Oriel Professor of the Interpretation of Holy Scripture at Oxford, 26 May 1977) he greets the 20th century separation of biblical studies from the domain of theology but concludes modestly: "Theological study of the Bible does take place in the context of the church; but that is not the only context is has" (29). He rejects only the extreme views that would either rule out theological conviction in interpretation, or non-theological conviction. The new emphasis in 1979 anticipates *Concept of BTh*, in which Barr wants a *mandatory* separation of disciplines (see chapter three).

[36] Barr, Bibelkritik, 33–34.

be compared to Jowett's.[37] Jowett makes two distinctions about inspiration. First, sound ideas about inspiration must derive from scripture. "There is no other source to which we can turn for information; and we have no right to assume some imaginary doctrine of inspiration like the infallibility of the Roman Catholic Church." Seen as a whole, the book itself attests considerable diversity, even outright contradiction. A doctrine of inspiration must therefore comprehend "imperfect or opposite aspects of the truth as in the book of Job or Ecclesiastes," and "inaccuracies."[38] How do all these divergences hold together? "A principle of progressive revelation admits them all."[39] Other, *a priori* or supernaturalistic doctrines mute scripture's testimony. Worse, they are culpably blind to its internal discrepancies. Second, "any true doctrine of inspiration must conform to all well-ascertained facts of history or of science. The same fact cannot be true and untrue." From science we know that many supposed facts in scripture, such as those pertaining to the formation of the world, are false. It would be foolhardy to pit biblical "truth" against scientific truth. Rather, "[a]s the idea of nature enlarges, the idea of revelation also enlarges; it was a temporary misunderstanding which severed them."[40] Just so with enlightened historical results. These "cannot be barred by the dates or narrative of Scripture; neither should they be made to wind round into agreement with them. Again, the idea of inspiration must expand and take them in."[41] The combined investigation of scripture and nature requires a dynamic, expansive doctrine of inspiration.

Barr agrees on both points with little qualification. First, approaches to scripture must on no account be *deductive*, he argues in 1983. They cannot work top down from a theory of inspiration. An *inductive* approach, on the other hand, rightly observes how little the Bible actually says about its authority, and it notes the diversity of content that inherently resists systematization. In this way, attention to the Bible guards against all forms of presuppositionalism, including that most confused manifestation of it, "canon criticism."[42] As for progressive revelation, there is a sense in which one can appreciate how the words of man to or about God became the words of God to man, but this concession is set firmly in a historical (sequential, horizontal) trajectory — "the primary direction of movement is *not from God to man, but from earlier to later*."[43] The most obvious departure from Jowett is in Barr's abandoning, rather

---

[37] Barr says Jowett is wrong about some things (e.g., Barr, Jowett and Reading, 38–39), but also holds Jowett up as the prime example of a non-historicist critic. Cf. Barr, Jowett and Original. What follows should justify a limited comparison.

[38] Jowett, Interpretation, 347.

[39] Ibid., 348.

[40] Ibid., 348.

[41] Ibid., 350.

[42] Barr, *Holy Scripture*, 22, 112, 166.

[43] Barr, Believing Communities, 29, my emphasis.

than merely expanding, dogmatic categories like revelation. As Barr writes already in 1966, "revelation ... introduces as a controlling theological concept one the function of which is quite out of harmony with the problems existing in the biblical situation." Belief in revelation might once have been excusable, but not in the critical age: "when modern theologians like Barth tried both to rehabilitate biblical authority in the Church and to do this on the basis of a controlling centrality of the concept of revelation ... they were introducing a damaging contradiction."[44] Indeed, for Barr there are few better illustrations of theology's diminution of biblical realities.

Second, the critically enlightened do not shy from untruth in scripture. At the heart of Barr's argument that modern scholars have not in fact been driven by a commitment to the literal sense is the premise that the literal sense is sometimes, perhaps often, false: "biblical criticism, taken in a broad sense, showed that the Bible, or some significant elements within it, was not literally true."[45] Critics have been "allegorical" in that they have continued to seek the truth of scripture *at some level*, that is, at a level different from the literal sense. Note that it is the *failure* of the text at the literal level that thrusts the pursuit of truth into an "allegorical" mode. Why adhere to the literal sense when the Bible is "literally" false at so many points? This would make the text a ghetto — and it makes moving "out of the plane of the text" an imperative. In all this Barr is not at all unlike Jowett on his own reading: "Jowett was a critic in the sense that the diversity of the Bible, and the *diversity and indirectness of its relation to fact and to theological truth*, were obvious to him from the beginning."[46] Is Barr speaking for Jowett, or for himself?

II. In Company with the Author: Or, In Pursuit of the Minds of Men

Along with making truth non-literal, Barr sometimes appeals to the situation of "men in biblical times" who did not have a Bible as we do. The Protestant principle of *sola scriptura* has a kind of logic but is actually a troubling anachronism given what we now known about the transmission of biblical tradition. Unlike some in the guild, Barr's response to this knowledge focuses neither on the literary strata, nor on the process itself; instead it invests exclusively in those "men" of but without the Bible. Criticism teaches that *they* broker biblical authority, not the text. "It no longer makes sense to speak of the authority of the Bible as if it meant the authority of the written documents,

[44] Barr, *Old and New*, 90.

[45] Barr, Literal, Allegorical, 8. Similarly Barton in 2007: "Critical inquiry does often involve taking the biblical text literally, but not taking it to be literally true" (Barton, *Nature*, 95).

[46] Barr, Jowett and Reading, 31, my emphasis. Again, "Biblical criticism ... was preoccupied not with discovering the history or the origins but with evaluating the character of the truth expressed in the Bible" (37).

quite apart from the persons and lives that lie behind them."[47] Biblical books are conduits of authority, but incidentally, not essentially. "*Christianity as a faith is not directed in the first place towards a book, but towards the persons within and behind that book*... The church is founded 'upon the foundation of the apostles and prophets' (Eph. 2:20), not upon the foundation of the books named after them."[48] In so saying Barr could hardly take a stance more directly opposite Childs.[49]

Now why Barr sets and makes a choice between biblical texts and persons is difficult to say. I doubt that in drawing the contrast this starkly Barr shares in the romanticism of Jowett who declared, famously, "The true use of interpretation is to get rid of interpretation, and leave us alone in company with the author."[50] Barr must have appreciated why getting rid of interpretation sounds naive in our time, and he will have had a distinct matrix of personal and cultural reasons for siding with biblical persons over and against biblical texts. One does wonder how he knows he has made the correct choice when faced with the non-identity of text and truth, and of text and person, but regardless, the initial point is simply that he makes it. Even if he were to call this "plain sense" exegesis, as Barton does,[51] the curious result is that Barr leverages a response to the literal sense's displacement (thereby providing confirmation of Frei's thesis in *Eclipse*). Although one misses Jowett's pathos, by traveling the old liberal path to biblical men Barr keeps company with Jowett and others who dispense with the text for the sake of biblical religion. Jowett thinks

[47] Barr, *Holy Scripture*, 47; cf. Barr, Believing Communities, 38–39.

[48] Barr, *Holy Scripture*, 48, my emphasis. Of the italicized line Kugel, *Guide*, 698, comments: "This statement would be true if, in place of 'Christianity,' one were to substitute the words 'Liberal Protestantism.'"

[49] Childs warns against easy identification with prophet or apostle. For a representative example see *OT Theology*, 137 (cf. *BTh in Crisis*, 130, *Struggle*, 312, and numerous places in between), and cf. Seitz, Not Prophets. As for Eph. 2:20, the nagging critical question is: who actually wrote the epistle? If not Paul, what could it mean to direct our attention to the "mind" purporting to be him? Contrast the analysis in *NT Introduction*, 311–328, and *Pauline Corpus*.

[50] Jowett, Interpretation, 384.

[51] Barton makes an odd matter-of-fact claim: "'Plain,' after all, does not mean 'obvious'" (Barton, *Nature*, 111). In resisting the efforts of Childs ("Sensus Literalis") and Greene-McCreight (*Ad Litteram*) to develop an understanding of *sensus literalis* in dialogue with its varied historical deployment — and Barton accepts the historical judgments of both — Barton thinks it better to work from the pragmatic notion, with a rather vaguer provenance, of "what the average reader will understand by the term." Plain is a better designation than literal because "plain sense" is more recoverable from "counterintuitive" use by theological readers (*Nature*, 101, cf. 100). This decision has three telltale consequences. First, it blocks an appreciation of what Childs and others mean by the literal sense. Second, since the use of "literal" by Origen, Augustine or the Reformers is equally counterintuitive to "us," it creates a serious obstacle to Barton's argument that "criticism" stands in continuity with critics of every age. His discussion of ancient biblical criticism (130–135) does not see the full extent of this difficulty, i.e., that for Calvin and Luther the literal sense of the Old Testament was Christ, but

"Scripture has one meaning — the meaning which it had to the mind of the prophet or evangelist."[52] While Barr is neither warm nor cold toward Jowett's notion of the "one sense,"[53] he agrees entirely about locating a text's meaning in the mind of the author.[54]

Prophetic in this regard is an early statement of Barr's on the relationship of scripture and theology. I quote from *The Semantics of Biblical Language*:

> No doubt there will always be some use of biblical language in theology, and I would not suggest it should be otherwise. But surely the most sound and reliable use will be that in which ample and unambiguous evidence from usage leads us to suppose that we use a word in a way that adequately conveys a deliberate and conscious purpose of communication performed in the sentences spoken or written by the men of the Bible.[55]

Here already is Barr's approach to scripture *in nuce*. Biblical language bears theological meaning in semantic or wider literary units — not at the level of individual words or syntax — because of its relationship to a generative theological mind. Despite other differences between Barr and Jowett they are quite alike in their singular focus on the minds of biblical authors as the absolute control on biblical interpretation.

To illustrate, we can sketch a rough parallel between "On the Interpretation of Scripture" and *The Semantics of Biblical Language*. Jowett protests the freighting of biblical Greek with later theological developments. Acts 16 cannot by itself support the practice of infant baptism. And the odd occurrence of επισκοπος is no warrant for the Episcopacy.[56] To borrow Barr's words, "The effect that disturbed him was a semantic one… Words of the Bible then came to be read as if the meanings of these same words, as they were used within later, theologically defined, usage, were the meanings within the Bible itself."[57] Barr's own argument in *Semantics* is similar because, by challenging a facile identification of language and thought, it debunks an erroneous method of supporting theological systems. Linguistic evidence must not be strained beyond what may reasonably be supposed to have given rise to the expression,

---

that today the same conclusion is by no means plain and obvious. Third, to say that "plain" is not "obvious" undercuts the common-sense appeal of his argument. Jowett spoke quite easily of the "plain and obvious meaning" of scripture (Jowett, Interpretation, 369). What can it mean that for Barton scripture's plain sense has ceased to be obvious? Maybe it is just the perception that the critic's elite sense is losing ground, to fundamentalist exegesis or to the more contemporary swell in theological exegesis — Barton's declared target.

52 Ibid., 378.

53 Barr, Jowett and Reading, 35–36; cf. Barr, Jowett and Original, 343.

54 Recall from chapter three, for example, that Barr believes "pan-biblical" theology is fated because "theology exists only in the minds of persons" (Barr, *Concept of BTh*, 214, cf. 4).

55 Barr, *Semantics*, 281.

56 Jowett, Interpretation, 360.

57 Barr, Jowett and Original, 434. Very like Barr and Barton, with Jowett the "emphasis again was not basically historical: it was semantic and literary."

and this appeal to best linguistic practice matches the call to read the Bible "like any other book." In fact Barr criticizes Jowett for failing to keep to his ideal. Jowett upholds the one sense to oppose many senses, yet he generates spiritual-philosophical readings in which the ties to scripture are just as dubious. "He was a critic in the sense that the meaning of scripture, as he believed, was very different from what traditional interpretations had maintained, and also in the sense that the relation between scripture and truth was not a constant but a variable one." At other times, though, he was "remarkably traditional." The "weakness lay above all in the failure to produce a convincing picture of what St Paul — or any other biblical writer — may probably have thought. This weakness derives … from a lack of historical perspective, and, above all, from the domination of a philosophical set of interests." Jowett rejected traditional interpretation, but he held to the idea of "the Bible as a special world" which as "[t]wentieth-century biblical theology" has shown can be taken in very traditional directions.[58] Jowett, Barr seems to say, was not fastidious enough about reading the Bible like any other book.

Allegory as a Matter of Semantics

Barr's 1989 essay "The Literal, the Allegorical, and Modern Biblical Scholarship" got a trial run in the conclusion of *The Bible in the Modern World* (1973), absent the suggestion that modern scholarship is furtively allegorical. Actually, the chapter "Word and Meaning, Letter and Spirit" tends to favor the literal over the allegorical, the very reverse of 1989. Source critics, for instance, in discovering J, E, D and P, "broke through the screen of ancient harmonizing and allegorizing interpretations."[59] Irrational people keep these old unifying strategies alive. "Literality, then, is only in part a fundamentalist characteristic; it is also an ingredient in critical scholarship."[60] Then again, seeds of Barr's creative redefinition of allegory in 1989 are also present. One concerns referentiality. "The normal use of 'literal' is referential in scope… Allegory is also referential in scope; the difference is that the referent is other than that suggested by the direct sense of the language, being in fact known only by an indirect process working from hints and hidden signals in the language."[61] Allegory has to do with indirect rather than direct reference. Another concerns the relation to linguistic signals. The relationship of letter and spirit is highly complex because allegory often "coexists with a very minute interest in the detailed verbal form of the text."[62] It is not always easy to differentiate the interests of allegorical and critical exegesis.

[58] Ibid., 437. Cf. Jowett, Interpretation, 419, 421, 416.
[59] Barr, *Modern World*, 170. The book was reissued in 1990.
[60] Ibid., 171.
[61] Ibid., 171–172.
[62] Ibid., 173.

Another common thread in Barr's remarks on the letter and the spirit running from 1973 to 1989 is the imperative to know the mind of writers.[63] Intentionality gets priority (it is the critical mode), though here again there is some overlap with allegory.

> The verbal form of the text is being used as evidence from which the mind and circumstances of the writers and traditionists is reconstructed. Considerations which may be valid for any purely referential use of the Bible may now be reversed, or may become entirely irrelevant. The question is not whether Jesus walked on water, but why the Gospel tradition depicted him as walking on water...
>
> When we look at things in this way, we immediately see that the verbal form of the text assumes much greater positivity and importance. Even on the referential level it had, as we have seen, much more positive importance than is usually supposed... But on the intentional level, working towards the minds of the tradition and of the writers, its positive importance is even greater... [For] we can be sure that we have no clues for the discovery of [a writer's] theology and his character as a writer other than these very patterns of verbal behaviour...
>
> This fact in turn is a main reason for the technical concern of biblical scholarship with the details of language, illustrated in the grammars of Hebrew and Greek, the concordances, the dictionaries, the monographs discussing patterns of parallelism and verse-structure, the word counts, and so on. *The detailed verbal evidence is the route to the mind of the writer.*[64]

Barr's intentionalism shares with allegorical-referential reading an acute interest in the detailed verbal form of the text, and this in a greater measure than is common in historical-referential reading. Still more, intentionalism and allegorism agree on the *indirectness* of the path from text to referent. In Barr's words, "we today in general do not move directly from biblical texts to external referents, but from biblical texts to the theological intentions of the writers and only from there indirectly to external referents. Thus the modern interpretative pattern is seldom or never a direct referential relation between the text and the entities referred to."[65] Formally, then, Barr's move from *text to mind* parallels the allegorist's move from *letter to spirit.*

In the chain of essays Barr writes contradicting Childs' 1977 claim that modern scholarship works with a "total commitment to the literal sense,"[66] it is a simple matter of rearranging the links already forged in 1993 to claim that, insofar as literal and allegorical suit the modern situation (they may not very well), the essence of biblical scholarship aligns better with allegory. Thus in 1989 the modern scholar is allegorical in his pursuit of a theological meaning. He is only rarely preoccupied with historical reference, with what really happened. Take creation as an example.

> What he wants to get at is the *theology*, the ideas and mind of the writers. The question is not: what exactly happened; but what was in their mind, what theology did they have, that led

[63] Ibid., 61–62.

[64] Ibid., 173–174, my emphasis.

[65] Ibid., 175.

[66] Childs, Sensus Literalis, 88.

them to express their ideas about creation… The precisions, the details, the literality of the story are supremely important, because they provide the hints and clues which lead us to this theology. But it's the theology, in the last resort, that explains the story and makes sense out of it. That's how the scholar works.

But as soon as we put it this way, we see that the operation of the scholar is, in terms of the older formulas, closer to allegorical exegesis than to literal or historical.[67]

It should be sufficiently obvious that "allegory" here is not primarily a negative label with which to brand biblical theologians. As Barr comes to define it, allegory in modern scholarship encompasses his own exegetical ideals.[68]

Barr's allegory is not medieval allegory. It operates on the conviction that the letter, because false, or often false, is ingredient in criticism only insofar as it points to truth *at another level*. This is a kind of multi-level reading of scripture. To repeat, the analogy is this: literal meaning is to spiritual meaning (the traditional view) as semantics to the author's mind (Barr's intentionalist view). The twist in Barr's case is that the letter, as conduit of theological truth, fails.

III. Conclusion: Allegory has Rules

There is another sense in which Barr's allegory is not at all like traditional allegory, and it has to do with whether or not the church's book is the word of God (see above). Barr puts it this way in *Modern World*:

The modern scholarly expositor of the Bible … concerns himself not with the flat literary relations on the surface of the biblical texts as it is, but with the intentions of the writer in his historical setting. It is within this process of study that historical [!] criticism has come into being, and one of its implications has been the breakdown of the old typological and allegorical interpretations, and therefore the breakdown of the unity of the Bible as it was once conceived.[69]

Allegory, here the traditional handmaiden of dogma, has broken down. Can biblical unity be reconstituted? Certainly not with a Barthian or neo-Barthian resuscitation of "revelation." But why not? Barr conceptualizes three approaches to the Bible as nodes on a triangle, thus:

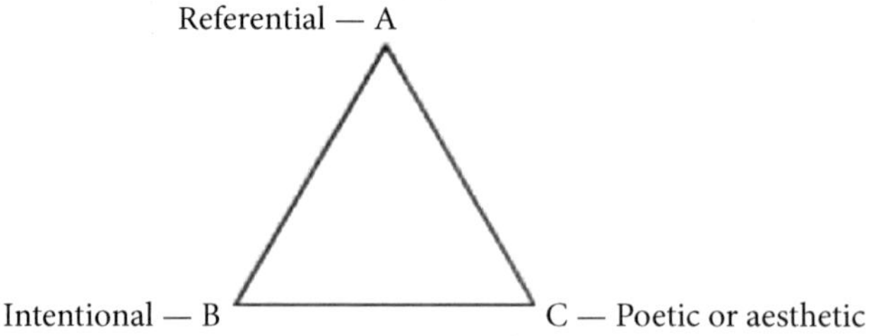

[67] Barr, Literal, Allegorical, 12.

[68] His conditions for allegory suggest as much: "All valid understanding of a passage as having allegorical features must depend on contextual considerations within the linguistic semantics, the literary context, the cultural background and the historical setting. These are exactly what the tradition of modern scholarship has provided" (ibid., 16, cf. 13–15).

[69] Barr, *Modern World*, 63, cf. 178.

Node (A) includes the search for historical entities (the kings of Judah) and theological entities (God, heaven) referred to by the text. At (B) we have "a study of the persons who wrote the books, and the quest for what was in their minds."[70] And (C) designates some literary trends in biblical study, such as the study of myths and images in the text as it stands. Only in the modern era have these nodes come apart. "This triangular distinction between different modes of study of the Bible is, however, comparatively new. The Bible offered a unity of myth and aesthetic pattern, extended throughout the Bible and the world by the typological and allegorical style of interpretation; but it was not supposed that anyone would savour this myth and pattern as a purely aesthetic experience."[71] Undoubtedly the pre-modern unity of the cosmos has dissolved, but Barr means much more than this. For him the dissolution is inevitable and proper. Any effort to reconstitute the unity — that of the universe under scripture — would be a grave mistake.

Barr's eventual claim that allegory lives on in criticism should not be seen as a softening of his anti-traditionalism. "Traditionally," he writes, "theology was primarily a referential form of study" (node A). Theology "sought to understand the entities like God and man, the events like creation and redemption. Its emphasis in using the biblical text was correspondingly referential: its interest lies in *that to which the text refers, that of which it speaks*. In modern times this point of view receives its most towering restatement in the Barthian theology." For Barr this order has passed away, permanently. But again, why? First, "the work of theologians is increasingly dependent on, and concerned with, the apex B of our triangle, the question of intention, the search for understanding of the mind of the writers." Here we encounter "one of the great differences in modern theological practice: even when theology is very definitely based on the Bible, it does not proceed from biblical texts straight to the entities referred to; rather, it proceeds indirectly, and adumbrates its referential interpretation only *after* consideration of the mind and purpose of the writers."[72] Barr even takes the appeal to a biblical/Hebrew mentality as evidence that a watershed has occurred: that habit signals "a drastic shift of emphasis from the referential use of language to the mentality from which it issued, from point A of our triangle to point B."[73]

One could call this shift the death of providence. Once upon a time "the Bible was traditionally tied up with a whole view of the world as God's world; and through this it furnished a worldview, a total orientation for life." Symptoms of the present crisis include the "demand for biblical theologies, and oth-

---

[70] Ibid., 62. We have seen ample evidence that this is not only a description of where modern scholars work, but where they ought to work in Barr's view.

[71] Ibid., 62.

[72] Ibid., 91, original emphasis.

[73] Ibid., 92.

er kindred approaches, and the whole modern reassertion of biblical authority." But the old order has died. It *must* die. The triangle is not to be reconstituted. For "in fact the attempt to reassert biblical authority in modern times is a nostalgia for the good old days."[74] Today, then, in the modern world, "can anything *rational* be said about the status of the Bible in the church?" One can only hope, because hope is the last remaining option. The alternatives are "either that we abandon the whole concept of any special status of the Bible and admit that it no longer matters very much; or that we continue to affirm for it the sort of special status that it used to have, but do so in an essentially irrational way."[75] The second course is not much of an option, obviously. The first course, on the other hand, remains open to Barr, should hope ever falter. How far does he go down this road?

I have said that allegory has rules. By this I mean at least three different kinds of rules. One would affirm dogmatic rules in the form of church creeds and confessions. Jowett, Barr and Barton reject this emphatically.[76] Another would affirm a rule of common sense, or reason. Barton, Barr and Jowett all embrace some version of this (hence for Barr the Bible is not the church's book, except in surrender to the university). A third would affirm scripture itself as a rule of life and faith. As seen at the start, this is Jowett's firm preference. Barr makes another important departure from Jowett at this point, however; thinking of "the Bible as a special world" is a mistake confirmed by the theology of the confessing church and the biblical theology movement which ensued. Mercifully Jowett was not dogmatic, but he was inconsistent and uncareful, and he left himself open to the return of dogma's heavy hand.

In other words, truthful reference in the interpretation of scripture is much less direct for Barr than for Jowett. (Is it by chance that one vouches for allegory, even if a touch facetiously, while the other does not?) Put it in terms of the triangle, only one aspect of one node is disqualified from modern discourse. Reference (A) is admissible — it is actually theologically requisite — but *direct* reference is not welcome, either as an overlay of philosophical interests, or of church dogmatics. That I quote *Semantics* shows just how far back this conviction lies. Karl Barth, writes Barr in 1961, has generally encouraged "the interpretations of linguistic phenomena which I have criticized [and which] are attempts to make such phenomena not 'merely' words or linguistic mechanisms but to make them 'point to' something beyond their linguistic function":

[74] Ibid., 110. On this reading Childs is *nostalgic*. For my case against this assessment see Driver, Later Childs.

[75] Barr, *Modern World*, 111, original emphasis.

[76] "Except in extremely conservative circles, however, people would now be unwilling to think that these creeds and confessions, however worthy of respect, are the right hermeneutical keys and dispose of the complexities of the Bible into a clear pattern of truth" (ibid., 158, cf. 86).

> The language Barth uses about "pointing to" and about "immanent linguistic context" and so on is purely philosophical-theological and entirely distorting when referred to units of a language system... All such units have a "pointing" or semantic function; *they have no further function beyond this*; but what Barth means by "pointing to" *is* something beyond the normal semantic function of linguistic units; he is therefore certainly referring to something other than such units, or he is making nonsense of them.[77]

Sense and nonsense is very much at issue. If the one non-negotiable rule for biblical interpretation is that exegetes must never overstep the bounds of what was probably in the mind of an author, then allegory in traditional dress must also go, for the same reason that Barthian reference must go. Each makes folly of semantics. Anything that distorts the linguistic evidence for patterns of verbal behavior in time is in danger of being "used as an instrument in the imperialism of dogmatic method toward biblical exegesis."[78]

B. Childs' Proposal for Multi-level Readings of Scripture

Canon provides no hermeneutical guidance, no *rule* for exegesis, according to Barr in 1983. "The essential hermeneutical guide did not come from within the canon, but from without, from the priorities of the various directions that the religion might take and did take."[79] Scripture and religion developed in parallel yet did not necessarily have anything to do with one another. Scripture could change while religion remained constant, or religion's structures could alter but leave the literary deposits of older traditions untouched. "Thus the canonical text of scripture is not a faithful index of the religious changes which affected its own development... And, most importantly of all, ... the essential hermeneutical guides, which determined the modes in which scripture might be understood, did not lie within the canon at all but outside it, in the religion."[80] And so it remains.

In reporting this as a defeater for the canonical approach, Barr sweeps subtle and unmissable aspects of Childs' argument under the rug. To take a subtle example first, Childs also posits a track parallel to but not identical with the literary history. Since for Childs and Barr an invisible history explains the relationship of scripture to religion, it is regrettable that instead of interacting with Childs' very different account Barr merely offers a rival interpretation of scripture alongside religion. There is a far more glaring oversight in *Holy Scripture*, though. Barr feels imprecision in Childs' use of "canon" is his first mistake, so he deduces three different senses of canon in Childs' work: canon 1 (as a list of

---

[77] Barr, *Semantics*, 277, my emphasis.
[78] Ibid., 278.
[79] Barr, *Holy Scripture*, 98, cf. 67.
[80] Ibid., 95.

books), canon 2 (the final form) and canon 3 (the authority principle). Reviewing *Holy Scripture* Childs writes that "the level of misunderstanding" is "disturbing": "It is troubling when an author scarcely recognizes his own profile in another's mirror." Childs sees that *none* of these three definitions of canon get at "the major phenomenon for which the term is used," for the process of canonical shaping.[81] What has happened? Does Barr simply overlooked this ubiquitous fourth use of canon in *Introduction to the OT*?

"Bibelkritik" outlines Barr's alternative approach, but "Believing Communities" shows the workings of his screed against Childs more clearly than anything else. So far as I can tell it is the only place Barr countenances Childs' argument for canonical shaping in the Old Testament. Barr rejects the joining of scripture and canon. "Contrary to some recent opinion, the category 'canon' is not essential to the category 'scripture.'"[82] This aligns well with later comments: "Scripture is essential, but canon is not."[83] But contrary to the assertion in 1983 that the authority of canon (3) has nothing intrinsic to do with canons 1 and 2, at this earlier time Barr identifies yet another sort of canon. He writes,

> the Bible is not a mere collection of varying and contrary opinions that happened to be held. Rather, it is a graded and selected presentation... It is not just tradition as it happened to be, but tradition shaped and edited in such a way as to present *to* the believing community an adequate and necessary presentation of that tradition, as the older community wanted it to be known to the later community. In this sense it is a sort of canonical tradition. From this point of view the older idea, that scripture was something that came from God through his own appointed and inspired representatives and was given as an address *to* the community, was not so wrong after all.[84]

Conservatives set entirely too much weight on this perspective for Barr's taste, but it finds at least some justification. Scripture, as it was collected, shaped and edited, accrued real authority that was intended to guide subsequent generations. In some acceptable sense of the word, scriptural tradition became canonical. Still, a little further down he writes, "If ... we take the word 'canon' in another sense, as *the standard or basis for the life of the community and its interpretation of its written sources*, then this is a function provided, within the early community, *not* by a *list* of accepted books but by the essential religious structure, by the fundamental faith of the believing community."[85] Here one sees the split opening up between what Barr will soon call canon 3 and canon 1. "That structure of faith [canon 3] remains after scripture is in existence, and theological interpretation of scripture works with this structure, arranging and

---

[81] Childs, Review of Holy Scripture, 67.

[82] Barr, Believing Communities, 33. A little later *Introduction to the OT* is cited directly.

[83] Barr, *Holy Scripture*, 63. He continues, "Canon is a derivative, a secondary or tertiary, concept, of great interest but not of the highest theological importance." This begs the question, however.

[84] Barr, Believing Communities, 29, original emphasis.

[85] Ibid., 34, my emphasis.

ordering the biblical materials in relation to it. Thus the principal 'canon' of theological interpretation in this sense is not the canon of scripture [canon 1?] but something more like the *regula fidei*."[86] But this forecloses on a basic question: just what is the relation of canon (*regula*) to scripture?

On the surface Barr actually accepts Childs' interpretation of the evidence for canonical shaping — at times "Believing Communities" sounds like a paraphrase of *Introduction to the OT*, as we have just seen. Barr never refutes this by reasoned argument. Rather, he quietly rejects the notion of the canon *as* a rule by subordinating it to an externalist account of biblical authority. Barr's denial (canon ≠ rule) crystalizes almost at the moment he glimpses the theological implications of Childs' proposal (canon ≈ rule). Thus at the root of Barr's case against canon we seem to have the raw assertion of a different rule, a rule with no intrinsic relation to the canon of scripture.

To understand what it means for Childs to move toward allegory, it is imperative to see the positive work he attempts by invoking the canon or rule of faith. It is not nearly so blunt an instrument as Barr would lead one to expect. Also in his response to *Holy Scripture*, Childs explains why his use of canon should not be dumped into a tributary of Reformation orthodoxy, now channeled by Barth:

> my understanding of canon was offered as a major criticism of late seventeenth and eighteenth century Reformed orthodoxy which tended to place the authority of a divinely inspired book *apart from its reception in the community through the work of the Spirit.* By defining canon as those sacred writings which were received, treasured, and shaped by a community of faith, I proposed a very different dynamic from that, say, of Charles Hodge, but one which was akin to the early Church Fathers' view of a rule-of-faith. In my opinion, the discussion … is thus skewed from the start.[87]

Similarly, in *OT Theology* Childs feels that Barr misses the mark because of definitions: Barr posits a "simple, common-sense" hiatus between revelation and reason and then rejects revelation as untenable, where as Childs accepts the term revelation, for lack of a better one, as "an inadequate shorthand expression which seeks to encompass an enormous range of activities related to God's relation to his people."[88] The word has been overburdened in its past usage. Yet its continued use finds a warrant in the way the literature was transformed in the biblical period. Revelation

> is not set in an appositional relationship to tradition, reason or experience. Indeed one of the central goals of emphasizing the role of the canon is to stress the horizontal dimension of the reception, collection and ordering of the experiences of the divine by a community of faith. A

[86] Ibid., 34.
[87] Childs, Review of Holy Scripture, 67, my emphasis.
[88] *OT Theology*, 22.

canonical approach would be equally critical of a stance which stressed only the vertical dimension of divine truth, as if word and tradition were always in tension…[89]

Still, a vertical dimension, understood here as reflection on the divine referent, propels Childs beyond merely social explanations. The Bible has a human form, and yet as such it is inseparable from the divine address it carries, which must not be domesticated.

To summarize, when Barr says "the principal 'canon' of theological interpretation … is not the canon of scripture but something more like the *regula fidei*," he denies from the outset the transfer between *regula* and κανών — translational equivalents — which Childs employs to get scripture and normative theology back under the same umbrella. This is a large part of the advantage to Childs in selecting the cipher "canon." For him it became increasingly evident that the process (the unacknowledged canon 4) by which an earlier generation gave all later generations the final form of scripture (canon 2) had everything to do with the Bible's authority (canon 3), partly because of figural dimensions on both sides of the canonical divide (e.g., in the shape of Chronicles). Contra the intuitions of not a few biblical scholars, the list (canon 1) on this understanding turns out to be canon's least important aspect.

I will unpack Childs' sense of the rule of faith at the end of this section (B), and in the concluding section (C) I will contrast Barr's and Childs' respective trinitarian dogmas. Meanwhile, my purpose in the next sub-section is to outline the way Childs' work handles the compunction to hear the literal sense of the OT as Jewish scripture and at the same time to hear the OT as a witness to Christ, which for him involves a turn from midrash to allegory. Later in his career Childs undertook a thorough study of allegory in historic Christian exegesis and developed in tandem an earnest proposal for the recovery of allegory in the modern world.

I. Call it Allegory

The preface to *Struggle* attests Childs' increased regard for allegory. Upon the completion of his Isaiah commentary he felt he had not done justice to the history of that book's interpretation. *Struggle* is an effort to close that gap. After working on the project for several months he "discovered a major hermeneutical problem that increasingly cried out for attention. One component of exegesis common to all the Church Fathers has been the application of figurative meanings — call it allegory." Thus Childs "became convinced that unless one could gain a new understanding of allegory, the enterprise of recovering a usable exegetical Christian tradition was doomed from the outset. To put it bluntly: for better or worse, allegory is constitutive of patristic interpretation.

---

[89] *OT Theology*, 23. Childs makes remarkably little use of terms like revelation and inspiration, but see the important discussion in Chapman, Reclaiming Inspiration.

But then how is one to proceed when starting at the beginning of the twenty-first century?"[90] The question reverberates throughout the ensuing study. Is a form of allegorical reference avoidable?

Childs delivered an earlier version of these remarks in April 2000 at the University of St Andrews, in an unpublished paper entitled "Allegory and Typology within Biblical Interpretation." Much of this made its way either into the preface of *Struggle* (above) or into the book's chapter on Origen, and its articulation of the basic problem is identical.[91] The paper highlights the centrality of figuration to the problems Childs addresses, and it serves as a benchmark for his "new understanding of allegory." Childs distinguishes his work from the vulnerable revival of typology in the post-war period, over which "Barr pronounced an obituary,"[92] and aligns himself instead with advances in the study of typology made by Catholic theologians and patristic specialists. In this newer research he summarizes "several lines of consensus," though these often read like a gloss on his own hermeneutical inclinations.

There are four points. First, the distinction between allegory and typology is a recent invention without roots in the tradition. Distinctions were made and can still be appreciated, but the relationship is more subtle. Allegory is not necessarily fanciful or arbitrary. Instead — here Childs, following Louth, speaks more programmatically — "the function of allegory is related to the *struggle to understand the mystery of Christ*. It is a way of relating the whole of Scripture to that mystery."[93] Second, a "distinction between the so-called literal sense and the figurative/allegorical cannot correctly be defined in terms of historicity… Rather, the heart of the problem of allegory turns on the nature of referentiality of the biblical text."[94] Origen, for example, saw that multiple senses means multiple referents. Third, allegory has a context. "The appeal to allegory is not a device by which to avoid difficulties in the text, as often suggested, or to allow unbridled use of human imagination. Rather, its use functions within a rule of faith (its *theoria* in Greek terminology) as the language of faith seeks

---

[90] *Struggle*, x.

[91] "Had the Christian church simply been led astray during all these years [of Isaiah's use] and stumbled in darkness without any serious theological guidance from this book? Is there no coercion from the text of Sacred Scripture providing true instruction? I had long since rejected the modern historical critical consensus that nothing of any real exegetical significance had occurred prior to the 19th century, but then what kind of light was earlier present? How did and does Scripture actually function for a community of faith and practice?" (Childs, Allegory, 1–2).

[92] Ibid., 5. Barr's critique of the modern differentiation of typology from allegory (by Goppelt, Daniélou, Lampe and Woollcombe, Hanson, and others) in 1966 is about where his contribution to the modern appreciation of allegory ends for Childs. Barr's articles of 1989, 1993 and 1996 are simply not discussed.

[93] Ibid., 6, my emphasis. Childs cites Louth, *Mystery*, 119, 121. See the discussion of *Struggle*, below.

[94] Childs, Allegory, 6–7.

to penetrate into the mystery of Christ's presence." It is "a means of appropriation" by which "the Holy Spirit continued to address each new generation."[95] Finally, the old contrast between Antiochene and Alexandrian exegesis has needed reevaluation. The Antiochenes were not literalists per se, much less historicists. They "resisted a type of allegory that destroyed textual coherence, that is to say, which distorted the overarching framework (its *theoria*) and thus failed to grasp its true subject matter, its *hypothesis*."[96] At each point the incidence of distinctive Childsian vocabulary ("struggle," "referentiality," "context," "rule of faith," "generation," "mystery," "framework," and "subject matter") reveals an overlap in his description of the ancient situation with the thrust of allegory under canonical hermeneutics.

This is not to suggest a straightforward identification of Childs with traditional allegory. Far from it. The bulk of the St Andrews paper interacts with Origen's spiritual exegesis, a world "strange and even bizzare [sic]," yet with much to teach modern exegetes. Three lessons are drawn: first, for Origen scripture is "a living and continuous vehicle of divine revelation," one which, in contrast to the Enlightenment legacy, supposes that the text can "transcend its single historical context"; second, Origen keeps the literal sense and the spiritual sense in tension; and third, Origen's figuration is vertical as well as horizontal — "Scripture, as it were, provides a keyboard for each new hearer to play and to receive new variations on the one unified story of God in Christ to be rendered in liturgy, private devotions, music, and art."[97] Childs then concludes: "I strongly feel that there is a *family resemblance* in the responses of the Church in spite of the enormous diversity with the Christian exegetical tradition. Obviously much hard work still needs to be done, not least in recovering the richness in the use of the Bible often forgotten."[98] In the case of Isaiah, fortunately, he lived to see some of this work through.

The most basic point is that Childs comes to agree wholeheartedly with Frances Young, whom he cites twice to this effect: "Without a form of allegory that at least allows for analogy, the biblical text can only be an object of archaeological interest."[99] He is content to call it allegory because of the mistaken mid-twentieth century compromise between history and typology, and because this is often what the Christian tradition called its figurative extension of the literal sense. Under the next four sub-headings I will trace the way allegory, or figural reading, is incorporated into Childs' approach from the point of his broken alliance with midrash.

---

[95] Ibid., 7.

[96] Ibid., 7.

[97] Ibid., 13.

[98] Ibid., 14, my emphasis.

[99] Young, *Biblical Exegesis*, 3, cited Childs, Allegory, 13 and *Struggle*, 68.

"A Historically Referential Reading is Theologically Inadequate"

Little in *OT Theology* would lead one to expect a revival of figuration in Childs' later work. For the most part, allegory and typology surface in discussions of the shape of the text itself — Moses is a type, David is a type — or as characterizations of traditional readings.[100] However, there is a new conviction about how different the dynamics of midrash are when contrasted with the christologically centered function of scripture in the church: "much of the confusion in the history of Old Testament theology derives from the reluctance to recognize that it is a Christian enterprise."[101] Also, the book shows an openness to variety in the biblical text's contemporary appropriation, which is a natural extension of *Introduction to the OT*'s argument that the Old Testament became a self-actualizing document. "The canonical process thus built in a dimension of flexibility which encourages constantly fresh ways of actualizing the material." Canon "provides a warrant for applying a similar element of flexibility in its modern actualization which is consonant with its shape."[102] An illustration latent with such figural possibilities surfaces in a discussion of the theological role of priesthood. The final form subordinates the underlying pre-history of priesthood and instead

> the post-exilic form of the Israelite priesthood has been made normative. The canonical shape reflects a variety of moves by which to render its witness, such as schematizing, idealizing and typologizing the tradition. For this reason an interpretation which is directly dependent on a historically referential reading is theologically inadequate. It reorders the text diachronically and in so doing misses the Old Testament's unique message.[103]

To paraphrase, sometimes letter contains figure; types and other actualizing tropes have been built into the literal sense. A sensitive theological exposition would have to make something of them (since a strict "historically referential reading is theologically inadequate"). All on its own, the literal sense of scripture pressures theological readers to consider a figural sense. Rather than allegory or typology, however, the most common figurative concept deployed in *OT Theology* is "intertextuality," which will prove too imprecise.

Barthian Reference Revisited

In 1989 Childs revised his 1969 lecture on Barth for another occasion at Yale, also unpublished.[104] Though the revisions are fairly significant, the recollec-

---

[100] *OT Theology*, 111, 117, 120, 212. At one point, a moralistic reading is said to sponsor "fanciful allegory" (196).

[101] *OT Theology*, 8.

[102] *OT Theology*, 13.

[103] *OT Theology*, 153, cf. 130.

[104] Atop the manuscript Childs has written "Lecture at YDS 1969, revised 1989 (unpublished)." It was delivered at the Beecher Lectures in 1990–1991. Childs was one of four

tions and personal tone still come through, especially in the first quarter of the lecture. Childs clearly continued his reading of the *Church Dogmatics* in the intervening years. Some of the most basic points of agreement between Childs and Barth — the Bible's reference, its living voice — remain:

> Barth continually reminds the exegete that the primary task is to penetrate to the *Sache* — to its subject matter. The witness of Scripture points beyond the text to its object, and therefore exegesis can never rest content with talking about the "Deuteronomic view of covenant," or of "Paul's concept of faith." Rather the goal is to move from the witness to its content — to talk about covenant, and faith, and love — the reality itself. Of course, *once exegesis has understood that it is not an antiquarian exercise, but a struggle with the truth of the Christian faith*, then preaching is no insurmountable problem. There is no impassible, ugly ditch separating the ancients from the present, but the temporal walls separating the first century from the 20th are collapsed by the power of the proclaimed Gospel.[105]

As for the move toward allegory, Barth's exegesis (the small print) does and does not resemble multi-level readings of scripture. On the one hand, Barth commonly assumes "that the text makes one point," a point "not different from the text."[106] This is why his exegesis often simply retells the story. On the other hand, Barth can seem to work with multiple levels, multiple *contexts* for interpretation. "He often assumed that an incident in the life of Jesus had been retained by the evangelists in a form close to its original occurrence, but that the original narrative had been transmitted within a larger and subsequent narrative framework." Barth was not a redaction critic; he did not reconstruct the motives of editors. Instead "he envisioned the larger framework as a transmission of the story within the broader apostolic witness which reflected a deeper grasp of the content of the Gospel. His exegesis of a given passage received its great vitality by allowing, as it were, these two levels of the story — the original level and its larger canonical reflections — to interact with each other." In a sense we do have multi-level reading in Barth. "Moreover, there was a certain compatibity [sic] of his interpretation — a family resemblance — with the whole Christian exegetical tradition. Much as one might react to Augustine's treatment of the Psalter, even when one could not accept much of his detailed exegesis, one still sensed that Augustine was offering a profoundly Christian reflection on some level of the Gospel."[107] Seen with hindsight Barth becomes a prototype of the search for a family resemblance in *Struggle*, and an indicator that something — Childs does not yet voice the word allegory — reflects a need to hear the Bible in multiple contexts. Barth takes seriously the challenge of hearing the Hebrew scriptures as an evangelical witness.

Divinity faculty who filled in for Leander Keck, who had originally been scheduled but who suffered a car accident and had to postpone for a year (see http://www.library.yale.edu/div/beecher.html, accessed 23 April 2008). On the 1969 lecture see chapter three.

[105] Childs, Barth: Exegete, 8, my emphasis.

[106] Ibid., 9.

[107] Ibid., 16–17.

Since Barthian reference is a crucial point of difference between Childs and Barr, here we can add a note on Childs' solitary response to Barr's revisioning of the literal and the allegorical. Childs cites Origen as an example of the radical difference between historical critical and traditional scholarship.

> The biblical text possessed for him different levels of meaning by which divine truth was reached. These levels stemmed intentionally from the divine author who had so formed Scripture as to provide a multiple entry into the mysteries of the faith. Regardless of which level of the text was being heard, the mode of revelation was *immediate and truthful*. Origen remains a classic example of an exegete who held to a theory of verbal inspiration.
>
> Precisely at the point of referentiality biblical scholars of the Enlightenment broke sharply with the tradition. The biblical text was no longer considered to be a *direct* channel of divine revelation, but rather and foremost a product of human culture... The task of interpretation was, therefore, to employ newly won historical tools to discover the author's meaning by setting him within his age...[108]

Barth and Childs retain a sense of the immediate, direct and truthful witness of scripture in Christian life. Barr's use of allegory stands quite in contrast. As Childs sees it in 1990, "Barr is correct when he sees a certain analogy between traditional allegory and the work of some ... post-critical scholars. However, I would argue that the similarity between the two is superficial and is an almost accidental congruence arising from very different assumptions. Any identification obscures the fundamental differences which separate traditional allegory from modern exegesis.[109] The issue turns on the directness of biblical reference, the perspicuity of the letter, or the plainness of the plain sense.

Biblical Theology: Extending Through Figuration

Biblical Theology addresses "the question of understanding the unity of the Bible's witness to the reality of divine redemption in Jesus Christ."[110] The unity of the two testaments does not have to do with threads of continuity in religious development. It is neither primarily formal nor aesthetic. Yet the unity of Christian scripture is real. "The task of Biblical Theology is therefore not just descriptive, but involves a *Sachkritik* which is called forth by the witness to this reality."[111] The very identity of God compels a confrontation with *ontic* as well as noetic dimensions of scripture.

Hermeneutically the issue has often turned on the relation of literal and figural. The Reformers appealed to the literal sense over and against what they saw as excesses in the church's evocation of the figurative. "However, what was offered as a defense of the truth of the gospel in the sixteenth century took on

---

[108] Childs, Barr's Understanding, 4, my emphasis.

[109] Ibid., 8.

[110] *Biblical Theology*, 723.

[111] Ibid., 721.

a different face in the nineteenth."[112] The literal sense came to be limited to one sense closely bound to an investigation of the author. "The result was that the opposite error was committed. If the traditional exegesis had falsely pulled apart the figurative sense from its literal meaning, now only the literal sense of scripture was recognized as legitimate, and this sense was increasingly identified with a historical meaning."[113] Historically the church has needed to strike a balance between attention to the text and to its theological content. Both prove necessary.

> The productive epochs in the church's use of the Bible have occurred when these two dimensions of scripture constructively enrich and balance each other as establishing an acknowledged literal sense. Unfortunately, the history of exegesis has more often been characterized by severe tension between a flat, formalistic reading of the text's verbal sense which is deaf to its theological content — this was Luther's attack on Erasmus — or by a theological and figurative rendering of the biblical text which ran roughshod over the language of the text to its lasting detriment — this was Calvin's attack on the Libertines (*Inst.*I.IX.i). However, *when the figurative sense is grounded on the literal and is a faithful rendering of both the content and witness of the written word, there is no theological reason for denying the legitimacy of multiple senses within the ongoing life of the church.*[114]

Figural extensions of the text are permissible so long as the letter provides the foundation: in fact this defense of figuration contrasts with the Reformers, too, as the "however" just barely anticipates. More on that in a moment.

Childs then advances the canonical approach as a natural home for figural reading in the modern day. Canon, as a rule of faith, bounds interpretation. "It establishes parameters of the apostolic witness within which area there is freedom and flexibility." This means it admits more than just one sense.

> The role of the canon as scripture of the church and vehicle for its actualization through the Spirit is to provide an opening and a check to continually new figurative applications of its apostolic content as it extends the original meaning to the changing circumstances of the community of faith (cf. Frei, *Eclipse*, 2–16). These figurative applications are not held in isolation from its plain sense, but an extension of the one story of God's purpose in Jesus Christ.[115]

Canon is in fact directly related to Christ, "God's true man, who is testified to in both testaments, [and] is the ultimate criterion of truth for both testaments."[116] This is why the canonical approach is not a form of biblicism. Childs resists mimicry of Paul's interpretation, of the New's use of the Old, on *figural* grounds. He wants to reflect on the entire two testament canon in light of the fullness of God's reality in Christ, but his "reasons are far different from the biblicist attempt to recover the one true interpretation in which the Old Testament's hidden agenda was always Jesus Christ." Childs' reasons involve

---

[112] Ibid., 723–724.

[113] Ibid., 724. Cf. *Struggle*, 64 and also Frei, *Eclipse*.

[114] Ibid., 724–725.

[115] Ibid., 724.

[116] Ibid., 591.

> the ability of biblical language to resonate in a new and creative fashion when read from the vantage point of a fuller understanding of Christian truth. Such a reading is not intended to threaten the *sensus literalis* of the text, but to extend through figuration a reality which has been only partially heard. It is for this reason that allegory or typology, when properly understood and practised, remains an essential part of Christian interpretation and reflects a different understanding of how biblical reality is rendered than, say, midrash does within Judaism.[117]

Thus the consummation in *Biblical Theology* of Childs' turn from midrash, coupled with a sharper apprehension of the entire Christian Bible's subject matter as God in Christ, finally produces an affirmation of and return to the ancient technique of figuration — allegory or typology — within a canonically ruled domain. It appears quite suddenly under that name, but then again, its theoretical contours are nothing especially new for Childs.

The Necessity of Multiple Level Interpretation

In about 1997 Childs produced three versions of an outline for a multiple level approach to the interpretation of scripture, one in response to Rendtorff's review of *Biblical Theology*, one in "Toward Recovering Theological Exegesis" — reprinted in 2000, this is perhaps the best statement overall — and one at a conference sponsored by Scholarly Engagement with Anglican Doctrine (published in 1998). Despite variations in all three, there is much verbatim repetition and so I will quote them interchangeably.[118] It is notable at the outset that figuration, as in *Biblical Theology*, invariably arises in connection with the problem of the Old Testament's relation to the New. Just so a fourth essay from the 1990s, "On Reclaiming the Bible for Christian Theology," which comments on the two testaments and their one *Sache* without mentioning the need for multi-level readings, nonetheless pleads for a "recovery of the church's exegetical tradition."[119] This too entails the recovery of at least an appreciation for allegory.

Although Childs would "defend the need for a multilevel reading of Scripture according to different contexts," he does not advocate the simple resuscitation of medieval allegory. "I am not suggesting for a moment that we merely return to a traditional fourfold interpretive scheme of the Middle Ages, which continually dissolved the biblical text into fanciful allegory."[120] The Reformers were right to criticize these excesses. "Nevertheless, in spite of its shortcomings, traditional medieval exegesis correctly sensed the need for interpreting Scripture in ways that did justice to its rich diversity in addressing different

---

[117] Ibid., 87–88. For Childs' take on Richard Hays' more sophisticated attempt to capitalize on the NT's use of the OT, which is resisted as an illegitimate form of allegory, see 84.

[118] For an earlier form of the proposal, to be discussed in the conclusion, cf. ibid., 379–383.

[119] Childs, On Reclaiming, 17.

[120] Childs, Christian Bible, 122.

contexts, and in serving a variety of functions when instructing the Church in the ways of God."[121] The most basic context for Childs is of course the canonical context, though this is by no means the only point of entry. Childs in fact delineates three main "contexts" or "entrances." He lists them in order of more to less familiar, insisting that no principle establishes a fixed order in actual operation: for "the unity of one interpretation is assumed throughout."[122]

I will call the first *res*$_1$. A primary set of contexts involves the *sensus literalis*. "In order to hear the voice of the Old Testament's witness in its own right, it is essential to interpret each passage within its historical, literary, and canonical context." Prophecy does not equal fulfillment; the biblical witnesses are discrete witnesses. Yet "even when restricting oneself to the to the Hebrew Bible according to its canonical shape, the serious interpreter is still constrained to relate the text's verbal sense to the theological reality which confronted historical Israel in evoking this witness."[123] The *sensus literalis* is no *sensus trivialis.*[124]

Far and away the most important statement of Childs' here remains "The Sensus Literalis of Scripture" (1977), which among other things argues that historical criticism reduced the *sensus literalis* to the *sensus originalis*. The study even makes allowance for figuration. "Viewed from the context of the canon the literal and the figurative sense of the text are not in stark tension, but serve different functions as a unified text within the community of faith. The literal sense of the text is the indispensable key for the hermeneutical task of actualizing the tradition because in its shaping of the tradition it has critically rendered the material into a form suitable for future accommodation."[125] In the background one can only suppose further conversations with Frei.[126]

Second is *res*$_2$. Another point of entry extends the literal/historical without contradicting it. This level "seeks to pursue a relationship of content."

> For example, in terms of an understanding of God, it inquires as to what features the two Testaments hold in common respecting the mode, intention and goal of God's manifestations. *A comparison is made, but not just on a conceptual level.* Instead, a theological enterprise is engaged in which neither witness is absorbed by the other, nor are their contents fused. Once again, a theological relationship is pursued both on the level of textual witness and that of the discrete subject matter (*res*) of the two collections.[127]

It is not clear to me whether *OT Theology* could be classed at this level since, although its structure is more thematic or systematic than *Introduction to the*

---

[121] Ibid., 122, cf. another address at the same session, Childs, Christ the Lord, 12.

[122] Childs, Christian Bible, 122.

[123] Childs, Witness to Christ?, 61.

[124] I am not sure who coined the latter term. Nils Dahl apparently used it. It appears at least three times in Childs work: Barth: Exegete, 20; Biblical Theology, 39; On Reclaiming, 16; conceptually cf. Elijah.

[125] Childs, Sensus Literalis, 93.

[126] See Frei, Literal.

[127] Childs, Toward Recovering, 23, my emphasis.

OT,[128] it confines itself fairly exclusively to the Old Testament's first context. It seems likely that much of Childs' work falls under the pursuit of res_1, though far from all of it. Numerous illustrations of res_2 and res_3 are on offer in part six of *Biblical Theology*, which constitutes about half the tome. We will look at one of these in closing.

Third is res_3. A final avenue to the biblical text reverses direction. Instead of moving from the text to the theological reality, it moves from the reality back to the text. There is a need "for the interpreter to encounter the biblical text from the full knowledge of the subject matter gained from hearing the voices of both Testaments. The interpreter now proceeds in a direction which moves from the reality itself back to the textual witness."[129] Here Childs tends to speak of an ongoing "pressure" or "coercion" of scripture, and he names two examples especially. One is trinitarian dogma. The other is the *Christuszeugnis* of the Old Testament.

To clarify, one way in which Childs' approach is ontic as well as noetic surfaces in the second and third contexts. "The text of Scripture, when infused by the Spirit with the full ontological reality of God, resonates with a fresh voice and evokes from its readers the response of praise and wonder. This voice, which transcends historical origins, calls forth the hymns, liturgy, and art of the Church in ever-changing forms of grateful response."[130] Biblical interpretation is ontic by virtue of the fact that it is pneumatic, and this is what it means for him to claim the Bible as the church's book. "Its genre is confession, not apologetics; its function is worship, not disputation; its content is eschatology, not time-bound history; and its truth is self-affirming, not analytical demonstration."[131] It is in these ecclesial modes that the recurrent metaphor of scriptural witnesses as voices in a choir, or as notes in the score of a symphony which is replayed in different theaters (cathedrals?), most fully applies. Childs' figuration is irreducibly Christian.

II. Wilhelm Vischer and the Christuszeugnis *of the OT*

One of the disagreements Barr has with Childs turns on whether or not Wilhelm Vischer read the OT allegorically or not: to Childs' yes Barr said no.[132] Stefan Felber, whose 1999 monograph about Wilhelm Vischer (1895–1988)

---

[128] But see *OT Theology*, 15–16.

[129] Childs, Christian Bible, 124.

[130] Ibid., 124–125.

[131] Ibid., 125.

[132] Childs, OT in Germany, cf. Barr, Vischer, who decides — not unlike his damning verdict on Childs — that Vischer probably did "not have a *method*, but rather a mixture of quite contradictory methods, held together by the fact that they appeared to produce a Reformational Christ. [Porteous said his theology was muddled.] … He *was* muddled" (53, original emphasis, cf. 50).

was the first of its kind, finds that Barr is strictly correct. Vischer renounced allegory. Felber adds, however, that it is another question "ob damit Childs wirklich widersprochen ist."[133] Childs sees that to speak of *Christuszeugnis* is to speak in a form of allegory, and even though he and Vischer do not classify this move the same way they appear to be on the same page. In fact they are not quite, though Childs mulled over Vischer's legacy often in the 1990s, and though it is no mistake that Felber opens with a block quote from Childs and concludes the central section of his study, "Wilhelm Vischer als Ausleger der Heiligen Schrift," with a comparison of Vischer and Childs.[134]

The title of Vischer's controversial *Das Christuszeugnis des Alten Testaments* neatly captures the apparent link between Vischer and Childs. Of course, Eichrodt and von Rad also maintain that Christ is somehow the subject matter of the Old Testament — each also gets special consideration by Felber[135] — though it was von Rad who did much to damage Vischer's reception in an early review of *Christuszeugnis.*[136] But if Childs from 1992 begins to invite comparison with Vischer, and if through the 1990s Childs revisits a dispute which would have been more current in his student days,[137] one should add immediately that, like Eichrodt and von Rad before him, he departs from Vischer in crucial respects. Childs includes "a postscript of a personal nature" at the end of his study of the OT in Germany from 1920–1940:

> Only after I had completed this essay did it occur to me how much my own attempt to resolve the hermeneutical problems of Old Testament interpretation according to a new canonical approach has been unconsciously influenced by the German struggle of the 30s. Along with many confessing Christians I too felt the full force of the powerful challenge of Barth, Vischer, and Hellbardt for the Old Testament to be heard as a theological witness to Christian Faith. Yet

---

[133] Felber, *Vischer*, 335, cf. 204.

[134] Ibid., 14, 292–304. In the comparison Felber finds a "weitreichenden Konsens" (304) but concedes that a major difference involves whether the NT's hearing of the OT is secondary (Childs) or more direct (Vischer). Childs takes a stronger position against christologizing the OT (that Childs' solution has to do with multiple levels of interpretation arises as if by accident, in the middle of a long citation from *Biblical Theology*). And Childs takes a more *historical* route on Felber's reading: "Vischers alttestamentliche Hermeneutik ist, obwohl er auf historisch-kritische Arbeit nicht verzichtet hat, entschieden einfacher" (302). Childs' reasons for parting company with Vischer are theological as well as historical, however; see below.

[135] In total there are six "confrontations" between Vischer and other prominent exegetes; the remaining three are Delitzsch, von Hofmann, and Calvin.

[136] Rad, Christuszeugnis. Then again, von Rad concludes his lecture on typology by saying that we must speak of a *Christuszeugnis* in the OT after all. See the conclusion of chapter three, and compare Moberly, *Bible, Theology, Faith*, esp. 143: with Vischer, von Rad agrees that "the historical sequence from Israel to Christ may be reversed hermeneutically when it comes to reading Israel's scripture as Christian scripture."

[137] Note Childs' discussion of Vischer in 1958, in one of his very first publications: Childs, Prophecy and Fulfillment, esp. 270. Vischer is defended for recognizing that both testaments share the same reality in Jesus Christ, but is criticized for the abstract manner in which Christ is discovered in the OT.

I was also forced to agree with von Rad, Eichrodt, and Zimmerli that Vischer's solution was seriously flawed and that there must be another alternative between the sharp polarity which he set up between modern historical critical exegesis and a repristination of 16th century Reformation theology.[138]

Somewhere in the process of writing *Biblical Theology*, however, Childs came to the realization that his approach sat atop an old controversy about the significance of biblical criticism for Christian theology, acutely felt in OT studies, and furthermore that his answers put him somewhere *between* Vischer and von Rad. "It would be the height of arrogance and sheer folly to suggest that the canonical approach offers the correct solution, but I would argue that the issues included under the cipher 'canonical' raise those basic theological factors, strangely missing in the previous debates, without which no truly theological solution between the church's Scripture and modernity can ever be reached."[139] In other words, as he puts it in a reprise essay on "OT in Germany," today's context is very different compared to that in Europe between the wars, but "many of the hermeneutical issues that evoked such controversies in the 1920s and 1930s still remain unresolved, and, with the erosion of the post-World War II consensus, have returned with a vengeance."[140]

Thus the outline of multi-level readings that responds to Rendtorff, "Does the Old Testament Witness to Jesus Christ?," centers on Vischer to affirm one part of his vision and to push back against another. The "recently renewed interest in Biblical Theology" is only "superficially" a "throwback to the Vischer era."[141] Entry at res_1 insists on hearing the OT on its own since "to read back into the story the person of Jesus Christ, as Vischer did, or to interpret the various theophanies as manifestations of the second person of the Trinity, is to distort this witness and to drown out the Old Testament's own voice."[142] And "to speak of the *Christuszeugnis* in the sense being proposed is ... far removed from Vischer's."[143] But one must in the end speak of the *Christuszeugnis*. Rendtorff's *Doktorvater* saw this, too, in a limited way.

Von Rad initially agreed with Vischer's call for a new theological approach, and later in life he freely admitted that Vischer had indeed sounded the alarm, especially in light of the threat from National Socialism after 1933. However, in his review he attacked Vischer as harshly as any of Vischer's liberal detractors, and concluded that his exegetical approach was quite hope-

[138] Childs, OT in Germany, 245, cf. Childs, On Reclaiming, 4.

[139] Childs, OT in Germany, 245. It is probable that Childs means to include von Rad in the period of "theological compromise" here.

[140] Childs, On Reclaiming, 4.

[141] Childs, Witness to Christ?, 57.

[142] Ibid., 61.

[143] Ibid., 63.

less. Moreover, it was significant that *von Rad did not really attack him theologically, but from the perspective of the historical-critical method.*[144]

Von Rad's theological compromise with historical-critical method trips him up here, though his good instincts about the christological scope of OT exegesis remain intact.

On his own account Childs departs from Vischer in two respects: he does not ignore the genuine advances of the critical era (here he stands closer to von Rad), and so he refuses to repristinate a bygone era.[145] And by returning to multiple senses Childs departs from the Reformers — for exactly the same reason he departs from Vischer: it is a mistake to "christianize" the Old Testament's voice. Calvin dealt with the unity of the testaments by defining the one sense of scripture so broadly that he did not need allegory.[146] This makes Calvin's effort to unite the witness of the two testaments unsatisfactory. He is right about "an overarching unity between the two." But the "exegetical caveat is that Calvin's approach runs the danger of projecting backward into the biblical narrative a meaning that is not derived from the Old Testament. The effect is that he christianizes the Old Testament by a form of psychologizing the unexpressed motivation of its characters."[147] It is not wrong to engage the Bible at the level of res_2 or res_3 prior to res_1, but it would be a serious error to factor res_1 out of the equation. The canonical OT is a pre-Christian witness to Christ.

Childs' mature theory blends the traditional with the critical — multiple senses of scripture are combined with a lesson historical criticism teaches on the *sensus literalis* that offers a corrective to Reformation understandings, even though criticism took the lesson too far. Childs' late revisiting of Vischer represents his effort to identify past mistakes and work beyond them.

III. "Family Resemblance": A Spiritual Reading of Spiritual Reading

The one who reads *Struggle* for instances of modern allegory will come away disappointed. It is much more a modern appreciation of traditional allegory than a modern allegorical reading of Isaiah — though as will be seen Childs proffers a muted multi-level reading in his Isaiah commentary. I will discuss *Struggle* first, though, as it rounds out this discussion of Childs' hermeneutics

144 Childs, On Reclaiming, 2, my emphasis. For Rendtorff's take on Vischer and von Rad, see *Canon and Theology*, 76–91.

145 I argue elsewhere that Childs is no arcadian. See Driver, Later Childs. Somewhat like Barth (cf. Smend, Nachkritische) Childs is genuinely post-critical.

146 *Struggle*, 211: "Calvin's notion of the literal sense is deep enough not to need another textual level to carry a spiritual meaning by means of allegory. Rather, the literal sense is the true and genuine meaning of scripture. In contrast to Luther, Calvin does not relate the two aspects of the literal sense in a dialectical fashion between the spiritual and the carnal." Cf. Childs, Sensus Literalis, 87.

147 *Struggle*, 217. Cf. Childs, Genre of Commentary, 191.

of allegory. It revisits these in service of "the enterprise of recovering a useable exegetical Christian tradition" in the twenty-first century and is a reading of the tradition reading Isaiah, a search for a "family resemblance" in the church's accommodation of the prophet.[148] And Childs does find "some basic and constitutive features" in the church's reception of Isaiah, which he catalogues in a sentence that comes as close as possible to a thesis statement: "the authority of scripture, its literal and spiritual senses, scripture's two testaments, its divine and human authorship, its Christological content, and the dialectical nature of history."[149] Typically, whether or not an exegete struggles (wrestles) with these six challenges determines whether the exegesis belongs to the family not.

Struggle, then, is an exercise in typology of another sort: it drafts a typology of Christian readers. A given profile can either be one of continuity or of breach.[150] Also, though Childs does not abandon the Jewish exegetical tradition,[151] he is preoccupied with the particular challenges arising from the affirmation of a two-part Christian Bible; Christian resources naturally come to the fore. The Jewish voice of Isaiah must be heard, but the driving question for Childs in 2004 is how to read its testimony to God's work in Christ. Another characteristic of this typology is the way it spans the entire Christian tradition. Although the advent of criticism (the Enlightenment) is undeniably a watershed, its secondary importance when compared to the search for continuity across the Christian exegetical tradition permits Childs to move between modern and pre-modern interpreters at will. No wall blocks a comparison of Hengstenberg or Brueggemann to, say, Origen or Thomas. So on the one hand it is possible to assess traditional readers from a modern perspective. Jerome is criticized for "historical rationalism"; Thomas conducts "an ontological interpretation" (this phrasing is recognized as anachronistic); Luther was on the brink of seeing a break in Isaiah between chapters 39 and 40; Calvin overly christianizes the Old Testament.[152] But it is equally possible to do the reverse — to weigh a modern exegete against a traditional perspective. Gerhard von Rad's typology, to take a poignant example, has been compared by some with Theodoret's. For Childs the comparison is suggestive — there is a "family resemblance" between them — even though von Rad appears not to have been directly informed by Theodoret. But there are notable differences.

---

[148] Wittgenstein employed the term *Familienähnlichkeit*, as did Nietzsche, and presumably others in turn before him (Needham, Polythetic, 367n1). I do not see that this pedigree has much impact on Childs' usage. In all likelihood the term is learned from Frei, who seems to have read Wittgenstein in greater depth (e.g., *Eclipse*, 27 and cf. Dawson, *Christian Figural Reading*, 146, 151, 157).

[149] *Struggle*, 322.

[150] For an example of this leading up to *Struggle* see Childs, Vitringa.

[151] In the same year as the Vitringa piece see Childs, Benno Jacob (and see the discussion of Childs and Jacob in chapter six). Cf. idem, Interpretation in Faith, 449n26, in 1964.

[152] *Struggle*, 97, 160, 193 and 216–217, respectively.

Theodoret spoke of the active and supernatural role of the Holy Spirit in illuminating the sacred Word to faithful recipients. Conversely, von Rad spoke of the spirit more in terms of the charismatic dimension of human interpretation seeking to reinterpret the past through fresh and creative applications. In sum, one can only surmise that von Rad might have been aided in his hermeneutical reflections if he had had the occasion to probe deeply into the writing of Theodoret.[153]

Had von Rad read Theodoret, he might have gained a better sense of how his sense of the "charismatic" in interpretation differed from a more classical doctrine of the Holy Spirit's activity, and perhaps fell short of it.

By way of such cross-comparison Childs hovers around certain hallmarks of good interpretation. Time and again he touches on the relationship of letter and spirit. Justin sounds mystical notes foreign to the historical, or economic character of the OT, thus threatening the relationship of the testaments and giving rise to a "serious misunderstanding of Judaism."[154] Clement of Alexandria's faults parallel Justin's, though he can follow the literal sense more closely.[155] Origen understands that allegory has to do with the nature of reference (so F. Young) and can honor and extend the literal sense without contrivance.[156] Jerome made a kind of advance by placing letter before spirit, but his extensions are often "arbitrary" and have the effect of "weakening the unity" of OT and NT.[157] John Chrysostom made few hermeneutical gains, yet he models the way allegory can aid preaching when restrained by the proper rules.[158] Cyril of Alexandria, despite a reputation to the contrary, takes an interest in the spiritual sense, and he constructs a "tight morphological fit" between both testaments. He seeks not to impose doctrine on scripture, but to facilitate a fresh hearing of the word of God in the present.[159] Theodore of Mopsuestia is critiqued even more harshly than Jerome for failing to connect OT and NT.[160] Theodoret breaks out of this legacy, however, and manages

[153] Ibid., 146.

[154] Ibid., 41.

[155] Ibid., 59.

[156] Ibid., 68, 71.

[157] Ibid., 101, 102. With Jerome Childs hints at the link between a good understanding of eschatology and a limiting view of biblical prophecy. "In contrast with Justin, Irenaeus, and Augustine, Jerome appeared to have little grasp of biblical eschatology" (102). He "may have had far too narrow a view of biblical history, which was lost in his simple correspondence theory of prophecy and fulfillment" (97).

[158] Ibid., 106.

[159] Ibid., 124.

[160] Ibid., 133. To me this is one of the more astonishing biblical theological judgments in *Struggle*. Famous for finding Christ in only four or five psalms, Theodore got himself into trouble. "Because of his concern to avoid the danger of excessively symbolic, figurative interpretation, he fell into an overly literal reading that hindered serious attention to the metaphors and similes of John's Gospel. Also, he could not fully attain a consistent interpreta-

non-arbitrary figurative extensions.[161] Thomas, via Augustine, brings the *res* or coercive pressure of scripture into the foreground. He works with the literal sense, and yet of equal importances is his non-literal mode of interpretation.[162] Nicholas of Lyra lacks an organic link between his two literal senses.[163] Luther changed allegory by means of "dialectic" and, like Thomas, still managed to heed the existential and ontological force of *res*. Calvin majors on the plain sense of scripture, though his is large enough to accommodate a figural dimension.

Efforts to extend the letter echo into the post-Reformation period, to be sure (witness Vitringa). Generally, though, after the Enlightenment things fall apart. The christological center cannot hold. Severed from typology, the ontology of scripture becomes increasingly strained. In the modern period generally, the *dissolution of struggle* becomes a serious setback. Despite his failings, von Rad is one of a few important exceptions.[164]

Childs recognizes that he offers a spiritual reading *of* spiritual reading. This awareness comes through most clearly in his discussion of Cyril.

> I am fully aware that this interpretation of the rationale behind the spiritual sense remains an eschatological ideal, and largely unrealized within the Christian church throughout much of its history. Perhaps the most troubling failure of all lies in the persistent attacks on Judaism throughout the centuries, illustrated in a particularly painful form by Cyril. Crucial to the hermeneutical analysis above is the point that the church's spiritual reflection on scripture according to its ontic wholeness falls into the genre of praise, worship, and self-criticism rather than apologetics and polemics. Only in the light of a deeper engagement with the substance of God's will disclosed in scripture will the repentant church be prepared to speak meaningfully on the faith it shares with Judaism.[165]

What is the "rationale" more precisely? Cyril shows this too, despite his anti-Semitism. He "comes to the text from a *holistic understanding* of the theological substance of Christian scripture" — we could call this res_3 — and he "then seeks to find further illumination of God's revelation by *rethinking the subject matter from within* as he intertwines Old and New Testament texts into new configurations" — res_2 with some regard for res_1. "Lying at the heart of this exegetical procedure is the conviction that scripture is a living Word continually activated by the Spirit to speak to each generation of a faithful church."[166]

---

tion of the Old Testament prediction while affirming a genuine correspondence between the testaments." This contradicts a common view of Theodore as a front-runner of things historical critical or ecumenical (e.g., see the discussion of Brunert chapter eight).

161 Ibid., 137–138.

162 Ibid., 148, 159–160, 162, 164. Cf. *Biblical Theology*, 40–42.

163 *Struggle*, 177–178.

164 Like Origen, for example (ibid., 71), Delitzsch struggled (277). Increasingly from the seventeenth and eighteenth century, others did not (cf. 267, 282, 287, 315).

165 Ibid., 125.

166 Ibid., 125, my emphasis.

As in the 2000 essay on allegory, Childs' hermeneutical ideals drive his sourcing of the tradition. The procedure of spiritual reading described here belongs to Childs every bit as much as to Cyril of Alexandria.

Defining Allegory

Finally, a word about how Childs defines allegory in *Struggle*. As a start Childs accepts Jon Whitman's definition: "allegory says one thing, and means another."[167] The core issue lies elsewhere, however. When discussing Luther, Childs negotiates some of the attempts to pin down Luther's understanding of figuration. Ebeling, following Jülicher, puts it as follows:

> Allegorical interpretation is the rendering of a text under the assumption that what it says clearly hides something else which obtains its meaning from somewhere else. The effect is that the actual words and larger units of the text have been replaced more or less completely by a comparative rendering by means of concepts which belong to a foreign sense of the text and derive from an intention independent of its literary composition.[168]

But clearly this will not do. "It is one thing to make a literary judgment that allegory says one thing but means something else." Luther goes this far himself. "It is quite another to suggest that the allegorical rendering is by definition 'foreign' to the text." To say this is to import prejudices foreign to the concept. "In contrast, the Church Fathers measured the truth of the figurative sense not as foreign, but as stemming from the *res* (substance) of the text itself. The source of the figurative was not separated from the text and assigned to an alien 'from somewhere,' but rather regarded as a different and true dimension of the selfsame reality." This time, perhaps in contrast to Cyril, Childs' reading finds a precedent in the secondary literature (see Christine Helmer's sophisticated exploration of "Luther's Trinitarian Hermeneutic and the Old Testament"). Allegory on Ebeling's understanding wrongly suggests "that the literal/historical is the one true interpretation, and the figurative is a substitute and alteration falsely imposed from some other source than the text."[169] Probably for Luther, and certainly for Childs, this is not the case.

And the *res* is Christ. Allegory or figurative reading carries readers from the canonical testaments to the very reality of the triune God. Precisely here Louth's plea for a modern return to allegory resonates most strongly with Childs. "The literal meaning is the fundamental meaning," Louth explains. Through this "allegory is firmly related to the *mystery of Christ*, it is a way of relating the whole of Scripture to that mystery, a way of making a synthetic vision out of the images and events of the Biblical narrative."[170] Naturally, it

[167] Whitman, *Allegory*, 2. Cf. *Struggle*, 66, 183–184.

[168] Ebeling, *Evangelienauslegung*, 48, cited as translated in *Struggle*, 184.

[169] *Struggle*, 184.

[170] Louth, *Mystery*, 121, my emphasis; cf. *Struggle*, 66, 302.

"does not *prove* anything, but it is not meant to."[171] In Childs' words, the genre is confession, not apologetics; its truth self-affirming, not an analytical demonstration. By the Holy Spirit it provides those inside the community of faith with a means of access to the reality they confess. In short, to move from res_1 to res_2 to res_3 and back again is not an evasion of the text, nor necessarily a warping of the same; ruled rightly, allegory penetrates into the very depths of signification.

IV. Conclusion: "A Rule of Faith Called Canon"[172]

I conclude with a comment about how canon as a rule of faith governs Childs' proposed multi-level reading, at least in theory. If allegory is mystical, how does one know when it verges on fanciful? Is not the danger always that it becomes uncontrolled, unruly? Childs has a very clear answer. Up to now I have avoided the most central plank in canonical figuration, the *regula fidei*. Since it is one of the first traditional concepts to wind up in Childs' proposal (canon ≈ rule), it is a good place to end a discussion of Childs' sourcing of the tradition. We end near to where he began. That is, in all versions of multi-level proposals from 1992 onwards Childs emphasizes the priority of the rule of faith over figuration, and suggests that the rule is a counterpart to the foundational *sensus literalis*. The Bible's "salvific meaning is not esoteric or hidden, but plain and forthright. Careful attention must be paid to its syntax and style. Yet the literal sense is to be balanced by a ruled reading — a reading informed by its subject matter and its confessional content."[173] Figural extensions of the literal operate *within* this more basic framework and are never independent of it. This rule enables him to speak of the "unity of one interpretation." It is also why for Childs the secret sense of allegory is an *open* secret.

"In its original sense," writes Childs in 1970, "canon does not simply perform the formal function of separating the books that are authoritative from others that are not, but is the *rule* that delineates the area in which the church hears the word of God."[174] The normative dimension of canon remains its most important sense because the exact shape of the canon has always fluctuated. Canon is thus rightly seen as a kind of confession. "In speaking of canon the church testified that the authority of its Scriptures stemmed from God, not from human sanction. Canonicity as the 'rule of faith' was a confession of the divine origin of the gospel that had called the church into being."[175] Here for the first time one sees the close correspondence of canon and rule.

---

[171] Ibid., 121.

[172] The phrase comes from Childs, Response to Reviewers, 52.

[173] Childs, Christ the Lord, 12.

[174] *BTh in Crisis*, 99, my emphasis.

[175] *BTh in Crisis*, 105.

Scalise rightly points to Barth as one source for this idea,[176] but the move to join them also occurs in the context of a discussion of of Hans von Campenhausen's *Die Entstehung der christlichen Bibel* (1968), from which Childs appears to have gleaned a preliminary understanding of Irenaeus' interpretive framework.

> The one rule and guideline, the only "canon" which Irenaeus explicitly acknowledges, is the "canon of truth," that is to say: the content of the faith itself, which the Church received from Christ, to which she remains faithful, and by which she lives. By this is meant neither a *Summa* of dogmatic propositions nor an unchangeable confessional formula nor even the sacred Scripture as such, however certain it may be that the latter teaches and contains truth.[177]

Another important source, chased up by Childs following the publication of *BTh in Crisis* and undergirding von Campenhausen's analysis, is Bengt Hägglund's "Die Bedeutung der 'regula fidei' als Grundlage theologischer Aussagen" (1958). Childs first discusses the article in 1972, in connection with von Campenhausen.[178] Through the patristic era, Hägglund explains, "Es ist nicht von ungefähr, dass das griechische Wort für 'regula,' κανών, mehr und mehr zu einer festen Bezeichnung für die heilige Schrift wurde. Das ursprüngliche Zeugnis ist nicht nur deshalb 'kanonisch,' weil es mit der Authorität der Propheten und Apostel ausgestattet ist, sondern auch weil es Träger der Offenbarung, Vermittler der Heilswirklichkeit ist."[179] According to von Campenhausen and Hägglund, for Irenaeus and for Tertullian the rule of truth or faith is prior to the Bible, larger than the Bible, and therefore not strictly identical with the Bible, but nonetheless works *only when coupled with the Bible's prophetic and apostolic witness*. In Hägglund's words again, "Die Aufgabe, eine 'fundamentum' der Lehrüberlieferung zu sein, erfüllt die 'regula' nur durch die Vermittlung der heiligen Schrift."[180] This is the theological background for Childs' use of Barth-like language of canon as vehicle, witness or transparency to the divine reality.

From the very first time "canon" is proposed as a better context for biblical theology in the critical era, it binds theological reflection on scripture to a living God who, by the prophets and apostles, still speaks to God's people, thus making scripture's textual authority indispensable but ancillary. The best analogy is the interpretive framework developed in the patristic period. As Ter-

[176] See section A.II of chapter three.

[177] Campenhausen, *Formation*, 182, cf. 183, 288–290.

[178] Childs, OT Scripture of Church, 713, cf. 711. The first thing Childs affirm in the ancient church is their confession of canon: "A particular set of writings is judged to contain the church's living tradition — the rule of faith — in which the life of the community is grounded. Our faith is established on the witness of the prophets and apostles..." (713–714).

[179] Hägglund, Die Bedeutung, 39.

[180] Ibid., 39.

tullian puts it, "It is your faith, says Christ, which has made you whole, not busying yourself with the scriptures."[181] By this Tertullian does *not* mean

> that the exegesis of Scripture must be subjected to an external norm, laid down by the Church, but that Scripture is to be read from within the faith with which the believer is already familiar, and that when it is so read scripture [sic] itself simply confirms that faith over and over again. The closest modern counterpart to this definition of the *regula veritatis* is the concept of the "canon within the canon" — but only if this is understood as a "guide" to a right understanding, and not as a critical principle by which to scrutinize the Scripture. The indestructible unity and homogeneity of the Scriptures of the Old and New Testaments is for Tertullian, as for all the Fathers from Irenaeus onwards, the fundamental biblical dogma in their fight against the gnostics. It is a dogma which was not seriously imperilled until the rise of modern historical criticism, and it gave Tertullian, like most of the theologians of the early Church, relatively little trouble.[182]

In full view of the rise of historical criticism, having gained from it a keen sense of the diversity and historical shape of the biblical material, Childs seeks to recover an ancient understanding of the unity of scripture in its witness to the one true God. It is why for him κανών and *regula* are always coextensive, and why biblical theology nonetheless entails a modified kind of *Sachkritik* of the canon, one with an eye to its divine subject matter or *Sache*.

Apart from Seeligmann's essay on midrash, I suspect that no other single article had more impact on Childs early on than Hägglund's. Its importance only grows in the allegory phase of Childs' career. "Die Bedeutung" is listed in *Introduction to the OT*,[183] footnoted occasionally in articles,[184] referenced in a discussion of Irenaeus in *NT Introduction*,[185] named at the start of a longer discussion of Irenaeus and the rule in *Biblical Theology*,[186] and featured in a chapter on Irenaeus as a biblical theologian (the first) in *Struggle*.[187] (Finally, the phrase "rule of faith" appears seven times in *Pauline Corpus*, and "regula fidei" twice more.)[188] Harnack and other nineteenth century church historians tended, mistakenly, to identify the rule of faith with a baptismal rite. In fact it had more to do with the grounding of biblical hermeneutics. For Hägglund,

---

[181] Praescr. 14.3–4 (CCSL I, II), cited in both Campenhausen, *Formation*, 289 and Hägglund, Die Bedeutung, 20.

[182] Campenhausen, *Formation*, 290.

[183] *Introduction to the OT*, 69, cf. 81, 83.

[184] E.g., Childs, Endform, 246n5.

[185] *NT Introduction*, 28.

[186] *Biblical Theology*, 30–32.

[187] *Struggle*, 47, cf. 48, 51–53.

[188] *Pauline Corpus* shows as well as anything the marrying of key concepts from Hägglund and Seeligmann, though neither are named there. One of the tests of canonicity for Paul's letters was orthodoxy, "the 'canon of truth/faith' (*regula veritatis/fidei*)," although "this criterion was not a later *superadditum* imposed in a political struggle for power, as is sometimes argued, but its roots lay deep within the church's oral tradition preceding its stage of a written Scripture" (23–24).

Die "regula fidei" ist nicht mit dem Symbol, auch nicht mit einer bestimmten Auslegung dieses Symbols identisch. Der Begriff — der nicht konkret, sondern abstrakt zu fassen ist — bezieht sich auf die ganze Lehre der Kirche, die Lehre die von den Aposteln und Propheten verkündigt worden und in der heiligen Schrift niedergelegt ist. Taufbekenntnis (als kurze Zusammenfassung des Inhalts der Offenbarung), heilige Schrift, apostolische Überlieferung — alles ist in der "regula fidei" oder "regula veritatis" inbegriffen. Deshalb kann diese "regula" mit der einen oder der anderen Grösse gleichgestellt werden, ohne dass doch beide ganz identisch sind.[189]

With Irenaeus, according to Childs, "the rule of faith was a summary of the apostolic faith that was held as central to the church's confession. It provided the grounds of the church's faith and worship over against deviant Gnostic speculation. The rule was *not identical with scripture*, but was that sacred apostolic tradition, both in oral and written form, that comprised the church's story... [It] was a *holistic rendering* of the apostolic faith according to its proper order."[190] Within the rule Irenaeus is free to employ a variety of interpretive techniques and methods.[191] But the rule is prior.

Hägglund's study makes a fascinating biblical theological proposal in itself, recommending a return to such a rule in dogmatic and historical theology. The correspondences with Childs' approach cannot detain us, however. The point for Childs is that *the space between rule and letter establishes the space in which figuration can be tried.* In 1977 we see a hint of this possibility. Figure and letter are "not in stark tension," although letter is "indispensable." Other moves are out of bounds — allegory must not disfigure the letter, criticism must not destroy the way that letter has been configured. "In terms of classic Christian theology, the church's *regula fidei* encompasses both text and tradition in an integral unity as the living Word of God."[192] In 2004 the point is stronger. "The canonical shape provides the larger framework of scripture — a rule of faith — within which the interpretive function of exegesis is guided."[193] In aid of the "multiple textual meanings" that the church increasingly pursued, the "great strength of Irenaeus, in spite of certain ambiguities in his approach, was in providing a rule of faith (*regula fidei*) as a framework for Christian interpretation that emphasized the theological content of scripture."[194] Today, I scarcely need to add, the canonical approach hopes to restore this early insight about scripture to the church.

The rule of faith also underscores why Childs speaks of a framework instead of a method. Rowan Greer, a Yale colleague who wrote on the rule, argues that in the early church all roads lead to Irenaeus because he was the first to work out a *framework* within which to read the scriptures of the Jews.

---

[189] Hägglund, Die Bedeutung, 3–4.
[190] *Struggle*, 47, my emphasis.
[191] Ibid., 52, cf. 306.
[192] Childs, Sensus Literalis, 93. Cf. idem, Witness to Christ?, 60.
[193] *Struggle*, 317.
[194] Ibid., 303. So with the four gospels and one gospel (Childs, Christ the Lord, 5).

"The quest for a framework of interpretation is a quest not as much for method as for a way of finding coherence between the Hebrew Scriptures and the Christian story."[195] This, according to Greer, kept one eye on the unity of the Christian story and one eye on the reality of Christ, and Irenaeus called it the rule of faith. "Irenaeus offers a Christian transformation of the Hebrew Scriptures that makes them wholly integral to a Christian Bible."[196] Once established, the framework was not questioned. "The church after Irenaeus accepts his basic platform and remains committed to what we should call theological exegesis by regarding the church's faith as the key to unlock the meaning of Scripture."[197] Obviously this left a great many particulars undecided, as controversies over the Trinity or the nature of Christ would shortly demonstrate. The first *method* also came later. Applied within Irenaeus' basic framework, the method was devised by Origen.[198]

Seen in this light, Childs spent decades laboring to re-establish an approach to scripture that had been imperilled (von Campenhausen) and inverted (Frei) in the critical era. Only later in his career did he work toward figuralism or allegory, since this first needed a framework. In a sense the hermeneutical move from *Introduction to the OT* to *Biblical Theology* follows the move from Irenaeus to Origen. Suggestively, Greer also observes that the function of the rule of faith was largely negative. It said "no" to heresy and, somewhat more positively, established the bounds of faithful interpretation. (However the needfulness of Childs' critique is judged, one wants to say that his "sustained polemic" bears a certain family resemblance to early church controversies.) Childs saw a diminishment of tacit rules that set an enormous challenge — total overhaul of a discipline he knew from the inside, or short of that, the sounding of a whistle to remind the field, and Christian exegetes in particular, why certain rules and not others have traditionally been in play.

A final point. In addition to establishing a regulative framework within which the literal sense can be heard, the rule of faith organizes what Childs so often calls a holistic rendering of scripture's witness. While the rule's foundation is quite absolute, it has a degree of abstraction that arises from the flawed human perception of its content and that accommodates the great variety of the biblical material without requiring its harmonization. What can this unity mean? A trend in some of the more recent literature has been to equate the rule of faith with the storied world of scripture or the Christian metanarrative, as if the rule's purpose is "to capture the *narrative* wholeness of Scripture."[199] This has rightly been challenged and does not do justice to Childs' under-

[195] Kůgel and Greer, *Early*, 151.
[196] Ibid., 154. Cf. *Struggle*, 53.
[197] Kugel and Greer, *Early*, 176.
[198] Ibid., 178–179.
[199] Blowers, Regula Fidei, 220, my emphasis, cf. 202, 205–215.

standing of *regula* anymore than biblical narrative (Frei) does to canonical shape.[200] Childs does at times speak of the rule in terms of the church's story, perhaps under Greer's tutelage. But the rule is more than salvation history. Its purpose as canon is to govern human access to scripture's framework (*theoria*) and true subject matter (*hypothesis*) as well as to testify to dispensations in the divine economy (*oikonomia*, which Childs interchanges with *Heilsgeschichte*). The church's acts of praise and repentance partake in the "ontic wholeness" of scripture, a reality that transcends and encloses the church's cognition of economic realities.

C. Noetic and Ontic Trinitarianism

This final section brings the two measures of allegory discussed above — Barr's and Childs' — into dialogue on the doctrine of the Holy Trinity. The question is: what impact does each (allegorical) approach to scripture have on the Christian affirmations each each make of trinitarian dogma? As before, we will take Barr first.

I. Barr: Trinitarian Rather Than Christological

Immediately after Barr describes modern, post-war typology as "a bridge which reaches neither side of the river" (1966),[201] he considers the function of the two testaments in the work of salvation. He contends that a Christian approach to the Old Testament needs to be "Trinitarian *rather than* Christological."[202] This is not meant to deny that Jesus Christ and the God of Israel are the same God. Indeed, the argument begins with an affirmation that "Christian use of the Old Testament seems to depend on the belief that One God who is the God of Israel is also the God and Father of Jesus Christ. All our use of the Old Testament goes back to this belief."[203] But this is also not an affirmation of a direct path from the Old Testament to Christ, let alone the opposite. In some sense "the God of Israel … foreknew his Son," Barr explains. "But there is no actual prediction or prophecy of which we can say that Jesus is the intended content. Our use of the texts should relate to the intended content because it was through the intended content that his purpose was moved for-

---

[200] For a wider analysis of the literature and a critique, see MacDonald, Israel and the OT Story. MacDonald remarks suggestively: "With his attention to the shape of the canon, we can justly speak of Irenaeus as the first canonical interpreter. There is a genuine diversity to Scripture, expressed in the different parts of the canon, but the Rule of Faith points to the Scripture's unity in the story of Jesus Christ" (293–294).

[201] Barr, *Old and New*, 132.

[202] Ibid., 153, my emphasis.

[203] Ibid., 149.

ward, even if the intended content does not comprehend that purpose."[204] Barr's intentionalism compels him to voice a strong "not yet" which excludes any talk of the Old quite reaching the New. "This may be prejudiced," he writes, "but I have always found this language of 'looking forward to,' 'pointing towards' and so on, very unconvincing. It at once leads us into questions of purpose and intention, and purpose and intention cannot really be otherwise expressed than as the purpose and intention of the writers at the time of writing."[205] So then, even though we see that the God of Israel is the Father of Christ our Lord — all language Barr embraces — the mind of the Old Testament is so closely identified with the minds of its human authors that its purpose and intention cannot *directly* reveal anything about the purpose and intention of the God of Israel, including especially the purpose of the Father with respect to the One who is Son.

There are difficulties with this view. How does Barr suppose he has access to the purposes of God to begin with? Barr's theological reason for excluding Christ from the "intended content" of the Old Testament is "because it was through the intended content that his purpose was moved forward." Who is "his"? God the Father? In that case what does the Son have to do with the Father's purpose? And just who or what is the passive subject moving the divine purpose forward? The next clause is even more confusing: "it was through the intended content that his purpose was moved forward, *even if the intended content does not comprehend that purpose.*" Is Barr suggesting that the humanly intended content of the Old Testament could get caught up in a purpose it did not in the first instance comprehend? If so, one could begin to doubt the adequacy of a strict intentionalist model. When Barr says interpretation of the Old Testament is trinitarian rather than christological, he emphasizes the (human) lack of the knowledge of Christ before His birth. How then does he connect the testimony of the Old to the one divine work of salvation witnessed to by the New?

Barr amplifies his doctrine of God in terms of "reality" and encounters more problems. The Old Testament touches the real because it records "the reality of God's original contact with Israel." But to what extent is the Old Testament caught up in the reality of Christ which the church now confesses? Barr states:

> God was known in Israel. We believe that his work with Israel worked also for the purpose which we see fulfilled in Jesus Christ. But the way he worked for this purpose was by contacts with Israel which were real in themselves. These contacts worked also afterwards through the after-effects in later interpretation of the texts which they produced. But our interest in the original setting of the texts is an interest in the reality of God's original contact with Israel.[206]

[204] Ibid., 153.
[205] Ibid., 152.
[206] Ibid., 155.

Is Jesus Christ different from the God who was known in Israel? How? Is the Father's purpose fulfilled in Christ different from the work of Christ itself? On what basis would one know? And if the text is a by-product of "situations of actual contact with God,"[207] whatever that might mean, why did the text have after-effects in the life of Israel and beyond? Conversely, in view of the text's after-effects, why is "our interest" so obviously limited to the "original setting"? What makes the original setting of the words more real?

Thoughts about the nature of the real in Christianity lead Barr to comment on the *indirect* applicability of the Old Testament to the Christian life. For him, we delude ourselves if we think that the NT is more proximate to reality, more immediately accessible in the life of faith, than the OT.[208] Both testaments are distant, though the OT is slightly more distant from modern Christians. "There are, indeed, even from a theological point of view, reasons why the Christian's relation to the Old Testament is less direct than his relation to the New. This has to be balanced by his recognition that the achievement of our salvation depends, if we may so put it, on those aspects which to us are less direct as much as on those which are more direct."[209] If this view mitigates some perceived inter-faith crisis, it does little to explain why the Old and New Testaments should be considered *together* in the work of salvation. True enough, in historical terms the world of the Old established the matrix into which the incarnation supposedly appeared. Yet theologically Barr wants "to suggest a way in which the Old Testament and the humanity which it by its religious-historical aftermath has conditioned are taken up into the incarnation and become a functional agent in atonement through rejection and crucifixion,"[210] while at the same time insisting that our "direction of thought is from God to Christ, from Father to Son, and not from Christ to God."[211] In what sense is the Old Testament a functional agent in the church's knowledge and experience of *Christ's* atonement? Does the functionality of the OT or the humanity in it continue today? Nothing suggests that the noetic-historical sequence, Old to New, should ever be reversed for Barr. But assuming OT sacrifice and redemption have a real integrity apart from the NT, why would a person want to talk of *the work* of salvation in Old and New Testaments, work in the singular, and with a definite article, as in the title of Barr's chapter?

Barr's commitment to intentionalism, to certain limits on the real, to an indirect reading of biblical texts, and simultaneously to at least a semblance of unity in the Godhead, informs his thesis "that the growth and development of

---

[207] Ibid., 155.

[208] Ibid., 149. Cf. Seitz, *Figured Out*, 4–6.

[209] Barr, *Old and New*, 156.

[210] Ibid., 159.

[211] Ibid., 153–154.

the tradition is soteriologically functional."[212] Salvation history could function this way. If it did, one wants to know more about how this very non-traditional account addresses some long-standing questions. On what basis can the church speak of the unity of God? What of the unity of salvation? Can one say that the tradition is "soteriologically functional" and still invoke the Trinity? Again, it might make sense, but after this problematic attempt I do not find Barr making major efforts to work out how it could.[213]

Childs' Critique

Childs addresses Barr's theology in "Old and New Testaments in the Work of Salvation" more tersely. "In my opinion," writes Childs in the Prolegomena to *Biblical Theology*,

> Barr has mounted a strong case against the sharp methodological separation of typology and allegory and demonstrated its relation to a peculiar modern theology of divine acts in history. Yet I am far from convinced that Barr's analysis has really touched to the heart of the theological problem related to biblical typology. The issue turns on the nature of the biblical referent and the effort of both the Old Testament and the New Testament authors to extend their experience of God through figuration in order to depict the unity of God's one purpose (cf. especially H. Frei's illuminating discussion in *Eclipse*, 2ff.). Barr's own treatment of the relation of the testaments (*Old and New in Interpretation*, 149ff.), correctly emphasizes the role of the Old Testament as a testimony to the time before Christ's coming, but fails to deal adequately with the theological claim of an ontological as well as soteriological unity of the two testaments, which lies at the heart of the New Testament's application of the Old (cf. John 1.1–5; Col. 1.15–20; Heb. 1.2–3). Barr speaks of his "Trinitarian" approach, but seems to confine himself to the "economic" rather than also to the "immanent" Trinity as well.[214]

Note again that the relationship between the testaments is a figural issue for Childs. Whatever attenuated form of allegory Barr winds up with, however, does not do justice to the ontological unity of the testaments. Barr does not grasp "the nature of the biblical referent," which, as Childs maintains with Origen's precedent, can legitimately be multiple, and can be fully real in senses not contained by the mind of an author.[215]

---

[212] Ibid., 156. The quote continues, "We do not only have a series of divine acts, the interpretation and presentation of which constitutes the tradition; we have a growth of tradition, the existence of which provides the matrix for the coming divine acts and the impulse for their very occurrence." What does Barr mean that a growing tradition impells the "very occurrence" of divine acts?

[213] Topping, *Revelation, Scripture and Church* gives a measured analysis and critique of Barr (along with Ricoeur and Frei). He argues that Barr's qualified (non-Barthian) theology of inspiration, augmented with a sense of "cumulative tradition" (see 26–29), is a poor stand-in for a robust doctrine of revelation, and that Barr's position breaks down here and elsewhere.

[214] *Biblical Theology*, 14.

[215] Topping, *Revelation, Scripture and Church*, 97–99 supports Childs' critique of Barr, linking a sequential understanding of the Godhead to Sabellianism (98).

II. Childs: God's Redemptive Will from the Beginning

In identifying Jesus Christ as the one scope of the Old and New,[216] Childs puts forward a fundamentally different doctrine of the Trinity. He first addresses the OT understanding of God, which of course shows variety and complexity, focusing on God's name, his covenant with his people, his transcendence ("monotheism" is not wrong but "theologically inert"[217]), and his passibility. He gives a preliminary nod to the subject matter.

> It is not by chance that the early church struggled with the Old Testament when it sought to bear witness to the sheer mystery of the God of Israel who in Jesus Christ "emptied himself, taking the form of a servant, and became obedient unto death." Jesus brought no new *concept* of God, but he demonstrated in action the full extent of God's redemptive will for the world which was from the beginning.[218]

In contrast to Barr, Childs takes care not to transfer observations about the historical unfolding and development of concepts in time directly to the identity of God Himself, though noetic differences in the biblical reports are duly noted. After a brief look at Jewish understandings of God in the second temple period, Childs turns to the New Testament's understanding of God's identity. Here one finds both continuity and discontinuity with the Old. In many cases the original contexts of NT material have been subordinated to the canonical context in the "shape of the whole collection. The result is that the diversity shown between early communities has been relativized and later readers of the New Testament saw tensions more as complementary than as antagonistic."[219] As in the OT there are many complications in detail. Sometimes the Old seems to be "using" the New, shaping its understanding and idiom, but sometimes the trajectory works in the reverse: "the doctrine of God in the New Testament is frequently developed as a coefficient of christology which strongly affects how the Old Testament was heard and used."[220] Yet before the canonization of the NT the early church expressed its confession of Christ largely in terms of Israel's faith, understood through Israel's scriptures. This was part of its "struggle to understand the relationship between Jesus Christ whom it confessed as Lord, and God who had revealed himself to Israel," and the same challenge "lay at the heart of the development of Trinitarian theology."[221] The reality of the church's confession entailed "serious wrestling" with the witness and content of the Old.

Childs then moves into biblical theological reflection which deals with the historical, discrete forms of the testaments but is not hamstrung by sequence.

---

[216] Ibid., 49, 91, 721, 725. On this language see Sheppard, Scope of Biblical Books.

[217] *Biblical Theology*, 355, cf. now MacDonald, *Deuteronomy*.

[218] *Biblical Theology*, 358, my emphasis.

[219] Ibid., 361.

[220] Ibid., 366.

[221] Ibid., 368.

In older forms of Biblical Theology "it was a fatal mistake ... when dealing with the identity of God to feel that it could reflect on the subject only in terms of its historical sequence. This appeal to the so-called 'economic Trinity' would restrict the doctrine of God to the divine workings within a historical trajectory of past, present and future: God, Christ, Spirit."[222] This does not deny the importance of economic workings (Heb. 1:1) but seeks to preserve necessary conditions in the reasoning by which "the church's reflection on God found itself inexorably drawn into Trinitarian terminology."[223] Otherwise it becomes very difficult, if not impossible, to talk about the God of Old and New as a unified being. (This is principally what Childs means when he invokes an "ontological" dimension. Ontology, as Childs defines it in another context, "refers to a mode of speech in relation to a subject matter which disregards or transcends temporal sequence."[224]) And surely it only helps Childs' case that the tradents, or canonical shapers in his terminology, so often appear to have made sequence a secondary or tertiary concern.

Having summarized a number of points at the biblical theological level, Childs steps into the arena of trinitarian dogma (*res*$_3$). God has spoken in many and various ways. However: "The church's struggle with the Trinity was not a battle *against* the Old Testament, but rather a battle *for* the Old Testament, for the one eternal covenant of God in both unity and diversity." In historical terms, the church's initial christological confession eventually lead to a fuller understanding of the Trinity; so, for example, "when the church lost interest in the doctrine of the Trinity during the course of the nineteenth century as if it were idle speculation, its christological focus was also blurred and suffered serious distortion."[225] Barr does not feature in Childs' treatment of "The Identity of God," but the inherent relatedness of christology and trinitarianism is precisely why Barr cannot have an approach to the Old Testament that is "Trinitarian *rather than* Christological." Even in sheer developmental terms, you do not get one without the other.

The Trinity and Multi-level Readings

Childs concludes his discussion of God's identity with his first defense of "the need for a multiple-level reading of scripture according to differing contexts."[226] This leads to remarks on Vischer, the *sensus literalis*, and other topics touched on already. Scripture's witness is not identical with the reality itself, and therefore (contra Vischer) promise and fulfillment must not be fused. In

[222] Ibid., 370.
[223] Ibid., 369.
[224] Childs, Witness to Christ?, 60.
[225] *Biblical Theology*, 376.
[226] Ibid., 379.

other words, the ontic leaves space for the noetic.[227] A first level of entry to the text is the literal/historical, the canonical context of Old before New — very roughly, what might probably have existed in the minds of the people who wrote and compiled the scriptures of Israel. A second level of entry extends the first, relativizing sequence. Traditionally called typology, here "[a] comparison is being made, but neither witness is absorbed by the the other, nor their contexts fused." Can one go further? "Is there a level of interpreting the biblical text in which the full-blown reality of God gained from a reading of the entire Bible is used? Is it not constitutive to Christian faith to confess that the God revealed in the Old Testament is also the Father of our Lord Jesus Christ? Indeed God is known as Father only in the Son." Why then cannot a knowledge of Christ have some place in actual exegesis of OT texts? Is this always an "allegorical trap"?[228]

In partial answer, Childs suggests that the "fact that the Christian church has continued to be drawn back to allegory in a way that is not the case for Judaism, could well be an indication of a genuine search for a level of exegesis which has not been satisfactorily met."[229] Triunity sets "monotheism" down a new but old path. As Barth has it,

> faith in that Word means faith in the One whom this very Judaism with its monotheism rejected as a sinner against its monotheism, a blasphemer against God. This is the gulf which separates Christian monotheism, if we can use the term, from Jewish monotheism and monotheism of every other kind. It is strange but true that confession of the one and only God and denial of Him are to be found exactly conjoined but radically separated in what appears to be the one identical statement that there is only one God.[230]

So the mystery of Israel has further iterations within a pursuit of the mystery of Christ. The differences between midrash and allegory are only symptoms of a paradoxical rift. A decision for one "monotheism" or the other would, for Childs, have to be textually mediated and self-authenticating. "There is no objective criterion by which this knowledge [of a living God] can be tested beyond that of the reality of God himself. If the church confesses that the spirit of God opens up the text to a perception of its true reality, it also follows that the Spirit also works in applying the reality of God in its fullness to an under-

---

[227] A parallel discussion of Vischer stipulates a more complex understanding of the relationship of Christ to the OT witness. "On the one hand, it is clear that the witness of the early church proceeded *noetically* first from a knowledge of the resurrected Christ and only then turned back to the Old Testament as a vehicle for its proclamation. On the other hand, the New Testament formulated its witness *ontically* as a fulfilment of a previously announced reality which had been prefigured in the old covenant and only later was fulfilled according to the fulness of time" (ibid., 477, my emphasis, cf. 520–521). Again, for Childs the ontic "disregards or transcends temporal sequence."

[228] Ibid., 380.

[229] Ibid., 381.

[230] *CD* II/1, 453–454, cited in *Biblical Theology*, 373.

standing of the text. The two movements cannot be separated."[231] Readers, it seems, have to be converted.

Thus, contra Barr, the Bible is not a book the church keeps only by giving away to a global community of elite readers. Fundamental to Childs' approach is the church's receptive posture. "Scripture accrues its proper authority when it is read and celebrated in the community of the church. The Bible is the book of the church, but not in the erroneous sense that it belongs to the church; rather, when received as a divine gift to believers, the Bible becomes a guide for faith and practice."[232] Allegory is not an acrobatic means of salvaging the text for theological purpose. It is part of a response to God that moves toward deeper understanding of a received text, according to its canonical rule, from faith to faith.

A "Morphological Fit" in Isaiah 53

Let me conclude with an example from *Isaiah*. Already in 1992 the testimony of Isaiah 53 "cannot be correctly heard if this witness is directly identified with the passion of Jesus Christ… Yet to know the will of God in Jesus Christ opens up a profoundly new vista on this prophetic testimony… For those who confess the Lordship of Jesus Christ there is an immediate morphological fit."[233] In his subsequent Isaiah commentary Childs works hard to do justice to the discrete voice of Isaiah, and yet does not hesitate to speak of the divine reality which for him gives rise to this figural or morphological fit. It is intriguing to see how immediately he switches from one mode to the next.

Generally speaking, in 2001 Childs restricts his comments to issues pertaining to Isaiah in its own historical context — entry at res_1. Occasionally he addresses Isaiah's message from the context of the larger Christian Bible, and at these points one spots a readiness to speak in terms appropriate to res_3 or res_2. Moreover, on two such occasions Childs rehearses a turn of phrase used three decades prior — "the mystery of Israel." The phrase first accompanies a discussion of Isaiah 6. The prophet's difficult commission involves a "mystery of divine hardening" lodged firmly "with God in the mystery of his inscrutable will."[234] "How long?" asks Isaiah, but there is no limit. "All of Israel must perish: 'houses without people.' … There is no continuity from the old to the new." Yet Isaiah himself experiences death and rebirth, outlives total destruction, names his son appropriately (7:3). "Thus the mystery of the remnant continues, and these ancient readers saw in the stump that remained standing when felled (cf. 11:1) the hope of the new."[235] Isaiah is one "whose cleansing by fire

---

[231] *Biblical Theology*, 382.
[232] Childs, Cultural Change, 210.
[233] *Biblical Theology*, 382.
[234] *Isaiah*, 56.
[235] Ibid., 58.

and whose restoration makes him the paradigm of new things arising from the old." Mingled with the unbelief of Ahaz "there appears a testimony to the emergence of a faithful remnant, which springs from the ashes of Israel's destruction, a new creation of God and his Messiah."[236] Turning to the New Testament, Childs sees that although the hardening motif is rendered variously, it "is seen as an integral part of the selfsame struggle of God with Israel already witnessed to in the entire Old Testament. The rejection and crucifixion of Jesus was the ultimate climax to a history that extended through Israel's history (Acts 7). Indeed, the *mystery of Israel remains the death of the old and the rebirth of the new.*"[237] If the shift to the present tense signals a more mysterious claim, of another order — not about a perception in Paul or John or Acts, a claim at the conceptual level, but a claim of direct theological reference — it derives as nearly as possible from a holistic reading of the Isaianic corpus, the wider prophetic corpus, and the full canonical scriptures of ancient Israel. This for Childs provides the soundest basis for Christian reading of the Old Testament.

Later, confronting the contested servant texts in Isaiah 41:8 and 42:1, Childs insists that their juxtaposition leads to "the obvious implication that *in some way* Israel is the servant who is named in 42:1."[238] In what way? Childs defers his answer: "the mystery of Israel as the servant remains yet unresolved up to this point in the book."[239] The discussion is resumed after the exposition of Isaiah 53, at which point an excursus is again made for the New Testament witness. Scholarly literature on the problem falls into two camps. "Both sides argue pro and con about the 'mind of Jesus' on the issue. Moreover, both sides distinguish between Jesus' own self-understanding and that voiced by the various witnesses of scripture. Both therefore seek to ground their positions on a historical-critical reconstruction of the history of tradition." One camp argues that the Old Testament texts were determinative, the other that New Testament understandings were "retrojected back into the Old Testament."[240] In a sense, both sides have a point. Nonetheless, the real function of Isaiah 53 has been obscured. First, "the authority of the biblical witness is not determined by its being anchored in 'the mind of Jesus.'" Neither is the text a clairvoyant prediction of Christ. Does that make the text's *Wirkung*, its historic reception in the church, merely a specious, "imaginative construal"?[241]

Childs argues to the contrary "that the canonical shape of the book of Isaiah shows a suffering servant figure who was not simply viewed as a figure of the past, but assigned a central and continuing theological role in relation to the

[236] Ibid., 59.
[237] Ibid., my emphasis.
[238] Ibid., 325, original emphasis.
[239] Ibid., 326.
[240] Ibid., 421.
[241] Ibid., 422. Cf. *Struggle*, 322.

life of the redeemed community of Israel. Thus, there was a coercion exerted by the biblical text itself, as authoritative scripture, that exercised pressure on the early church in its struggle to understand the suffering and death of Jesus Christ."[242] This is not really the movement of prophecy to fulfillment.[243]

> Rather, an analogy was drawn between the redemptive activity of the Isaianic servant and the passion and death of Jesus Christ. The relation was understood "ontologically," that is to say, in terms of its substance, its theological reality. To use classic Christian theological terminology, the distinction is between the "economic" Trinity, God's revelation in the continuum of Israel's history, and the "immanent" Trinity, the ontological manifestation of the triune deity in its eternality.[244]

Childs then holds that various New Testament witnesses participate in this understanding. Revelation 13:8 is a prime example — "the lamb slain before the foundation of the world." Then, lest there be any doubt about whether the mind of an apostle evangelist is his terminus, Childs modulates once again into first-order, biblical theological discourse. "The morphological fit between Isaiah 53 and the passion of Jesus continues to bear testimony to the common subject matter within the one divine economy." And: "The suffering servant retains its theological significance within the Christian canon because it is inextricably linked in substance with the gospel of Jesus Christ, who is and always has been the ground of God's salvation of Israel and the world."[245] To say this is to make a christological *and* a trinitarian judgment, and on Childs' understanding, a judgment in a directly referential allegorical mode.

Barr's recourse to allegory amounts to a provocation, really. It is subsidiary to biblical criticism as an approach (not a mere method!), but it drives home the point that for Barr biblical reference has an indirect bearing on theology. The authoritative *regula fidei* exists in the life of community, outside and with a non-obvious relation to the canonical "list." As a Christian minister, though, Barr ventures into constructive theological territory in 1966, including into trinitarian dogma. That attempt raises questions he later pursues only rarely, and without vigor.[246] A model of strict noetic sequence has implications for one's understanding of the person of Christ, and I worry that Barr's formulation is insufficiently christological to qualify as trinitarian. With others (e.g., Topping), from a Christian vantage I far prefer the "ontology of scripture" that

---

[242] *Isaiah*, 422–423.

[243] Or not in the first instance: "in a broad sense, Isaiah 53 does *continue* to function as prophecy since the chapter is bracketed within the eschatological framework of an unfolding divine economy" (ibid., 423, my emphasis, cf. 191–192).

[244] Ibid., 423.

[245] Ibid.

[246] A 2000 essay (Barr, *History and Ideology*, 161–178) follows the trinitarian work of Peter Hodgson, a Vanderbilt colleague, with the barest "Scriptural Foundations" — just two pages. Barr is noncommittally positive about Hodgson, saying that certain "questions would require much more work on them than I have been able to do" (179).

allows Childs to speak to an economic and immanent Trinity in New and Old, although I am not convinced that Childs' model is absolutely coherent either. I can understand a contrast between Barr's noetic trinitarianism and Childs' noetic and ontic trinitarianism if it means that in the latter case one does move from Christ to the Old Testament, but what does it actually mean to say that the Old or New Testament is "ontically" formed? Is the *Christuszeugnis* of the Old necessarily figural or allegorical? If so, is trinitarian dogma the product of allegorical reading? Just how directly does the OT literal sense bring Christ? Why does the literal sense have to be pared back? Where else than Isaiah 53 — to most Christians so obvious — can one find a "morphological fit"? Could the church not, affirming the canonical context for its interpretation of scripture, go on in that context to engage the mystery of Christ in the details of the laws for childbirth in Leviticus 12, for example — a direction Ephraim Radner has indicated?[247] If not, why not? Childs did not say as much about such questions as he might have, leaving plenty of room for debate among those scholars and exegetes for whom Christian theology is the goal. Debate is needful on several fronts, internally and externally, in the church's scripturally inscribed life and its relationships with the university and the synagogue and others. But on the home front at least, I would suggest that of the two rules considered here the rule of faith called canon holds more promise. Up to now it has certainly been more productive.

[247] Interacting with Jacques-Joseph Duguet (1649–1733), a Jansenist, Radner suggests: "The Scriptures themselves, written by a sublime author, reflect his order and coherence and unity amid diverse parts and periods. And they do so in the ways that reveal the echoes and shadows and figures of Christ, resonating within Old and New Testaments, thematically organizing, imagistically interconnecting, narrationally weaving a unified vision of God's being within the world that is perfectly given in the incarnation. And thus, to enter this orchestrated and divine reality is to be changed by an encounter with a grace that converts the intellectual and spiritual being of the reader. When in Leviticus 12, for instance, we hear of the laws governing the purification of women after childbirth, we are invited into a search for Christ amid the details of birth, blood, and sacrifice, whose traverse must inform the depths of our souls" (Radner, *Hope among the Fragments*, 97; cf. idem, *Leviticus*, 120–134).

CHAPTER 8

"For a Generation to Come": The Scope of Psalm 102 in Reception and Research

"On whatever day I call upon you, hear me quickly." Peter prayed, Paul prayed, the other apostles prayed, the faithful prayed in those early days, the faithful prayed in the ages that followed, the faithful prayed in the time of the martyrs, the faithful pray in our own time, and the faithful will pray in the day of our descendants.
— Augustine, on Psalm 102:2

Like faithful Israel who awaited the salvation of its covenant God, we Christians also live in hopeful expectation of our redemption and that of "all Israel" with whom we will be finally united in God's time. — Brevard Childs

As a way of drawing threads of the argument together, I will close with a short example. Psalm 102 has been worked quite heavily of late. In addition to articles and commentaries, the text has been the subject of no less that two monographs.[1] Compared to this my discussion will be highly abbreviated. I restrict myself to the question of the scope of Psalm 102, and even this must be selective. The term "scope" has resonances within patristic and reformation commentary,[2] but to begin with I use it simply to index perceptions of the compass of the biblical text in time and subject matter. How far does Psalm 102 reach? As per the title, "generation" in verse 19 is my focal point. Gunkel is is a convent point of departure because of his general influence and the retrospective he provides in this study (chapter four). He will be followed by two representatives of the shift to emphasize textualization of the tradition (Steck, Childs). In the middle section Augustine represents the Christian exegetical tradition, and I will close with remarks about whether the twain shall meet.

A. Recent Critical Discussion

For the last century, consider a pair of contrasts. About a hundred years ago Hermann Gunkel began to apply the logic of forms to the Psalter. Previous

[1] Brüning, *Mitten im Leben* (1992) and Brunert, *Psalm 102* (1996).
[2] See Sheppard, Scope of Biblical Books and idem, Scope of Isaiah.

psalms research had stagnated, in his view, because ancient poetry had not yet been set in its proper context: "if someone researching the past wants to obtain the true picture of what happened, that researcher first has to disregard the context in which the items came to us more or less accidentally. Rather, the researcher's goal is to observe things in the contexts in which they were originally found."[3] The problem is especially acute in the canonical Psalter, where principles governing internal arrangement are difficult to come by, if indeed they can be discerned at all.[4] Israel's literary witnesses come down to us in an intrinsically secondary, artificial context, because their true provenance is "nicht auf dem Papier, sondern im Leben."[5] For Gunkel this ties into a theory of the rise of cultures, wherein primitive nations such as Israel had not yet attained literary expression conceivable "on paper" in the first instance.[6] On the whole, psalms had their living context in the cult.

Concerning Psalm 102, however, Gunkel sees a certain distance from the cult. It is classed as an individual complaint song, but as a later and freer instance of the type and at some remove from the oldest rites. As Gunkel's *Auseinandersetzung* with Mowinckel makes clear, this understanding has quite a bit do to with the triumph of the poetic individual. The "I" of the psalmist in the first section (1–12) must on no account be explained as the "I" of the liturgical community supposed to lie behind the second section (13–23).[7] Again, although the Psalm is one of the best examples Gunkel finds to show that תְּפִלָּה (verses 1, 2, 17) is a terminus technicus for the individual complaint song as a genre, he predicates: "It is only questionable whether the superscription intends the original use of the complaint song or whether it characterizes

[3] Gunkel and Begrich, *Introduction*, 3 = *Einleitung*, 4. That the canon is in view is made explicit in the next sentence: "it should be irrelevant initially whether these songs are found inside the canon or outside the canon, or even whether they are found within Israel or outside Israel." But on Gunkel's own "Gefälle" toward Israel, and ultimately toward canon, see chapter four.

[4] See esp. Gunkel and Begrich, *Introduction*, §13, "The Collection of the Psalms."

[5] *RGG*^{2}, 3:1679. See chapter four.

[6] "The literary witness of the natural times and environments can be distinguished from those of more developed nations. Those literary witnesses of more developed nations are only conceivable on paper, but these witnesses arise in the real life of persons and have their setting therein. In real life women sing the victory song to those returning, triumphant armies. In real life some of the professional mourners strike up the moving dirge over the one who has passed away" (Gunkel and Begrich, *Introduction*, 7 = 10).

[7] Compare ibid., 122–123 = 173–175 with Mowinckel, *Psalms*, 1:221, 223–227. "Rather," Gunkel explains, "it is quite natural that the pious poet would also consider his own people when he had finished with himself, or that he first speaks of Israel and then himself, or that he mixes the two together" (Gunkel and Begrich, *Introduction*, 123 = 175). It is only a short step from here to what Gunkel feels is the Psalter's enduring value — the creative expression of the pious individual.

the psalm according to its usage in later worship services where the more original life setting and the later performance type need not correspond."[8]

As for the scope of Psalm 102, since Gunkel finds prophetic influences at work this derives almost wholly from his estimation of the prophets. "Sometimes," he explains, "eschatology appears in trace amounts in the complaint song. The singer in Ps 102 comforts himself in the hope *which is already granted to Israel in the present*."[9] When a psalmist expresses his faith in future deliverance, we are not to understand the plaintiff as one "gaining comfort and certainty for the present by a deduction based upon YHWH's assurance for his people in the distant future… Rather, the context is spontaneous and immediate."[10] Gunkel finds support for this general characterization in Psalm 102:14 — "You will rise up and have compassion on Zion, for it is time [עֵת] to favor it; the appointed time [מוֹעֵד] has come."

Thus when Gunkel comes to verse 19 — "Let this be recorded for a generation to come, so that a people yet unborn may praise the Lord" — emphasis falls on the salvation "das sicherlich nun bald hereinbrechen wird."[11] A record is made for posterity based on the exuberant conviction that the hour is nigh. The people about to be created [עַם נִבְרָא] are identified with the *next* generation [דּוֹר אַחֲרוֹן], for indeed the next generation is also the last.

Fast forward to 1990. In contrast to Gunkel, Odil Hannes Steck argues that Psalm 102 instantiates "Fernerwartung" — expectation for the distant future. After advancing a careful reading of time in the Psalm, in which the psalmist in the present ("Redegegenwart") perceives God's permanence and salvation, Steck argues against seeing the Psalm as collective adventism ("kollektive Naherwartung"). Individual and collective threads correlate to the individual's complaint and the anticipated collective salvation. According to Steck, the Psalm's argument turns on the contrast of a single person in jeopardy of death and the durable God who secures the fate of the sons of His servants (verse 29).

Wenn Jahwe bei der Heilswende Jerusalems dereinst kollektiv so handeln wird, wie V. 18 erwartet, kann er auch in der Zeit davor das jetzige Bitten des Beters um dessen Lebenslänge nicht ungehört lassen… Die an der Gewißheit kollektiver Fernerwartung exemplifizierte

---

[8] Nogalski's translation is in error here (ibid., 193 = 259). It renders "decken" as "be hidden" without recognizing that when the verb is being used reflexively, with "sich," it means to correspond or coincide. I have modified his translation accordingly.

[9] Ibid., 192 = 258, my emphasis.

[10] Ibid., 270–271 = 353. The quote continues, "The present time grows increasingly gloomy as its particular references approach the gruesome image that the prophets have presented for the days before YHWH's intervention. When this happens, then far from letting itself be discouraged and oppressed, eschatological faith sees a majestic confirmation of that which it believes. Specifically, it sees an undeniable sign that the last days have begun" (271 = 354).

[11] Gunkel, *Psalmen übersetzt*, 437. For what follows see 439–440.

Langzeitigkeit Jahwes (V. 13, 14–23) wird als Gegensatz zum Beterschicksal mit seiner vorzeitigen Todesnähe vorgebracht.[12]

Accordingly, כִּי in 14b must be translated "when" rather than "for" — "have compassion on Zion *when* it is time to favor it, *when* the appointed time has come."[13]

Unlike a great many critics, Gunkel and Steck think Psalm 102's apparent "Uneinheitlichkeit" nevertheless arose from a single conceptual universe.[14] But rather than a certain mixing of genres, Steck sees the confluence of two streams of tradition, late prophecy and late wisdom.[15] Religious-historically, it stems in part from the world of Trito-Isaiah.[16] That the psalmist is aware of prophetic visions of a new heavens and a new earth, but yet probably stands outside the circles that developed the prophetic literature in this direction, may explain why, in line with late wisdom circles, eschatological hope has been deferred from the next to a much later generation.

Verse 19, then. "Was wird wann aufgeschrieben für ein künftiges Geschlecht?" What is written for a future generation is "die Gewißheit dieser künftigen Rettung jetzt, wie sie prophetische genährt in der Gegenwart V. 14ff. ausspricht, damit die Heilsempfänger das Widerfahrnis der Heilswende als Erfüllung der Rettungsgewißheit ihrer Vorfahren, die in der Redegegenwart des Psalms leben, wahrnehmen."[17]

It is unclear if this first contrast, "Fernerwartung" vs. "Naherwartung," has any straightforward correlation to the most obvious contrast between Steck and Gunkel, namely, their point of departure vis-à-vis the final form. Steck represents well the turn from *man* to *text*, yet in the case at hand Gunkel and Steck both accept Psalm 102 as more or less a unit. Their disagreements turn on how to read the intent of its author, and where to locate his notion of eschatology in its historical development. Does Steck admit a broader scope for the Psalm? Perhaps. His psalmist certainly takes a more forward-looking

[12] Steck, Ps 102, 364.

[13] The same adjustment would seem to be required in 20a. Hossfeld counters this move in Hossfeld and Zenger, *Psalmen 101–150*.

[14] For Steck the view is consistent with his position that we should assume biblical texts to be coherent until proven guilty, "despite our impressions to the contrary" (Steck, *Prophetic Books*, 30).

[15] Steck, Ps 102, 371: "In Psalm 102 stehen also nicht verschiedene literarische Schichten zusammen, sondern zwei nebeneinander gegebene, traditionelle Sprachfelder — späte Weisheits- und späte prophetische Tradition — treten in einem einheitlichen Text zusammen." Psalm 102 is thus unlike Psalms 22 or 69, which for Steck do contain primary and secondary individual and collective strata.

[16] 102:26f provides a striking intertext for the vision of a new heaven and a new earth, if indeed it is not explicitly drawing on the language of Isaiah 66:22 and 65:9, 17. An allusion to Isaiah 59:19 in 102:16 seems especially probable because of the shared constellation of וְיִירְאוּ + אֶת־שֵׁם יהוה + אֶת־כְּבוֹד (ibid., 368).

[17] Ibid., 362.

view. But what sort of further associations does the text have? For Gunkel, ancient literature was immature — sometimes childlike, sometimes childish. On balance it bears little analogy for the mature individual reading today, although it does occasionally "transcend itself": the Psalter, which "is not a contemporary book and therefore cannot possibly voice modern thoughts and feelings," can sometimes teach us how to pray in a proper spirit of piety.[18] Steck's contrasting emphasis on the textuality of the Psalm opens up a broader range of affiliation in the ancient context. But at first glance Steck's reading is equally archaeological. Elsewhere he argues that late prophetic "Fortschreibung" advanced on the conviction of a "surplus value" in the sacred text that invited new readings.[19] If one were so inclined, one could perhaps approach biblical prophecy similarly today without contravening the tradents' intent. As he hazards once: "within the canon, in the final versions of the prophetic books, material that is not contemporary again becomes contemporary material in a higher sense *for all later generations* who wish to orient themselves toward the Bible."[20] An analogous point is not explicitly drawn with respect to Psalm 102, however.

At this juncture a second contrast can be drawn, between Steck and Brevard Childs. Childs mentions Psalm 102 in 1979.[21] He then discusses it further in an article-length study of the formula "it shall be recorded for a future generation," a "canonical formula" as he has it, in 1990, the same year Steck's article appeared. For Childs Psalm 102 attests the way in which Israel's traditions acquired an enduring significance as scripture. His essay's thesis "is that the process of the canonization of the Hebrew Bible was closely related to the concern to render the sacred tradition in such a way as to serve future generations of Israel as authoritative Scripture."[22] This relates immediately to the question "What is the status of the Hebrew canon for the Christian church?"[23] So the scope of verse 19 extends directly to the contemporary debate about the hermeneutical significance of canon. Lest this maneuver be hastily dismissed as a dogmatic imposition or gloss, a look at Childs' reading is in order.

Not just the psalms chapter but all of *Introduction to the OT* is written under the same thesis as the essay of 1990. The Introduction explores the various ways biblical material has been transmitted and shaped "in such a way that its authoritative claims be laid upon all successive generations of Israel."[24] Childs argues against critical research on the psalms in general because of its doubly negative outcome: increasingly it locked the psalms in their ancient

[18] Gunkel, *Water*, 161. Again, recall the fuller discussion in chapter four.

[19] Steck, *Prophetic Books*, 47, 148–190.

[20] Ibid., 186; my emphasis.

[21] *Introduction to the OT*, 518.

[22] Childs, Generation, 358.

[23] Ibid., 357.

[24] *Introduction to the OT*, 78.

context, a move which had the effect of making "traditional use of the Psalter by the synagogue and church [appear] highly arbitrary and far removed from the original function within ancient Israel."[25] His positive argument to the contrary sees a variety of impulses shaping the literature, but also discerns a unifying result: "psalms do not need to be cultically actualized to serve later generations. They are made immediately accessible to the faithful."[26] The Psalter, like the rest of the Old Testament, was sown with the seeds of its own continuing actualization.[27] Hence a "modern interpreter" has "a warrant for breaking out of the single, narrowly conceived mode of exegesis which is represented by most modern critical commentaries."[28]

In 1990 Childs presumes the analysis advanced in *Introduction to the OT* but comes at Psalm 102 from an angle more reminiscent of his early form-critical studies. He first covers the semantic range of the word דּוֹר. The next step is to identify the stereotyped formulas in which the term typically functioned. This leads to a reiteration of one of Childs' most foundational insights:

> If in early Israel the transmission and actualization of Israel's sacred tradition occurred in the context of the cult, increasingly in the late pre-exilic and post-exilic periods Israel's tradition was given a written form and transmitted by scribal schools… [T]here was a growing tendency toward the textualization of the tradition.[29]

In a third, exegetical step, verse 19 is taken as the key to the Psalm. "Although the promise was addressed originally to the exilic community, the dimension of the promise had already transcended that generation."[30] Finally, hermeneutical implications are drawn, one of which revisits the challenge critical scholarship made to scripture's continuing relevance. "The divine promise is not a coefficient of the past, but a witness recorded for future generations. The concern of the psalm is not 'traditional,' that is, simply preserving the past, but rather 'kerygmatic,' a bearing of testimony to the enduring power of God's promise for the future."[31] In this manner Childs feels he "follows the Old Testament's witness beyond itself to its subject matter, who is God, and thus provides a critical basis for genuine theological reflection."[32]

---

[25] *Introduction to the OT*, 510.

[26] *Introduction to the OT*, 521. In the context Childs is discussing psalms ascribed to David, especially through superscriptions, but the point is quite consistent with his overall thesis. Hence he concludes, "The canonical shape of the Psalter assured future generations of Israelites that this book spoke a word of God to each of them in their need. It was not only a record of the past, but a living voice speaking to the present human suffering" (523). Or again, he sees "a *growing consciousness* of the Psalter as sacred scripture" (521).

[27] Compare *Introduction to the OT*, 79 and passim.

[28] *Introduction to the OT*, 522–523.

[29] Childs, Generation, 360.

[30] Ibid., 361.

[31] Ibid., 363.

[32] Ibid., 363–364.

To summarize, despite sharing with Steck an emphasis over against Gunkel on the textuality of biblical traditions, Childs has a unique sense of Psalm 102's *immediate* applicability. Steck is probably open to an analogical extension of the text into the present, but his analysis of the text in question lacks proof of it. What separates Childs and Steck could, in a word, be called the perspicuity of Scripture. The scope of Psalm 102 for Childs enfolds the long history of interpretation in the church and synagogue and catches up the present generation as well.

B. Augustine's Interpretation

Now to the tradition.[33] Augustine is a suitable representative among Christian readers and must suffice at present. Of verse 19 (Latin 101:18) he writes, "At the time of writing [the things written] were not profitable to the people among whom they were written, for their purpose was to foretell the New Covenant among people who were living under the Old."[34] Yet the Old Covenant (*Vetus Testamentum*) pertains to one generation, the New to another. In *all* generations God's promise holds for the just. As Augustine's second exposition of Psalm 102 demonstrates beautifully, generations of the righteous in created time (like so many "dried-up leaves ... underfoot") begin with Adam, include Abel, Seth and Enoch, then Noah and his offspring, Abraham, Isaac and Jacob, the patriarchs, the prophets, and at last Christ himself; and after Christ the apostles, then other saints; "and now today all who are holy are holy in the name of Christ, as will all those be who after us will be saints, even

[33] There are special reasons to turn to the tradition in a study of Childs, who associates Gunkel's view that the Psalter has nothing immediate to say in our time with Gunkel's underrating of pre-critical exegesis. "One of the major reasons for working seriously in the history of biblical exegesis is to be made aware of many different models of interpretation which have all to frequently been disparaged through ignorance. With all due respect to Gunkel, the truly great expositors for probing the theological heart of the Psalter remain Augustine, Kimchi, Luther, Calvin, the long forgotten Puritans buried in Spurgeon's *Treasury*, the haunting sermons of Donne, and the learned and pious reflections of de Muis, Francke and Geier. Admittedly these commentators run the risk, which is common to all interpretation, of obscuring rather than illuminating the biblical text, but because they stand firmly within the canonical context, one can learn from them how to speak anew the language of faith" (*Introduction to the OT*, 523).

[34] Augustine, *Expositions 99–120*, 61–62; CCSL, 1438; PL, 1304–1305. "Quando scribebantur haec, non ita proderant eis inter quos scribebantur; scribebantur enim ad prophetandum Novum Testamentum, inter homines qui vivebant ex Vetere Testamento. Sed et illud Vetus Testamentum Deus dederat, et in illa terra promissionis populum suum collocaverat. Sed quoniam *memoriale tuum in generationem et generationem*, non iniquorum est, sed justorum: in una generatione pertinet ad Vetus Testamentum; in alia autem generatione pertinet ad Novum Testamentum."

to the world's end. From all these innumerable generations you may pick out all the holy offspring in each, and make of them one generation, and in this *generation of generations*, says the psalm, *your years abide*."[35] Why then does Psalm 102 pertain to generations under the New Testament more than to those under the Old? The explanation is exegetical: because it was written for a people yet to be created. And who are these? It can only mean those who are in Christ, Augustine explains, the same new creation to which the apostle refers in 2 Corinthians 5.

Though Augustine clearly wants to work by means of the "plain sense" — *per litteram*[36] — he is alive to multiple dimensions of the psalm. He does not immediately identify the poor man praying in the first part with Christ, for the man seems at times too poor to be so great and exalted a Lord. Augustine does indeed call the man Christ, but reluctantly: "It is he, yet it is not he."[37] In this manner Christ speaks with and on behalf of his bride, the Church. The two become one flesh, and so they also become "one voice" (*voce una*). Christ is the head, the Church his members, but they speak with the same voice. "Let us listen, then, to the prayer offered by the head and the body, the bridegroom and the bride. Christ and the Church together are one person, but the Word and flesh do not form one nature."[38] Augustine frames it dramatically in his exposition of the previous psalm: "We are Christ"![39] But lest the supplicant in Psalm 102 speak words too base for the head, Augustine qualifies, "I have prefaced my sermon with these remarks so that if you do hear anything of the kind, you may discern in it the sound of the body's weakness and realize that the head is speaking in the voice of its members." The invitation is for the Church to enter the psalm through Christ. "Let us listen; and, more than that, let us hear ourselves in these words. If we perceive ourselves to be outside them, let us do our best to be within."[40] So the three voices of the Psalms, the "I," Christ and the Church, are all in fact one voice.

In a study of the *Enarrationes* Michael Cameron comments aptly,

> Augustine thus awakened his hearers to themselves as subjects of the paschal mystery and participants in its dynamic of charity. Unwittingly, he also gave an intriguing reply to the hermeneutical conundrum created by the modern division between participant and observer,

---

[35] Ibid., 72.

[36] As Cameron, Enarrationes in Psalmos, explains, "His custom was not to focus on 'the letter,' or the literal sense, of the psalm (*solemus non ad litteram atendere*), but to reach 'through' the letter, as it were, to search out the mysteries within (*sed per litteram scrutari mysteria*: 131.2)" (291). Cf. Greene-McCreight, *Ad Litteram*.

[37] Augustine, *Expositions 99–120*, 47; CCSL, 1426; PL, 1295.

[38] Ibid., 47; CCSL, 1427; PL, 1295. "Jam ergo audiamus quid oret caput et corpus, sponsus et sponsa, Christus et ecclesia, utrumque unus: sed Verbum et caro non utrumque unum; Pater et Verbum utrumque unum; Christus et ecclesia utrumque unus."

[39] Ibid., 33.

[40] ExP, 48; CCSL, 1427; PL, 1295–1296.

subject and object, positing their conjunction not by mere fiat but by uncovering the engine of participation in the structure of redemption itself.[41]

Such a mechanism led to a text having multiple senses as a matter of course. If the attendant allegory sounds odd or even perverse on modern ears,[42] it hardly needs to be said that Augustine has none of the problem with application that was seen in the previous section. The epigraph vividly articulates Augustine's sense of Christ and the Church praying together in all generations, past, present, and to come. For Augustine, and with very few exceptions for Christian readers before the rise of critical method, scripture's scope comprehends the expositor's generation immediately. The seismic crisis of relevance that marks the present age, Childs not excluded, had not yet transpired.

C. Reprise

In a seventy page survey of the reception history of Psalm 102, Gunild Brunert affords an example of how someone fully engaged with critical research might understand the tradition, and so can help draw together sections A and B, above. Brunert credits Augustine with developing a theological foundation for significant Christian reception of the Psalter, but he adds a serious charge: "Das ändert aber nichts daran, daß er die christliche Tendenz fortgesetzt hat, den jüdischen Psalmen jeden Eigenwert abzusprechen. Er hat sie im Gegenteil verstärkt."[43] So whatever relevance issues *Psalmus vox totius Christi, capitis et corporis* may solve, one cannot sidestep the thorny legacy of Christian supersessionism. This, in fact, this is the gold standard against which Brunert weighs traditional readings. Does a Christian reader accord the Jewish psalm

---

[41] Cameron, Enarrationes in Psalmos, 293. See further idem, Totus Christus; Fiedrowicz, Introduction; Fiedrowicz and Müller, Enarrationes.

[42] Taking just one example, Augustine offers a double reading of the psalm's three birds (pelican, owl, sparrow) in three habitats (solitary places, ruined walls, rooftop). In the first instance they represent an aspect of Christ's body. Christian ministers have three tasks in three different locations: one goes to non-Christians, another to the backslidden, another to those near the Church but lukewarm. Then again, the same figures can refer to Christ, who was alone like the pelican in being born of a virgin, who like the owl in the ruins was crucified, and who like a sparrow on the roof was resurrected. But cf. Byassee, *Praise Seeking*, 128.

[43] Brunert, *Psalm 102*, 27. Brunert cites verse 19 as his only example, but see above. Augustine's comments are driven by intertextual associations with a later generation, yet to be created, which on his logic resonates across the the Testaments with apostolic indicators of a new creation. Fiedrowicz, Introduction, 23–24, seems not to mark the difference either. On the other hand, even if this is not what happens at verse 19, other remarks are more egregious. At the Christological reading of the owl among the ruins, for instance, Augustine suggests Christ was crucified "by the Jews' benighted ignorance and in the tottering walls of their ruin" (Augustine, *Expositions 99–120*, 54; CCSL, 1432; PL, 1300: "tanquam in nocte ignorantiae ipsorum, et tanquam in parietinis ruinae ipsorum").

any independent value (*jüdischen Eigenwert*)?[44] Augustine fails the test. So does virtually everyone else.

Prior to the world wars Brunert names just four exemplars: Theodore of Mopsuestia, Calvin and Hengstenberg in restricted senses, and Delitzsch. Gunkel opens up fresh debate and sets the critical agenda for much of the 20th century, but like Wellhausen and others fails roundly on the Jewish question. To affirm even these few Brunert must perform some precarious acrobatics — for Calvin as for Luther the subject matter, literal sense and scope of the Old Testament actually *is* Christ.[45] It could be wondered, too, how much lasting value there is in Delitzsch, or in Hengstenberg, whose messianic revelation-historical exegesis has christological accents anyway.[46] Brunert has less trouble with contemporary application than many others, though, and he does not neglect to draw out the significance of his work on Psalm 102 for the church. She is neither *the* new people of God, nor even *a* new people; rather, alongside Israel she is half of the people of God:

> solange Israel glaubt, daß sich die in diesem Buch konzentrierten Hoffnungen in der laufenden Geschichte noch nicht erfüllt haben, daß also Jesus von Nazareth nicht der Heilskönig war, auf den es wartet, so lange sollte die Kirche sensibel genug sein, in den Texten über ihr eigenes Selbstverständnis (vor Israel, vor dem gemeinsamen Gott und vor den Völkern) Formulierungen zu wählen, die die Glaubensentscheidung Israels respektieren und die Würde dieses Volkes nicht verletzen… [Die Kirche] wartet nicht allein auf den Tag, an dem alle Völker mit einer Stimme den Herrn anrufen (nostra aetate 4), sondern sie darf darauf vertrauen, daß Israel diesen Tag auch erwartet; sie ist nicht allein auf dem Weg zu Gott, sondern sie geht ihn gemeinsam mit Israel. Das ist die theologische Botschaft des vierten Psalmenbuches an die Kirche…[47]

Little wonder that Erich Zenger guided Brunert's dissertation.[48] How to treat the Scriptures of Israel as a Christian reader, what even to call them, have, after Auschwitz, become hermeneutical and theological problems of the first order.

Childs' ruled approach moves in a very different direction. In Brunert's view, following Manfred Oeming, Childs' theological approach to Psalm 102

---

[44] See Brunert, *Psalm 102*, 27, 28–29, 30, 33, 35, 39, 42, 47, 58–60, 62, 63, 293–294, 307.

[45] For Brunert, "*Die reformatorische Rückbesinnung* auf die Schrift und ihre *Betonung des Literalsinnes* setzt sich bei der Auslegung dieses Psalmes also nur zögernd durch. Erst Calvin nimmt auf der Basis des sensus litteralis eine historische Deutung vor, während Luther an der allegorischen Interpretation festhält" (ibid., 35, original emphasis).

[46] Ibid., 47: "Dem Grundkonsens, der sich bei allen Differenzen im einzelnen in Bezug auf die Notwendigkeit zeitgenössisch-jüdischer Deutung gebildet hatte, versucht sich seit der zweiten Hälfte des 19. Jahrhunderts noch einmal eine hier durch Hengstenberg und Delitzsch vertretene Linie entgegenzusetzen. Ihre Versuche, die Ergebnisse der kritischen Forschung durch messianisch-offenbarungsgeschichtliche Exegese wieder stärker in den kirchlichen Umkreis zu integrieren, haben sich aber nicht durchgesetzt."

[47] Ibid., 307.

[48] To the claim that "Psalm 102 vor allem ein jüdisches Gebet ist" (ibid., 14), compare the programmatic statements in Zenger, Nach Auschwitz.

amounts to a "dogmatische Flucht aus den Schwierigkeiten des historisch-kritischen Geschäfts."[49] (If he had noticed the christological apparatus supporting and surrounding Childs' reading he surely would have added a strong theological objection as well: Childs gives too much play to traditional, supersessionist readings of Jewish scripture.) Brunert does not follow Oeming in making another criticism, however. Oeming comments:

> Wenn Childs die Notwendigkeit des hermeneutischen Geschäfts des "Wiederverständlichmachens" von der final form her für überflüssig hält, vermag ich ihn nicht mehr zu begreifen. Wie kann man angesichts der tiefgreifenden Entfremdung des säkularen Zeitalters von der Bibel und angesichts des bedrückenden Unverständnisses für die Normativität heiliger Schriften gerade auch des Alten Testaments glauben, eine Rückwendung zur kanonischen final form löse alle Probleme?[50]

Can the Bible, especially the Old Testament, say anything immediate to our day at all? Or in terms of Psalm 102:19, which generation to come — which people "being created" — falls within the scope of the text? For Brunert, what is written refers to the fourth book of psalms, lives on quite naturally and appropriately in post-biblical Israel, but is killed almost without exception by the church. He must in essence reject the Christian tradition to save Jewish scriptures from the church, for the church.[51] Yet the strategy requires that he salvage at least part of the tradition, I think, for the following reason: if Brunert's were the first Christian generation to hear the Psalm's true message, he would have no reason to include himself in its implied readership, as one of the עַם נִבְרָא. Without a Theodore, on what basis could Brunert make the subtle but significant switch to the present tense, as above? The truly perplexing

[49] Brunert, *Psalm 102*, 72, citing Oeming, *Gesamtbiblische*, 209 [= ^{3}216]; on Oeming see further chapter two. Brunert seems not to recognize that Childs posits the same two literary strata in 1979 as he does in 1990. This leads him to make the implausible but not altogether atypical suggestion that Childs lapses into historical-critical mode in 1990. It is simply not true that in the later article "geht er insofern über sein ausschließliches Interesse am kanonisierten Endtext hinaus." Interest in a so-called depth dimension is there from the beginning. Neither is Childs indifferent ("gleichgültig") to the details of the Psalm's prehistory. Earlier stages of the tradition are of course subordinate to the final form for Childs, but they also have an important place in establishing a warrant for continuing re-application of Israel's traditions as they have been scripturally rendered. Still, remarks made toward the end of the *Introduction to the OT* chapter on the psalms voice a difficult question: "The question arises, did the later refashioning do violence to the original meaning? One's answer depends largely on how one construes 'doing violence.' Certainly the elements of continuity between the earlier and later interpretations are evident. Nevertheless, the original meaning is no longer an adequate norm by which to test the new" (*Introduction to the OT*, 522).

[50] Oeming, *Gesamtbiblische*, ^{2}208 [= ^{3}215].

[51] On his own understanding, this is where his real contribution lies. "Das wirklich Neue an der christlichen Form der holistischen Psalmenexegese scheint jedenfalls nicht der Blick über den Einzelpsalm hinaus bzw. auf den Gesamtpsalter zu sein, sondern das Bemühen, potentielle übergreifende Botschaften (innerhalb) des Psalters nicht christlich zu vereinnahmen" (Brunert, *Psalm 102*, 294).

dilemma here is whether a person expressly standing inside the church can so easily presuppose the perspicuity of Scripture *and at the same time* reject the *Christuszeugnis* of the Old Testament. Again, if the Jewish significance of Psalm 102 was consistently thwarted throughout Christian history, would not a more likely deduction be that the church simply has no title to it whatsoever? This would seem to be a more consistent application of Brunert's chief criterion, which in any event sits uneasily alongside an important, tacit recognition that for a psalm to speak in the church, it must also have spoken.

Childs leaves vital space for this dynamic with a confession that bears some resemblance to Augustine. "Thus, the church prays, as did Israel, with the words of the Psalter, but instinctively understands that the Lord, who is our shepherd (Ps 23:1), is also the good shepherd of John 10:11. Like faithful Israel who awaited the salvation of its covenant God, we Christians also live in hopeful expectation of our redemption and that of 'all Israel' with whom we will be finally united in God's time."[52] There have been a few recent efforts to read Augustine on the Jews sympathetically.[53] Childs' view of Israel is more subtle than the bishop's and is alert to the fact that the church's sorry history in this area is one of the great challenges now before it, but the vision is also totally uncompromising in its confession of Christ the Lord. It would have to include Augustine, as Brunert does not, in the church's hearing of Psalm 102. This is a hard position to take. But if Christian biblical theology has a future, it may at last prove necessary.

At the end of chapter six a question arose about how far Childs goes — maybe not far enough (Kugel, Zimmerli), at least up to the 1979 *Introduction*, or else maybe too far (Albertz, Rendtorff), from *OT Theology* or *Biblical Theology*. I have shown how much further he goes than some think, toward allegory even, and a major point has been that regardless of its success, the movement had to happen. The logic of Childs' ruled approach compels it, in a way. Still, it can be difficult to see how the major phases of Childs' work fit together, as shown by sympathetic readers who nevertheless take one part of his work to be more essential than another.[54] To me the most graphic reminder of this possibility is the way that his last two titles on Isaiah sit side by side on my bookshelf, ostensibly doing very different things — there is a technical modern commentary, and there is a long look at scripture's impress in the church's life. The two appear to exist quite separately. Take your pick. Psalm 102 raises the same problem in microcosm, for Childs' 1990 form-critical "Analysis of a Canonical Formula: 'It Shall be Recorded for a Future Generation'" directly contributes only to this chapter's first section. *Wirkungsgeschichte* does not

---

[52] Childs, *Pauline Corpus*, 193.

[53] Byassee, *Praise Seeking*, 149–193 and Fredriksen, *Augustine and the Jews*.

[54] Provan, Canons, for example, tends to see the canonical (churchly) dimension of Childs' work as less crucial than its protracted engagement of critical scholarship.

come into it, except insofar as Childs shows that the Psalm was made for it, that it was meant for future generations, and stands as God's witness. Again, Childs believes he "provides a critical basis for genuine theological reflection."[55] If it is fair to compare such framing with Irenaeus' achievement in his *regula fidei*, then Childs is still some way short of Origen's method. Yet some will no doubt wonder: once one gets to Origen, does one still need to do the work of Irenaeus? Or more pointedly: does Childs actually need to set a *critical* basis for *theological* reflection? Is a critical basis even comparable to Irenaeus? Why not put the whole thing in Christian theological terms?

Some do so incline. Consider in closing Jason Byassee's *Praise Seeking Understanding: Reading the Psalms With Augustine* (2007), which sees itself as part of a diverse "'return to allegory' movement" — with Louth and the mystery of Christ near the head — and tries to discover if "it is now possible to read the way Augustine does."[56] Byassee quite rightly notes that "[t]he viability of allegory is finally an ecclesiological issue."[57] He explores the challenge of doing allegory today, outlining what it cannot as well as what it might hope to achieve. He highlights the beauty and advantage of Augustine's hermeneutic for the psalms, too. But he shows little interest in matters of canon formation, even though the canonical association of psalms has been an important and theologically promising development.[58] At one point Byassee says, "By keeping Augustine in pride of place in the church's memory we thereby *enshrine his exegesis* in the church's practice as well."[59] The wording here is careless at best. What it shows in the extreme is the danger of repristination, as if an attenuated literal sense and the demise of allegory formerly secured by historical criticism were loss without remainder. Childs is rightly wary of this. More than just habits of training drive him back to a study of דּוֹר אַחֲרוֹן and related formulae in 1990. In other words, I do not think that Childs had any intention of pulling up the ladder behind him.[60] Canon and history stay in dialectical tension right

[55] Childs, Generation, 364. This is the last line of the essay. Why does he stop here?

[56] Byassee, *Praise Seeking*, 53. He very much thinks that "we should read the Psalter like St. Augustine" (a carefully qualified proposal, 11), centered on a return to christological allegory, but wonders if the world is set up to do this sort of thing anymore. So he asks, in the next sentence, "Where are the communities to which one may go to learn to do this?" (53, cf. 269).

[57] Ibid.

[58] Byassee's allegory has room for historical criticism to make contributions — it made the Bible "strange" once allegory domesticated it (ibid., 2), and it has a task "as part of a larger project of determining the *construction of the letter*" (248) — but in curtailment. As a recent example of good work on the Psalter as such, let me offer one that has been too little noted in English discussions: Ballhorn, *Zum Telos des Psalters*.

[59] Byâssee, *Praise Seeking*, 90, my emphasis.

[60] It is a little silly for Byassee to call Childs' work a "dogmatic argument for historical criticism" and to lump it in that category with the work of Käsemann, Watson and Vanhoozer (ibid., 256). The slight point here is obscured by Byassee's overall misreading. He thinks that Childs *rejects* allegory: "a specifically Christian dogmatic category — canon — is mobilized to

to the end; and reconstructive history is there from 1952 to 2008 (see chapter one). It will not do to put "history" away.

Byassee does note an important comment by Childs on Augustine's interpretation of the psalms, and a relatively early one at that (1977). It occurs in *Old Testament Books for Pastor and Teacher*, s.v. "Psalms":

> At the head of any list stands the *Enarrationes* of Augustine... Augustine provided the prism through which the Psalter was refracted during the larger part of Christian history. The exposition is not easy reading and runs counter to everything that the historical critical method assumes as obvious. Augustine does not interpret the text to discover what the Biblical author originally meant, but he replays the chords of the text as one plays an organ in order to orchestrate one's praise to the God and Father of Jesus Christ. The exposition is not for beginners, but for the serious pastor who wrestles with Scripture in a search for the presence of God.[61]

The introduction to these remarks gives an indication of Childs' receptive posture toward the tradition, of the way he long saw its contemporary use both as a challenge and an imperative. It reads:

> Probably the gravest indictment against the historical critical method is that it has effectively blocked all access to the richness of pre-critical interpretation of the Bible, both Jewish and Christian. To some extent the church's liturgical use of the Old Testament Psalms has been able to survive the impact of critical exegesis. In my judgment, it is absolutely imperative for the serious and theologically robust use of the Psalms once again to regain this lost heritage. Obviously traditional forms cannot be simply repristinated in the post-critical age, but neither can the great giants of the past be simply ignored without serious impoverishment of the Christian church.[62]

For the sourcing of Christian exegetical tradition, if there is a path between Brunert's minimalism (just Theodore and Calvin before the critical era) and Byassee's enshrining of Augustine, Childs wants to find it. Risks include on the one hand the dissolution of the historic church — for sight of which the late developing notion of a "family resemblance" is paramount — and on the other hand lack of attention to the text itself and the legitimate gains criticism lends an understanding of it. As with Vischer, it always remains possible to take allegory (or if not by that name christologizing exegesis) too far. For Childs, though, with a "critical basis" in place and a deep sense and knowledge of a "lost heritage," the trouble most often is getting allegory off the ground.

---

insist that Christians not interpret the Old Testament christologically" (260). Ironically, to say "the canon rules out allegory" (265) overlooks the way canon (literally!) rules allegory in.

[61] *OT Books*, 62–63. The paragraph concludes, "Along with Augustine the commentary of Jerome probably should be mentioned, but there is no comparison in the profundity of the two." I am not sure that Byassee has seen the full context; he indicates that the passage is cited by Michael Cameron, on whose analysis he relies (*Praise Seeking*, 257n27).

[62] *OT Books*, 62.

CHAPTER 9

Epilogue

> Quo vadis, *biblical theology? ... All biblical exegetes should be aware of the reality that under no circumstances can they avoid being theologians... In some sense every serious Bible reader is converted into a theologian. Thus biblical theology is not a luxury but a natural element among the people who should know God and serve him. It is a necessity for a community that knows of the need to be critical of itself in order to be faithful to the task assigned to her in the world.*
>
> — Markus Barth

Having moved from Switzerland to the United States in 1953, New Testament theologian Markus Barth was in a unique position to assess *Biblical Theology in Crisis*. His review, probably the most significant first response to that title, made a comparison with H.-J. Kraus' analysis of the European situation in *Die Biblische Theologie: Ihre Geschichte und Problematik*, which had also appeared in 1970. It drew on Barth's direct experience of the American scene, too — he had taught in Dubuque, Chicago, and Pittsburgh over nearly the same time Childs was establishing himself in Plymouth (Wisconsin) and New Haven. The large amount of agreement between Kraus and Childs was not lost on the reviewer; neither was the fact that the American, perhaps for the while less optimistically, was speaking out of another context and so had told a different story.

Barth framed his comments with a simple question: whither biblical theology? His main worry about *BTh in Crisis* was that too much emphasis had been set on "crisis, end, and demise." "If there is a more profound way of doing theology," he suggested, "it need not worry about its survival."[1] Still, he welcomed the book's ardour, particularly because he saw that, willy-nilly, some fashion of biblical theology results whenever the scriptures of synagogue or church are pursued. To read the Bible is to become a theologian. And as a theologian of the church, "a community that knows of the need to be critical of itself in order to be faithful to the task assigned to her in the world," the younger Barth understood that genuinely Christian biblical interpretation must bear witness to the Triune God made known in Christ.[2] He heralded Childs both for the critique of past efforts and for the outline of constructive work.

---

[1] M. Barth, Whither Biblical Theology?, 353–354.

[2] Ibid., 354.

Quo vadis, biblical theology? After surveying Childs' total corpus the question can be asked today as well as it could forty years ago. In truth it has more force now, since by several accounts the crisis has not abated. With the benefit of hindsight Childs appears more optimistic about the health of biblical theology than Kraus, who abandoned it in favor of systematic theology.[3] Nor did Childs take Brett's point in 1991, that a state of crisis in method ought to be welcomed. Still, we have seen those who, after 1992, hesitate about Childs' zeal for a project that to them smells like food past its sell-by date.[4] Through the 1990s, even as OT and biblical theology show signs of a broader revival, leading practitioners like Brueggemann and Rendtorff express concerns of their own about what Childs had achieved in his magnum opus. (Brueggemann supposes that 1970 was the year of Childs' most "satisfying" attempt.)[5] Still more recently, to some would-be practitioners the very name must seem out of vogue, as evidenced by the attempt to correlate the older "biblical theology movement" with active developments in "theological interpretation of scripture."[6] Naturally there are also those who, for a host of reasons, object more fundamentally to the notion of biblical theology, and to its reconfiguration or continuation in new guise. Doubt, from within and without, besets the enterprise as much as ever. So where does Childs stand on this contested landscape? Does his biblical theological work amount to the protracted death throes of a dying field? Is it desirable in principle but flawed in execution? Is it just hermeneutically perverse? Is it important, unavoidable, maybe even suggestive and full of promise, but finally dissatisfying? By any measure the work is imposing. To what extent (if any) does it offer clarity and insight?

In the main I think it still too early to say what Childs' long-range impact will be, although it has already been broad, reaching many who approve his vision, many who do not, and a great many in between. Basic misconceptions about Childs' approach persist, however. Too many who reject Childs have not seen to the bottom of what he has actually done, or tried to do. In 2009, for example, Leo Perdue, citing earlier critique by James Barr and himself, writes that "Childs's theology comes under criticism in many circles for his confusing definition of canon, canonical approach, and believing community and for his failure to include Judaism and history in his theological work." Perdue finds, too, that he is unable "to adjudicate between the three major canons of Catholicism, Judaism, and Protestantism, which hold differences in the collec-

---

[3] Compare *Biblische Theologie* to Kraus' 1983 title *Systematische Theologie*.

[4] Fretheim, Review of *Biblical Theology*, discussed in chapter one.

[5] Brueggemann, *Theology of the OT*, 90.

[6] E.g. Treier, Biblical Theology and/or Theological Interpretation of Scripture? (though of course Childs' second Festschrift is called *Theological Exegesis*). Interestingly, the phrase *regula fidei* — so central to Childs' conception of canonical interpretation — has lately risen in popularity; see Treier, Reading within the Rule(s), in his *Introducing Theological Interpretation*.

tion of books and in the order of their arrangement."[7] True enough, Childs' deliberately broad definition of "canon" has not helped his reception, and variations on the vague phrase "believing community" have exposed him to some justified criticism, most notably from Jewish scholars like Levenson and Kugel who in other respects show sympathy.[8] But as I have demonstrated, these very ciphers have also enabled Childs to hold certain difficult theological matters in tension — the mystery of Israel, to which the church is bound in the act of receiving its first testament from the synagogue; the mystery of Christ, the Lord, revealed across a two testament canon — simultaneously affirming what he judges to be a catholic orthodoxy while yet allowing for search and struggle. Indeed, to my mind one of his most successful formulations here is the "search for the Christian Bible": "The church struggles with the task of continually discerning the truth of God being revealed in the scripture and at the same time she stands within a fully human, ecclesiastical tradition which remains the tradent of the Word."[9] His handling of the problem of the Christian Bible's scope is remarkably subtle, even as, on well considered theological grounds, he affirms the Masoretic Text as the best "vehicle" for recovering the Old Testament.[10] As for Childs' "failure to include Judaism and history," it is precisely here that he toils hardest and longest: Judaism from his early reappraisal of Wellhausen on midrash; history from the 1952 seminar paper that, revised and expanded, makes it into his famous Exodus commentary. These concerns persist. (They mark the entire opus.) Those who care about the future of biblical theology can be strangely careless in handling the thought of the person who is arguably the twentieth century's greatest biblical theologian.

And yet canon in biblical interpretation has acquired "Raum und Bedeutung," as Dohmen puts it. In a recent article Hermann Spieckermann argues for the maintenance of a more careful distinction between the history of Israelite religion and Old Testament theology. "OT theology needs to be considered — broadly speaking — a canon-related discipline, which takes the normative claims developed within the biblical texts seriously."[11] He criticizes Albertz for too exclusively using the OT text as the basis of his history because doing so blurs the necessity of dealing with two very different disciplines, one "descriptive," the other "norm-abiding."[12] The historian of Israelite religion

[7] Perdue, Old Testament Theology, 114. For the earlier, more measured criticism from which these judgments derive see idem, *Collapse of History*, 182–193.

[8] For a different and challenging take on "community of faith" in sight of a church in disarray, see Radner, Absence of the Comforter (second FS for Childs). To Radner, the "vague references" Childs never identifies do not need to be, "according to a long post-Reformation Protestant tradition in which such ecclesial referents are deliberately peripheral" (356, cf. 371).

[9] *Biblical Theology*, 67. See the discussion above, pages 193–197.

[10] *Introduction to the OT*, 96–101, cf. 659–671.

[11] Spieckermann, "YHWH Bless You and Keep You," 165.

[12] Ibid., 174.

should rely on extra-biblical sources as much as possible, using the OT sparingly, cautiously.[13] There is common ground, but at heart OT theology is a different thing. It needs to be informed by the history of religion. It also needs the freedom to pursue its own ends.

> It is bound to those sources, which gained normative repute and were rendered canonical as the Tanakh in the Jewish and the Old Testament in the Christian tradition. The scriptures have become *the Scripture*. Perceiving the authoritative rank of Scripture means to recognize the claim beyond the limits of historical description. The authoritative claim is not confined to a certain time. It bridges the gap between the *in illo tempore* and every presence. The recognition of the normative claim of Scripture, perceived as the claim to the ultimate truth of God's relation to his creation, constitutes the very difference between OT theology and the approach of the history of religion.[14]

Canon in this sense includes the shape of scripture as received and the shaping of scripture as it works its effects in every generation of church and synagogue. By according norm-abiding historical realities their own integrity, Spieckermann steps well clear of the canonical half-measures of Hermann Gunkel.[15] And Childs, who adopts a distinction between *Historie* and *Geschichte*,[16] contends above all for the latter space, for canon.

I see room for growth of understanding here. Karel van der Toorn, for instance, has produced one of the freshest books on canon in recent years. *Scribal Culture and the Making of the Hebrew Bible* (2007) spans many competencies, first analyzing ANE sources and then attempting to correlate findings in that realm to the complex formation of the Hebrew Bible. It will be impossible to do justice to his study at present. I simply wish to highlight some of the overlap with Childs, who in the late 1960s started to reflect on the effect of the transformation of biblical tradition in the exilic and late post-exilic period, an effect sparked by the textualization of oral tradition. Childs would later remark, tersely, that "[t]he history of Israel comes to a close in the Hebrew Bible with the restoration of worship under Ezra. The full significance of this fact has seldom been explored."[17] Van der Toorn has now (without reference to Childs) taken up this very point, exploring in detail the closure of the canonical era and Ezra's place in it. He makes intriguing suggestions about the occa-

---

[13] To wit, "the danger to be trapped into the selective strategy of biblical redactors in presenting their view of Israel's history of religion is always lurking around" (ibid., 181).

[14] Ibid., 182.

[15] See the above discussion of Gunkel's tacit canon, pages 116–121.

[16] See above, pages 18–21.

[17] *Biblical Theology*, 164. In the short discussion that follows he explains, "In my judgment, the problem at issue illustrates another case in which the effect of the canonical process has not been correctly understood. Obviously, Israel's history with God did not end with Ezra. Yet from the perspective of Israel's tradition, the events which occurred after Ezra are no longer given an independent place, but attached in various ways to the writings of other periods and according to different literary genres. This is to say, the relationship between history and tradition has been altered" (ibid., 165).

sion, motive and warrant of scribal activity right up to the final canonization of Hebrew scripture. His account falls short, however, in suggesting that the production of the canon ultimately resulted from the scribal "intention to put the ancestral heritage in the hands of a lay readership," that the key is "likely to have been the increasing demand for a national literature by an educated public."[18] Absent from this conclusion is a consideration of the *religious* aspect of scribal motives. At issue is what sort of canon consciousness lies in the formation of the literature. Canon, in other words, is one place the historian of religion and the theologian cannot help meeting. There are times when one thinks Childs' theology would have been well served by a deeper awareness of material findings at Ugarit or Qumran. Equally, there are times when historians of biblical religion could profit from attention spent on relevant developments in theological reflection on the Bible.

Other research has made the connection with the Book of the Twelve prophets. Most recently Seitz (2009), in a highly theological account, writes of the achievement of association in canon formation. He demonstrates how newer work on the Twelve goes beyond what Childs did thirty years ago by addressing them in their Masoretic order. At the same time, along with nuanced discussion of the value *regula fidei* holds for a theological approach to Israel's scriptures, Seitz extends a notion Childs had long before adapted from Seeligmann: in the formation of the Twelve (and Isaiah) "one is made conscious of the reality of affiliation and association within a diverse witness."[19] Also Rendtorff, with his own canonical sensibilities, has offered a subtle account of how to read the Twelve as a theological unit.[20] Those familiar with the debate will know what an array of literature exists on the subject, representing many shades of opinion. Interestingly, though, even someone like Aaron Schart, who follows an intensely reconstructive approach to the Twelve's formation, begins by noting that *Introduction to the OT* "represents an important shift in the research on prophetic books."[21] Seitz, Rendtorff and Schart all recognize 1979 as a landmark year, and know they work in the wake of the change it brought.[22] Each, of course, also plots his own course from there.

In any event, Childs' own approach to scripture is irreducibly confessional. If this point is not always explicit, it is an unmissable keystone of his thought.[23]

---

[18] Toorn, *Scribal Culture*, 260, 259.

[19] Seitz, *Goodly Fellowship*, 52. Another set of markers, Law and Prophets, is "no curiosity but belongs to decisions deeply rooted in the history of the material" (62). For a retrospective on Childs' thinking about the Twelve in 1979 see 74–75.

[20] Rendtorff, How to Read.

[21] Schart, Reconstructing the Redaction History, 34.

[22] Childs did not address the Twelve again, but *Isaiah* parallels what he might have done.

[23] Moberly cites part of the following passage in 2009. He observes, "Although the thought is basic to Childs's work, its expression is untypical, as Childs generally eschews such first-person 'confessional' terminology" (*Theology of Genesis*, 7n3).

So an early chapter in *OT Theology* asks "How God is Known." "I would like to start talking about God in the Old Testament, but how do I do this?" Do I imagine myself at the beginning, he asks, or do I admit that I already know a fuller story? His answer falls in the category of confession:

> I do not come to the Old Testament to learn about someone else's God, but about the God we confess, who made himself known to Israel, to Abraham, Isaac and to Jacob. I do not approach some ancient concept, some mythological construct akin to Zeus or Moloch, but our God, our Father. The Old Testament bears witness that God revealed himself to Abraham, and we confess that he has also broken into our lives. I do not come to the Old Testament to be informed about some strange religious phenomenon, but in faith I strive for knowledge as I seek to understand ourselves in the light of God's self-disclosure. In the context of the church's scripture I seek to be pointed to our God who has made himself known, is making himself known, and will make himself known.
>
> I do not come to a hitherto unknown subject, but to the God whom we already know. I stand in a community of faith which confesses to know God, or rather to be known by God. We live our lives in the midst of confessing, celebrating and hoping. Thus, I cannot act as if I were living at the beginning of Israel's history, but as one who already knows the story, and who has entered into the middle of an activity of faith long in progress.
>
> I belong to a community of faith which has received a sacred tradition in the form of an authoritative canon of scripture. There is a rule of faith and practice which has been formed because God is known. The Old Testament assumes the reality of God.[24]

Joining Anselm, Childs takes the stance of *fides quaerens intellectum*. In other words, the "we" here is patently Christian, although "community of faith" remains — a little problematically — generic. Whether this latter decision aids the cause of ecumenism is a legitimate question. For his part Childs does not look for contact on the basis of some lowest common denominator. Again, the last sentence of *The Struggle to Understand Isaiah as Christian Scripture* is nothing short of a confession: "By reviewing the history of the church's biblical interpretation, we can derive new confidence in confessing with the creed: I believe in one holy catholic and apostolic church."[25] I do not think this is meant to foreclose on conversation with less overtly confessional church historians. Still, it may. What Childs hopes to discern is *Familienähnlichkeit* — a family resemblance across Christian interpretation of Isaiah, and indeed of all the church's Bible. Where judgment in this mode eclipses better history (not to say ostensibly more neutral description), historians will be within their rights to rule the spiritual reading of spiritual reading out of bounds.

Family resemblance is the most important conceptual development in Childs' later work, and yet long a student of the Christian tradition, he gave hints about the ancient roots of his governing vision in his earliest proposals for canon as context. Rarely perceived — it is perhaps indicative that Yale colleague David Bartlett wrote to Childs in October 1997 for clarification on a

---

[24] *OT Theology*, 28–29.

[25] *Struggle*, 323.

basic point, while working on a book about biblical studies and preaching — the thread is nonetheless there. Citing *Introduction to the OT*, Bartlett pressed for an explanation of what exactly Childs meant by canonical shape. He got the following reply.

> On the basis of the final form of the Scriptures, the interpreter strives to discern the "canonical shape"... By canonical shape I mean the attempt to discern those theological forces which were exerted in the shaping of the Scriptures in order to provide guidelines by which to aid its present and future readers toward its "proper" interpretation, that is to say, one which is faithful to its true subject matter (*res*). The Greek Church Fathers expressed this concern in terms of *skopus*. In a sense, one has to know what one is looking for in order to find it.[26]

Canon, *res*, scope: all such language issues from a reading of the Fathers. In other words, the form of scripture relates to its shape (or "function," Childs says a little earlier in the letter — form critical terminology lurks vaguely in the background), as it relates to its shaping, in respect of "theological forces." In terms more native to Christian theology these forces must be coterminous with the activity of the Holy Spirit, who in the formation of scripture and in its proper hearing evokes a response, and points to the *res* or *skopus*, namely, to God as definitively known in Christ. True, in full trinitarian terms the point is masked in 1979, but it is implicit in the 1970 affirmation of canon *as* rule — a christological rule no less. Like canon for OT and NT, family resemblance is a means of expressing and searching out the unity of canon and church.

One sometimes hears an accusation that Childs is rather Protestant, which in a basic sense is true enough. In another sense, though, he reaches for much more with a phrase like "community of faith," and most profoundly with his discernment of family in all the church's exegetical life. His is a very catholic Christianity. In fairness one has to allow that Childs' respect for and use of tradition — Jewish as well as Christian, though not quite in the same way — puts him in a very different category than that of a baldly biblicist champion of *sola scriptura*. Is it *merely* Protestant to say "we are not prophets or apostles," or that scripture is distinct from commentary? Once again Childs draws a theological conclusion from a deep reading of history and tradition. The matter (like so many others) goes beyond anything I am able to settle, and calls for wider deliberation. It is certainly an area where the limits of an approach that has drawn respectful attention from Catholics and Jews can yet be tested.

Many elements contribute to Childs' project, and it has been convenient to speak of two major turns in the development of his thought. The first is his reorientation of form criticism toward the final form, a break with his teachers that was underway in the late 1960s and firmly in place in *BTh in Crisis*. On this score his early (1967) and later (1979, 2001) work on Isaiah makes a useful counterpoint. The second turns on two interrelated things he called, on occa-

[26] A shorter excerpt is cited in Bartlett, *Between the Bible and the Church*, 65 (cf. 9). Childs added a copy of the whole exchange to his archival box at Princeton.

sion, mysteries; above all it concerns how Christ can be revealed in the scriptures of Israel. The "recht starken Angriff" Childs got from Neusner's account of canon and midrash in 1983 did challenge some of his assumptions about the presumably shared canon he had just introduced, though there were other analyses (Leiman). Recognizing difference in Jewish attitudes to canon helped pave the way for his ownership of a *Christuszeugnis* in the Old Testament, and eventually for a tentative recovery of allegory. This development has troubled some readers of *Biblical Theology*, where it first comes into play unavoidably, despite the fact that the sight of Christ in the OT is profoundly traditional and even has some precedent in biblical theology's not too distant past. Childs does not break with his teachers in every respect.

In the final analysis what is the sum of these parts? Is it, as I asked at the outset, an inconcinnity? That premature conclusion proves far too simplistic. The contours of Childs' work are better described as a long progress marked by struggle, discipline and care. Through each adjustment persists a remarkable consistency, as in this thread running back to the conclusion of his first book (1960): "The great challenge to Old Testament scholarship in our time is to retain and extend our vast knowledge of Israel's total life which has been opened up by historical research, while at the same time to use this understanding in such a way as to recover the Old Testament for the Christian Church."[27] The challenge of historicism would alter, though not dissolve, as its hegemony waned in the decades to come. It characterizes much of Childs' moment. The challenge to hear the scriptures aright is something every generation of the church faces anew. Biblical theology, as Markus Barth rightly sees, is as durable as the church. Childs describes the situation in his last book, about the canonical Paul (2008).

> The Christian canon is not a fixed deposit of traditions from the past, but a dynamic vehicle by which the risen Lord continues through the Holy Spirit to guide, instruct, and nourish his people. The imperative "to search the Scriptures" reveals the need for its continuous interpretation. The activity of hearing, reading, and praying is required, indeed mandated by the Scripture itself. In every successive generation new light has been promised for those seeking divine illumination to provide fresh understanding, new application to changing cultures, and a call for repentance for persistent failure in living out the imperatives of the gospel. In this constant struggle to live a faithful Christian life, the Scriptures of the church afford the abiding context from which to grow into the image of Christ. It is thus a theological gyroscope for maintaining one's direction when buffeted by the ever-shifting winds of change.[28]

Exegetes, theologians, teachers of the church live from faith to faith, held by one Lord in an incomplete and ever-renewed apprehension of the church's one Bible.

---

[27] *Myth and Reality*, 105 (^{2}106).

[28] *Pauline Corpus*, 26.

APPENDIX 1

Two Letters to James Barr

On 1 April 1996 Childs sent copies of two letters for inclusion in an archival box he had deposited at Princeton Theological Seminary the summer before. The box is introduced on page 13, above. The letters are discussed in the context of the "long chain of disagreements" between Professors Barr and Childs, starting on page 211.

A. First Letter

Sept. 3, 1982

Dear Jim,

I appreciated receiving a copy of your article on Jowett which I have studied carefully. I found many of the broad lines by which you described Jowett's position fully compatible with my own understanding of his work. Therefore, I reread my own essay to see how you were led to interpret the point of my article as you did. I have tried to reflect further on our agreements and disagreements respecting the contribution of Jowett.

First to review the main point of my article.[1] In section I, I discussed the long struggle prior to the Reformation — by both Jews and Christians — to define the nature of the plain sense of the text. In section II, I attempted to describe the effect of the rise of the historical critical approach on the question. I agreed with Hans Frei that the new approach (better to speak of approaches) was characterized by an attack on the identity of the explicative sense and its historical reference, the unity of which had been assumed by the Reformers.

I did not have time in the article to pursue all the various ways in which the breaking apart of the identity of text and reference occurred, but assumed that Frei's book was readily available. My basic concern was with the fact of such a split, however it occurred. I did, however, make mention of Spinoza and Wolff who were examples of interpreters who attacked the identity of the two elements in terms of an "ideal reference" (the terminology is Frei's). For Spinoza

[1] [A handwritten note in the margin states:] "The Sensus Literalis of Scripture," *Festschrift W Zimmerli*, Göttingen 1976, 80–93.

the ideal which transcended all the accidents of history was recovered by brilliant appeals to historical discrepancies within the Bible, psychological insights (cf. the chapter on prophecy), and philosophical axioms.

I then turned to see the effect of the historical critical method on the sensus literalis which I had discussed in the first section of the paper. Among the Reformers sensus literalis and sensus historicus were often used interchangeably. What was the effect of the new approach? Obviously there were many different approaches combined under the rubric of the historical critical approach. At this point (p.89) the briefness of my article has caused misunderstanding. My major point was to point out the increasing separation of text from referent which 19th century scholarship engendered.

In my judgment, Jowett was a classic example of an English, Victorian scholar who was in line with those 18th century and early 19th century scholars who appealed to an ideal reference, and thus departed significantly from the characteristic hermeneutical understanding of the Reformers. I have followed Frei's language in including the use of an ideal reference under the broad rubric of historical reference. It certainly is not to be identified with the later, technical sense of history. I bear some blame in my article for not distinguishing more sharply between Jowett's ideal reference and W.R. Smith's strictly historically reconstructed reference. In 19th century England the two approaches to referentiality were not clearly distinguished in practice. As I understand Lightfoot's criticism of Jowett, the point lay in Lightfoot's demanding a far more rigorous distinction, especially when calling Jowett a philosopher rather than a historian. Very shortly, and again for a variety of reasons, historical criticism in Britain became increasingly dominated by the search for a truly historical reference used in the strict sense. (Much more of course needs to be said at this point. The need for a large scale monograph on the subject akin to that of Reventlow's is a desideratum. Certainly Westcott had much of the ideal reference in his *Introduction to the Study*... which by 1880 had been largely replaced by the rise of the Oxford school. Still the change was done in true English style without a real confrontation. Lightfoot's position also needs careful delineations. In what sense was his attack on Baur dominated by his desire to have a more accurate historical referentiality? Still I remain impressed with the theological penetration of Lightfoot which gave his historical work great balance. I remain far more critical of Hort's textual principles, but that is another matter).

I would fully agree that Jowett stands under the influence of Schleiermacher and not Ernesti. (In the article I claimed no direct literary influence. The expression he used had been in the air since the late 18th century.) I would include Schleiermacher as a major figure in the development of historical criticism, but clearly he used a form of ideal reference along with other features which had begun to creep also into Jowett's position. (cf. 401ff.) Moreover his use of historical critical techniques was to aid him in recovering this ideal reference. Therefore, John's Gospel, not the Synoptics, was the key to understanding the real Jesus, and I Timothy was judged to be "unecht" and so confused the reader's true apprehension of Pauline faith.

One of my criticisms of your article is that you have overinterpreted my use of the term historical reference. You appear to understand this only in its strict sense (like W.R. Smith) and rule out the ideal reference from its inclusion. I had thought it obvious that Jowett was not a historical critic in the sense of Baur, nor was he ever concerned with the modern issue of the layering of tradition upon the biblical text.

It would seem that we do not agree on what Jowett was actually after nor what comprised his method. In the passage which I quoted from Jowett, my point was not to suggest Jowett's interest lay in reconstructing the original in the sense of Baur. He needed the original text as a vehicle for recovering his ideal reference. Tradition was viewed as an alien, interpretative accretion which obstructed the path to the ideal reference the recovery of which was the goal of exegesis. Jowett's appeal to read Scripture "like any other book" was both a negative foil to block off any support for traditional interpretation on the grounds of a special hermeneutic, and a positive claim regarding the multiplicity of avenues to universal truth.

What is the nature of Jowett's ideal reference? He explicates it fully in the latter part of his essay. He is not only dependent on Schleiermachers' [sic] "inner and outer" contrast, or his "actual and ideal," but on C.G. Heyne's category of the growth of human consciousness from childhood to maturity (pp.331, 387, 416). Jowett's concern for anachronism (354, 359ff) does not derive from Baur's historical sense, but is used to clear the deck from the wrong, traditional ecclesiastical questions and prepare for a correct interpretation. He is naturally unconcerned with discrepancies in Scripture not does he see any need for harmonizing the parts of the Bible. His vision of the text's true reference is unaffected by such trifles. Even his appeal to the author's original intent (p.378) is not for strictly historical purposes in the modern sense. Rather, the goal of interpretation is to recover the truth of the Unity of God and perfection of Christ (386f.). His emphasis on the need for understanding the original languages of Scripture derives largely from his concern to check ecclesiastical anachronisms. He does not limit the text's sense to its verbal significance, but "the real meaning … seems to lie deeper and to be more within" (401). Again, "Christian truth is not dependent on the fixedness of modes of thought" (402). Thus, I fully agree with your characterization of his lack of concern with historical detail. I would extend it to language as well.

I do not feel that classifying Jowett among the historical critics who appeal to an ideal reference affects the argument of my essay in any way. Nor do I think that Jowett has anything in common with the concerns of the "canonical critics". (I gather that your remarks were meant facetiously). His interpretation disputes seeing Scripture's unique role faithfully to render divine reality, but sees it as another vehicle — when properly removed from the church's claim for a unique function — by which to illuminate universal truth, divorced from the accidents of time and place (412) and to activate Christ's moral power (425). Jowett's understanding of interpreting the Bible "like any other book" differs indeed from Smith's, but the effect from a canonical perspective is the same.

Thank you again for the stimulation of your article. With warmest regards to you and Jane.

As ever,
Brevard

B. Second Letter[2]

March 21, 1996

Prof. James Barr
Vanderbilt University

Dear James,

Thank you for your kindness in sending me your latest essay on "Allegory and Historicism" (*JSOT* 1996). I have read it with interest. I am happy that you have had the chance to express in detail your position on these matters. For my part, I shall not pursue the matter, but let this debate lapse. I fear that we are like two ships passing in the night.

In respect to your argument, the initial problem is that we do not share in common one definition of historicism. You define it as "the idea that, in order to understand something, the essential mode is to get at its origins" (p.106). My understanding is a very different one. It has been been shaped by the European debate and is largely compatible, say, with the entries in the *RGG*, 2nd and 3rd editions. In a word, historicism is an approach to the critical study of history which assumes that historical reality has been formed solely from forces with the phenomenological world — to use Kant's terminology, or must conform to the rules of analogy or uniformity common to human experience — to use Troeltsch's language.

I would further argue that the discussion of the relation between the diachronic and synchronic dimensions of history has emerged as a "post-modern" debate, of course, greately [sic] aided from your own contribution. But, in

[2] [A handwritten note at the top states:] This is a typed copy of a letter I sent handwritten to James Barr in response to his letter & essay. [Barr's letter, unfortunately, was not included.]

my judgment, this distinction is only indirectly related to the problem of historicism since both practitioners of diachronic and synchronic analysis can still reflect the assumptions of historicism, as classically defined.

It is evident that I have always felt that historicism, as I have defined it, is a threat to any serious handling of the Bible. Yet this negative judgment does not carry over to a negative assessment of the value, indeed necessity, of proper historical study. Moreover, along with most serious historians I feel that the search for origins is often of great value and remains a central element in all historical research. In a word, I do not share your fundamental objections to diachronic historical analysis, although I recognize the important contributions of the post-modern discussion. I have profited greated [sic] from study of Dilthey, Collingwood, and Gadamer, among others.

From my perspective to be anti-historicist (according to my definition) and yet also be interested in proper historical research is in no way inconsistent. I suspect that this is a position shared by many competent historians.

I am happy to hear that you have been able to work out with Vanderbilt a one semester-per-year arrangement. That certainly gives you the best of both worlds.

Ann has just returned from a 3 week trip to India with a British group. She had a glorious time and was one of the few who survived without becoming sick. She even had a 3 day camel ride across the desert.

She joins me in sending you and Jane warmest greetings,

Cordially yours,
BS Childs

APPENDIX 2

Translation of German Words & Quotations

Page 5

Alttestamentler: Old Testament scholar

Page 6

Neutestamentler: New Testament scholar

Seit ihrer Entstehung ... der Hebräischen Schriften: From its inception, it was characteristic of Old Testament theology that it always had to contend with serious methodological uncertainties. Although it was often called the crowning achievement of the whole discipline, it appeared as though its leading practitioners were always glancing warily about at other subdisciplines, full of concern that some new literary, historical, or philological discovery might threaten the enterprise... Not only was the discipline loosely defined and constantly shifting, but *certain fundamental tensions* continue to pose questions as to what form an Old Testament theology should take. Is this academic discipline only descriptive, or does it necessarily include an element of constructive theology? What is the relation between an Old Testament theology and a history of Israel? Are its structuring principles historical, systematic, or an eclectic combination of both? And finally: what is the relation between Jewish and Christian theological interpretations of the Hebrew Scriptures?

Ich möchte so ... Fragen angehen: I would like to address some of these agonizing methodological questions in some other way.

Page 9

Christuszeugnis: witness to Christ

his *gesamtbiblische* theology: his comprehensive biblical theology (a Biblical Theology embracing both Old Testament and New Testament)

Allerdings bleibt ... der Biblischen Theologie: To be sure, it remains hard to specify what it means to find a reference to Christ in the Old Testament, and struggling with this problem cuts to the heart of biblical theology.

Page 11

quälenden methodologischen Fragen: agonizing methodological questions

im Alten Testament einen Hinweis auf Christus zu finden: to find a reference to Christ in the Old Testament

dogmatische Flucht aus den Schwierigkeiten des historischen Geschäfts: dogmatic flight from the difficulties of historical-critical work

Page 13

sorgfältige und wohlüberlegte Arbeit mit verständlichem Urteil: careful, well considered work with insightful judgment

Page 14

Gedächtnisfeier: memorial celebration

weidewechselnde Wanderhirten: wandering shepherds who lead their flocks from one pasture to another

Page 22

Kanonbewußtsein: canon consciousness

vielmehr hebt ... bezeichnet werden: rather, the term highlights the norming function of books and collections of books that are already available and designated by a variety of terms, such as *scripture*, *holy scripture* (or *books*), *Miqra*, *Law*, *Torah*, and *Prophets*

Page 28

Es ist nicht von ungefähr ... Vermittler der Heilswirklichkeit ist: It is no accident that the Greek word for "regula," κανών, increasingly became a firm designation for holy scripture. The original witness is therefore not only "canonical" because it represents the authority of the prophets and apostles, but also because it is the bearer of revelation, mediating the reality of salvation.

Christuszeugnis: witness to Christ

Page 29

gesamtbiblische: pertaining to the Bible as a whole

Kanonbewußtsein: canon consciousness

Page 30

Kanonbewußtsein: canon consciousness

Pages 35–36

Es ist erschreckend ... ***Krise der Biblischen Theologie:*** It is alarming how strongly the distancing effect of a "theology" that treats its subject matter as a historical object and merely catalogues phenomena isolates academic study of the Old Testament. Within the structures of theological instruction and research it is thereby branded as an inert historical discipline. This comment is to be understood as a further contribution to the discussion evoked by the claim of B. S. Childs and R. E. Clements that there is a *crisis in Biblical Theology.*

Page 57

Ausbildung: education

Page 60

der literarischen … von entscheidender Bedeutung: the literary distinctiveness of biblical literature the … theme of the *canon* is of decisive importance

Man entdeckte … geschehener Geschichte: One discovers, *and constantly rediscovers afresh*, the difference between the biblical mode of presenting history and history consisting of mere facts.

Ergänzungen und Fortschreibungen: supplements and updatings

Die Intention dieses Nachwortes … eingeordnet werden: The intention of this Epilogue is clear. The critical, open-minded thinker Qohelet is to be integrated into the Bible's classic wisdom literature.

Die Unabgeschlossenheit des Alten Testament: The Old Testament's Lack of Closure

Der Abschluß des Kanons: The Closing of the Canon

Inspirationslehre: doctrine of inspiration

der größten Hindernisse der historischen Bibelkritik: the largest obstructions to historical criticism of the Bible

Page 60n123

Die Bibel ist aber kein absolutes, sondern ein historisches Buch: The Bible, however, is not a book of absolutes but a book of history.

Streit um das Alte Testament: dispute about the Old Testament

Page 60n124

Traditionsliteratur: literature derived from tradition

Autorenliteratur: literature composed by an author

Page 61

vielmehr hebt der Begriff … ***Propheten*** **bezeichnet werden:** rather, the term refers to the norming function of books and collections of books that are already available and designated by a variety of terms, such as *scripture*, *holy scripture* (or *books*), *Miqra*, *Law*, *Torah*, and *Prophets*.

die Frage nach dem Kanon … Fragestellung behandelt worden ist: for a long time, the question of the canon has been handled more or less as an exclusively historical issue

Erst in den vergangenen vier Jahrzehnten … Forschung zu behandeln sind: Only in the last four decades have questions about the canon been opened up and, by North American canon studies, freed from their confinement to the category of purely historical issues, so that today it is generally acknowledged that the problems of the biblical canon can only be dealt with in conversations between biblical, historical, and systematic theological research.

Funktion für eine Gemeinschaft: function for a community

Page 61n128

denn das, was uns als Kanon begegnet, ... zum Ausdruck bringt: for that which encounters us as canon is, of course, not to be separated from the idea of that which gives norms and orientation, expressed in the aspect of the canon as a *normative collection of writings* and a *collection of normative writings*

Page 62

B. S. Childs kommt ... bezeichnet als "Kanonisierung": The work of B. S. Childs leads him to the insight that the concept of canon cannot be limited to final decisions regarding the normative scriptures, but that the canon ultimately involves something inherent *in the writings themselves* and not imposed upon them externally. Thus what Childs here has in view is that which constitutes traditional literature as such, namely the stance of the tradents who collect, update, and hand on the literature. Since this is constitutive for a later canon, Childs suggests a terminology that applies the term canonical to the whole, while distinguishing two aspects: the process of writing and handing on the tradition on the one side — designated the "canonical process" — and the conclusion of this process on the other side — described as "canonization."

lief meist ohne Regeln ab: mostly runs its course without rules

Pages 62–63

Weil die gegebene Überlieferung im Grundsatz unantastbar war ... intaktes Textbild zu stoßen: Because the given tradition was basically unchallengeable — that is, until the critical era — the interpreter is in the happy situation of being able to work like archaeologists making a test probe. If they remove the later strata, they may expect to uncover an older, intact form of the text.

Page 62n130

Einmal ins Rollen gebracht, ... eine neue Schicht: Once it starts to roll, with every turn it gains a new layer

Der Schneeball mußte irgendwann zur Ruhe kommen: The snowball must eventually come to a stop

Page 63

zu einem der wichtigsten Themen der Bibelwissenschaft avancierte: advanced to one of the most important themes of biblical scholarship

Raum und Bedeutung: space and importance

Page 63n132

ist religionsgeschichtlich keineswegs originell: from the point of view of the history of religions, it is by no means original

Page 63n135

Von hierher … in Verbindung zu bringen: From this point of view it is also evident that one of the most frequent criticisms of this basic approach of canonical biblical interpretation, that it is ahistorical or fundamentalist because it begins with the extant, final form of the biblical text, is completely wide of the mark. The basic approach of canonical interpretation of scripture is the attempt to relate the literary and historical particularities of biblical literature to their distinctive theological role.

Aufklärung: Enlightenment

Pages 63–64

Die Bewahrung der Schrift geschah ja *nicht* um ihrer selbst willen: The preservation of the Scriptures was *not* a matter of what the Scripture itself wills.

Page 64

die *Anfänge der Wissenschaft*: the *beginnings of science*

Wissenschaft: *science,* a scientific approach

Wir nehmen … von Brevard S. Childs entzündet: We will take the controversial discussion in German-speaking countries as an opportunity to familiarize our readers with the discussion of this problem in the USA, where it has been ignited especially by the theses of Brevard S. Childs.

daß die Kanonbildung nicht eine späte kirchliche Setzung ist, sondern: that the issue of the formation of the canon is not a matter that was only settled by a later ecclesiastical decision, but "a consciousness deep within the literature itself."

Page 66n148

Das wichtigste theologische … die christliche Theologie: The most important theological event of the second half of this century is the discovery of the importance of Judaism for Christian theology

Pages 68–69

Wer sich mit ausländischen Beiträgen … diese Arbeiten stehen: Those who deal with the contributions to the discussion from the scholarship of another country must be very cautious in their assessments, since they often do not have sufficient knowledge of their contexts.

Page 69

Aus der Sorge … positiven Kanon: The concern for the theological responsibility of historical exegesis, and the attempt, so to speak, to heal historical criticism from within, tends increasingly toward a disdain for historical work. At the same time, there is an increasing dogmatism with which the canon is claimed to be the solution to all current problems... This second phase of the canonical approach tends to become a *dogmatic flight from the difficulties of historical-critical work* into a positivistic view of canon, the importance of which is vastly overrated.

einer gut amerikanischen … ist von sicherem Wert…: a good American esteem for positivism. Only what can hold in one's hands, in black and white, the final text empirically present, is truly valuable.

Meiner Meinung nach … meiner Darlegungen: In my opinion, M. Oemings' latest analysis of my canonical approach … completely misses the meaning of my explanations.

Page 69n165

dogmatische Flucht: dogmatic flight

Page 70

Kanonhermeneutik … die Glaubensgemeinschaft(en), haben: Canonical hermeneutics … is the reflection of the special conditions and problems for understanding posed by the fact that the biblical writings have the form and function of a canon, i.e. a (relatively) closed collection of writings with normative and/or formative function for the believing community(-ies).

Page 72

***Methodisierung* des kanonhermeneutischen Ansatzes:** methodization of the canonical-hermeneutics approach

ist also nicht ein primär … ***hermeneutischen Zentralkategorie*****:** is thus not a primarily historical-descriptive term, but becomes a *central category of hermeneutics*

Page 72n180

Wirkungsgeschichte: the history of effects (in later interpretation)

Page 73

fordert, um verstanden zu werden, gesamtbiblische Intertextualität: requires for its understanding an intertextuality that embraces the whole Bible

Entstanden sind beide [Testamente] … sind kaum schon gezogen: Each [Testament] obviously consists of many books. The question, however, is whether they remained this way after their combination. In each group of books there is, despite all their variations, a stable pattern, and moreover, so many supporting literary connections, that one must reckon with more than merely a series of independent books. Each canon forms a self-contained meaning system. This has first been shown by the research of our own time, but appears to be already adequately demonstrated. Thereby, within the two groups of books a new, more intensive kind of intertextuality has come into being. This has major consequences for the meaning of each book, even for the particular statements within them. The consequences have hardly been realized.

neue, intensivere Art von Intertextualität: a new, more intensive kind of intertextuality

gesamtbiblische: relating to the Bible as a whole

Habilitation: second dissertation qualifying for university teaching

gesamtbiblische: pertaining to the Bible as a whole

***konturierte Intertextualität*:** contoured (nuanced) intertextuality

Page 73n185

In der katholischen Exegese ... *theologische Methodologie*: To be sure, in Roman Catholic exegesis there has been an elaborated reflection on methodology, but not a *theological methodology* driven with the same intensity.

Page 73n187

Die Entwicklung ... dringend erfordert: The development of a more sophisticated theory would be urgently required both for the "systematic" division of theology (oriented to normative topical issues) and for its "exegetical" division (oriented to the structure of the texts).

Page 74

verrät eine Ambivalenz; ... das (noch) Schemenhafte: betrays an ambivalence; "vision" describes that which is fascinatingly new, but also that which is (still) unreal

Intertextualität: intertextuality

Lektüre: reading

Allein im zweiten Fall ... Rezeptionsprozeß zur Geltung: Only in the second case does the canon become effective as the normative standard for an open-ended reception process.

das Maß des Gebens ist nicht das Maß des Nehmens: the standard/measure of giving is not the standard/measure of reception (what is given is not necessarily what is received)

der Fokus nicht die Vergangenheit, ... für zukünftige Rezeption ist: the focus is not on the past, but on the present and the openness for future reception

Page 75

lexematische Übereinstimmungen: lexical agreements

Anwesenheit: presence

Von einer kanonisch-intertextuellen ... die Genese des Textes: From a canonical intertextual reading of a text, as set forth in the eight studies of the preceding section, no direct path leads to insights into the genesis of the text.

Am plausibelsten ... groß ausgebauten Pentateuch: In my view, the agreements discovered by canonical-intertextual readings can most plausibly be explained by the fact that the author of Gen 22 intentionally alludes to these texts. The indicated text-text relations are, at least for the most part, intended by the author. Gen 22 is a parade example of an author who works intertextually, who to a certain extent elaborates his text on the basis of a Pentateuch already largely developed.

Page 75n197

Frage nach der Sinnkomplexion für den Hypertext: inquire after the meaning complex of the hypertext

Page 75n200

Im Aufbau stets ... verschiedener Hypotexte beleuchtet: In the construction of ever new text-text relations, the hypertext is repeatedly illuminated afresh under the influence of different hypotexts.

Page 75n201

Quellenforscher: source analyst

Page 76

Die historische Analyse ... in der Bibel gefunden hat: Historical analysis is thus not bracketed out, but realigned. It is no longer a matter of "targeting" a point behind the text, in order to make visible the truth of the text. The concept of canon is related to an appreciation of the text in the specific form it has found in the Bible.

Operationalisierungskonzept: concept of operationalization

lehrbar und lernbar: teachable and learnable

Page 76n206

einer kanonisch-intertextuellen Lektüre ... begriffen würde: a canonical intertextual reading would be misunderstood if it were understood as a variation of a work-immanent or holistic interpretation [*Werkimmanent Interpretation* is a technical term of German literary criticism insisting that interpretation remain within the framework of the literary work itself.]

Page 79

raffiniert: sophisticated

Page 82

Es gibt bisher ... von Brevard Childs: To date there is only one thoroughly worked out "Biblical Theology," namely the 1992 volume of Brevard Childs.

[Es] zeichnet sich ... heute immer lauter gefordert wird: An even more distant goal of our efforts looms before us, namely that of a "Biblical Theology," in which the dualism of an Old

Testament theology and a New Testament theology in mutual contrast would be overcome. Just how such a biblical theology might be presented is still difficult to imagine. It is encouraging, however, that the calls for such a theology become louder and louder.

Wird ein Weg ... jetzt die Frage: Will a way be found by which this split can be overcome? That is now the question.

gesamtbiblische: pertaining to the Bible as a whole

Page 83

gesamtbiblische: pertaining to the Bible as a whole

Page 84

Es gibt bisher nur eine einzige wirklich ausgearbeitete 'Biblische Theologie': To date there is only one thoroughly worked out "Biblical Theology"

Page 87

gesamtbiblische Theologien: theologians concerned with the Bible as a whole

Page 96

eher konservativ: rather conservative

bestimmten dogmatischen Voraussetzungen: certain dogmatic presuppositions

An dieser Stelle ... Childs' Position zu verstehen: At this point I must abandon the role of reporter, because I have difficulty understanding Childs' position.

Über die Frage der "Arbeitsteilung" ... nicht zum Christuszeugnis: Different opinions can coexist as to how the "division of labor" among the theological disciplines should be regarded. I agree with Childs when he says this is more a matter of strategy than principle, even if I would sort out the tasks differently. What I do not understand and cannot accept is that dogmatic decisions precede exegetical analysis. Above all, I do not understand what is being said when it is claimed that the Old Testament bears witness to Christ. I by no means deny that there are theologically legitimate ways of reading the Old Testament with the New Testament as one Christian Bible, thereby interpreting the Christian Bible as a whole from the Christ event as the point of orientation. But this does not mean that the Old Testament itself becomes a witness to Christ.

Daß das Alte Testament Christus bezeugt ... nicht nachvollziehbar: I do not understand what it means to claim that the Old Testament testifies to Christ (not a coming Messiah, but Jesus Christ). A hermeneutic that ignores basic historical facts is incomprehensible to me.

ausschließlich eine christliche Disziplin: exclusively a Christian discipline

Für mich ist dies ... nicht nachvollzogen werden könnten: For me, this is a crucial point. I try never to make statements about the Old Testament that could not be understood and affirmed by a Jew.

Aber meine Antworten, ... akzeptabel sein: But my answers, i.e. my exposition of the text, must be understandable and acceptable to a Jew.

Page 97

Christuszeugnis: witness to Christ

Integretät: integrity

Theologie *im* Alten Testament: theology *in* the Old Testament

Page 98

historisch ein verhältnismäßig spätes Produkt: historically a relatively late product

Page 98n85

was das Alte Testament enthält: what the Old Testament contains

Page 99

eine Art theologische Literaturgeschichte des Urchristentums: a kind of "history of early Christian literature"

viel konsequenter 'kanonisch' zu arbeiten, als Childs in diesem Buch tut: to work much more consistently "canonically" than Childs does in this book

Wirkungsgeschichte: the history of effects (in later interpretation)

Page 100

So muß also … AT gesprochen werden: So we must therefore truly speak — to finally utilize the controversial word — of the Old Testament's witness to Christ.

Auseinandersetzung: dispute, debate

Page 105

Ursprünglich haben die ältesten [Gattungen] … Aufnahmefähigkeit der alten Hörer: Originally, the oldest [genres] … played a particular role in the life of the Israelites, of which they represent an important part. This was precisely because they were not written on paper, but in the lives of the people, and also because the oldest units were so short, corresponding to the ancient hearer's capacity to appropriate them.

nicht auf dem Papier, sondern im Leben: not on paper, but in life

Page 107

die großen Schriftstellerpersönlichkeiten: the great literary personalities

haben eine ähnliche oder dieselbe Geschichte erlebt: have experienced a similar or the same history

nicht auf dem Papier, sondern im Leben: not on paper, but in life

Page 108

die großen Schriftsteller, die sich der altertümlichen Gattungen bemächtigen: the great authors, who took control of the ancient genres

höchst individuelle Worte: highly individual words

die Sammlung der Sammlungen, der Kanon, entsteht: the collection of collections, the canon, takes shape

Page 111

Männer: men

Einzelpersönlichkeiten: individual personalities

er habe sein ganzes Leben nach seinem verlorenen Kinderglauben gesucht: he had sought his whole life long to recover the lost faith of his childhood

Page 112

Kulturprotestantismus: culture Protestantism

Page 114

Menschheit: humanity

Volkes Schmerz: the people's pain

Nun hebe wieder ... rede leise: Now raise [your voice] again in the old way, / And where you find [sensitive, receptive] hearts, speak softly

Page 116

Wir haben in diesen Sagen *die Anfänge der Religionsgeschichte*: In these sagas we have *the beginnings of the historiography of religion*

Page 119

Schranken des Kanons: canonical boundaries

die gesamte Geschichte der israelitisch-jüdisch-urchristlichen Religion als Einheit: the whole history of Israelite-Jewish-early Christian religion as a unity

Pages 119–120

zugleich aber tat man ... oder gar voreingenommen gewesen war: at the same time the mental floodgates were opened to everything foreign that could contribute anything at all to understanding the Bible, which was happily welcomed. All this was in strong contrast to the past, when the non-biblical was regarded indifferently or even with prejudice.

Page 120

Wenn wir also damals 'Religionsgeschichte' ... der biblischen Religion: So if we then inscribed "history of religion" on our banner, we did not think of the history of religions in general, but a history of biblical religion.

Die babylonische Religion ... Geschichte gehabt zu haben: In *Schöpfung und Chaos*, Babylonian religion appeared only in a negative light, and God appeared to have had a special history with Israel.

liegt hier ein Problem, ... systematische Kraft besaß: here lies a problem for which ... even in the following years and decades Gunkel did not have adequate systematic strength to resolve

Theologisch gesehen, ... Menschheitsgeschichte als Offenbarungsgeschichte begreift: Regarded theologically, Gunkel here calls for a theology oriented to the history of religions, a theology that does not understand the revelation of God as an isolated act for a particular people or for individuals within this people, but which sees God's action in the whole history of humanity as revelation, i.e. that perceives human history as such as the history of revelation.

Page 121

Indem Gunkel eine ... nach dem Gefälle dieser Geschichte virulent: When Gunkel calls for an investigation of Holy Scripture from the point of view of ... literary history and study of the history of religions, aiming at a purely historical representation, he guards against the danger that critical analysis of the canon will dissolve it from within, leaving only a variety of sources and religious beliefs. The unity of the Holy Scriptures is attributed to the history lying behind them. But then ... the question is, what is the unifying factor in this history. The question of the "gradient" of history (its tendency and goal) becomes virulent.

kommt die gesamtbiblische theologische Problematik hier überhaupt nicht in Sicht: the problematic of a theology that embraces the whole Bible does not come into view at all

Page 121n79

Betrachtet man das 'Gefälle' der Geschichte ... sinnenfällig ins Auge: If one regards the "gradient" of history just right, it becomes obvious that God's revelation in Israel is incomparably greater than in e.g. Babylonia or Egypt, however much a true knowledge of God is also present there.

Page 122

lebendige, aus dem Herzen kommende Religion: living, heart-felt religion

großen religiösen Personen: great religious figures

Die Erscheinung, ... Geschichtsforschung zu treten beginnt: The phenomenon that our generation has experienced, that Biblical Theology has been replaced by "the history of the religion of Israel," is thus explained by the fact that now the spirit of historical research is beginning to replace the doctrine of inspiration.

In welchem Sinne … die Dogmatik zu handeln haben: In what sense we can continue to speak of revelation, when biblical religion is considered from the point of view of the history of religions, is an issue that must be dealt with by systematic theology.

Bibelwissenschaft: academic study of the Bible

der in der Bibel gesammelten Schriften: the writings assembled in the Bible

Bibelkritik: Biblical criticism

eine Geschichte des Volkes Israel auf allen seinen Lebensäußerungen: a history of the Israelite people in all its manifestations

Seine höchste Aufgabe … 'Biblischen Theologie.': The scholar then finds his or her highest duty in a history of Israelite religion and ethics, the replacement of the former "Biblical Theology."

biblische Religionsgeschichte: history of biblical religion

Page 123

großen religiösen Persönlichkeiten: great religious personalities

die eigentlichen Träger der israelitischen Religion: the real bearers of Israelite religion

Nur so gewinnen wir … mit Recht die "Religionsgeschichte Israel" getreten: Only so will we attain a truly historical and vivid understanding of the various religio-ethical beliefs and ideas that always encounter us as members of a spiritual organism, as is the case with the individual periods of the religious life in Israel and the development of Israelite religion in general. Thus the "history of Israelite religion" properly takes the place of "Biblical Theology."

Krone: crowning achievement

biblische Theologie: Biblical Theology

biblische Religionsgeschichte: history of biblical religion

Alle andern alttestamentlichen Disziplinen … Bedürfnis des Glaubens entspricht: All other Old Testament disciplines should serve this one task, a requirement that proceeds from the nature of the Old Testament itself, in which religion is the real center, and which also corresponds to what faith needs.

Pages 123–24

hat der Umschwung … neben der Religionsgeschichte geführt: the reversal of the theological situation since 1918, especially the emphasis on the rootedness of the whole Scripture in the revelation of the *one* God in Jesus Christ (W. Vischer), along with the impossibility of settling truth questions purely by historical research, has led to the call for a revitalization of Biblical Theology alongside the study of the history of religions.

Page 124

Fundamentaltheologisch: in terms of fundamental theology

ungeklärte Nebeneinander … und normativem Anspruch: unresolved juxtaposition of historical methodology (in the sense of the "history of religions school") and normative claim

die Frage nach der Korrelation … hermeneutischen Prinzip: the question of the correlation between revelation and history with its hermeneutical principle

***Geltung* (Verbindlichkeit der Schrift):** validity (binding force of the Scripture)

***Genese* (Entstehung der Überlieferungsvielfalt):** genesis (origin of the tradition's diversity)

Neuorientierung der Disziplin: reorientation of the discipline

Der Entwurf einer BTh … ***eine zweigeteilte christl. Bibel sein will*****:** The design of a Biblical Theology acknowledges a biblical canon consisting of the two testaments, and proceeds on this basis. The factual existence of this canon is relevant for a comprehensive biblical theology. This results from the fact that a theologically-determined relation of the two Testaments to each other was already presupposed for the origin of the Christian canon… In this process it becomes clear that the New Testament, by its own hermeneutic of Scripture, does not understand itself as a canon that can be read independently of the Old Testament, as though it were an additive to the Old Testament canon that had already been closed, but, together with that first part (later named the "Old Testament" as a result of this process), has in view a two-part Christian Bible.

Page 125

Formgeschichte: form criticism

Gattungen: genres

vor allem: above all

ältesten und reinsten Ausprägungen nach Form und Inhalt: oldest and purest expressions of form and content

Wurzeln im Leben: roots in the life

Page 125n95

gesamtbiblische theologische Problematik: the problematic of a comprehensive biblical theology

Page 130

kanonhermeneutische Debatte seit Gerhard von Rad: debate about canonical hermeneutics since Gerhard von Rad

Page 132

gesamtbiblische theologische Problematik: the problematic of a comprehensive biblical theology

Page 133

gesamtbiblische: pertaining to the Bible as a whole

kanonhermeneutische Debatte: debate about canonical hermeneutics

Page 133n140

wenn von Rad selbst … im Gefälle einer gesamtbiblischen Theologie: if in his *Theology of the Old Testament* von Rad himself did not specifically reflect on the hermeneutical problem of the canon, and thus can be taken as a reference for canonical theology only in a limited sense, his reflections still lie on the gradient that tends toward a comprehensive biblical theology.

Page 134

Ich habe ihn gar nicht verstanden: I do not understand him

Christuszeugnis: witness to Christ

Page 135

Glaubensgeschichte: religious history

Page 145

Kanonbewußtsein: canon consciousness

In der bisweilen opak … die Ebenen ohne explizite Hinweise: Childs sometimes uses "canon" in an "extended," effectively obscure way. Two basic viewpoints can be distinguished, which I would call the *semiotic* concept and the *functional* concept. I will explain these below. In order to include all aspects of canon he considers important, Childs combines a theory of meaning of the canon with a theory of how it functions, alternating between these as required by the plane of the discussion, and without any indication that he does so.

Kanon (1) = *Kanon als* (der kanonisierte) *Text* (der Bibel): Canon (1) = *Canon as* (the canonized) *text* (of the Bible)

Kanon (2) = *Kanon als Metatext* (Metasprach/metalinguistischer Rahmen): Canon (2) = *Canon as metatext* (meta-language, meta-linguistic framework).

Beides sind extrinsische Vorgänge, … an den Text herangetragen: Both are extrinsic processes that are not in the text itself, but are brought to the text.

Page 146

[eine autoritative] Begrenzung des Sinns: [an authoritative] limitation of the meaning

So wird die interpretatorische Kreativität angeregt und zugleich begrenzt: Interpretative creativity is thereby both encouraged and limited.

Page 147

man mit mehr rechnen muß als nur einer Reihe von in sich selbständigen Büchern: one must reckon with more than merely a series of independent books

Daß 'Kanonisierung' ... nicht genügend beachtet: That "canonization" means not only "selection and compilation of authoritative writings," but is reflected in the text itself ... does not generally receive adequate attention.

Funktionstheorie: function theory

Bedeutungstheorie: meaning theory

Kanonisierung ist nicht nur ... einen Niederschlag gefunden: Canonization is not only an external declaration that defines the selection and arrangement of normative documents; it has — as recent canon research has worked out — left its imprint within the text itself.

Page 148

einer Zusammenführung und Fokussierung verschiedener Traditionsstränge: a merging and focusing of various strands of tradition

der disparaten Traditionen der älteren kanonischen Bücher: of the disparate traditions of the older canonical books

Ist man durch die Einsichten ... derart disparate Sammlung abgeschlossen werden: If, through insights into the process of formation of the first two parts of the canon, one becomes aware that the canon grows from within and that indications of completion are found in the text itself, so that canon formation does not take place as an external declarative act, then the question is raised whether something analogous is not also true for the third part of the canon. For this part of the canon, the problem of closure is posed in a particular way: How can such a disparate collection be concluded?

Das letzte Buch ... des dreiteiligen Kanons: The last book of the third part thus connects this part back to the two preceding parts, and opens up a comprehensive perspective on the tripartite canon centered on the Torah.

Page 148n40

Der 'kanonische Prozeß' ... als entscheidendem Faktor der 'Schriftwerdung': The "canonical process" understood as the incorporation and updating of each new acquisition of the biblical traditions is to be distinguished from the "canonization" that brings this inner-biblical process to a conclusion. On the "canonical process" as decisive factor in the "shaping of Scripture"

***[m]ethodisch* wichtig:** methodologically important

der Herausbildung einer Kanontheorie: the formation of a theory of the canon

Page 149

selbstreferentielles: self-referential

Page 151

gemeinsame Nenner der verschiedenen Stimmen: common denominator of the different voices

interpretatorisch relevante Bezugspunkt ist der Text: the text is the relevant interpretative point of reference

Page 152

schriftgelehrte Prophetie: *scribal prophecy*

Page 153

kanonisch-intertextuelle Lektüre: canonical-intertextual reading

sehr enge traditionelle: very narrow traditional

Analogie: analogy

Exempel: example

Typologie: typology

Überbietung: surpassing

Wie eine entsprechende theoretische Hermeneutik … Schriftsinn nicht genügend Atem: How a corresponding theoretical hermeneutic would look would at first have to be worked out step by step. I am not aware of any existing theories that would correspond to this approach and would also rest on exegetical experience. In the final analysis, the theory of multiple meanings of Scripture probably also ran out of breath.

Page 154n79

enge traditionelle: narrow traditional

Page 159

Kanonbewußtsein: canon consciousness

Page 160

Könnte es nicht sein, … Modifikationen erfährt: Could it not be the case that the canonical understanding of the "Bible as a whole," whose canonicity the Christian community affirms, experiences significant modifications?

Page 161

Schriftgelehrten: scribes

Kanonbewußtsein: canon consciousness

Page 165

Das Neue Testament ist kein Midrasch zum Alten Testament: The New Testament is no Midrash on the Old Testament.

Page 167

***Christuszeugnis*:** witness to Christ

Page 167n32

***Kanonbewußtsein*:** canon consciousness

Page 168

niemals Aussagen über das Alte Testament … werden könnten: never to make statements about the Old Testament that could not be understood and affirmed by a Jew.

Je mehr es die Theologie … Keim des Antijudaismus in sich: The more it is concerned to make the theology of the Old Testament a matter of interpreting the Old Testament in relation to the New, the more it is in danger of co-opting it as Christian... The theology of the Old Testament thus contains the seeds of anti-Judaism in itself.

Die Einsicht von B.S. Childs … für den christlich-jüdischen Dialog: The insight of B.S. Childs is probably inevitable: The Theology of the Old Testament is "Essentially a Christian discipline" and therefore defined confessionally. This makes it unsuitable for Christian-Jewish dialogue.

Page 170–71

Wenn irgendeine biblische … auch im Christentum: If any biblical interpretation can no longer base its view on the biblical text itself, but only on later traditions, this is a sign of serious weakness, both in Judaism and in Christianity.

Page 173

***Kanonbewußtsein*:** canon consciousness

das Verhältnis darlegen … Verständnis von beiden: to explain the relationship between the origins of midrashic exegesis and biblical literature, and thereby to make a contribution to a better understanding of both.

Wie erwähnen zuerst … der Interpretation geradezu herausfordert: We mention first the extraordinary malleability of narrative and the literary motif in the Bible, as well as the playful aspect of the Semitic or Hebraic mind, then a pronounced tendency toward borrowing and adapting thoughts and ideas that derive from a foreign environment or a different time, transforming them to fit their own place and time, and finally the emergence of a canonical consciousness: the changeable currents of tradition in transmission coagulate and become Holy Scripture. In particular, the concept of Torah becomes loaded with a content that cries out to be interpreted.

die Doppelsinn des Wortes, Gleichklang und Wortspiel: the double meaning of a word: homonyms and wordplays

Page 174

völlig anderer Art: completely different kind

ein Element der Bewusstheit in die Vorgänge: an element of awareness into the process

Ein späteres Geschlecht … Zeit an zu passen: A later generation is not content with taking over the old word, but changes the meaning — sometimes, the text itself — in order to adjust it to the thought and feeling of a new time.

wurzelt im Midrasch … in der Zeit des Erklärers: is rooted in Midrash, and the goal of Midrash is to actualize the biblical text, i.e. to show that the old biblical word refers to historical events in the time of the interpreter.

aber noch nicht als Auslegung … zum Abschluss gekommene Literatur: but still not qualify as interpretation in the real sense. The playful element colors the way the motif is modified, the quote is transposed by adaptation, but all these phenomena are involved with a river of tradition still in flux, not "congealed," a stream that has not yet reached its goal.

Page 174–75

nicht der *äussere* Prozess der Kanonisierung, … Bedeutung und Autorität beilegt: not the *external* process of canonization, but the shift in consciousness that attaches new meaning and authority to an old word

Page 174n52

Amos sieht Obst (קיץ) …aufsteigen zu lassen: Amos sees some fruit (קיץ), and that is enough to evoke the idea of the end (קץ).

Page 175

Wandel im Bewußtsein: change in consciousness

Einerseits will er … für jeden neuen Tag: On the one hand, he wants to explain a self-contained text that, even in this form, possesses the highest authority. On the other hand, he strives to keep this same text open … to protect against petrification and to fill it with new life — for every new situation and every new day!

Page 175–76

Midrasch liest und deutet … von Israel: Midrash reads and interprets [an] expression of an individual as the testimony of the community of Israel.

Page 175n61

***Vergegenwärtigung*:** actualization

Page 177

Schriftgelehrten: scribes

Page 183

auf den biblischen Text selbst gründen kann: can be based on the biblical text itself

spätere Traditionen: later traditions

ernsthaften Schwäche sowohl im Judentum als auch im Christentum: serious weakness in both Judaism and Christianity

Page 190

recht starken Angriff: a rather strong attack

"Biblische Theologie und jüdische Auslegung des Tanach": "Biblical Theology and Jewish Interpretation of the Tanach"

dem ersten apostolischen Zeugnis und jeder folgenden kirchlichen Tradition: the first apostolic witness and each subsequent ecclesiastical tradition

Mitte der Schrift: center of the Scripture

sei es ein Wesen, ein Kerygma … mitbestimmt sind: whether it is an essence, a kerygma, or a historical line of development, which are often co-determined by a philosophical system (idealism, existentialism, ontology)

Für das Christentum, … ***Kanon in der Christologie***: For Christianity, as opposed to Judaism, the canon is rooted in Christology

Page 191

Christuszeugnis: witness to Christ.

Erstens werden die Hebräischen Schriften … Verständnis von Schrift-Autorität führt: First, the Hebrew Scriptures are not understood as a closed entity, and also not as standing in a dialectical relationship with later rabbinical tradition. Rather, there is an unbroken continuity between Scripture and tradition that leads to a different understanding of the authority of Scripture.

bewirkt das jüdische Verständnis … (*in Gestalt des Midrasch*): the Jewish understanding of the role of *oral tradition as an authoritative commentary on the written tradition (in the form of Midrash)* effects a very different dynamic in comparison to that of Christianity

Meine Position, … ***Midrash in Context*** **hinnehmen müssen:** My position, that the subject matter of the biblical disciplines are the canonical writings of the Jewish synagogue regarded from the perspective of Christian theology, has recently suffered a rather strong attack in Jacob Neusner's latest work, *Midrash in Context.*

Page 192

Muss man nicht deutlicher … endgültigen literarischen Fixierung: Should we not distinguish more clearly between the time when the material originated and the time of its final literary fixation?

Die Idee eines Kanons, … recht verschieden aussahen: The idea of a canon, i.e. a limited collection of authoritative writings, is not simply a Christian idea, but is also Jewish, even if their respective contents and roles look quite different.

***Kanonbewußtsein*:** canon consciousness

***Christuszeugnis*:** witness to Christ

spätere rabbinische Tradition… gemeinsamen Schrift zu untergraben: later rabbinic tradition. Both lead to undermining the possibility of serious theological dialogue between Jews and Christians on the basis of a common document.

Page 193

***Kanonbewußtsein*:** canon consciousness

Page 194

Jüdische Kanons: Jewish canon

einfache Kontinuität: simple continuity

***Christuszeugnis*:** witness to Christ

Das Neue Testament ist kein Midrasch zum Alten Testament: The New Testament is no Midrash on the Old Testament.

Die Identität Jesu … Alten Bund geschlagen: The identity of Jesus Christ is made completely understandable in the terminology of the Old Testament. However, the continuity of God's comprehensive work of redemption is perceived solely from the standpoint of the New Testament, and the bridge to the Old Testament is spanned only from the New Testament side.

Page 195

kunstvolle Dialektik: artful dialectic

Die sorgfältige Beachtung … einen christologischen Mitte überein: Careful consideration of the Christian canon leads to theological reflection on both Testaments, a reflection that can be satisfied neither with the categories of an unbroken continuity nor with those of a radical discontinuity. Only that theological reflection which straightforwardly uses both categories squares with the one christological center.

***Sachkritik*:** content criticism or subject criticism (criticism that deals with the theological subject matter of the text itself)

***Christuszeugnis*:** witness to Christ

Der modern Christ … Zeugnis für den einen Herrn ablegt: The modern Christian reads the Old Testament exactly as did the early church, as pointing to Jesus Christ. The Old Testament is part of the Scripture of the church, because it bears witness to the one Lord.

Allerdings bleibt es schwer bestimmbar, … Herz der Biblischen Theologie: Moreover, it remains hard to specify what it means to find a reference to Christ in the Old Testament, and struggling with this problem cuts to the heart of biblical theology.

Mitte: center

Page 195n162

aus dem kanonischen Rang … in eigenem Recht: out of the Old Testament's canonical rank as an independent witness to Jesus Christ in its own right

Page 196

Die Gefahr der katholischen Position, … ***es vom jüdischen unterscheidet,*** **zuwider:** The danger of the Catholic position, amply illustrated in the history of the church, was, of course, the danger of making the word of God a prisoner of religious traditions — often in the name of piety. Does not an appeal to tradition in itself, without allowing the content of the biblical witness to exercise its critical role, go against the unique Christian understanding of the canon, *which distinguishes it from the Jewish understanding*?

Page 196n167

Ein ebenso wichtiges Argument … Tradenten dieser Tradition: An equally important argument was the theological ground/occasion for solidarity with the Jews, the chosen bearers of this tradition.

Page 197

verständlich und akzeptabel: understandable and acceptable

***Schriftgelehrte*:** scribes

Page 199

recht starken Angriff: rather strong attack

verständlich und akzeptabel: understandable and acceptable

Page 200

interpretatorisch relevante Bezugspunkt ist der Text: the text is the relevant interpretative point of reference

Page 201

theologischen Interesse des Schriftverständnisses: theological interest in understanding the Scripture

Gesamtbiblische: pertaining to the Bible as a whole

Page 201–2

Man wird immerhin die Frage stellen, ... ***nicht unwesentliche Modifikationen erfährt***: The question will still be raised whether in a presentation so resolutely oriented to theological understanding of canon it is legitimate to almost completely neglect the area on in which the author's own understanding of the canon is based... *Could it not be the case that a canonical understanding of the "Bible as a whole," whose canonicity is affirmed by the Christian community, experiences significant modifications?*

Page 202

Bleibt die Frage ... doch ein Hauptanliegen des Buches ist: Does the question of the canonical shape of the individual Old Testament books still remain, if they (as in the *Introduction*) are discussed without pursuing the issue of the comprehensive canonical understanding of the Bible as a whole? Is there not still a "historical" job to be done? After all, a major concern of the book is to distance itself from such a historical approach.

Page 204

Gesamtbiblische: pertaining to the Bible as a whole

Page 205n203

Frühkatholizismus: early Catholicism

Page 215

auch eine Weltanschauung, ... Geschichte der Theologie steht: also a world view that stands in precisely the same multi-sided relation to philosophy, literary analysis, and especially the history of theology

Page 216

Literaturverständnis: literary understanding

Page 217

Kritik ist kein neutraler Begriff, ... der Interpretation vollkommen zu bestimmen: Criticism is not a neutral term, nor is it a method or academic realm such as those represented by an Introduction to the Old Testament or New Testament. The concept of criticism refers to freedom. It is not a method, but the freedom to accept the results of the method. One can apply "modern methods" without being in the least touched by the spirit of criticism. Criticism means the willingness not only to apply methods, but to follow them wherever they lead. Applied to the Bible, this means in particular: the freedom to come to exegetical results that differ from earlier theological exegesis. In this sense, criticism is a child of the Enlightenment, but at the same time also a child of the Reformation, for in this sense the theology of the Reformation was outspokenly "critical." The theological tradition was no longer in a position to entirely determine the possibilities of interpretation.

Page 219

Mit dem Auftreten der Bibelkritik ... die Forschung: With the advent of biblical criticism there was thus a shift in the criteria for what constituted correct exegesis. The answers to critical questions were no longer measured by the standards of church doctrine, but by the standards of scholarship.

Page 237

***Sachkritik*:** content criticism or subject criticism (criticism that deals with the theological subject matter of the text itself)

Page 242

ob damit Childs wirklich widersprochen ist: whether thereby Childs is actually contradicted

Christuszeugnis: *witness to Christ*

Page 242n134

weitreichenden Konsens: wide-ranging consensus

Vischers alttestamentliche Hermeneutik ist, ... entschieden einfacher: Vischer's Old Testament hermeneutic is decidedly simpler, although he has not given up on historical criticism.

Page 243

Christuszeugnis: witness to Christ

Doktorvater: "doctor father," the supervisor of a student's doctoral work, especially the dissertation

Page 250

Es ist nicht von ungefähr, ... Vermittler der Heilswirklichkeit ist: It is no accident that the Greek word for "regula," κανών, increasingly became a firm designation for holy scripture. The original witness is therefore not only "canonical" because it represents the authority of the prophets and apostles, but also because it is the bearer of revelation, mediating the reality of salvation.

Die Aufgabe, eine 'fundamentum' ... der heiligen Schrift: The "regula" fulfills its responsibility of being a "fundamentum" of the teaching tradition only through the mediation of the Holy Scriptures.

Page 251

***Sachkritik*:** content criticism or subject criticism (criticism that deals with the theological subject matter of the text itself)

Page 252

Die "regula fidei" ... doch beide ganz identisch sind: The "regula fidei" is identical neither with the creed nor with a particular interpretation of the creed. The term — which is to be understood abstractly, not concretely — refers to the doctrine of the church as a whole, the doctrine proclaimed by the apostles and prophets and deposited in the Holy Scripture. The baptismal confession (as a short summary of the contents of revelation), Holy Scripture, apostolic tradition — all this is included in the concept of "regula fidei" or "regula veritatis." Thus this "regula" can be used as the equivalent of one or the other of these normative guidelines, without being identified with any one in particular.

Page 266

***Auseinandersetzung*:** debate, dispute

nicht auf dem Papier, sondern im Leben: not on paper, but in life

Page 266n3

Gefälle: gradient

Page 267

das sicherlich nun bald hereinbrechen wird: that certainly will arrive soon

Fernerwartung: expectation in the long-term future

kollektive Naherwartung: collective expectation for something in the near future

Redegegenwart: the speaker's present time

Pages 267–68

Wenn Jahwe bei der Heilswende Jerusalems ... vorzeitigen Todesnähe vorgebracht: If YHWH will one day act for the collective salvation of Jerusalem, as expected in v. 18, he can not fail to hear the plea of the one who presently prays for his life ... The confidence that God will act for Israel collectively in the distant future, exemplified by YHWH whose days "endure through all generations" (vv. 13, 14–23), is contrasted with the fate of the one who prays facing death in the near future.

Page 268

Uneinheitlichkeit: inconsistency

Was wird wann aufgeschrieben für ein künftiges Geschlecht: What is written, and when, for a future generation?

die Gewißheit dieser künftigen Rettung ... Redegegenwart des Psalms leben, wahrnehmen: the certainty of this future deliverance is prophetically nourished in the present as expressed in vv. 14ff. This means that the recipients of salvation, who live in the time when the psalm is proclaimed in the cult, perceive the experience of God's saving act in the speaker's present time as the fulfillment of their ancestors' confidence in salvation to come.

Fernerwartung: expectation in the long-term future

Naherwartung: expectation in the near future

Page 268n15

In Psalm 102 stehen also … in einem einheitlichen Text zusammen: It is thus not the case that Psalm 102 has brought together different literary layers, but that two traditional parallel linguistic fields — late wisdom traditions and late prophetic traditions — come together in a unified text.

Page 269

Fortschreibung: updating

Page 273

Das ändert aber nichts … im Gegenteil verstärkt: This changes nothing in regard to the Christian tendency to deny the Jewish psalms any intrinsic value. He not only continues this tradition, but strengthens it.

Page 274

solange Israel glaubt, … Psalmenbuches an die Kirche…: so long as Israel believes that the hopes concentrated in this book have not yet been fulfilled in ongoing history, and thus that Jesus of Nazareth is not the promised savior king for whom Israel waits, so long should the church be sensitive enough to choose formulations in their own texts that set forth their own self-understanding (before Israel, before their common God, and before the peoples of the earth) that respect Israel's decisions of faith and do not violate the dignity of this people… [The church] is not the only believing community waiting for the day when all nations will call on the Lord with one voice (Nostra Aetate 4), for they may be sure that Israel also is looking forward to that day. The church is not alone on the path to God, but walks it together with Israel. That is the theological message of the fourth book of Psalms to the church.

Page 274n45

***Die reformatorische Rückbesinnung* … an der allegorischen Interpretation festhält:** The reformational return to Scripture and its emphasis on the literal sense can be carried through in the interpretation of this psalm only with caution. Calvin was the first to advocate a historical interpretation on the basis of the sensus literalis, while Luther held fast to the allegorical interpretation.

Page 274n46

Dem Grundkonsens, … haben sich aber nicht durchgesetzt: Since the second half of the 19th century the approach of Hengstenberg and Delitzsch has once again opposed the basic consensus that had been formed (despite all the differences in detail) in reference to the necessity of contemporary Jewish interpretation. But their attempts to integrate the results of critical research into church contexts through Messianic revelation-historical exegesis have not prevailed.

Page 274n48

Psalm 102 vor allem ein jüdisches Gebet ist: Psalm 102 is first and foremost a Jewish prayer

Page 275

dogmatische Flucht aus den Schwierigkeiten des historischkritischen Geschäfts: dogmatic flight from the difficulties of historical-critical work

Wenn Childs die Notwendigkeit ... löse alle Probleme: When Childs considers the hermeneutical project's necessity of "making the text understandable again" from the point of view of the final form of the text, I can no longer understand him. How can one, in view of the profound alienation from the Bible in this secular age, and in view of the dismal lack of understanding of the normativity of sacred writings, especially of the Old Testament, believe that a return to the canonical final form will resolve all problems?

Page 275n49

geht er insofern über sein ausschließliches Interesse am kanonisierten Endtext hinaus: here he goes beyond his exclusive interest in the canonical final form of the text

Page 275n51

Das wirklich Neue ... des Psalters nicht christlich zu vereinnahmen: In any case, what seems to be really new in the Christian form of holistic exegesis of the Psalms is not its view of individual psalms or of the psalter as a whole, but the effort to avoid monopolizing the potential ripple effects within the Psalter for Christian interpretation.

Page 276

***Wirkungsgeschichte*:** the history of effects (in later interpretation)

Page 281

Raum und Bedeutung: room and significance

Page 286

recht starken Angriff: rather strong attack

Christuszeugnis: witness to Christ

Page 289

unecht: inauthentic

Bibliography

A. Brevard Springs Childs

Books by Childs are listed by abbreviation at the front (page xiii). The slim paperback *Biblical Theology: A Proposal* (Minneapolis: Fortress, 2002) was not, strictly speaking, authorized (Childs learned of its existence when someone handed him a copy with the request for an autograph), and I have not referenced the title since it merely excerpts the 1992 *Biblical Theology*.

Those with an interest in unpublished works and letters should consult "The Brevard S. Childs Manuscript Collection," housed in the Princeton Theological Seminary archives. A finding guide is online (http://libweb.ptsem.edu/collections/ead/childs_brevard_s.html). I have posted this link, along with many others to full-text books and articles, on a hyperlinked bibliography on my website, http://www.danieldriver.com/bsc/.

Dissertation & Books

Childs, Brevard S. "Der Mythos als theologische Problem im Alten Testaments." Basel, 1953. Resubmitted as "A Study of Myth in Genesis I–XI." ThD diss., Basel, 1955. Revised and published as *Myth and Reality in the Old Testament.* Studies in Biblical Theology 27. London: SCM, 1960. 2nd ed. London: SCM, 1962.

— *Memory and Tradition in Israel.* Studies in Biblical Theology 37. London: SCM, 1962.

— *Isaiah and the Assyrian Crisis.* Studies in Biblical Theology, Second Series 3. London: SCM, 1967.

— *Biblical Theology in Crisis.* Philadelphia: Westminster, 1970.

— *The Book of Exodus: A Critical, Theological Commentary.* Louisville: Westminster, 1974.

— *Old Testament Books for Pastor and Teacher.* Philadelphia: Westminster, 1977.

— *Introduction to the Old Testament as Scripture.* Philadelphia: Fortress, 1979.

— *The New Testament as Canon: An Introduction.* Philadelphia: Fortress, 1984.

— *Old Testament Theology in a Canonical Context.* Philadelphia: Fortress, 1985.

— *Biblical Theology of the Old and New Testaments: Theological Reflection on the Christian Bible.* Minneapolis: Fortress, 1992.

— *Die Theologie der einen Bibel. Bd. 1: Grundstrukturen; Bd. 2: Hauptthemen.* Translated by Manfred and Christiane Oeming. 2 vols. Freiburg: Herder, 1994–1996.

— *Isaiah: A Commentary.* Louisville: Westminster John Knox, 2001.

— *The Struggle to Understand Isaiah as Christian Scripture.* Grand Rapids: Eerdmans, 2004.

— *The Church's Guide for Reading Paul: The Canonical Shaping of the Pauline Corpus.* Grand Rapids: Eerdmans, 2008.

Articles & Select Papers

1955

— "A Study of Glory." *Mission House Seminary Bulletin* 2 (1955): 34–43.
— "Jonah: A Study in Old Testament Hermeneutics." *Scottish Journal of Theology* 11 (1958): 53–61.
— "Prophecy and Fulfillment: A Study of Contemporary Hermeneutics." *Interpretation: A Journal of Bible and Theology* 12/3 (1958): 257–271.
— "The Enemy from the North and the Chaos Tradition." *Journal of Biblical Literature* 78/3 (1959): 187–198.

1960

— "Adam," "Eden, Garden of," "Eve," "Orientation," "Tree of Knowledge, Tree of Life." In *The Interpreter's Dictionary of the Bible.* Edited by George Arthur Buttrick et al. 4 vols. Nashville: Abingdon, 1962.
— "A Study of the Formula, 'Until This Day.'" *Journal of Biblical Literature* 82 (1963): 279–292.
— "Interpretation in Faith: The Theological Responsibility of an Old Testament Commentary." *Interpretation: A Journal of Bible and Theology* 18/4 (1964): 432–449.
— "The Birth of Moses." *Journal of Biblical Literature* 84/2 (1965): 109–122.
— "A Survey of Recent Books in Old Testament." *Yale Divinity News* 62/3 (1965): 13–14.
— "Deuteronomic Formulae of the Exodus Traditions." Pages 30–39 in *Hebräische Wortforschung: Festschrift zum 80. Geburtstag von Walter Baumgartner.* Edited by George W Anderson et al. Leiden: Brill, 1967.
— "Karl Barth as Interpreter of Scripture." Pages 30–39 in *Karl Barth and the Future of Theology: A Memorial Colloquium Held at Yale Divinity School January 28, 1969.* Edited by D L Dickerman. New Haven: Yale Divinity School Association, 1969.
— "Psalm 8 in the Context of the Christian Canon." *Interpretation: A Journal of Bible and Theology* 23/1 (1969): 20–31.

1970

— "A Traditio-historical Study of the Reed Sea Tradition." *Vetus Testamentum* 20/4 (1970): 406–418.
— "Psalm Titles and Midrashic Exegesis." *Journal of Semitic Studies* 16/2 (1971): 137–150.
— "Midrash and the Old Testament." Pages 45–59 in *Understanding the Sacred Text.* Edited by John Reumann. Valley Forge, Pa.: Judson Press, 1972.
— "The Old Testament as Scripture of the Church." *Concordia Theological Monthly* 43 (1972): 709–722.
— "A Tale of Two Testaments." *Interpretation: A Journal of Bible and Theology* 26/1 (1972): 20–29.
— "The Etiological Tale Re-examined." *Vetus Testamentum* 24/4 (1974): 387–397.
— "The Old Testament as Narrative." *Yale Alumni Magazine* 38/4 (January 1975): 30–32.
— "God Leads a People to Freedom: Studies in Exodus." *Enquiry* 9/1 (1976): 1–33.
— "Reflections on the Modern Study of the Psalms." Pages 377–388 in *Magnalia Dei: The Mighty Acts of God: Essays on Bible and Archaeology in Memory of G. E. Wright.* Edited by Frank Moore Cross et al. New York: Doubleday, 1976.
— "The Search for Biblical Authority Today." *Andover Newton Quarterly* 16 (1976): 199–206.
— "The Sensus Literalis of Scripture: An Ancient and Modern Problem." Pages 80–93 in *Beiträge zur alttestamentlichen Theologie: Festschrift für Walther Zimmerli zum 70. Geburtstag.* Edited by Herbert Donner et al. Göttingen: Vandenhoeck & Ruprecht, 1977.

— "Symposium on Biblical Criticism" [response to Paul Minear]. *Theology Today* 33/4 (1977): 358–359.
— "The Canonical Shape of the Book of Jonah." Pages 122–128 in *Biblical and Near Eastern Studies: Essays in Honor of William Sanford LaSor*. Edited by Gary A Tuttle. Grand Rapids: Eerdmans, 1978.
— "The Canonical Shape of the Prophetic Literature." *Interpretation: A Journal of Bible and Theology* 32/1 (1978): 46–55. Repr. pages 41–49 in *Interpreting the Prophets*. Edited by James Mays and Paul Achtemeier. Philadelphia: Fortress, 1987. Repr. pages 513–522 in *"The Place is Too Small for Us": The Israelite Prophets in Recent Scholarship*. Edited by Robert P Gordon. Winona Lake, Ind.: Eisenbrauns, 1995.
— "The Exegetical Significance of the Canon for the Study of the Old Testament." *Supplements to Vetus Testamentum* 29 (1978): 66–80.
— "Background Material on Exodus." In "Studies in Exodus and Psalms," by John A. Bowe. *New Ventures in Bible Study* 1/2 (Winter 1978–1979): 3–64.

1980

— "On Reading the Elijah Narratives." *Interpretation: A Journal of Bible and Theology* 34/2 (1980): 128–137.
— "A Response [to James Mays et al.]." *Horizons in Biblical Theology* 2 (1980): 199–211.
— "Response to Reviewers of *Introduction to the OT as Scripture*." *Journal for the Study of the Old Testament* 16 (1980): 52–60.
— "Differenzen in der Exegese: Biblische Theologie in Amerika." *Evangelische Kommentare* 14 (1981): 405–406.
— "Some Reflections on the Search for a Biblical Theology." *Horizons in Biblical Theology* 4/1 (1982): 1–12.
— "Wellhausen in English." *Semeia* 25 (1982): 83–88.
— "Anticipatory Titles in Hebrew Narrative." Pages 57–65 in vol. 3 of *Isac Leo Seeligmann Volume: Essays on the Bible and the Ancient World*. Edited by A Rofé and Y Zalovitch. 3 vols. Jerusalem: E. Rubinstein, 1983.
— "Gerhard von Rad in American Dress." Pages 77–86 in *The Hermeneutical Quest: Essays in Honor of James Luther Mays on his 65th Birthday*. Edited by Donald G Miller. Allison Park, Pa.: Pickwick Publications, 1986.
— "Die Bedeutung des Jüdischen Kanons in der Alttestamentlichen Theologie." Pages 269–281 in *Mitte der Schrift: ein jüdisch-christliches Gespräch — Texte des Berner Symposions vom 6–12 Januar 1985*. Edited by Martin Klopfenstein et al. Translated by Ulrich Luz and Eva Ringler. Judaica et Christiana 11. Frankfurt am Main/New York: Peter Lang, 1987.
— "Death and Dying in Old Testament Theology." Pages 89–91 in *Love and Death in the Ancient Near East*. Edited by John H Marks and Robert M Good. Guilford, Conn.: Four Quarters Publishing Company, 1987.
— "Die theologische Bedeutung der Endform eines Textes." *Theologische Quartalschrift* 167/4 (1987): 242–251.
— "Biblische Theologie und christlicher Kanon." Pages 13–27 in *Zum Problem des biblischen Kanons*. Edited by Ingo Baldermann et al. JBTh 3. Neukirchen-Vluyn: Neukirchener, 1988.
— "Karl Barth: The Preacher's Exegete." Paper presented at The Lyman Beecher Lectureship on Preaching, Yale University. New Haven, 1989.
— "Reflections on the Reissue of William Perkins' *Commentary on Galatians*." Pages xiv–xvi in *A Commentary on Galatians, William Perkins*. Edited by Gerald T Sheppard. Pilgrim Classic Commentaries. New York: Pilgrim, 1989.
— "The Struggle for God's Righteousness in the Psalter." Pages 255–264 in *Christ in Our Place*. Edited by Trevor Hart and Dan Thimell. Allison Park, Pa.: Pickwick Publications, 1989.

1990

— "Analysis of a Canonical Formula: 'It Shall be Recorded for a Future Generation.'" Pages 357–364 in *Die hebräische Bibel und ihre zweifache Nachgeschichte*. Edited by Erhard Blum et al. Neukirchen-Vluyn: Neukirchener, 1990.
— "Critical Reflections on James Barr's Understanding of the Literal and the Allegorical." *Journal for the Study of the Old Testament* 46 (1990): 3–9.
— "Die Bedeutung der hebräischen Bibel für die biblische Theologie." *Theologische Zeitschrift* 48/3 (1992): 382–390.
— "Leander E. Keck: A Tribute." Pages xix–xxi in *The Future of Christology: Essays in Honor of Leander E. Keck*. Edited by A Malherbe and W Meeks. Minneapolis: Fortress, 1993.
— "Biblical Scholarship in the Seventeenth Century: A Study in Ecumenics." Pages 325–333 in *Language, Theology, and the Bible: Essays in Honour of James Barr*. Edited by Samuel E Balentine and John Barton. Oxford: Clarendon, 1994.
— "Old Testament in Germany 1920–1940: The Search for a New Paradigm." Pages 233–246 in *Altes Testament, Forschung und Wirkung: Festschrift für Henning Graf Reventlow*. Edited by Peter Mommer and Winfried Thiel. Frankfurt am Main: Peter Lang, 1994.
— "Die Beziehung von Altem und Neuem Testament aus kanonischer Sicht." Pages 29–34 in *Eine Bibel — zwei Testamente: Positionen biblischer Theologie*. Edited by Christoph Dohmen and Thomas Söding. Translated by U. Dohmen. Paderborn: Ferdinand Schöningh, 1995.
— "Old Testament Theology." Pages 293–301 in *Old Testament Interpretation: Past, Present and Future: FS Gene M. Tucker*. Edited by James L Mays et al. Edinburgh: T & T Clark, 1995.
— "On Reclaiming the Bible for Christian Theology." Pages 1–17 in *Reclaiming the Bible for the Church*. Edited by Carl E Braaten and Robert W Jenson. Grand Rapids: Eerdmans, 1995.
— "Retrospective Reading of the Old Testament Prophets." *Zeitschrift für die alttestamentliche Wissenschaft* 108/3 (1996): 362–377.
— "Does the Old Testament Witness to Jesus Christ?" Pages 57–64 in *Evangelium, Schriftauslegung, Kirche: Festschrift für Peter Stuhlmacher zum 65. Geburtstag*. Edited by Jostein Ådna et al. Göttingen: Vandenhoeck & Ruprecht, 1997.
— "The Genre of the Biblical Commentary as Problem and Challenge." Pages 185–192 in *Tehillah le-Moshe*. Edited by Mordechai Cogan et al. Winona Lake, Ind.: Eisenbrauns, 1997.
— "Interpreting the Bible Amid Cultural Change." *Theology Today* 54 (1997): 200–211.
— "Toward Recovering Theological Exegesis." *Pro Ecclesia* 6 (1997): 16–26.
— "Jesus Christ the Lord and the Scriptures of the Church." Pages 1–12 in *The Rule of Faith: Scripture, Canon, and Creed in a Critical Age*. Edited by Ephraim Radner and George Sumner. Harrisburg, Pa.: Morehouse Publishers, 1998.
— "The Nature of the Christian Bible: One Book, Two Testaments." Pages 115–125 in *The Rule of Faith*. Edited by E Radner and G Sumner. Harrisburg, Pa.: Morehouse Publishers, 1998.
— "The One Gospel in Four Witnesses." Pages 51–62 in *The Rule of Faith*. Edited by E Radner and G Sumner. Harrisburg, Pa.: Morehouse Publishers, 1998.
— "The Almost Forgotten Genesis Commentary of Benno Jacob." Pages 273–280 in *Recht und Ethos im Alten Testament — Gestalt und Wirkung: Festschrift für Horst Seebass zum 65. Geburtstag*. Edited by Stefan Beyerle et al. Neukirchen-Vluyn: Neukirchener, 1999.
— "Hermeneutical Reflections on C. Vitringa, Eighteenth-century Interpreter of Isaiah." Pages 89–98 in *In Search of True Wisdom: Essays in Old Testament Interpretation in Honour of Ronald E Clements*. Edited by Edward Ball. Sheffield: Sheffield Academic, 1999.

2000

— "Allegory and Typology within Biblical Interpretation." Paper presented at St Mary's College, University of St Andrews. St Andrews, 2000.

— "Toward Recovering Theological Exegesis." *Ex Auditu* 16 (2000): 121–129.
— "A Tribute to the *Book List* of SOTS." Pages 90–94 in *Reading from Right to Left: Essays on the Hebrew Bible in Honour of David J.A. Clines*. Journal for the Study of the Old Testament Supplement 373. Edited by J Cheryl Exum and HGM Williamson. London: Sheffield Academic, 2003.
— "Critique of Recent Intertextual Canonical Interpretation." *Zeitschrift für die alttestamentliche Wissenschaft* 115/2 (2003): 173–184.
— "The Canon in Recent Biblical Studies: Reflections on an Era." *Pro Ecclesia* 14/1 (2005): 26–45. Repr. pages 33–57 in *Canon and Biblical Interpretation*. Edited by Craig Bartholomew et al. Grand Rapids: Zondervan, 2006.
— "Speech-act Theory and Biblical Interpretation." *Scottish Journal of Theology* 58/4 (2005): 375–392.

Select Reviews[1]

— Review of James Barr, *Semantics of Biblical Language*. *Journal of Biblical Literature* 80/4 (1961): 374–377.
— Review of Martin Noth, *Exodus: A Commentary*. *Journal of Biblical Literature* 81 (1962): 428.
— Review of Gerhard von Rad, *Genesis: A Commentary*. *Journal of Biblical Literature* 81/1 (1962): 103.
— Review of Lothar Perlitt, *Vatke und Wellhausen*. *Journal of Biblical Literature* 84/4 (1965): 470.
— Review of Gerhard von Rad, *The Problem of the Hexateuch and Other Essays*. *Journal of Biblical Literature* 85/3 (1966): 390.
— Review of Otto Eissfeld, *The Old Testament: An Introduction*. *Journal of Biblical Literature* 85/1 (1966): 130.
— Review of Werner Klatt, *Hermann Gunkel: Zu seiner Theologie der Religionsgeschichte und zur Entstehung der formgeschichtlichen Methode*. *Journal of Biblical Literature* 88 (1969): 508–509.
— Review of Hans-Joachim Kraus, *Geschichte der historisch-kritischen Erforschung des Alten Testaments*. *Journal of Biblical Literature* 89 (1970): 96–98.
— Review of James Sanders, *Torah and Canon*. "A Call to Canonical Interpretation." *Interpretation: A Journal of Bible and Theology* 27/1 (1973): 88–91.
— Review of Gerhard von Rad, *Genesis: A Commentary*. *Religious Studies* 10 (1974): 360–362.
— Review of Otto Kaiser, *Introduction to the Old Testament*. *Journal of Semitic Studies* 22 (1977): 220–221.
— Review of Walther Zimmerli, *Old Testament and the World*. *Theology Today* 34 (1977): 130–132.
— Review of Rolf Rendtorff, *Das überlieferungsgeschichtliche Problem des Pentateuch*. *Journal of Biblical Literature* 97/2 (1978): 272–273.
— Review of James Crenshaw, *Gerhard von Rad*. *Journal of Biblical Literature* 100 (1981): 460.
— Review of James Smart, *The Past, Present, and Future of Biblical Theology*. *Journal of Biblical Literature* 100 (1981): 252–253.
— Review of James Barr, *Holy Scripture: Canon, Authority, Criticism*. *Interpretation: A Journal of Bible and Theology* 38/1 (1984): 66–70.

[1] I have selected only those reviews with a direct bearing on this study. For a complete list, with full-text links where available, go to http://www.danieldriver.com/bsc-reviews/.

— Review of Michael Fishbane, *Biblical Interpretation in Ancient Israel. Journal of Biblical Literature* 106/3 (1987): 511–513.
— Review of Walter Brueggemann, *Theology of the Old Testament: Testimony, Dispute, Advocacy. Scottish Journal of Theology* 53/2 (2000): 228–233.

Select Audio Recordings

— "The Recovery of Biblical Narrative." *Catalyst: A Resource for Christian Leaders* 11/8 (16 May 1979).
— "The Recovery of Biblical Narrative: The Samson Cycle." *Catalyst: A Resource for Christian Leaders* 11/9 (13 June 1979).
— "Biblication Theology in the Context of the Christian Canon." Princeton, NJ: Princeton Theological Seminary, Educational Media, 1981.
— "The Canonical Problem of the New Testament." Princeton, NJ: Princeton Theological Seminary, Educational Media, 1981.
— "The Canonical Shape of the Gospels." Princeton, NJ: Princeton Theological Seminary, Educational Media, 1981.
— "The Present Impasse in the Study of the Bible." Princeton, NJ: Princeton Theological Seminary, Educational Media, 1981.
— "The Unity of the Fourfold Witness." Princeton, NJ: Princeton Theological Seminary, Educational Media, 1981.
— "The Rise and Fall of Biblical Theology." Yale University Divinity School Memorabilia, Record Group No. 53, Box 74. New Haven, n.d.
— "Old Testament Interpretation." Yale University Divinity School Memorabilia, Record Group No. 53, Box 74. New Haven, 1982.
— "On Using the Old Testament Theologically." Nils W. Lund Memorial Lectureship, 25–26 October 1983. 4 cassettes. Chicago: North Park Theological Seminary, 1983.
  — Lecture 1: "Old Testament Theology as Christian Discipline."
  — Lecture 2: "How God Makes Himself Known."
  — Lecture 3: "The Expression of the Will of God in the Law."
  — Lecture 4: "Distinguishing Between True and False Prophecy."
— "Interpreting the Bible in the Midst of Cultural Change." Cheney Lectures. Yale University Divinity School Memorabilia, Record Group No. 53, Box 61. New Haven, 1996.

Notable Items in the Princeton Archives

— Notes taken for Otto A. Piper's "The Parables of Jesus." Princeton Theological Seminary, Spring 1949.
— "The Deliverance of Israel at the Crossing of the Sea (Exodus 13:17–15:21)." Paper written for Walter Baumgartner. University of Basel, 1952.
— "A Study of Myth in Genesis I–XI." Partial publication of ThD dissertation. Plymouth, Wis.: self-published, 1955. [copies are also held at Yale University and the Universität Basel]
— "Canon and Criticism: The Old Testament as Scripture of the Church." James Sprunt Lectures, Union Theological Seminary. Richmond, Va., January 1972 .
  — Lecture 1: "The Canon as a Historical and Theological Problem." [paper body missing]
  — Lecture 2: "'II Isaiah' in the Context of the Canon."
  — Lecture 3: "The Canonical Shape of the Psalter."
  — Lecture 4: "The Crossing of the Sea in its Canonical Context."
  — Lecture 5: "Daniel in the Context of the Canon."
— "Toward Recovering Biblical Exegesis." Manuscript submitted to *Pro Ecclesia*. May 13, 1995.
— Correspondence between Childs and Jonathan Mark Isaac, a masters student. The letters accompany Isaac's MA thesis, Mennonite Brethren Biblical Seminary, May, 1994.

—Addendum: Two letters from Childs to James Barr. September 3, 1982; March 21, 1996. [transcribed in the appendix, above]
—Addendum: Two letters between Childs and David Bartlett (of Yale Divinity School) about Childs' understanding of the canon. October 21, 1997; October 26, 1997.

B. Other Works Consulted

Aichele, George. *Sign, Text, Scripture: Semiotics and the Bible*. Sheffield: Sheffield Academic, 1997.
Albertz, Rainer. *A History of Israelite Religion in the Old Testament Period, Vol. 1: From the Beginnings to the End of the Monarchy*. Translated by John Bowden. London: SCM, 1994.
— "Religionsgeschichte Israels statt Theologie des Alten Testaments! Plädoyer für eine forschungsgeschichtliche Umorientierung." *Jahrbuch für Biblische Theologie* 10 (1995): 3–24.
Allert, Craig D. *Revelation, Truth, Canon and Interpretation: Studies in Justin Martyr's Dialogue with Trypho*. Leiden/Boston: Brill, 2002.
— *A High View of Scripture? The Authority of the Bible and the Formation of the New Testament Canon*. Grand Rapids: Baker Academic, 2007.
Alt, Albrecht. "Die Ursprünge des israelitischen Rechts." Pages 278–332 in *Kleine Schriften*. Munich: Beck, 1953.
— "The Origins of Israelite Law." Pages 79–132 in *Essays on Old Testament History and Religion*. Translated by R A Wilson. Oxford: Basil Blackwell, 1966.
Alter, Robert. *The Art of Biblical Narrative*. New York: Basic Books, 1981.
Anderson, Bernhard W. "From Analysis to Synthesis: The Interpretation of Genesis 1–11." *Journal of Biblical Literature* 97/1 (1978): 23–39.
—, with Steven Bishop. *Contours of Old Testament Theology*. Minneapolis: Fortress, 1999.
Auerbach, Erich. *Mimesis: The Representation of Reality in Western Literature*. Translated by Willard R Trask. Princeton: Princeton University Press, 1953.
— *Dante, Poet of the Secular World*. Translated by Ralph Manheim. Chicago: University of Chicago Press, 1961.
— "Figura." Pages 11–76 in *Scenes from the Drama of European Literature*. Edited by Wlad Godzich and Jochen Schulte-Sasse. Translated by Ralph Manheim. Gloucester, Mass.: Peter Smith, 1984.
Augustine, Saint. *Expositions of the Psalms (99–120)*. Translated by Maria Boulding. The Works of Saint Augustine III/19. Hyde Park/New York: New City, 2003.

Baeck, Leo. "Das Judentum auf alten und neuen Wegen." *Judaica* 6 (1950): 133–148.
Baentsche, Bruno. "Bibelwissenschaft: I. Altest Testament, D. Biblische Theologie." *Religion in Geschichte und Gegenwart* 1 (1909): 1194–1197.
Baldermann, Ingo et al., eds. *Zum Problem des biblischen Kanons*. Jahrbuch für biblische Theologie 3. Neukirchen-Vluyn: Neukirchener, 1988.
Ballhorn, Egbert, and Georg Steins, eds. *Der Bibelkanon in der Bibelauslegung: Methodenreflexionen und Beispielexegesen*. Stuttgart: Kohlhammer, 2007.
Barr, James. *The Semantics of Biblical Language*. Oxford: Oxford University Press, 1961.
— *Old and New in Interpretation: A Study of the Two Testaments*. London: SCM, 1966.
— *Fundamentalism*. London: SCM, 1977.
— "Childs' Introduction to the Old Testament as Scripture." *Journal for the Study of the Old Testament* 16 (1980): 12–23.

— "Does Biblical Study Still Belong to Theology?" Pages 18–29 in *Explorations in Theology 7: The Scope and Authority of the Bible*. London: SCM, 1980.
— *Fundamentalismus*. Munich: Chr Kaiser, 1981.
— "The Bible as a Document of Believing Communities." Pages 25–47 in *The Bible as a Document of the University*. Edited by Hans Dieter Betz. Chico, Calif.: Scholars, 1981.
— "Bibelkritik als theologische Aufklärung." Pages 30–42 in *Glaube und Toleranz: das theologische Erbe der Aufklärung*. Edited by Trutz Rendtorff. Gütersloh: Gütersloher Verlaghaus Mohn, 1982.
— "Jowett and the 'Original Meaning' of Scripture." *Religious Studies* 18/4 (1982): 433–437.
— "Jowett and the Reading of the Bible 'Like Any Other Book.'" *Horizons in Biblical Theology* 4/2 (1982): 1–44.
— *Holy Scripture: Canon, Authority, Criticism*. Oxford: Oxford University Press, 1983.
— "The Theological Case Against Biblical Theology." Pages 3–19 in *Canon, Theology, and Old Testament Interpretation: Essays in Honor of Brevard S. Childs*. Edited by Gene M Tucker et al. Philadelphia: Fortress, 1988.
— "The Literal, the Allegorical, and Modern Biblical Scholarship." *Journal for the Study of the Old Testament* 44 (1989): 3–17.
— *The Bible in the Modern World*. London: SCM, 1990.
— Review of Mark Brett, *Biblical Criticism in Crisis? Journal of Theological Studies* N.S. 43/1 (1992): 135–141.
— *The Garden of Eden and the Hope of Immortality*. London: SCM, 1992.
— "Wilhelm Vischer and Allegory." Pages 38–60 in *Understanding the Poets and Prophets: Essays in Honour of George Wishart Anderson*. Edited by A Graeme Auld. Journal for the Study of the Old Testament Supplement Series 152. Sheffield: JSOT, 1993.
— "Allegory and Historicism." *Journal for the Study of the Old Testament* 69 (1996): 105–120.
— *The Concept of Biblical Theology: An Old Testament Perspective*. Minneapolis: Fortress, 1999.
— *History and Ideology in the Old Testament: Biblical Studies at the End of a Millennium*. Oxford: Oxford University Press, 2000.
Barth, Hermann. *Die Jesaja-Worte in der Josiazeit: Israel und Assur als Thema einer produktiven Neuinterpretation der Jesajaüberlieferung*. Wissenschaftliche Monographien zum Alten und Neuen Testament 48. Neukirchen-Vluyn: Neukirchener, 1977.
Barth, Karl. *Die kirchliche Lehre von der Taufe*. Zürich: Evangelischer, 1943.
— *The Teaching of the Church Regarding Baptism*. London: SCM, 1948.
— *Church Dogmatics, 1/2: The Doctrine of the Word of God*. Translated by G T Thomson and Harold Knight. Edinburgh: T&T Clark, 1956.
Barth, Markus. *Die Taufe, ein Sakrament?* Zürich: Evangelischer, 1951.
— "Whither Biblical Theology?" Review of Brevard Childs, *Biblical Theology in Crisis*. *Interpretation: A Journal of Bible and Theology* 25/3 (1971): 350–354.
Barthel, Jörg. "Die kanonhermeneutische Debatte seit Gerhard von Rad: Anmerkungen zu neueren Entwürfen." Pages 1–26 in *Kanonhermeneutik: Vom Lesen und Verstehen der christlichen Bibel*. Edited by Bernd Janowski. Neukirchen-Vluyn: Neukirchener, 2007.
Bartlett, David L. *Between the Bible and the Church: New Methods for Biblical Preaching*. Nashville: Abingdon, 1999.
Bartholomew, Craig, and Michael Goheen. "Story and Biblical Theology." in *Out of Egypt: Biblical Theology and Biblical Interpretation*. Edited by Mary Healy et al. Scripture and Hermeneutics Series 5. Grand Rapids: Zondervan, 2004.
Barton, John. *Reading the Old Testament: Method in Biblical Study*. London: Darton, Longman & Todd, 1984.
— "Canon and Old Testament Interpretation." Pages 37–52 in *In Search of True Wisdom: Essays in Old Testament Interpretation in Honour of Ronald E Clements*. Edited by Edward

Ball. Journal for the Study of the Old Testament Supplement Series 300. Sheffield: Sheffield Academic, 2000.

— "Intertextuality and the 'Final Form' of the Text." *Supplements to Vetus Testamentum* 80 (2000): 33–37.

— "Canonical Approaches Ancient and Modern." Pages 199–209 in *The Biblical Canons*. Edited by J-M Auwers and H J De Jonge. Bibliotheca ephemeridum theologicarum lovaniensium 163. Leuven: Leuven University Press, 2003.

— *The Nature of Biblical Criticism*. Louisville/London: Westminster John Knox, 2007.

Bauckham, Richard. "Biblical Theology of the Old and New Testaments: Theological Reflections on the Christian Bible." *Biblical Interpretation* 2 (1994): 246–250.

Baumgartner, Walter. "Zum 100. Geburtstag von Hermann Gunkel." *Supplements to Vetus Testamentum* 9 (1963): 1–18.

Berger, Klaus. *Einführung in die Formgeschichte*. UTB 1444. Tübingen: Francke, 1987.

Beuken, W A M. "Isa. 56:9–57:13 — An Example of the Isaianic Legacy of Trito-Isaiah." Pages 48–64 in *Tradition and Re-interpretation in Jewish and early Christian Literature: Essays in Honour of Jürgen C H Lebram*. Edited by Jan W van Henten et al. Translated by W Quarles van Ufford. Studia post-biblica 36. Leiden: Brill, 1986.

Bloch, Renée. "Midrash." Pages 29–50 in *Approaches to Ancient Judaism: Theory and Practice (1)*. Edited by William Scott Green. Translated by M H Callaway. Missoula, Mont.: Scholars, 1978.

Blocher, Henri. "'The Analogy of Faith' in the Study of Scripture." *Scottish Bulletin of Evangelical Theology* 5 (1987): 17–38.

Blowers, Paul M. "The Regula Fidei and the Narrative Character of Early Christian Faith." *Pro Ecclesia* 6/2 (1997): 199–228.

Blum, Erhard. "Formgeschichte — A Misleading Category? Some Critical Remarks." Pages 32–45 in *The Changing Face of Form Criticism for the Twenty-First Century*. Edited by Marvin A Sweeney and Ehud Ben Zvi. Grand Rapids/Cambridge: Eerdmans, 2003.

Bockmuehl, Markus. *Seeing the Word: Refocusing New Testament Study*. Grand Rapids: Baker Academic, 2006.

Boyarin, Daniel. "'The Eye in the Torah': Ocular Desire in Midrashic Hermeneutic." *Critical Inquiry* 16 (1990): 532–550.

— *Intertextuality and the Reading of Midrash*. Bloomington, Ind.: Indiana UP, 1990.

— *A Radical Jew: Paul and the Politics of Identity*. Berkeley: University of California Press, 1994.

Brandscheidt, Renate. "Psalm 102: Literarische Gestalt und theologische Aussage." *Trierer theologische Zeitschrift* 96 (1987): 51–75.

Brandt, Peter. *Endgestalten des Kanons: Das Arrangement der Schriften Israels in der jüdischen und christlichen Bibel*. Bonner biblische Beiträge 131. Berlin: Philo, 2001.

Braulik, Georg. "Die Tora als Bahnlesung: zur Hermeneutik einer zukünftigen Auswahl der Sonntagslesungen im Lektionar der römischen Eucharistiefeier." Pages 50–76 in *Bewahren und Erneuern: Festschrift für Hans Berhard Meyer SJ zum 70. Geburtstag*. Edited by R Meßner et al. Innsbruck: Tyrolia, 1995.

Brett, Mark G. *Biblical Criticism in Crisis? The Impact of the Canonical Approach on Old Testament Studies*. Cambridge: Cambridge University Press, 1991.

— "The Future of Old Testament Theology." *Supplements to Vetus Testamentum* 80 (2000): 465–488.

Brueggemann, Dale. "Brevard Childs' Canon Criticism: An Example of Post-critical Naiveté." *Journal of the Evangelical Theological Society* 32/3 (1989): 311–326.

Brueggemann, Walter. *Theology of the Old Testament: Testimony, Dispute, Advocacy*. Minneapolis: Fortress, 1997.

— "Against the Stream: Brevard Childs's Biblical Theology." *Theology Today* 50/2 (1993): 279–284. Repr. pages 165–170 in *The Book That Breathes New Life: Scriptural Authority and Biblical Theology*. Edited by Patrick D Miller. Minneapolis: Fortress, 2005.

Brunert, Gunild. *Psalm 102 im Kontext des Vierten Psalmenbuches*. Stuttgarter biblische Beiträge 30. Stuttgart: Katholisches Bibelwerk, 1996.

Brüning, Christian. *Mitten im Leben vom Tod umfangen: Ps 102 als Vergänglichkeitsklage und Vertrauenslied*. Bonner biblische Beiträge 84. Frankfurt a.M.: Anton Hain, 1992.

Bruns, Gerald L. "Midrash and Allegory: The Beginnings of Scriptural Interpretation." Pages 625–646 in *The Literary Guide to the Bible*. Edited by Robert Alter and Frank Kermode. London: Collins, 1987.

Budde, Achim. "Der Abschluss des alttestamentlichen Kanons und seine Bedeutung für die kanonische Schriftauslegung." *Biblische Notizen* 87 (1997): 39–55.

Bultmann, Rudolf. *Die Geschichte der synoptischen Tradition*. 2nd ed. Göttingen: Vandenhoeck & Ruprecht, 1931.

— *Die Exegese des Theodor von Mopsuestia*. Stuttgart: Kohlhammer, 1984.

Buss, Martin J. *Biblical Form Criticism in its Context*. Journal for the Study of the Old Testament Supplement Series 274. Sheffield: Sheffield Academic, 1998.

— "Gunkel, Hermann (1862–1932)." Pages 487–491 in *Historical Handbook of Major Biblical Interpreters*. Edited by Donald K McKim. Downers Grove, Ill.: InterVarsity, 1998.

Byassee, Jason. *Praise Seeking Understanding: Reading the Psalms with Augustine*. Radical Traditions. Grand Rapids: Eerdmans, 2007.

Cameron, Michael. "'Totus Christus' as Hermeneutical Center in Augustine's Enarrationes in Psalmos." Paper presented at The Harp of Prophecy: The Psalms in Early Christian Exegesis. Notre Dame, Ind., 1998.

— "Enarrationes in Psalmos." Pages 290–296 in *Augustine Through the Ages: An Encyclopedia*. Edited by Alan Fitzgerald. Grand Rapids: Eerdmans, 1999.

Campenhausen, Hans freiherr von. *Die Entstehung der christlichen Bibel*. Tübingen: Mohr, 1968.

— *The Formation of the Christian Bible*. Translated by John Austin Baker. London: A and C Black, 1972.

Carroll, Robert. "Canonical Criticism: A Recent Trend in Biblical Studies?" *Expository Times* 92 (1980): 73–78.

Chapman, Stephen B. "The Canon Debate: What It Is and Why It Matters." Paper presented at SBL, Theological Hermeneutics of Christian Scripture session. San Diego, 2007.

— *The Law and the Prophets: A Study in Old Testament Canon Formation*. Forschungen zum Alten Testament 27. Tübingen: J C B Mohr (Paul Siebeck), 2000.

— "A Canonical Approach to Old Testament Theology? Deuteronomy 34:10–12 and Malachi 3:22–24 as Programmatic Conclusions." *Horizons in Biblical Theology* 25/2 (2003): 121–145.

— "Reading the Bible as Witness: Divine Retribution in the Old Testament." *Perspectives in Religious Studies* 31/2 (2004): 171–190.

— "Reclaiming Inspiration for the Bible." Pages 167–206 in *Canon and Biblical Interpretation*. Edited by Craig Bartholomew et al. Scripture and Hermeneutics Series 7. Grand Rapids: Zondervan, 2006.

Clements, Ronald E. *Isaiah and the Deliverance of Jerusalem*. Journal for the Study of the Old Testament Supplement Series 13. Sheffield: JSOT, 1980.

Collins, John Joseph. "Is a Critical Biblical Theology Possible?" Pages 1–17 in *The Hebrew Bible and its Interpreters*. Edited by William Henry Propp et al. Winona Lake: Eisenbrauns, 1990.

— *Encounters with Biblical Theology*. Minneapolis: Fortress, 2005.

Countryman, William. "Tertullian and the Regula Fidei." *Second Century* 2 (1982): 208–227.

Crenshaw, James L. *Gerhard von Rad*. Waco, Tex: Word Books, 1978.

Daniélou, Jean. *Origen*. Translated by Walter Mitchell. London: Sheed and Ward, 1955.
— *From Shadows to Reality: Studies in Biblical Typology of the Fathers*. London: Burns & Oates, 1960.
Davies, Philip R. *Scribes and Schools: The Canonization of the Hebrew Scriptures*. Louisville: Westminster John Knox, 1998.
— *Whose Bible is it Anyway?* London/New York: T&T Clark, 2004.
Davis, Ellen F, and Richard B Hays, eds. *The Art of Reading Scripture*. Grand Rapids/ Cambridge: Eerdmans, 2003.
Dawson, John David. *Allegorical Readers and Cultural Revision in Ancient Alexandria*. Berkeley: University of California Press, 1992.
— "Figure, Allegory." Pages 365–368 in *Augustine through the Ages: An Encyclopedia*. Edited by Allan D Fitzgerald. Grand Rapids: Eerdmans, 1999.
— "Plato's Soul and the Body of the Text in Philo and Origen." Pages 89–107 in *Interpretation and Allegory: Antiquity to the Modern Period*. Edited by Jon Whitman. Leiden: Brill, 2000.
— *Christian Figural Reading and the Fashioning of Identity*. Berkeley: University of California Press, 2002.
De Villiers, Pieter G R. "Hermann Gunkel as Innovator." *Old Testament Essays* 20/2 (2007): 333–351.
— Review of Hermann Gunkel, *Creation and Chaos in the Primeval Era and the Eschaton: A Religio-Historical Study of Genesis 1 and Revelation 12*, translated by K William Whitney, Jr. *Review of Biblical Literature* [http://www.bookreviews.org] (2007).
Dohmen, Christoph. "Vom vielfachen Schriftsinn: Möglichkeiten und Grenzen neuer Zugänge biblischen Texten." Pages 13–74 in *Neue Formen der Schriftauslegung?* Edited by Thomas Sternberg. Quaestiones disputatae 140. Freiburg: Herder, 1992.
— "Wilhelm Vischer als Ausleger der Heiligen Schrift." *Theologische Literaturzeitung* 126/9 (2001): 947–949.
— Review of Stephen Chapman, *The Law and the Prophets*. *Biblica* 83/3 (2002): 409–412.
— "Der Kanon des Alten Testaments: Eine westliche hermeneutische Perspektive." Pages 277–297 in *Das Alte Testament als christliche Bibel in orthodoxer und westlicher Sicht*. Edited by Ivan Z Dimitrov et al. Wissenschaftliche Untersuchungen zum Neuen Testament 174. Tübingen: Mohr Siebeck, 2004.
— *Exodus 19–40*. Herders Theologischer Kommentar zum Alten Testament. Freiburg/Basel/ Vienna: Herder, 2004.
— *Die Bibel und ihre Auslegung*. 3rd, revised edition. Munich: C H Beck, 2006.
—, and F Mussner, eds. *Nur die halbe Warheit? Für die Einheit der ganzen Bibel*. Freiburg: Herder, 1993.
—, and Manfred Oeming. *Biblischer Kanon — warum und wozu? Eine Kanontheologie*. Quaestiones disputatae 137. Freiburg: Herder, 1992.
—, and Thomas Söding, eds. *Eine Bibel — zwei Testamente: Positionen biblischer Theologie*. Paderborn: Ferdinand Schöningh, 1995.
—, and Günter Stemberger. *Hermeneutik der Jüdischen Bibel und des Alten Testaments*. Stuttgart: Kohlhammer, 1996.
Driver, Daniel R. "Later Childs." *Princeton Theological Review* 38 (2008): 117–129.
— Review of Egbert Ballhorn and Georg Steins, eds., *Der Bibelkanon in der Bibelauslegung: Methodenreflexionen und Beispielexegesen*. *Review of Biblical Literature* [http://www.bookreviews.org] (2008).
—, and Nathan MacDonald. "Canonical Criticism HB/OT" and "Childs, Brevard S." Forthcoming in *Encyclopedia of the Bible and its Reception*. Edited by H Spieckermann et al.

Droge, Arthur J. *Homer Or Moses? Early Christian Interpretation of the History of Culture*. Hermeneutische Untersuchungen zur Theologie 26. Tübingen: JCB Mohr (Paul Siebeck), 1989.

Dunn, James D G. Review of John Barton, *The Nature of Biblical Criticism*. *Review of Biblical Literature* [http://www.bookreviews.org] (2008).

Eagleton, Terry. *Literary Theory: An Introduction*. Minneapolis: University of Minnesota Press, 1996.

Ebeling, Gerhard. *Evangelische Evangelienauslegung: Eine Untersuchung zu Luthers Hermeneutik*. Munich: Albert Lempp, 1942.

— "The Meaning of 'Biblical Theology.'" Pages 79–97 in *Word and Faith*. Translated by J W Leitch. London: SCM, 1963.

— *Wort und Glaube*. 3rd ed. Vol. 1. Tübingen: J C B Mohr, 1967.

— "The Bible as a Document of the University." Pages 5–23 in *The Bible as a Document of the University*. Edited by Hans Dieter Betz. Chico, Calif.: Scholars, 1981.

Eichrodt, Walther. "Ist die typologische Exegese sachgemässe Exegese?" *Theologische Literaturzeitung* 81/11 (1956): 641–654.

— *Theology of the Old Testament*. Translated by John Baker. London: SCM, 1961.

Ellis, Edward Earle. *The Old Testament in Early Christianity: Canon and Interpretation in the Light of Modern Research*. Wissenschaftliche Untersuchungen zum Neuen Testament 54. Tübingen: J C B Mohr, 1991.

Esler, Philip F. *New Testament Theology: Communion and Community*. Minneapolis: Fortress, 2005.

Farmer, William R. "Galatians and the Second-century Development of the Regula Fidei." *Second Century* 4/3 (1984): 143–170.

Felber, Stefan. *Wilhelm Vischer als Ausleger der Heiligen Schrift: eine Untersuchung zum Christuszeugnis des Alten Testaments*. Göttingen: Vandenhoeck und Ruprecht, 1999.

— "Zur Autorität des Alten Testaments." Pages 25–40 in *Festhalten am Bekenntnis der Hoffnung*. Edited by Christian Herrmann and Eberhard Hahn. Erlangen: Martin Luther, 2001.

Fiedrowicz, Michael. "General Introduction." Pages 13–66 in *Expositions of the Psalms (1–32)*. Translated by Maria Boulding. The Works of Saint Augustine, III/15. 1–32. Hyde Park/New York: New City, 2000.

—, and Hildegund Müller. "Enarrationes in Psalmos." *Augustinus-Lexikon* II:5–6 (2001): 804–858.

Fishbane, Michael. "Torah and Tradition." Pages 275–300 in *Tradition and Theology in the Old Testament*. Edited by Douglas A Knight. London: SPCK, 1977.

— *Biblical Interpretation in Ancient Israel*. Oxford: Clarendon, 1985.

— *The Garments of Torah: Essays in Biblical Hermeneutics*. Indiana studies in biblical literature. Bloomington, Ind.: Indiana University Press, 1989.

— "Types of Biblical Intertextuality." *Supplements to Vetus Testamentum* 80 (2000): 39–44.

— "Inner-biblical Interpretation and the Development of Tradition." Pages 25–35 in *Das Alte Testament und die Kultur der Moderne: Beiträge des Symposiums »Das Alte Testament und die Kultur der Moderne« anlässlich des 100. Geburtstags Gerhard von Rads (1901–1971) Heidelberg, 18.–21. Oktober 2001*. Edited by Manfred Oeming et al. Altes Testament und Moderne 8. 1901–1971. Münster: Lit, 2004.

— "Midrash and the Meaning of Scripture." Pages 549–563 in *Interpretation of the Bible*. Journal for the Study of the Old Testament Supplement Series 289. Sheffield: Sheffield Academic, 1998.

Fowl, Stephen E. "The Canonical Approach of Brevard Childs." *Expository Times* 96 (1985): 173–176.

— *Engaging Scripture: A Model for Theological Interpretation*. Oxford: Blackwell, 1998.

Frankemölle, Hubert. *Frühjudentum und Urchristentum: Vorgeschichte — Verlauf — Auswirkungen*. Stuttgart: Kohlhammer, 2006.

Frei, Hans. "Karl Barth: Theologian." Pages 5–13 in *Karl Barth and the Future of Theology: A Memorial Colloquium Held at Yale Divinity School January 28, 1969*. Edited by D L Dickerman. New Haven: Yale Divinity School Association, 1969. Repr. in *Reflection* 66/4 (1969): 5–9. Repr. pages 167–176 in *Theology and Narrative*.

— *The Eclipse of Biblical Narrative: A Study in Eighteenth and Nineteenth Century Hermeneutics*. New Haven: Yale University Press, 1974.

— *The Identity of Jesus Christ: The Hermeneutical Bases of Dogmatic Theology*. Philadelphia: Fortress, 1975.

— "The 'Literal Reading' of Biblical Narrative in the Christian Tradition: Does it Stretch Or Will it Break?" Pages 36–77 in *The Bible and the Narrative Tradition*. Edited by Frank McConnell. Oxford: Oxford University Press, 1986.

— *Types of Christian Theology*. New Haven: Yale University Press, 1992.

— *Theology and Narrative: Selected Essays*. Edited by G Hunsinger and W Placher. New York/ Oxford: Oxford University Press, 1993.

Fretheim, Terence E. Review of Brevard Childs, *Biblical Theology of the Old and New Testaments*. *Catholic Biblical Quarterly* 56 (1994): 324–326.

Gabler, Johann Philipp. "J P Gabler and the Distinction Between Biblical and Dogmatic Theology: Translation, Commentary, and Discussion of His Originality." Translated and discussed by John Sandys-Wunscha and Laurence Eldredge. *Scottish Journal of Theology* 33 (1980): 133–158.

Gerstenberger, Erhard. Review of Rolf Rendtorff, *Leviticus 1:1–10:20*. *Review of Biblical Literature* [http://www.bookreviews.org] (2007).

Gese, Hartmut. "Tradition and Biblical Theology." Pages 301–326 in *Tradition and Theology in the Old Testament*. Edited by Douglas A Knight. London: SPCK, 1977.

Goppelt, Leonhard. *Typos, the Typological Interpretation of the Old Testament in the New*. Translated by Donald H Madvig. Grand Rapids: Eerdmans, 1981.

Grant, Robert McQueen. *The Letter and the Spirit*. London: SPCK, 1957.

Grech, Prosper S. "The Regula Fidei as a Hermeneutical Principle in Patristic Exegesis." Pages 589–601 in *Interpretation of the Bible*. Journal for the Study of the Old Testament Supplement Series 289. Sheffield: Sheffield Academic, 1998.

Greene-McCreight, Kathryn. *Ad Litteram: How Augustine, Calvin, and Barth Read the "Plain Sense" of Genesis 1–3*. Issues in Systematic Theology 5. New York: Peter Lang, 1999.

Greer, Rowan. *The Captain of Our Salvation: A Study in the Patristic Exegesis of Hebrews*. Tübingen: J C B Mohr (Paul Siebeck), 1973.

—, and James Kugel. *Early Biblical Interpretation*. Philadelphia: Westminster, 1986.

Groves, Joseph W. *Actualization and Interpretation in the Old Testament*. Society of Biblical Literature Dissertation Series 86. Atlanta: Scholars, 1987.

Gunkel, Hermann. "Die Richtungen der alttestamentlichen Forschung." *Christliche Welt* 36 (1922): 66.

— "Der Micha-Schluß: Zur Einführung in die literaturgeschichtliche Arbeit am Alten Testament." *Zeitschrift für Semitistik* 2 (1924): 145–178.

— *Die Psalmen übersetzt und erklärt*. Göttingen: Vandenhoeck & Ruprecht, 1926.

— "Bibelwissenschaft: I. des AT, 7. Übersicht über die gegenwärtigen Arbeitsgebiete." *Religion in Geschichte und Gegenwart* 1 (1927): 1073–1074.

— "Biblische Theologie und biblische Religionsgeschichte, I. des AT." *Religion in Geschichte und Gegenwart* 1 (1927): 1089–1091.
— "Die 'Christliche Welt' und die alttestamentliche Wissenschaft." Pages 151–156 in *Vierzig Jahre 'Christliche Welt': Festgabe für Martin Rade zum 70. Geburtstag 4. April 1927*. Edited by Hermann Mulert. Gotha: Leopold Klotz, 1927.
— *What Remains of the Old Testament*. Translated by A K Dallas. London: G Allen & Unwin, 1928.
— "Individualismus: II. Individualismus und Sozialismus im AT." *Religion in Geschichte und Gegenwart* 3 (1929): 234–239.
— "Literaturgeschichte, Biblische, 2. LG des ATs." *Religion in Geschichte und Gegenwart* 3 (1929): 1677–1680.
— *The Influence of the Holy Spirit: The Popular View of the Apostolic Age and the Teaching of the Apostle Paul*. Translated by Roy Harrisville and Philip Quanbeck II. Philadelphia: Fortress, 1979.
— *The Folktale in the Old Testament*. Sheffield: Almond, 1987.
— *The Stories of Genesis*. Translated by John J Scullion. Vallejo, Calif: BIBAL, 1994.
— *Genesis*. Translated by Mark E Biddle. Macon, Ga.: Mercer University Press, 1997.
— "The Religion of the Psalms." Pages 134–167 in *Water for a Thirsty Land: Israelite Literature and Religion*. Edited by K C Hanson. Minneapolis: Fortress, 2001.
— *Water for a Thirsty Land: Israelite Literature and Religion*. Translated by A K Dallas and James Schaaf. Fortress classics in biblical studies. Minneapolis: Fortress, 2001.
— *Creation and Chaos in the Primeval Era and the Eschaton: A Religio-historical Study of Genesis 1 and Revelation 12*. Translated by K William Whitney Jr. Grand Rapids/Cambridge: Eerdmans, 2006.
—, and Joachim Begrich. *Einleitung in die Psalmen: die Gattungen der religiösen Lyrik Israels*. Translated by James Nogalski. Göttingen: Vandenhoeck & Ruprecht, 1933.
—, and Joachim Begrich. *Introduction to Psalms: The Genres of the Religious Lyric of Israel*. Translated by James Nogalski. Macon, Ga.: Mercer University Press, 1998.

Hägglund, Bengt. "Die Bedeutung der 'regula fidei' als Grundlage theologischer Aussagen." *Studia theologica* 12 (1958): 1–44.
Hanson, Richard Patrick Crosland. *Allegory and Event: A Study of the Sources and Significance of Origin's Interpretation of Scripture*. London: SCM, 1959.
Harnack, Adolf von. *The Origin of the New Testament and the Most Important Consequences of the New Creation*. Translated by J R Wilkinson. London: Williams & Norgate, 1925.
Harrisville, Roy A. "What I Believe My Old Schoolmate is Up To." Pages 7–25 in *Theological Exegesis: Essays in Honor of Brevard S. Childs*. Edited by Christopher R Seitz and Kathryn Greene-McCreight. Grand Rapids: Eerdmans, 1999.
—, and Walter Sundberg. *The Bible in Modern Culture: Baruch Spinoza to Brevard Childs*. 2nd ed. Grand Rapids: Eerdmans, 2002.
Hartzfeld, David F. "Gerhard von Rad, Brevard S Childs: Two Methodologies." PhD diss., University of Sheffield, 1989.
Hasel, Gerhard F. *Old Testament Theology: Basic Issues in the Current Debate*. Grand Rapids: Eerdmans, 1991.
Hays, Richard B. *Echoes of Scripture in the Letters of Paul*. New Haven: Yale University Press, 1989.
Helmer, Christine. "Luther's Trinitarian Hermeneutic and the Old Testament." *Modern Theology* 18/1 (2002): 49–73.
— "Biblical Theology: Bridge Over Many Waters." *Currents in Biblical Research* 3/2 (2005): 169–196.

—, and Christof Landmesser, eds. *One Scripture Or Many? Canon from Biblical, Theological, and Philosophical Perspectives*. Oxford: Oxford Universit Press, 2004.

—, and Taylor G Petrey, eds. *Biblical Interpretation: History, Context, and Reality*. Atlanta: SBL, 2005.

Hempel, Johannes. "Altes Testament und Religionsgeschichte." *Theologische Literaturzeitung* 81 (1956): 259–280.

Hertzberg, Hans Wilhelm. "Vischer, Wilhelm: Das Christuszeugnis des Alten Testaments." *Theologische Literaturzeitung* 61/24 (1936): 435–439.

— "Die Nachgeschichte alttestamentlicher Texte innerhalb des Alten Testaments." Pages 110–121 in *Werden und Wesen des Alten Testaments*. Edited by Paul Volz et al. Beihefte zur Zeitschrift für die alttestamentliche Wissenschaft 66. Berlin: A Töpelmann, 1936.

— *Beiträge zur Traditionsgeschichte und Theologie des Alten Testaments*. Göttingen: Vandenhoeck & Ruprecht, 1962.

Higton, Mike. *Christ, Providence and History: Hans W. Frei's Public Theology*. London: T&T Clark, 2004.

Hossfeld, Frank-Lothar, ed. *Wieviel Systematik erlaubt die Schrift? auf der Suche nach einer gesamtbiblischen Theologie*. Quaestiones Disputatae 185. Freiburg: Herder, 2001.

—, and Erich Zenger. *Psalmen 101–150*. Herders Theologischer Kommentar zum Alten Testament. Freiburg: Herder, 2008.

Hübner, Hans. "Vetus Testamentum und Vetus Testamentum in Novo Receptum: die Frage nach dem Kanon des Alten Testaments aus neutestamentlicher Sicht." *Jahrbuch für Biblische Theologie* 3 (1988): 147–162.

Hübner, Hans, and Bernd Jaspert. *Biblische Theologie: Entwürfe der Gegenwart*. Biblisch-theologische Studien 38. Neukirchen-Vluyn: Neukirchener, 1999.

Hunsinger, George. "Beyond Literalism and Expressivism: Karl Barth's Hermeneutical Realism." *Modern Theology* 3/3 (1987): 209–223.

Jacob, Benno. *The Second Book of the Bible: Exodus*. Translated by Walter Jacob. Hoboken, NJ: Ktav Publishing House, 1992.

— *Das Buch Exodus*. Stuttgart: Calwer, 1997.

Janowski, Bernd. "Biblische Theologie, I. Exegetisch." *Religion in Geschichte und Gegenwart* 1 (1998): 1544–1549.

— "The One God of the Two Testaments: Basic Questions of a Biblical Theology." *Theology Today* 57/3 (2000): 297–324.

— "Biblische Theologie heute: Formale und materiale Aspekte." Pages 17–32 in *Biblical Interpretation: History, Context, and Reality*. Edited by Christine Helmer and Taylor G Petrey. Atlanta: SBL, 2005.

— "Die kontrastive Einheit der Schrift: Zur Hermeneutik des biblischen Kanons." Pages 27–46 in *Kanonhermeneutik*.

—, ed. *Kanonhermeneutik: Vom Lesen und Verstehen der christlichen Bibel*. Neukirchen-Vluyn: Neukirchener, 2007.

Jeremias, Jörg. "Neuere Entwürfe zu einer 'Theologie des Alten Testaments.'" Pages 125–158 in *Theologie und Exegese des Alten Testaments / der Hebräischen Bibel*. Edited by Bernd Janowski. Stuttgarter Bibelstudien 200. Stuttgart: Katholisches Bibelwerk, 2005.

Jowett, Benjamin. "On the Interpretation of Scripture." Pages 330–433 in *Essays and Reviews*. London: John W Parker and Son, 1860.

Käsemann, Ernst. *Das Neue Testaments als Kanon: Dokumentation und kristische Analyse zur gegenwärtigen Diskussion*. Göttingen: Vandenhoeck & Ruprecht, 1970.

Kermode, Frank. "The Argument About Canons." Pages 78–96 in *The Bible and the Narrative Tradition*. Edited by Frank McConnell. Oxford: Oxford University Press, 1986.

Kertelge, Karl. "Biblische Exegese im Kontext katholischer Theologie." Pages 88–99 in *Dogma und Glaube*. Edited by K Backhaus. Mainz: Matthias Grünewald, 1993.

Klatt, Werner. *Hermann Gunkel: Zu seiner Theologie der Religionsgeschichte und zur Entstehung der formgeschichtlichen Methode*. Forschungen zur Religion und Literatur des alten und neuen Testaments 100. Göttingen: Vandenhoeck & Ruprecht, 1969.

Knight, Douglas A. "Revelation through Tradition." Pages 143–180 in *Tradition and Theology in the Old Testament*. Edited by Douglas A Knight. London: SPCK, 1977.

— "James Barr." *Proceedings of the American Philosophical Society* 152/3 (2008): 386–390.

Koch, Klaus. *Was ist Formgeschichte? Neue Wege der Bibelexegese*. Neukirchen-Vluyn: Neukirchener, 1964.

— *The Growth of the Biblical Tradition: The Form-critical Method*. Translated by S M Cupitt. London: A & C Black, 1969.

Kraft, Robert A. "Para-mania: Beside, Before and Beyond Bible Studies." *Journal of Biblical Literature* 126/1 (2007): 5–27.

Kratz, Reinhard Gregor. "Redaktionsgeschichte/Redaktionskritik I." *Theologische Realenzyklopädie* 28 (1997): 367–378.

— et al., eds. *Schriftauslegung in der Schrift: Festshcrift für Odil Hannes Steck zu seinem 65. Geburtstag*. Beihefte zur Zeitschrift für die alttestamentliche Wissenschaft 300. Berlin/New York: Walter de Gruyter, 2000.

Kraus, Hans-Joachim. *Geschichte der historisch-kritischen Erforschung des Alten Testaments*. 2nd ed. Neukirchen-Vluyn: Neukirchener, 1969. 3rd ed. Neukirchen-Vluyn: Neukirchener, 1982.

— *Die biblische Theologie: Ihre Geschichte und Problematik*. Neukirchen-Vluyn: Neukirchener, 1970.

— "Zur Geschichte des Überlieferungsbegriffs in der alttestamentlichen Wissenschaft." Pages 278–295 in *Biblisch-theologische Aufsätze*. Neukirchen-Vluyn: Neukirchener, 1972.

— *Systematische Theologie im Kontext biblischer Geschichte und Eschatologie*. Neukirchen-Vluyn: Neukirchener, 1983.

Krauter, Stefan. "Brevard S Childs' Programm einer Biblischen Theologie: Eine Untersuchung seiner systematisch-theologischen und methodologischen Fundamente." *Zeitschrift für Theologie und Kirche* 96 (1999): 21–48.

Kristeva, Julia. *Desire in Language: A Semiotic Approach to Literature and Art*. Translated by Thomas Gora. Oxford: Blackwell, 1980.

Kugel, James. "Two Introductions to Midrash." *Prooftexts* 3 (1983): 131–155.

— *How to Read the Bible: A Guide to Scripture, Then and Now*. New York: Free, 2007.

—, and Rowan Greer. *Early Biblical Interpretation*. Philadelphia: Westminster, 1986.

Lampe, G W H, and K J Woollcombe. *Essays on Typology*. Studies in Biblical Theology 22. London: SCM, 1957.

Landmesser, Christof et al. *Jesus Christus als die Mitte der Schrift: Studien zur Hermeneutik des Evangeliums*. Beihefte zur Zeitschrift für die neutestamentliche Wissenschaft 86. Berlin: Walter de Gruyter, 1997.

Lau, Wolfgang. *Schriftgelehrte Prophetie in Jes 56–66: Eine Untersuchung zu den literarischen Bezügen in den letzten elf Kapiteln des Jesajabuches*. Beihefte zur Zeitschrift für die alttestamentliche Wissenschaft 225. Berlin/New York: Walter de Gruyter, 1994.

Leiman, Sid Z. *The Canonization of Hebrew Scripture: The Talmudic and Midrashic Evidence*. Transactions 47. Hamden, Conn.: Archon Books, 1976.

Levenson, Jon Douglas. "Why Jews Are Not Interested in Biblical Theology." Pages 281–307 in *Judaic Perspectives on Ancient Israel*. Edited by Jacob Neusner et al. Philadelphia: Fortress,

1987. Repr. pages 33–61 in *The Hebrew Bible, the Old Testament, and Historical Criticism*.
— *The Hebrew Bible, the Old Testament, and Historical Criticism: Jews and Christians in Biblical Studies*. Louisville: Westminster John Knox, 1993.
— *The Death and Resurrection of the Beloved Son: The Transformation of Child Sacrifice in Judiasm and Christianity*. New Haven: Yale University Press, 1993.
— "Negative Theology." *First Things* 100 (2000): 59–63.
Levin, Christoph. *Die Verheißung des neuen Bundes in ihrem theologiegeschichtlichen Zusammenhang ausgelegt*. FRLANT 137. Göttingen: Vandenhoeck & Ruprecht, 1985.
— *Das Alte Testament*. 3rd, revised edition. Munich: C H Beck, 2006.
Levinson, Bernard M. *Legal Revision and Religious Renewal in Ancient Israel*. Cambridge: Cambridge University Press, 2008.
Lindbeck, George A. *The Nature of Doctrine: Religion and Theology in a Postliberal Age*. Philadelphia: Westminster, 1984.
Loewe, Raphael. "The Plain Meaning of Scripture in Early Jewish Exegesis." Pages 140–185 in *Papers of the Institute of Jewish Studies*. Edited by Joseph George Weiss. Jerusalem: The Hebrew University, 1964.
Lohfink, Norbert. "Eine Bibel — zwei Testamente." Pages 71–81 in *Eine Bibel — zwei Testamente: Positionen Biblischer Theologie*. Edited by Christoph Dohmen and Thomas Söding. Paderborn: Ferdinand Schöningh, 1995.
Louth, Andrew. *Discerning the Mystery: An Essay on the Nature of Theology*. Oxford: Clarendon, 1983.
Lubac, Henri de. "'Typologie' et 'Allegorisme.'" *Recherches de science religieuse* 34 (1947): 180–226.
— *Scripture in the Tradition*. Milestones in Catholic Theology. New York: Crossroad, 2000.
Lyons, William John. *Canon and Exegesis: Canonical Praxis and the Sodom Narrative*. Journal for the Study of the Old Testament Supplement Series 352. Sheffield: Sheffield Academic, 2002.

MacDonald, Nathan. "Israel and the Old Testament Story in Irenaeus's Presentation of the Rule of Faith." *Journal of Theological Interpretation* 3/2 (2009): 281–298. Paper presented in an earlier version at the Durham-Duke Symposium: Identity. Durham, England, 2008.
— *Deuteronomy and the Meaning of "Monotheism."* Forschungen zum Alten Testament II/1. Tübingen: Mohr Siebeck, 2003.
MacDonald, Neil B. "Illocutionary Stance in Hans Frei's the Eclipse of Biblical Narrative: An Exercise in Conceptual Redescription and Normative Analysis." Pages 312–328 in *After Pentecost: Language and Biblical Interpretation*. Edited by Craig G Bartholomew et al. Scripture and Hermeneutics Series 2. Carlisle/Grand Rapids: Paternoster/Zondervan, 2001.
— *Metaphysics and the God of Israel: Systematic Theology of the Old and New Testaments*. Grand Rapids: Baker Academic, 2007.
McConville, J G. "Biblical Theology: Canon and Plain Sense." *SBET* 19/2 (2001): 134–157.
McCormack, Bruce. *The Humility of the Son: An Exercise in Reformed Kenoticism*. Cambridge: Cambridge University Press, forthcoming.
— "Passibility in Mutability: The Failure of the Older Kenoticism." Paper presented at SJT/T F Torrance Lectures. St Andrews, 2007.
McDonald, Lee, and James Sanders, eds. *The Canon Debate*. Peabody, Mass: Hendrickson, 2002.
McKane, William. *A Critical and Exegetical Commentary on Jeremiah: Vol. 1, Introduction and Commentary on Jeremiah I–XXV*. Edinburgh: T&T Clark, 1986.
Miller, Patrick D. "Der Kanon in der gegenwärtigen amerikanischen Diskussion." Pages 13–27 in *Zum Problem des biblischen Kanons*. Edited by Ingo Baldermann et al. Jahrbuch für

Biblische Theologie 3. Neukirchen-Vluyn: Neukirchener, 1988.

Minear, Paul Sevier. *The Bible and the Historian: Breaking the Silence About God in Biblical Studies*. Nashville: Abingdon, 2002.

Moberly, R W L. "Did the Serpent Get it Right?" *Journal of Theological Studies* 39 (1988): 1–27.

— "The Church's Use of the Bible: The Work of Brevard Childs." *Expository Times* 99 (1988): 104–109.

— "The Earliest Commentary on the Akedah." *Vetus Testamentum* 38 (1988): 302–323.

— "The Canonical Approach" (review of Mark Brett, *Biblical Theology in Crisis?*). *Expository Times* 103 (1992): 119–120.

— *The Old Testament of the Old Testament: Patriarchal Narratives and Mosiac Yahwism*. Overtures to Biblical Theology. Minneapolis: Fortress, 1992.

— "Christ as the Key to Scripture: Genesis 22 Reconsidered." Pages 143–173 in *He Swore an Oath: Biblical Themes from Genesis 12–50*. Edited by Richard S Hess et al. 2nd ed. Carlisle/Grand Rapids: Paternoster/Baker, 1994.

— *The Bible, Theology, and Faith: A Study of Abraham and Jesus*. Cambridge: Cambridge University Press, 2000.

— "The Canon of the Old Testament: Some Historical and Hermeneutical Reflections From a Western Perspective." Pages 239–257 in *Das Alte Testament als christliche Bibel in orthodoxer und westlicher Sicht*. Edited by Ivan Z Dimitrov et al. Wissenschaftliche Untersuchungen zum Neuen Testament 174. Tübingen: Mohr Siebeck, 2004.

— *Prophecy and Discernment*. Cambridge Studies in Christian Doctrine 14. Cambridge: Cambridge University Press, 2006.

— "Biblical Criticism and Religious Belief." *Journal of Theological Interpretation* 2/1 (2008): 71–100.

— "Did the Interpreters Get it Right? Genesis 2–3 Reconsidered." *Journal of Theological Studies* NS 59/1 (2008): 22–40.

— "What is Theological Interpretation of Scripture." *Journal of Theological Interpretation* 3/2 (2009): 161–178.

— *The Theology of the Book of Genesis*. Cambridge: Cambridge University Press, 2009.

Moon, Joshua. "Restitutio ad Integrum: An 'Augustinian' Reading of Jeremiah 31:31–34 in Dialogue With the Christian Tradition." PhD diss., University of St Andrews, 2007.

Morgan, Donn F. "Canon and Criticism: Method Or Madness?" *Anglican Theological Review* 68/2 (1986): 83–94.

Mowinckel, Sigmund. *The Psalms in Israel's Worship*. Oxford: Blackwell, 1962.

Needham, Rodney. "Polythetic Classification: Convergence and Consequences." *Man* 10/3 (1975): 349–369.

Neusner, Jacob. *Midrash in Context*. Philadelphia: Fortress, 1983.

— *What is Midrash?* Guides to Biblical Scholarship. Minneapolis: Fortress, 1987.

— *Jews and Christians: The Myth of a Common Tradition*. London: SCM, 1991.

Nicholson, Ernest W. *The Pentateuch in the Twentieth Century: The Legacy of Julius Wellhausen*. Oxford: Clarendon, 1998.

Noble, Paul R. "The Sensus Literalis: Jowett, Childs, and Barr." *Journal of Theological Studies* 44/1 (1993): 1–23.

— *The Canonical Approach: A Critical Reconstruction of the Hermeneutics of Brevard S. Childs*. Biblical Interpretation Series 16. Leiden: Brill, 1995.

Oeming, Manfred. *Gesamtbiblische Theologien der Gegenwart: Das Verhältnis von AT und NT in der hermeneutischen Diskussion seit Gerhard von Rad*. 2nd ed. Stuttgart: W Kohlhammer, 1987.

— "Text — Kontext — Kanon: ein neuer Weg alttestamentlicher Theologie? Zu einem Buch von Brevard S Childs." *Jahrbuch für Biblische Theologie* 3 (1988): 241–251.
— *Das Alte Testament als Teil des christlichen Kanons? Studien zu gesamtbiblischen Theologien der Gegenwart.* 3rd ed. Zürich: Pano, 2001.
Olbricht, Thomas H. "Biblical Interpretation in North America in the 20th Century." Pages 541–557 in *Historical Handbook of Major Biblical Interpreters*. Edited by Donald K McKim. Downers Grove, Ill.: InterVarsity, 1998.
Outler, Albert Cook. "Origen and the Regulae Fidei." *Second Century* 4/3 (1984): 133–141.

Perdue, Leo. *The Collapse of History: Reconstructing Old Testament Theology*. Minneapolis: Fortress, 1994.
— "Old Testament Theology Since Barth's *Epistle to the Romans*." Pages 55–136 in *Biblical Theology: Introducing the Conversation*. Edited by Leo Perdue, Robert Morgan and Benjamin D Sommer. Nashville: Abingdon, 2009.
Perlitt, Lothar. *Vatke und Wellhausen*. Beihefte zur Zeitschrift für die alttestamentliche Wissenschaft 94. Berlin: Alfred Töpelmann, 1965.
Preus, Samuel. *From Shadow to Promise: Old Testament Interpretation From Augustine to the Young Luther*. Cambridge, Mass.: Harvard University Press, 1969.
Provan, Iain. "Canons to the Left of Him: Brevard Childs, His Critics, and the Future of Old Testament Theology." *Scottish Journal of Theology* 50 (1997): 1–38.
— Review of Paul Noble, *The Canonical Approach*. *Scottish Journal of Theology* 52/4 (1999): 530–533.

Rad, Gerhard von. "Das Christuszeugnis des Alten Testaments: Eine Auseinandersetzung mit Wilhelm Vischers gleichnamigem Buch." *Theologische Blätter* 14 (1935): 249–254.
— "Grundprobleme einer biblischen Theologie des Alten Testaments." *Theologische Literaturzeitung* 68 (1943): 225–234.
— "Typologische Auslegung des Alten Testaments." *Evangelische Theologie* 12 (1952): 17–33.
— "'Gerechtigkeit' und 'Leben' in den Psalmen." Pages 225–247 in *Gesammelte Studien zum Alten Testament*. Theologische Bücherei 8. Munich: Kaiser, 1958.
— *Das erste Buch Moses, Genesis*. 5th ed. Das Alte Testament Deutsch 2–4. Göttingen: Vandenhoeck & Ruprecht, 1958.
— *Genesis: A Commentary*. Translated by John H Marks. London: SCM, 1961.
— "Typological Interpretation of the Old Testament." Pages 17–39 in *Essays on Old Testament Interpretation*. Edited by Claus Westermann. Translated by John Bright. London: SCM, 1963.
— "'Righteousness' and 'Life' in the Cultic Language of the Psalms." Pages 243–266 in *The Problem of the Hexateuch and Other Essays*. Translated by Trueman Dicken. Edinburgh/London: Oliver & Boyd, 1965.
— *Old Testament Theology, Volume II: The Theology of Israel's Prophetic Traditions*. Translated by D M G Stalker. Edinburgh and London: Oliver and Boyd, 1965.
— *Genesis: A Commentary*. Rev. ed. Philadelphia: Westminster John Knox, 1971.
Radner, Ephraim. "The Absence of the Comforter: Scripture and the Divided Church." Pages 355–394 in *Theological Exegesis: Essays in Honor of Brevard S. Childs*. Edited by Christopher R Seitz and Kathryn Greene-McCreight. Grand Rapids: Eerdmans, 1999.
— *Hope among the Fragments: The Broken Church and Its Engagement of Scripture*. Grand Rapids: Brazos, 2004.
— *Leviticus*. Brazos Theological Commentary on the Bible. Grand Rapids: Brazos, 2008.
—, and George R Sumner. *The Rule of Faith: Scripture, Canon, and Creed in a Critical Age*. Harrisburg, Pa.: Morehouse, 1998.

Rendtorff, Rolf. *Gesammelte Studien zum Alten Testament*. Theologische Bücherei 57. Munich: Chr Kaiser, 1975.

— *Das überlieferungsgeschichtliche Problem des Pentateuch*. Beihefte zur Zeitschrift für die alttestamentliche Wissenschaft 147. Berlin: Walter de Gruyter, 1977.

— "Rabbinic Exegesis and the Modern Christian Bible Scholar." Pages 29–36 in *Proceedings of the Eighth World Congress of Jewish Studies*. Jerusalem: World Union of Jewish Studies, 1983.

— "Zur Bedeutung des Kanons für eine Theologie des Alten Testaments." Pages 3–11 in *"Wenn nicht jetzt, wann dann?" Aufsätze für Hans-Joachim Kraus zum 65. Geburtstag*. Edited by Hans-Georg Geyer. Neukirchen-Vluyn: Neukirchener, 1983.

— *The Old Testament: An Introduction*. Translated by John Bowden. London: SCM, 1985.

— *The Problem of the Process of Transmission in the Pentateuch*. Translated by John J Scullion. Journal for the Study of the Old Testament Supplement Series 89. Sheffield: JSOT, 1990.

— "Der Text in seiner Endgestalt: Überlegungen zu Exodus 19." Pages 459–470 in *Ernten, was man sät: Festschrift für Klaus Koch zu seinem 65. Geburtstag*. Edited by Dwight R Daniels et al. Neukirchen-Vluyn: Neukirchener, 1991.

— *Canon and Theology: Overtures to an Old Testament Theology*. Translated by Margaret Kohl. Minneapolis: Fortress, 1993.

— "Canonical Interpretation: A New Approach to Biblical Texts." *Pro Ecclesia* 3/2 (1994): 141–151.

— Review of Brevard Childs, *Biblical Theology of the Old and New Testaments*. *Jahrbuch für Biblische Theologie* 9 (1994): 359–369.

— "Die Bibel Israels als Buch der Christen." Pages 97–113 in *Eine Bibel — zwei Testamente: Positionen Biblischer Theologie*. Edited by Christoph Dohmen and Thomas Söding. Paderborn: Ferdinand Schöningh, 1995.

— *Theologie des Alten Testaments: ein kanonischer Entwurf*. 2 vols. Neukirchen-Vluyn: Neukirchener, 1998—2001.

— "How to Read the Book of the Twelve as a Theological Unity." Pages 75–87 in *Reading and Hearing the Book of the Twelve*. Edited by James Nogalski and Marvin Sweeney. Atlanta: Society of Biblical Literature, 2000.

— *Der Text in seiner Endgestalt: Schritte auf dem Weg zu einer Theologie des Alten Testaments*. Neukirchen-Vluyn: Neukirchener, 2001.

— *Leviticus 1:1–10:20*. Biblischer Kommentar Altes Testament 3/1. Neukirchen-Vluyn: Neukirchener, 2004.

— *The Canonical Hebrew Bible: A Theology of the Old Testament*. Translated by David E Orton. Leiderdorp: Deo Publishing, 2005.

— *Das Alte Testament: Eine Einführung*. 7th ed. Neukirchen-Vluyn: Neukirchener, 2007.

— "What Happened to the 'Yahwist'?: Reflections After Thirty Years." Paper presented at International SBL. [http://sbl-site.org/Article.aspx?ArticleID=553] Edinburgh, 4 July 2006.

Reventlow, Henning Graf. *The Authority of the Bible and the Rise of the Modern World*. Translated by John Bowden. London: SCM, 1984.

— *Problems of Old Testament Theology in the Twentieth Century*. Translated by John Bowden. London: SCM, 1985.

— *Problems of Biblical Theology in the Twentieth Century*. Translated by John Bowden. London: SCM, 1986.

Robeck, Cecil M. "Canon, Regulae Fidei, and Continuing Revelation in the Early Church." Pages 65–91 in *Church, Word and Spirit*. Grand Rapids: Eerdmans, 1987.

Römer, Thomas C. *The So-called Deuteronomistic History: A Sociological, Historical and Literary Introduction*. London/New York: T&T Clark, 2007.

Rowe, C Kavin. "Biblical Pressure and Trinitarian Hermeneutics." *Pro Ecclesia* 11/3 (2002): 295–312.
— "Luke and the Trinity: An Essay in Ecclesial Biblical Theology." *Scottish Journal of Theology* 56/1 (2003): 1–26.
— "For Future Generations: Worshipping Jesus and the Integration of the Theological Disciplines." *Pro Ecclesia* 17/2 (2008): 186–209.

Sanders, James. *Torah and Canon*. Philadelphia: Fortress, 1972. 2nd ed. Eugene, Ore.: Cascade Books, 2005.
— "Adaptable for Life: The Nature and Function of Canon." Pages 531–560 in *Magnalia Dei: The Mighty Acts of God: Essays on Bible and Archaeology in Memory of G. E. Wright*. New York: Doubleday, 1976.
— *Canon and Community: A Guide to Canonical Criticism*. Eugene, Ore.: Wipf & Stock, 1984.
— "Canon as Dialogue." Pages 7–26 in *The Bible at Qumran: Text, Shape, and Interpretation*. Edited by Peter W Flint and Tae Hun Kim. Studies in the Dead Sea Scrolls and Related Literature. Grand Rapids: Eerdmans, 2001.
Sandmel, Samuel. "The Haggada Within Scripture." *Journal of Biblical Literature* 80 (1961): 105–122.
Scalise, Charles. "Canonical Hermeneutics: The Theological Basis and Implications of the Thought of Brevard S Childs." PhD diss., Southern Baptist Theological Seminary, 1987.
— "The 'Sensus Literalis': A Hermeneutical Key to Biblical Exegesis." *Scottish Journal of Theology* 42 (1989): 45–65.
— "Canonical Hermeneutics: Childs and Barth." *Scottish Journal of Theology* 47 (1994): 61–88.
— *Hermeneutics as Theological Prolegomena: A Canonical Approach*. Studies in American Biblical Hermeneutics 8. Macon, Ga.: Mercer University Press, 1994.
— *From Scripture to Theology: A Canonical Journey into Hermeneutics*. Downers Grove, Ill.: InterVarsity, 1996.
Schart, Aaron. "Reconstructing the Redaction History of the Twelve Prophets: Problems and Models." Pages 34–48 in *Reading and Hearing the Book of the Twelve*. Edited by James Nogalski and Marvin Sweeney. Atlanta: Society of Biblical Literature, 2000.
Schmid, Konrad. "Ausgelegte Schrift als Schrift: Innerbiblische Schriftauslegung und die Frage nach der theologischen Qualität biblischer Texte." Pages 115–129 in *Die Kunst des Auslegens: zur Hermeneutik des Christentums in der Kultur der Gegenwart*. Edited by Reiner Anselm et al. Frankfurt am Main: Peter Lang, 1999.
— "Innerbiblische Schriftauslegung: Aspekte der Forschungsgeschichte." in *Schriftauslegung in der Schrift: Festshcrift für Odil Hannes Steck zu seinem 65. Geburtstag.*. Edited by Reinhard Gregor Kratz et al. Beihefte zur Zeitschrift für die alttestamentliche Wissenschaft 300. Berlin/New York: Walter de Gruyter, 2000.
Schnabel, Eckhard. "Die Entwürfe von BS Childs und H Gese bezüglich des Kanons." Pages 102–152 in *Der Kanon der Bibel*. Edited by Gerhard Maier. 1990.
Seckler, Max. "Über die Problematik des biblischen Kanons und die Bedeutung seiner Wiederentdeckung." *Theologische Quartalschrift* 180/1 (2000): 30–53.
Sedlmeier, Franz. "Psalm 102.13–23: Aufbau und Funktion." *Biblische Zeitschrift* 40 (1996): 219–235.
Seeligmann, Isac L. "Voraussetzungen der Midraschexegese." *Supplements to Vetus Testamentum* 1 (1953): 150–181.
Seitz, Christopher R. *Zion's Final Destiny: The Development of the Book of Isaiah: A Reassessment of Isaiah 36–39*. Minneapolis: Fortress, 1991.
— "The Old Testament as Abiding Theological Witness: Inscripting a Theological Curriculum." *Theology Today* 54 (1997): 216–223.

— "'We Are Not Prophets Or Apostles': The *Biblical Theology* of B S Childs." Pages 102–109 in *Word Without End.*
— *Word Without End: The Old Testament as Abiding Theological Witness.* Grand Rapids: Eerdmans, 1998.
— "Canonical Approach, I. Altes Testament." *Religion in Geschichte und Gegenwart* 2 (1999): 53–54.
— *Figured Out: Typology and Providence in Christian Scripture.* Louisville: Westminster John Knox, 2001.
— "Prophecy and Tradition-history: The Achievement of Gerhard von Rad and Beyond." Pages 29–52 in *Prophetie in Israel: Beiträge des Symposiums »Das Alte Testament und die Kultur der Moderne« anlässlich des Geburtstags Gerhard von Rads (1901–1971) Heidelberg, 18.–21. Oktober 2001.* Edited by Irmtraud Fischer et al. Altes Testament und Moderne 11. 1901–1971. Münster: Lit, 2003.
— "On Letting a Text 'Act Like a Man': The Book of the Twelve: New Horizons for Canonical Reading, With Hermeneutical Reflections." *Scottish Bulletin of Evangelical Theology* 22 (2004): 151–172.
— "The Canonical Approach and Theological Interpretation." Pages 58–110 in *Canon and Biblical Interpretation.* Edited by Craig Bartholomew et al. Scripture and Hermeneutics Series 7. Grand Rapids: Zondervan, 2006.
— *Prophecy and Hermeneutics: Toward a New Introduction to the Prophets.* Studies in Theological Interpretation. Grand Rapids: Baker Academic, 2007.
— *The Goodly Fellowship of the Prophets: The Achievement of Association in Canon Formation.* Grand Rapids: Baker Academic, 2009.
—, and Kathryn Greene-McCreight, eds. *Theological Exegesis: Essays in Honor of Brevard S. Childs.* Grand Rapids: Eerdmans, 1999.
Sheppard, Gerald T. "Canon Criticism: The Proposal of Brevard Childs and an Assessment for Evangelical Hermeneutics." *Studia Biblica et Theologica* 4 (1974): 3–17.
— "Wisdom and Torah: The Interpretation of Deuteronomy Underlying Sirach 24.23." Pages 166–176 in *Biblical and Near Eastern Studies: Essays in Honor of William Sanford LaSor.* Edited by Gary A Tuttle. Grand Rapids: Eerdmans, 1978.
— *Wisdom as a Hermeneutical Construct: A Study of the Sapientializing of the Old Testament.* Beihefte zur Zeitschrift für die alttestamentliche Wissenschaft 151. Berlin/New York: Walter de Gruyter, 1980.
— "Canonization: Hearing the Voice of the Same God Through Historically Dissimilar Traditions." *Interpretation: A Journal of Bible and Theology* 36/1 (1982): 21–33.
— "Barr on Canon and Childs: Can One Read the Bible as Scripture?" *TSF Bulletin* Nov–Dec (1983): 2–4.
— "Between Reformation and Modern Commentary: The Perception of the Scope of Biblical Books." Pages xlviii–lxxvii in *A Commentary on Galatians, William Perkins.* Edited by Gerald T Sheppard. Pilgrim Classic Commentaries. New York: Pilgrim, 1989.
— "Canonical Criticism." Pages 861–866 in vol. 1 of *The Anchor Bible Dictionary.* 6 vols. Edited by D N Freedman. New York: Doubleday, 1992.
— "The 'Scope' of Isaiah as a Book of Jewish and Christian Scriptures." Pages 257–281 in *New Visions of Isaiah.* Sheffield: Sheffield Academic, 1996.
— "Childs, Brevard (b. 1923)." Pages 575–584 in *Historical Handbook of Major Biblical Interpreters.* Edited by Donald K McKim. Downers Grove, Ill.: InterVarsity, 1998.
— "Biblical Wisdom Literature and the End of the Modern Age." *Supplements to Vetus Testamentum* 80 (2000): 369–398.
Smart, James D. *The Past, Present, and Future of Biblical Theology.* Philadelphia: Westminster, 1979.

Smend, Rudolf. *Wilhelm Martin Leberecht de Wettes Arbeit am Alten und am Neuen Testament*. Basel: Helbing & Lichtenhahn, 1958.

— *Die Entstehung des Alten Testaments*. Stuttgart: W Kohlhammer, 1978.

— "Questions About the Importance of the Canon in an Old Testament Introduction." *Journal for the Study of the Old Testament* 16 (1980): 45–51.

— "Nachkritische Schriftauslegung." Pages 212–232 in *Die Mitte des Alten Testaments: Gesammelte Studien, Bd 1*. Beiträge zur evangelischen Theologie 99. Munich: Chr Kaiser, 1986.

— "Theologie im Alten Testament." Pages 104–117 in *Die Mitte des Alten Testaments: Gesammelte Studien, Bd 1*. Beiträge zur evangelischen Theologie 99. Munich: Chr Kaiser, 1986.

— *Karl Barth als Ausleger der Heiligen Schrift*. Theologie als Christologie. Berlin: Evangelische Verlagsanstalt, 1988.

— "Gerhard von Rad." Pages 13–24 in *Das Alte Testament und die Kultur der Moderne: Beiträge des Symposiums »Das Alte Testament und die Kultur der Moderne« anlässlich des 100. Geburtstags Gerhard von Rads (1901–1971) Heidelberg, 18.–21. Oktober 2001*. Edited by Manfred Oeming et al. Altes Testament und Moderne 8. Münster: Lit, 2004.

Söding, Thomas. *Einheit der Heiligen Schrift? zur Theologie des biblischen Kanons*. Quaestiones disputatae 211. Freiburg: Herder, 2005.

Sommer, Benjamin D. *A Prophet Reads Scripture: Allusion in Isaiah 40–66*. Stanford: Stanford University Press, 1998.

Spieckermann, Hermann. "'YHWH Bless You and Keep You': The Relation of History of Israelite Religion and Old Testament Theology Reconsidered." *Scandinavian Journal of the Old Testament* 23/2 (2009): 165–182.

Spina, Frank A. "Canonical Criticism: Childs versus Sanders." Pages 165–194 in *Interpreting God's Word for Today: An Inquiry into Hermeneutics from a Biblical Theological Perspective*. Edited by Wayne McCown and James Earl Massey. Wesleyan Theological Perspectives 2. Anderson, Ind.: Warner, 1982.

Spriggs, D G. *Two Old Testament Theologies: A Comparative Evaluation of the Contributions of Eichrodt and von Rad to Our Understanding of the Nature of Old Testament Theology*. Studies in Biblical Theology 30. London: SCM, 1974.

Steck, Odil Hannes. "Theological Streams of Tradition." Pages 183–214 in *Tradition and Theology in the Old Testament*. Edited by Douglas A Knight. London: SPCK, 1977.

— "Zu Eigenart und Herkunft von Ps 102." *Zeitschrift für die alttestamentliche Wissenschaft* 102 (1990): 357–372.

— *Der Abschluß der Prophetie im Alten Testament. Ein Versuch zur Frage der Vorgeschichte des Kanons*. Biblische Studien 17. Neukirchen-Vluyn: Neukirchener, 1991.

— *Studien zu Tritojesaja*. Beihefte zur Zeitschrift für die alttestamentliche Wissenschaft 203. Berlin/New York: Walter de Gruyter, 1991.

— *The Prophetic Books and Their Theological Witness*. Translated by James D Nogalski. St. Louis, Mo.: Chalice, 2000.

Steins, Georg. *Die Chronik als kanonisches Abschlussphänomen: Studien zur Entstehung und Theologie von 1/2 Chronik*. Bonner biblische Beiträge 93. Weinheim: Beltz Athenäum, 1995.

— "Torabindung und Kanonabschluß: zur Entstehung und kanonischen Funktion der Chronikbücher." Pages 213–256 in *Die Tora als Kanon für Juden und Christen*. Edited by Erich Zenger. Herders Biblische Studien 10. Freiburg: Herder, 1996.

— *Die "Bindung Isaaks" im Kanon (Gen 22): Grundlagen und Programm einer Kanonisch-Intertextuellen Lektüre*. Herders Biblische Studien 20. Freiburg: Herder, 1999.

— "Das Lesewesen Mensch und das Buch der Bücher." *Stimmen der Zeit* 221/10 (2003): 689–699.

— "Der Bibelkanon als Denkmal und Text: Zu einigen methodologischen Aspekten kanonischer Schriftauslegung." Pages 177–198 in *The Biblical Canons*. Edited by J-M Auwers and H J De Jonge. Bibliotheca ephemeridum theologicarum lovaniensium 163. Leuven: Leuven University Press, 2003.

— "Das Wort Gottes wächst mit den Lesenden: Eine folgenreiche Rückbesinnung gegenwärtiger Bibelexegese." *Lebendige Seelsorge* 55/2 (2004): 74–81.

— "Bibel im Gespräch: Die verkannte Offenbarungskonstitution Dei Verbum." Pages 17–21 in *Das unerledigte Konzil: 40 Jahre Zweites Vatikanum*. Herder Korrespondenz Spezial. Freiburg: Herder, 2005.

— "Die Einheit der Heiligen Schrift — ein 'aufgegebenes' Thema der Bibelexegese." *Religionsunterricht an höheren Schulen* 48/3 (2005): 140–150.

— "Wort des lebendigen Gottes: Neue Brücken zwischen Bibelauslegung und Liturgie." *Theologie der Gegenwart* 48 (2005): 242–253.

— "Die Bibel als 'Ein Buch' lesen? Eine innerbiblische Lektüreanleitung." Pages 69–78 in *Verantwortete Exegese: Hermeneutische Zugänge — Exegetische Studien — Systematische Reflexionen — Ökumenische Perspektiven — Praktische Konkretionen. Franz Georg Untergaßmair zum 65. Geburtstag*. Edited by Gerhard Hotze and Egon Spiegel. Vechtaer Beiträge zur Theologie 13. Berlin: LIT, 2006.

— "Kanonisch lesen." Pages 45–64 in *Lesarten der Bibel: Beiträge zur Theorie der Exegese des Alten Testaments*. Edited by Helmut Utzschneider and Erhard Blum. Stuttgart: W Kohlhammer, 2006.

— "Der Kanon ist der erste Kontext: Oder, Zurück an den Anfang!" *Bibel und Kirche* 62/2 (2007): 116–121.

— "Kanon und Anamnese: Auf dem Weg zu einer Neuen Biblischen Theologie." Pages 110–129 in *Der Bibelkanon in der Bibelauslegung: Methodenreflexionen und Beispielexegesen*. Edited by Egbert Ballhorn and Georg Steins. Stuttgart: Kohlhammer, 2007.

— "Kanonisch-intertextuelle Bibellektüre — My Way." Pages 55–68 in *Intertextualität: Perspektiven auf ein interdisziplinäres Arbeitsfeld*. Edited by Karin Herrmann and Sandra Hübenthal. Aachen: Shaker, 2007.

Stemberger, Günter. *Introduction to the Talmud and Midrash*. Translated by Markus Bockmuehl. Edinburgh: T&T Clark, 1996.

Stern, David. *Parables in Midrash: Narrative and Exegesis in Rabbinic Literature*. Cambridge, Mass.: Harvard University Press, 1991.

Stuhlmacher, Peter. "Der Kanon und seine Auslegung." Pages 263–290 in *Jesus Christus als die Mitte der Schrift: Studien zur Hermeneutik des Evangeliums*. Edited by Christof Landmesser et al. Zeitschrift für die neutestamentliche Wissenschaft und die Kunde der älteren Kirche 86. Berlin: Walter de Gruyter, 1997.

Sundberg, Albert C. *Old Testament of the Early Church*. Harvard Theological Studies 20. Cambridge, Mass.: Harvard University Press, 1964.

Tanner, Kathryn. "Theology and the Plain Sense." Pages 59–78 in *Scriptural Authority and Narrative Interpretation*. Edited by Garrett Green. Philadelphia: Fortress, 1987.

Taylor, Marion Ann. *The Old Testament in the Old Princeton School (1812–1929)*. San Francisco: Mellen Research University Press, 1992.

Thompson, Thomas L. *Historicity of the Patriarchal Narratives*. Berlin/New York: Walter de Gruyter, 1974.

Toorn, Karel van der. *Scribal Culture and the Making of the Hebrew Bible*. Cambridge, Mass.: Harvard University Press, 2007.

Topping, Richard R. *Revelation, Scripture and Church: Theological Hermeneutic Thought of James Barr, Paul Ricoeur and Hans Frei*. Aldershot, England; Burlington, Vt.: Ashgate, 2007.

Torrance, Thomas F. *Baptism in the Early Church: Draft of Interim Report 1955 Containing Detailed References and Supporting Material Not Included in the Printed Report to the General Assembly*. Edinburgh: Church of Scotland, 1955.

— *The Biblical Doctrine of Baptism: A Study Document*. Edinburgh: St. Andrew, 1958.

Trebolle Barrera, Julio C. *The Jewish Bible and the Christian Bible: An Introduction to the History of the Bible*. Translated by Wilfred G E Watson. Grand Rapids: Eerdmans, 1998.

Treier, Daniel J. "Biblical Theology and/or Theological Interpretation of Scripture? Defining the Relationship." *Scottish Journal of Theology* 61/1 (2008): 16–31.

— *Introducing Theological Interpretation of Scripture: Recovering a Christian Practice*. Grand Rapids: Baker Academic, 2008.

Tucker, Gene M et al., eds. *Canon, Theology, and Old Testament Interpretation: Essays in Honor of Brevard S. Childs*. Philadelphia: Fortress, 1988.

Ulrich, Eugene. "The Notion and Definition of Canon." Pages 21–35 in *The Canon Debate*. Edited by Lee M McDonald and James A Sanders. Peabody, Mass: Hendrickson, 2002.

Van Seters, John. *Abraham in History and Tradition*. New Haven: Yale University Press, 1975.

— *The Edited Bible: The Curious History of the "Editor" in Biblical Criticism*. Winona Lake, Ind.: Eisenbrauns, 2006.

Vischer, Wilhelm. *The Witness of the Old Testament to Christ: Vol. 1, The Pentateuch*. Translated by A B Crabtree. London: Lutterworth, 1949.

— "Das Geheimnis Israels: Eine Erklärung der Kapitel 9–11 des Römerbriefs." *Judaica* 6 (1950): 81–132.

Wagner, Ross. "The Septuagint and the 'Search for the Christian Bible.'" Pages 17–28 in *Scripture's Doctrine and Theology's Bible: How the New Testament Shapes Christian Dogmatics*. Edited by Markus Bockmuehl and Alan J Torrance. Grand Rapids: Baker Academic, 2008.

Watson, Francis. "Canon and Criticism: A Response to Professor Childs." *Kings Theological Review* 87 (1985): 55–58.

— *Text, Church and World: Biblical Interpretation in Theological Perspective*. Edinburgh: T&T Clark, 1994.

— *Text and Truth: Redefining Biblical Theology*. Grand Rapids: Eerdmans, 1997.

Webster, John. "The Dogmatic Location of the Canon." Pages 9–46 in *Word and Church: Essays in Christian Dogmatics*. Edinburgh: T&T Clark, 2001.

— *Holy Scripture: A Dogmatic Sketch*. Cambridge: Cambridge University Press, 2003.

Wellhausen, Julius. *Prolegomena zur Geschichte Israels*. 6th edition. Berlin and Leipzig: Walter de Gruyter, 1927.

—, and William Robertson Smith. *Prolegomena to the History of Israel*. Translated by John Sutherland Black and Allan Menzies. Edinburgh: A & C Black, 1885.

White, Hayden. "Auerbach's Literary History: Figural Causation and Modernist Historicism." Pages 124–139 in *Literary History and the Challenge of Philosophy: The Legacy of Erich Auerbach*. Edited by Seth Lehrer. Stanford: Stanford University Press, 1996.

Whitman, Jon. *Allegory: The Dynamics of an Ancient and Medieval Technique*. Oxford: Clarendon, 1987.

Wilken, Robert Louis. "Allegory and the Interpretation of the Old Testament in the 21st Century." *Letter & Spirit* 1 (2005): 11–21.

Wolfenson, L B. "Implications of the Place of the Book of Ruth." *Hebrew Union College Annual* 1 (1924): 151–178.

Wolterstorff, Nicholas P. *Divine Discourse: Philosophical Reflections on the Claim That God Speaks*. Cambridge: Cambridge University Press, 1995.

Wood, Susan K. *Spiritual Exegesis and the Church in the Theology of Henri De Lubac*. Grand Rapids: Eerdmans, 1998.

Yeago, David S. "The New Testament and the Nicene Dogma: A Contribution to the Recovery of Theological Exegesis." Pages 87–100 in *The Theological Interpretation of Scripture: Classic and Contemporary Readings*. Edited by Stephen E Fowl. Cambridge, Mass.: Blackwell, 1997.

— "The Bible: The Spirit, the Church, and the Scriptures: Biblical Inspiration and Interpretation Revisited." Pages 49–93 in *Knowing the triune God*. Edited by James J Buckley and David S Yeago. Grand Rapids: Eerdmans, 2001.

Young, Frances M. *From Nicaea to Chalcedon: A Guide to Literature and Its Background*. Philadelphia: Fortress, 1983.

— "The Rhetorical Schools and Their Influence on Patristic Exegesis." Pages 182–199 in *The Making of Orthodoxy: Essays in Honour of Henry Chadwick*. Edited by Rowan Williams. Cambridge: Cambridge University Press, 1989.

— "Typology." Pages 29–48 in *Crossing the Boundaries: Essays in Biblical Interpretation in Honour of Michael D Goulder*. Edited by Stanley E Porter et al. Biblical Interpretation Series 8. Leiden: Brill, 1994.

— *Biblical Exegesis and the Formation of Christian Culture*. Cambridge: Cambridge University Press, 1997.

— "The Fourth Century Reaction Against Allegory." *Studia Patristica* 30 (1997): 120–125.

— "The 'Mind' of Scripture: Theological Readings of the Bible in the Fathers." *International Journal of Systematic Theology* 7/2 (2005): 126–141.

Zenger, Erich. *Das Erste Testament: Die jüdische Bibel und die Christen*. Düsseldorf: Patmos, 1991.

— "Thesen zu einer Hermeneutik des Ersten Testaments nach Auschwitz." Pages 143–158 in *Eine Bibel — zwei Testamente: Positionen Biblischer Theologie*. Edited by Christoph Dohmen and Thomas Söding. Paderborn: Ferdinand Schöningh, 1995.

— "Theologie des Alten Testaments: ein kanonischer Entwurf." *Biblische Zeitschrift* 43/1 (1999): 117–118.

— "Psalmenforschung nach Hermann Gunkel und Sigmund Mowinckel." Pages 399–435 in *Congress Volume Leiden*. Leiden/Boston: Brill, 2000.

Zimmerli, Walther. "Das Phänomen der 'Fortschreibung' im Buche Echeziel." Pages 174–191 in *Prophecy: Essays Presented to Georg Fohrer on his Sixty-fifth Birthday, 6 September 1980*. Edited by J A Emerton. Beihefte zur Zeitschrift für die alttestamentliche Wissenschaft 150. Berlin/New York: De Gruyter, 1980.

— Review of Brevard Childs, *Introduction to the Old Testament as Scripture*. *Vetus Testamentum* 31 (1981): 235–244.

Source Index

A. Old Testament

B. New Testament

Author Index

Subject Index